The Monarchy and the British N
1780 to the Present

C000246904

The monarchy has remained important in British public life long after monarchs ceased, in the early nineteenth century, to govern as well as to reign, and popular legitimacy came to be founded on representation, not the immutability of a sacred hierarchy. This book addresses two fundamental questions about the British monarchy in the modern period. What has been its function in the political and social life of the nation? Why, for much but by no means all of the modern period, has it been so popular with its subjects? Leading historians offer contributions on the monarchy and public values, the monarchy's popularity, the monarchy and Ireland, the monarchy and film, gender and the monarchy, the royal court and republicanism. These essays shed considerable new light on the monarchy's place in British public life and on the broader social and political history of modern Britain.

ANDRZEJ OLECHNOWICZ is Lecturer in Modern British History at the University of Durham. He is the author of *Working-Class Housing in England between the Wars: The Becontree Estate* (1997).

The Monarchy and the British Nation, 1780 to the Present

Edited by

Andrzej Olechnowicz

CAMBRIDGE
UNIVERSITY PRESS

CAMBRIDGE UNIVERSITY PRESS
Cambridge, New York, Melbourne, Madrid, Cape Town, Singapore, São Paulo, Delhi

Cambridge University Press
The Edinburgh Building, Cambridge CB2 8RU, UK

Published in the United States of America by Cambridge University Press, New York

www.cambridge.org
Information on this title: www.cambridge.org/9780521606356

© Cambridge University Press 2007

First published 2007

Printed in the United Kingdom at the University Press, Cambridge

A catalogue record for this publication is available from the British Library

ISBN 978-0-521-84461-1 hardback
ISBN 978-0-521-60635-6 paperback

Contents

Part III

Illustrations

Tables and graphs

Introduction

The monarchy has remained important in British political life long after monarchs ceased – in the early nineteenth century – to govern as well as to reign, and after popular legitimacy came to be founded on representation. Autobiographies, opinion polls and academic studies (as well as newspaper coverage) attest to its importance in the private, imaginative lives of many men, women and children. Yet the monarchy's political and cultural significance received little systematic historical analysis before the 1980s. The disciplines of sociology, social psychology, and cultural and media studies developed theoretical perspectives on the modern monarchy, though many of these pay too little regard to specific historical contexts to satisfy historians.

This collection of studies by intellectual, political, social and cultural historians combines original research, new approaches, and reassessments of the recent historiography in order to shed light on two fundamental and related questions. First, what has been the monarchy's role in the political and public life of the nation? Second, why for most of the last two centuries has the monarchy been popular with its subjects? These suggest further questions. What power or authority has the monarchy possessed? Has the gender of the monarch affected the institution's constitutional character and role? If the monarchy has a symbolic or representative function, what does it symbolize or represent? If it embodies national identity, how has it resolved the tension between 'Britishness' and ethnic identities? If the monarchy embodies certain moral values, has it failed to appeal to those who do not share them? Has its representative character been compromised by an upper- or middle-class lifestyle? Why has it not faced a greater challenge from republicanism? Has the monarchy survived because of its capacity to adapt and re-invent itself? Can its popularity be explained in rational terms or does it appeal only to atavistic human emotions? Finally, can the monarchy remain popular (and dignified) in the face of intrusive and sensationalist tabloid interest?

While there is, in fact, a very considerable measure of agreement among the contributors, it was not their object to seek this. Their purpose is

1

rather to stimulate debate and suggest new avenues for future research at a time when Buckingham and St James's Palaces are uncertain about the future direction of the monarchy and when the European Union, devolution, House of Lords reform and perhaps the possibility of Disestablishment present it with potentially difficult challenges.

The opening chapter accounts for the emergence of interest in the monarchy among historians in the 1980s, and surveys the existing historiography relating to the role of the monarchy, its popularity and the nature of republicanism. It emphasizes that a top-down approach has usually been adopted and that future research must endeavour to uncover ordinary people's perspectives in order to understand the appeal of monarchism. Thereafter the book is divided into three parts, each of three chapters.

The first part consists of three broad overviews. Jonathan Parry argues that the tendency of admirers and critics of the monarchy to focus on the irrational attraction of ceremonial and of mystique has obscured a more straightforward, rational and 'Whig' reason for its popularity: its ability to appear more or less representative of the nation, in terms of both its constitutional symbolism and its liberalism. In particular, it has played a crucial role in defining national identity against less liberal foreign regimes. Moreover, the monarchy has exemplified values which very many people have admired or shared – especially conventional bourgeois values. Yet Parry recognises that this achievement was sometimes in doubt, and that it was effected primarily by political events outside the monarchy's control. A key theme for the Victorian Liberal Party was the defence of the power of party and Parliament, and the assertion of civic republican ideas of political participation and public virtue in the face of monarchical influence. However, by the second quarter of the nineteenth century, monarchical influence was less threatening than several other vested interests that excited criticism, and by the fourth quarter, the traditional radical critique of the vested interest state had lost most of its power, thus safeguarding the position of the monarchy along with other 'Establishment' institutions.

Campbell Orr's chapter considers the significance of gender for the development of the monarchy. She argues that the monarchy was 'feminized' both in the sense of female rule and of feminine values; that constitutional rule is more easily accomplished by women than by men; and that the monarchy consists of several royal households at any one time, and therefore exemplifies different types of both femininity and masculinity as well as a different mix of upper-class and middle-class behaviours. The decline of the warrior-king ostensibly went hand-in-hand with the emergence of the constitutional monarch. Yet although Albert's respectability and domesticity assisted this, there were other types of masculinity, associated with the dandyism and celebrity culture of the Regency, which persisted throughout Victoria's reign; while Victoria herself adapted the warrior role to her own feminine version. The association of the monarchy with philanthropy was one aspect of its feminization, helped empower a certain kind of female activism, and involved a different style of royal masculinity. Nonetheless, feminization entailed only limited support for women's rights, and the double sexual standard persisted in royal life until the 1990s.

James Loughlin explores the relationship between monarchy and national identity in the case of Ireland under the Union. George III's refusal to endorse the promised Catholic emancipation that was supposed to accompany the Act of Union, was regarded in Ireland as a betrayal. Unlike other regions of the United Kingdom, Ireland combined constitutional integration with semi-colonial status, reflected in a centralized administrative system based on Dublin Castle, at the apex of which stood the monarchical 'substitute', the Viceroy. Conceived in Britain as the embodiment of an accepted constitutional order, in Ireland it meant that the monarchy was often identified with an administrative system alienated from the mass of the people. While opposition to the Union among Irish nationalists was enduring, it coexisted with a more complex attitude to the monarchy explicable in terms neither of simplistic acceptance nor of rejection, with O'Connell and Butt encouraging royal allegiance, Parnell often discouraging it, and Griffith looking to independence under a dual monarchy. However, by the time southern Ireland left the Union in 1922, a bloody civil war was fought over the issue of an oath of allegiance to the King.

The second part considers the extent of royal authority and the nature of republicanism, principally in the Victorian and Edwardian periods. David Craig argues that the widely held assumption that Bagehot simply gave the monarchy a ceremonial role, reads *The English Constitution* out of context. Rather, one of Bagehot's aims was to show that cabinet government was the best form of government, and that unroyal cabinet government was possible, a point which many contemporaries doubted. Nevertheless, Bagehot thought monarchy was important because while Britain already possessed a free polity – a republic – most of the population were not ready for it. It was only because the 'masses' deferred to what they thought a divine-right monarchy and to the aristocracy that this republic was possible. Prematurely shattering this illusion would end obedience to the law; but as education spread, monarchy would become redundant. Craig concludes that those commentators who invoke *The English Constitution* to bolster their support for the monarchy have unwittingly chosen an inappropriate prop.

Michael Bentley challenges the 'Whig' story of royal enfeeblement in the period 1830–1910. It is only by defining royal power as the ability to override politicians and officials and to make happen what its wielders want to happen, that the way is cleared to write off the British monarchy by 1850. Bentley argues instead for a persistent royal 'authority' well into the twentieth century. Those entrusted by the constitution with making policy could not do so without reference to what Queen Victoria wanted. A political career could depend on not making an enemy of the court. Making sure that the Queen did not get her way cost time, effort and temper which Prime Ministers tended not to have. For most, it was easier by far to let the Queen have her way when no critical aspect of policy came under threat.

Antony Taylor's chapter shows that for republicans, the boundaries between monarchy and the aristocracy were porous. They saw the key to power residing in formal structures of land-ownership and portrayed regal power as a usurpation of the throne by a roguish dynasty, supported by a corrupt Church, and an aristocratic mafia. Republicans projected debt and debauchery, frequently associated with the younger sons of aristocratic families, as the overriding characteristic of the heir to the throne, Albert Edward, and paid minute attention to the origins of aristocratic connection and position. To republican eyes, the people were deprived of their true rights and reduced to the position of internal exiles in their own land. However, republicans misunderstood the nature of the monarchical system they were opposing. Their insistence that aristocracy and monarchy were the same unmodified feudal force not only overlooked the tensions between them but also underestimated the new public ceremonial of the monarchy from the 1880s.

The third part explores the popularity of the monarchy, principally in the twentieth century. Philip Williamson argues that in response to a succession of severe challenges the monarchy was 're-invented' in the early twentieth century to become more secure and more popular. He considers that as for the first time monarchs began to make frequent public statements, the public language of the monarchy best reveals the meaning of the institution, and the nature of the support it cultivated; and that the abdication crisis should be understood as the test of what the monarchy had come to represent. This was to commend and uphold social solidarity, imperial unity, constitutionalism, Christian witness, and – the keystone of them all, over which Edward VIII stumbled – public duty. If this was an 'establishment' ideology, it commanded remarkable support among all classes and across a great range of opinion. The monarchy's place in public life turned on it being the only agency able to express and symbolize these public values convincingly, because it was now perceived to be above and outside sectional political, social and denominational divisions.

Jeffrey Richards argues that contrary to Bagehot's dictum that the monarchy's 'mystery is its life. We must not let daylight in upon the magic', the cinema and television have played a significant role in the creation of a popular monarchy. Different aspects of the visual media have played to different sides of the institution of monarchy but they have complemented each other. Newsreels and documentaries with their reverent and respectful coverage of great public events have created an enduring image of the monarchy as the epitome of a life of duty and service. Feature films, both British and American, have helped to humanize and mythologize the monarchy by turning past royal figures into stars and inviting the public to sympathize with their private tragedies and tribulations. For Richards, they have replaced the magic of distance with the magic of familiarity.

The final chapter charts the course of royal popularity over the last 130 years, noting that the monarchy has usually been very popular except possibly during the two world wars and in the 1990s. It turns to psychological models to understand why, in a highly inegalitarian society, those with least resources have so enthusiastically supported a Royal Family with among the most. It argues that two key processes are at work. First, the prominence of the monarchy in everyday life as well as its ubiquitous presence during national ceremonies makes conforming far less mentally wearing than resisting. Second, great sympathy is normally generated for 'ordinary' royals who have no choice but to live with the burdens, constraints and miseries of royal life and work, despite their immense wealth. It offers the immense compensation for all those forced to do what they would not choose to do by their lack of money, that even if they had great wealth, it would not bring them happiness or the freedom to do whatever they wanted. What royals have done and said has normally had the effect of reinforcing this wishful thinking, though the unpopularity of the 1990s demonstrates the dangers of any royals appearing to ignore their 'duty' and balk at 'sacrifice'.

1 Historians and the modern British monarchy

Andrzej Olechnowicz

Until the 1980s, academic historians of the nineteenth and twentieth centuries largely ignored the British monarchy as an object of research; David Cannadine's celebrated 1983 essay on the monarchy's 'invention of tradition' can reasonably be taken as starting the current round of scholarly interest.[1] There was no one decisive reason for this change. In part the timing reflected a run of royal events which demonstrated the immense popularity of the Royal Family: the Queen's Silver Jubilee in 1977, which saw street parties throughout the kingdom (6,000 in London alone, in rich and poor areas alike);[2] the Prince of Wales's wedding to Lady Diana Spencer in 1981, watched by an estimated world-wide television audience of 1,000 million; and comparable national and international excitement over the wedding of Prince Andrew in 1986. The monarchy manifestly commanded a range and depth of support which no political party, religion or national football team has perhaps ever matched. Such contemporary perceptions began to affect historical perspectives. As Walter Arnstein wrote, there now seemed something odd in most social historians being 'more fascinated with a small band of Lancashire woolcombers who sought to found a trade union than with the 30,000 school children who serenaded Queen Victoria at her Golden Jubilee pageant in London's Hyde Park'.[3]

It was no accident, however, that much of the early scholarly running was made by historians on the left. From the late 1970s onwards, national and international political events – notably the election of Mrs Thatcher's Conservative government in 1979 with a third of workers'

---

[1] D. Cannadine, 'The context, performance and meaning of ritual: the British monarchy and the "invention of tradition", c.1820–1977', in E. Hobsbawm and T. Ranger (eds.), *The Invention of Tradition* (Cambridge, 1983), pp. 101–64.

[2] P. Ziegler, *Crown and People* (Newton Abbot, 1979), pp. 172–93. Cannadine had published a first version of his 1983 essay in Jubilee year: 'The not so ancient traditions of monarchy', *New Society*, 2 June 1977.

[3] W. L. Arnstein, 'Queen Victoria's speeches from the throne: a new look', in A. O'Day (ed.), *Government and Institutions in the Post-1832 United Kingdom* (Lampeter, 1995), p. 131.

6

votes, and popular support for the 1982 Falklands War – coincided with scholarly reappraisals of British economic and social history to force a redirection in their thinking. Scepticism about the idea of the 'Industrial Revolution' and a new emphasis upon the long dominance of a southern 'gentlemanly capitalism' based around commerce, finance and services, cast doubt both on a Marxist-indebted history of the nineteenth century preoccupied with the socio-economic power of northern, industrial, bourgeois capitalism and with the activities of a labour movement, and on an orthodox Marxist view of aristocratic influence as surviving only because this was in the interests of the bourgeoisie. From the resulting reassessments, the monarchy emerged as a prime candidate in upholding anti-industrial and aristocratic values, containing class consciousness and socialism, and frustrating what these historians considered to be economic modernization (i.e. a more socialist economy), because of its role in shaping a particular kind of national identity. For example, in the 1978 Marx memorial lecture, Eric Hobsbawm explained the halt in the labour movement's advance exclusively in socio-economic terms; but shortly afterwards he shifted to placing greater emphasis on the influence of national culture, through the processes of the 'invention of tradition'.[4]

The most influential contribution came from the heterodox Marxist and Scottish nationalist Tom Nairn, whose *The Enchanted Glass: Britain and its Monarchy* (1988) developed his analysis in *The Break-up of Britain* (1977) of British 'over-traditionalism leading to incurable backwardness'.[5] With greater empirical depth, Linda Colley's *Britons: Forging the Nation, 1707–1837* (1992) presented Protestant Britons defining themselves as a single people in reaction to the Catholic, 'superstitious, militarist, decadent and unfree' French, and identified the monarchy as central to this process: under the Hanoverians it assumed 'many of the characteristics and much of the patriotic importance that it retains today'.[6] Nairn and Colley have influenced each other's work, and both were indebted to another heterodox Marxist, Arno Mayer, who in *The Persistence of the Old Regime: Europe to the Great War* (1981) argued that 'the rising business and professional classes' had failed to replace 'the landed and public service elites' as Europe's ruling classes, in large part because the European monarchies 'remained the focus of dazzling and minutely choreographed public rituals that rekindled deep-seated royalist sentiments while simultaneously exalting and relegitimating the old order

---

[4] E. Hobsbawm *et al.*, *The Forward March of Labour Halted?* (London, 1981), pp. 1–19; E. Hobsbawm, 'Introduction', in Hobsbawm and Ranger, *Invention of Tradition*, pp. 1–14.

[5] T. Nairn, *The Break-up of Britain* (London, 1977), pp. 40–2.

[6] L. Colley, *Britons* (New Haven, 1992), pp. 6–7, 193.

as a whole'. Britain, it was argued, had been no exception, remaining a traditional society into the reign of George V.[7]

Non-Marxist historians too came to explore the same terrain, as they 'dispersed the collectivity of class into various other alliances, mainly of a cross-class nature', producing analyses centred around discourses of 'community' and the 'populism' of popular constitutionalism.[8] Increasingly, the political realm was regarded as conditioning social identity, and inequality and exploitation largely disappeared from the academic agenda as British 'class' interests came to be seen as compatible, and 'class' relations as harmonious. A privileging of mainly political discourses also produced a new – albeit contested – periodization which ascribed a fundamental economic, political and social unity from the early seventeenth to the late nineteenth century. This emphasis on continuity saw early Victorian political history 'inverted from the familiar steady march toward representative democracy to a world where theatre and spectacle remained the prime source of political legitimation'.[9]

These two revisionist trends encouraged historians to expect a ceremonial monarchy which faced few ideological obstacles to loyalty among its subjects. Furthermore, inspired by John Pocock's notion of the United Kingdom as an 'Atlantic archipelago' and the work of early modern historians of the Scottish and Irish impact upon English politics – as well as revived political debates about devolution – historians of the nineteenth and twentieth centuries also began to examine the interaction of the four nations of the kingdom.[10] Here too the cultural role of the monarchy seemed important in fashioning a British identity, which satisfied a majority of subjects that it respected national differences and was more than English identity writ large.

One fundamental objection to the historical study of the monarchy is that British academic historians cannot write good royal history because they tend to treat the institution with 'a certain obsequiousness'.[11] The real issue is actually not obsequiousness but something altogether different. Many historians have been 'conformists': in the last analysis they

---

[7] A. J. Mayer, *The Persistence of the Old Regime* (New York, 1981), pp. 79, 81, 88–95, 135–9.

[8] For a summary of this shift, see R. Price, 'Historiography, narrative, and the nineteenth century', *Journal of British Studies* 35 (1996), 221, 229–31; and for criticism, 'Roundtable. Richard Price's *British Society, 1680–1880*', *Journal of Victorian Culture* 11 (2006), 146–79.

[9] Ibid., 221–2.

[10] E.g. K. Robbins, *Nineteenth-Century Britain* (Oxford, 1988); H. Kearney, *The British Isles* (Cambridge, 1989).

[11] This was the judgement of Robert Baldcock, a history editor at Yale University Press, in 1998.

see little wrong with the monarchy or the structures of the nation. More recent work, focusing on the examination of discourses, runs the risk of a naïve reading of the materials producing a similarly congratulatory history; it has always to be remembered that discourses were not innocent descriptions of reality, but weapons in contests for some form of power.

This essay considers three broad historiographical themes. First, it discusses studies of the monarchy's constitutional role, political power and social character by reviewing the genre of royal biography, the contribution of constitutional and political historians, and changing assessments of Bagehot's classic statement of the British monarchy's role in *The English Constitution* (1867). The second section examines how historians have sought to explain the monarchy's popularity, by assessing studies of philanthropy, ceremony, gender, religion, national identity, empire, media and 'soap opera'. The third section will outline historical understandings of the character of British republicanism. The conclusion will suggest that monarchism should be considered both as a pervasive cultural fact, which often goes unremarked, and as a distinctive ideology articulated in print and other media, which needs close historical investigation.

I

The official royal biography still carries authority in defining the character of individual monarchs and their public role. Nor is the genre extinct: in 2003 the Palace chose William Shawcross to write the Queen Mother's official biography. The biographies of George V by Harold Nicolson in 1952, George VI by John Wheeler-Bennett in 1958 and Queen Mary by James Pope-Hennessy in 1959 all sought to establish that the monarchs had been exemplary individuals, who had behaved in a constitutional manner and had not been hostile to the working class and the Labour movement. In these senses, they were patrician responses to a fear not of republicanism, but of confiscatory socialism. Nicolson, the most scrupulous of the three, quoted the advice of the King's private secretary in 1917 that the monarchy should induce the thinking working classes to regard it 'as a living power for good', and emphasised that the King took special trouble in 1924 to get to know his new Labour ministers personally.[12] Wheeler-Bennett praised George VI for developing 'a new concept of Royalty . . . closely identified with the people, genuinely interested in their affairs'.[13] Pope-Hennessy was less plausible: royal tours of mining

---

[12] H. Nicolson, *King George the Fifth* (London, 1952), pp. 301, 389.
[13] J. Wheeler-Bennett, *King George VI* (London, 1958), p. 172.

and industrial areas in 1912–13 were a success because 'the new King and Queen felt more at their ease with British working people than they ever did with members of London Society or with foreign royalties'.[14]

Such statements are hardly surprising given the purpose of the official royal biography, which is illuminated by Nicolson's diaries and letters. Concerned that he might be unable to tell the whole truth, George VI's private secretary, Sir Alan Lascelles, assured him that he would be shown 'every scrap of paper', but added that the book was 'not meant to be an ordinary biography. It is something quite different. You will be writing a book on the subject of a myth and will have to be mythological.' Nicolson would not be expected to say anything untrue, nor to praise or exaggerate, but would be expected 'to omit things and incidents which were discreditable'. When he asked what would happen if he did find something damaging, Lascelles replied that his 'first duty will always be to the Monarchy'. Nicolson did his duty, changing the wording of a 1914 memorandum in which George V threatened to refuse Royal Assent to the government's Irish Home Rule Bill.[15]

In the 1950s these three official royal biographies were 'almost impossible to contest' because government and royal records remained closed to other historians. Moreover, royal insiders abided by a code of silence with anyone other than entirely friendly outsiders. The breaking of this code has been the most dramatic development of the last thirty years of commentary on the Royal Family, making possible muck-raking biographies based on unsubstantiated and unattributable gossip. The genre of popular royal biography is hardly new, but such books used to be deferential and celebratory – 'mythological' in exactly the same way as official royal biographies. Some were written with assistance from the royal persons concerned, for example Kathleen Woodward's *Queen Mary: A Life and Intimate Study* and Lady Cynthia Asquith's *The Married Life of The Duchess of York*. The unauthorized (though still reverential) book by a royal governess, Marion Crawford's *The Little Princesses* (1950), conventionally marks the shift towards a more revelatory style. So far Kitty Kelley's *The Royals* (1997) represents the acme of this genre, using interviews with many 'current or former members of the royal household' to claim exposures of the Windsors' 'secrets of alcoholism, drug addiction, epilepsy, insanity, homosexuality, bisexuality, adultery, infidelity, and illegitimacy', and 'their relationship with the Third Reich'.[16]

[14] J. Pope-Hennessy, *Queen Mary 1867–1953* (London, 1959), p. 473.

[15] H. Nicolson, *Diaries and Letters, 1930–64*, ed. S. Olson (Harmondsworth, 1984), pp. 334, 343; P. Hall, *Royal Fortune* (London, 1992), p. 175, and see p. 173 for Nicolson's son avoiding the sensitive word 'mythological' in his own earlier edition of the diary.

[16] K. Kelley, *The Royals* (New York, 1997), pp. xii, 2–3; also 23–4 which broke one of the last taboos, criticism of the Queen Mother.

Historians rightly attacked Kelley's book for its tendentiousness.[17] But it raises the question of how historians studying the contemporary monarchy should approach such popular royal biographies. One strategy would be to ignore them. Another might be to treat them as texts involved in the construction of cultural understandings of royal life; what then becomes important is not their truth or falsity, but the tropes in which they present the Royal Family. But a critical and cautious engagement with their claims seems the most professional approach, especially since the much-disputed revelations in Andrew Morton's *Diana: Her True Story* (1992) proved to be accurate, and published with the Princess of Wales's approval. At the very least they can provide some corrective to the continuing flow of respectful semi-official biographies and studies, many using a very selective history of the House of Windsor.[18]

The present position makes the work of the official royal biographer unenviable. Philip Ziegler's *King Edward VIII: The Official Biography* (1990) was fortunate both in dealing with a figure cut off by the rest of the Royal Family – so his shortcomings could only reflect well on it – and in that the ground had been so well prepared by Frances Donaldson's well-documented biography in 1974.[19] Ziegler was therefore the first official biographer not to approach his task in terms of a 'mythological' narrative (though he still dutifully considered that his predecessors had 'demonstrated that it is possible to be "official" without being ponderously decorous or slavishly discreet').[20] Shawcross will have to prove whether an official life can still carry any authority in an age of 'openness'.[21] It is likely that the genre of royal biography that historians will continue to find most useful is that described by Cannadine as 'unofficial and non-commissioned, but sometimes with approved access to the royal archives'.[22] In biographies by Kenneth Rose and Sarah Bradford as well as Donaldson, historians have authoritative and sufficiently frank lives of the previous three monarchs,[23] though not yet for Victoria and Edward VII.

---

[17] Ben Pimlott in *Guardian*, 18 Sep. 1997; D. Cannadine, *History in Our Own Times* (New Haven, 1998), p. 6.

[18] E.g. E. Longford, *The Royal House of Windsor* (London, 1974); R. Lacey, *Majesty* (London, 1977); J. Dimbleby, *Prince Charles* (London, 1994).

[19] F. Donaldson, *Edward VIII* (London, 1974). He was singular also in that he published his memoirs, though these are disappointingly conventional on the extent of royal powers and are primarily, and misleadingly, self-justificatory: The Duke of Windsor, *A King's Story* (London, 1951).

[20] P. Ziegler, *King Edward VIII* (London, 1990), p. xii.

[21] It may, however, be noted that Shawcross left his original publisher, Penguin, because they published Paul Burrell's *A Royal Duty*: *Guardian*, 7 Jan. 2004.

[22] D. Cannadine, 'From biography to history: writing the modern British monarchy', *Historical Research* 77 (2004), 297.

[23] K. Rose, *King George V* (London, 1983); S. Bradford, *King George VI* (London, 1989). But this style of book is no guarantee against mythologizing; Robert Rhodes James's study of George VI stated that 'he had no prejudices': *A Spirit Undaunted* (London, 1998), p. 344.

Constitutional historians and lawyers share with official royal biographers an emphasis on the constitutional propriety of monarchs in a state 'headed by a sovereign who reigns but does not rule'.[24] Since the British constitution depends upon much conventional custom and practice, they have to adopt the historian's approach of analyzing the working of institutions over time and considering moments of conflict or tension[25] – though usually without extensive historical research, and often relying on official royal biographies for their understanding of particular political episodes. A common and long-standing view is that Queen Victoria – albeit against her will, in some versions – was the first constitutional monarch, and that her successors 'all sought to reign according to the fundamental precepts of constitutional monarchy as laid down by Bagehot'.[26] The fundamental trope is the substitution of influence for power.[27] The monarch was obliged to act on ministerial advice, a convention which over time altered in function from protecting the people from royal power to shielding the monarch from partisan criticism about ministerial decisions. Nonetheless, 'under normal conditions' the monarch held Bagehot's three rights or, in Rodney Brazier's reformulation, five rights – 'to be informed, to be consulted, to advise, to encourage and to warn'.[28] But exceptionally, when a government ends or a prime minister requests a dissolution of Parliament, the monarch has no ministerial advice and so is not bound by these conventions. The monarch also 'has the right (some would say duty) to exercise . . . discretion to ensure that the values which lie at the foundation of a constitutional system are preserved', and can do so by using the 'reserve powers' of insisting on a dissolution, dismissing ministers or refusing the Royal Assent. Vernon Bogdanor argues that this was how George V understood his duty during the Irish Home Rule crisis of 1911–14.[29]

Many constitutional writers find it unremarkable that the authoritative statements of constitutional rules consist of what Bagehot simply made up, what authorities like Anson or Jennings considered was the case, or what a monarch's private secretary wrote in a letter to *The*

---

[24] V. Bogdanor, 'The monarchy and the constitution', *Parliamentary Affairs* 49 (1996), 407.

[25] E.g. R. Brazier, *Constitutional Reform* (Oxford, 1998) and *Constitutional Practice* (Oxford, 1999).

[26] V. Bogdanor, *The Monarchy and the Constitution* (Oxford, 1995), pp. 40–1.

[27] E.g. ibid., p. 34; R. Brazier, 'The monarchy', in V. Bogdanor (ed.), *The British Constitution in the Twentieth Century* (Oxford, 2003), p. 76.

[28] E. Barendt, *An Introduction to Constitutional Law* (Oxford, 1998), p. 112; Bogdanor, 'Monarchy', pp. 414, 416; Brazier, 'Monarchy', pp. 75–8.

[29] Bogdanor, 'Monarchy', 413; Bogdanor, *Monarchy*, p. 65; Brazier, 'Monarchy', pp. 81–3.

Times.[30] The more fundamental issue is that such writers regard the conventions about the monarch's personal prerogatives as sufficiently clear not to compromise the principle that the monarch must remain neutral in a party political sense. Other writers have been less sure. Peter Hennessy found in the 1990s that the four officials who interpret constitutional conventions – the cabinet secretary, the clerk of the House of Commons, the Queen's private secretary, and the prime minister's principal private secretary – hold the view that 'if you have an unwritten constitution, you make it up as you go along'.[31]

As Robert Colls has put it, 'we have been asked to trust a constitution almost indistinguishable from the ascribed personality of the men we have invited to govern us'. For him it is the pervasive culture of 'state secrecy' which allows conventions to be interpreted in this way.[32] Yet such criticisms do not figure in traditional institutional approaches, which simply note that it is 'a fundamental condition of royal influence that it remains private' in order to safeguard the monarch's strict neutrality in public.[33] This culture's wider impact is unstudied, except in the area of royal finances. Philip Hall, though denied access to relevant royal and Treasury files, tenaciously followed clues in parliamentary debates, private papers and the National Archives to produce a long history of royal tax avoidance and transfer of public money into the monarch's private funds. The secrecy surrounding these transactions meant that official guides to the monarchy presented false information; and Hall further establishes that this secrecy was the product of collusion by the various layers of the political establishment, from royal advisers and civil servants to Chancellors of the Exchequer of all political parties who failed to report new arrangements to Parliament or misled MPs into believing that recent practices had always existed.[34]

Recent political historians interested in the modern monarchy have been especially drawn to Queen Victoria's reign. They have generally agreed that she regarded herself neither as neutral, nor as bound in normal circumstances by ministerial advice. Cannadine has argued that the

---

[30] See D. Cannadine's review of Bogdanor's *Monarchy*, in *Times Literary Supplement*, 3 Nov. 1995; and for *Times* letters, P. Hennessy, 'Searching for the "great ghost": the Palace, the premiership, the Cabinet and the constitution in the post-war period', *Journal of Contemporary History* 30 (1995), 222, and Bogdanor, *Monarchy*, p. 71.

[31] Hennessy, 'Searching', 213; and for earlier doubts see H. J. Laski, *Parliamentary Government in England* (London, 1938), ch. 8.

[32] R. Colls, 'The constitution and the English', *History Workshop Journal* 46 (1998), 100.

[33] Bogdanor, 'Monarchy', 417–9. Yet secrecy has generated royal conspiracy theories, collected in L. Picknett, C. Prince, S. Prior and R. Brydon, *War of the Windsors* (Edinburgh, 2002).

[34] Hall, *Royal Fortune*, pp. ix–xxi, 13–7, 34–6, 40, 52–62, 113–14.

Queen's Hanoverian influences and temperament together with Prince Albert's backward-looking concept of monarchical power meant that in the early decades of her reign the Queen attempted to reassert royal political power.[35] Some have noted the Queen's close interest in foreign policy, and argued that here she could exercise power through her contacts with her continental royal relatives.[36] Miles Taylor has recently shown that in imperial affairs too, the Queen, by communicating directly with governors, generals and Indian princes, exercised 'a considerable sway of personal influence'; it seems indicative that even before the 1876 Royal Titles Act, the Queen referred to herself as 'Empress' of India.[37] Moreover, Richard Williams has demonstrated that Victorian newspapers reveal no widespread sense of a politically neutral monarchy, and that on occasion – including over the Royal Titles Act – there was much public criticism of 'unconstitutional' ambitions.[38] In fact, it is clear that public awareness of the Queen's partisanship and political interventions fell short of the reality. It has long been known, from the Queen's letters published between 1907 and 1932, that she loathed and obstructed Gladstone, in practice exercising a 'right to instruct, to abuse, and to hector'.[39] The Queen was protected by the culture of secrecy, and the reticence of the politicians and her private secretaries. Gladstone, despite considerable ill-treatment, 'shielded the Queen from the consequences of her actions'.[40] One private secretary, Henry Ponsonby, noted that his tasks included translating the 'first violent reactions of the human being' into 'the cautious disapproval of the sovereign'.[41] The monarch's private secretaries were evidently of considerable political importance, but like other members of the court they have received little study. Kim Reynolds's study of the Queen's female household – with its conclusion that it played a role in 'reinforcing the Queen's political prejudices' – is the only thorough study of any part of her court.[42]

---

[35] D. Cannadine, 'The last Hanoverian sovereign?: the Victorian monarchy in historical perspective, 1688–1988', in A. L. Beier, D. Cannadine and J. M. Rosenheim (eds.), *The First Modern Society* (Cambridge, 1989), pp. 127–65.

[36] B. Harrison, *The Transformation of British Politics, 1860–1995* (Oxford, 1996), p. 50, and see e.g. R. R. McLean, 'Kaiser Wilhelm II and the British Royal Family: Anglo-German dynastic relations in political context, 1890–1914', *History* 86 (2001), 478–502; K. Urbach, 'Prince Albert and Lord Palmerston: a battle royal' (unpublished paper).

[37] M. Taylor, 'Queen Victoria and India, 1837–61', *Victorian Studies* 46 (2004), 266, 272.

[38] R. Williams, *The Contentious Crown* (Aldershot, 1997).

[39] H. C. G. Matthew, *Gladstone, 1875–98* (Oxford, 1995), pp. 260, 259–64.

[40] Ibid., p. 261.

[41] A. Ponsonby, *Henry Ponsonby* (London, 1942), p. 174.

[42] K. D. Reynolds, *Aristocratic Women and Political Society in Victorian Britain* (Oxford, 1998), pp. 190–217.

Was it, as Cannadine suggested, just bad Hanoverian blood that motivated the Queen to attempt to behave as an 'unconstitutional' monarch? It has been argued that she had a firm sense of the constitution as balanced between 'a monarchic, an aristocratical, and a democratic element', and of her duty to preserve this balance.[43] It seems clear that some politicians played on her beliefs for their own party purposes with, for example, Disraeli in 1868 and Salisbury in 1886 emphasizing her right to dissolve Parliament. She also appears to have believed that her temporal powers were a 'gift of God', and this sense of divine ordination certainly meant that she was very serious and active in her further role as governor of the Church of England.[44] Brian Harrison has suggested that her reiterated phrase 'my people' reflected a sense of personal responsibility for the national welfare.[45] Arnstein has noted that she was by temperament a 'warrior queen', regarding herself as a soldier's child, taking close interest in military matters, and decreeing a military funeral for herself.[46] That the Queen received large numbers of petitions – 800 a year in the 1850s – has been presented as evidence of a popular belief in a governing monarchy,[47] but it may also explain why she felt she understood the temper of the country. Historians need to understand her self-image more precisely, and assess if and how it shaped her understanding of her political responsibilities.

Yet there remains a need for caution over the effectiveness of Queen Victoria's political impact. Close study of particular episodes has found her more flexible towards political realities than rigid about her prerogatives. Particularly given the fluidity in the political system between 1851 and 1859, it is perhaps less surprising that the Queen and Prince Albert were tempted to pursue royal government, than that it advanced so little. It is evident that the Queen appreciated that she had limited room for manoeuvre: her power of dissolving Parliament could be used only in 'extreme cases and with a certainty of success', because 'to use this instrument and be defeated is a thing most lowering to the Crown and hurtful

---

43 G. H. L. Le May, *The Victorian Constitution* (London, 1979), pp. 2, 93; F. Prochaska, *The Republic of Britain, 1760–2000* (London, 2000), p. 136.

44 E. Longford, *Victoria R.I.* (London, 1966), pp. 711–2; G. I. T. Machin, *Politics and the Churches in Great Britain, 1869–1921* (Oxford, 1987), pp. 22, 70, 209; D. W. R. Bahlman, 'The Queen, Mr. Gladstone and church patronage', *Victorian Studies* 3 (1960), 349–80; Bahlman, 'Politics and church patronage in the Victoria age', *Victorian Studies* 22 (1979), 253–96.

45 C. Ford and B. Harrison, *A Hundred Years Ago* (London, 1994), p. 267.

46 W. L. Arnstein, 'The warrior queen: reflections on Victoria and her world', *Albion* 30 (1998), 1–28: Arnstein, *Queen Victoria* (Basingstoke, 2003), pp. 200–1.

47 D. M. Craig, 'The crowned republic? Monarchy and anti-monarchy in Britain, 1760–1901', *Historical Journal* 46 (2003), 177.

to the country'.[48] It is also difficult to see that the Victorian monarchy ever had a decisive and independent influence on the course of foreign policy; Karina Urbach points out that Palmerston prevailed against Albert on almost every issue.[49] Similarly in imperial affairs, the scope for royal intervention declined as Liberal policy reduced Crown patronage and the army was reformed. For Taylor, the 1876 formal adoption of the title 'Empress of India' ironically marks the moment when 'most of Victoria's imperial powers – both formal and real – had been reduced or removed'.[50] After the 1884 third Reform Act, although there was 'an increasing awareness of Victoria's partisanship' there were also 'no widely-held fears that it could be used to subvert the course of parliamentary politics'.[51] In practice the Queen feared being dragged publicly into partisan positions which might provoke questions about the monarchy's existence; so whatever her class sympathies or private convictions, she sought compromise and under pressure would offer arbitration. The monarchy has found survival in hedging and trimming.

Consequently, similar caution is needed with her successors. The journalist and biographer Simon Heffer, who used material in the Royal Archives, has argued that Edward VII's reign 'saw the last wholesale exercise of true political power in the Sovereign through the King's initiative in international alliances and his *de facto* control over the reform of the army'. He certainly pinpointed areas where the King took an interest and had some impact, such as honours or appointments in the diplomatic corps.[52] What Heffer will not entertain is the conventional but also well-documented view that Edward VII lacked the diligence and drive to be a consistently significant political player. Moreover, the diplomatic historian Roderick McLean doubts whether any change in the stance of the British monarchy 'was a decisive factor in the political estrangement between London and Berlin before 1914'. What McLean's work does suggest is a need for systematic investigation of foreign governments' understandings of the British monarchy's political influence: it appears that in July 1914 the Kaiser believed that 'Britain would not go to war against Germany because George V would not allow the British government to intervene.'[53]

---

[48] Victoria to Russell, 16 Jul. 1846, in W. C. Costin and J. S. Watson, *The Law and Working of the Constitution*, II (London, 1952), p. 393.

[49] Urbach, 'Albert and Palmerston'.

[50] M. Taylor, 'The imperial crown: the monarchy and the British Empire, 1801–76' (unpublished paper).

[51] Williams, *Contentious Crown*, p. 116.

[52] S. Heffer, *Power and Place. The Political Consequences of Edward VII* (London, 1999), pp. 2, 88, 94.

[53] McLean, 'Wilhelm and the British Royal Family', 487, 502.

On balance, the preoccupation with identifying the first constitutional monarch and with assessing the continuing scope of prerogative powers should be abandoned as unproductive and reductionist in a system where ultimately 'the British Constitution is what happens next'.[54] The prerogatives that remained were the ones that the monarchy could politically get away with. The monarchy should be seen as simply one – and in this period very rarely if ever the most important – of several institutions within the process of government, responding to the political possibilities opened up by party competition and by public reaction, concerned first and foremost to ensure its own continuance.

For the monarchy, this often meant seeking compromise and an arbitrating role when conflict broke out between the parties or within the realm.[55] The historian of British inter-party conferences notes this royal role in 1868–9 over the Irish Church question, in 1884 over the Reform Bill, in 1906 over the Education Bill, in 1910 over the finance and Parliament Bills, in 1913–14 over Irish Home Rule, in 1916 over the breakup of the Asquith coalition, in 1921 over the opening of the Northern Ireland Parliament, and in 1931 over the creation of the National Government.[56] Assessments of the effectiveness and prudence of royal arbitration have varied sharply. Bogdanor believes that the instincts of Edward VII and George V were correct in the crises of 1910–14. Colin Matthew is more critical, and argues that George V 'leaned too far towards the Unionists'.[57] Harrison sees George V's actions in 1931 being endorsed by voters in the following general election, but Ross McKibbin suggests that his behaviour was 'hardly prudent'.[58]

McKibbin maintains that the arbitrating role extended beyond politics to class interests: the monarchy became 'apparently . . . the even-handed guarantor of the class-neutrality of Parliament', ensuring that the rules of the game were followed. This, he argues, was acceptable to all classes: 'to the politically strong because the Crown undoubtedly represented a conservative force; to the politically weak because they, more than any, had an interest in seeing that the rules *were* followed'. He notes that even the language of the monarchy became 'engrossed by the stylised vocabulary of "fairness"'.[59] Harrison detects a still broader royal 'class-reconciling

---

[54] Hennessy, 'Searching', 227.   [55] Harrison, *Transformation*, p. 50.
[56] J. D. Fair, *British Interparty Conferences* (Oxford, 1980); B. Harrison, *Peaceable Kingdom* (Oxford, 1982), p. 351.
[57] Bogdanor, *Monarchy*, pp. 113–35; H. C. G. Matthew, 'Edward VII' and 'George V', *Oxford Dictionary of National Biography* (online edition), hereafter *ODNBO*.
[58] Harrison, *Peaceable Kingdom*, p. 351; R. McKibbin, *Classes and Cultures* (Oxford, 1998), pp. 5–6.
[59] McKibbin, *The Ideologies of Class* (Oxford, 1990), pp. 18–9.

role', integrating first the radical middle class in the nineteenth and then the organised working class in the twentieth century.[60]

The distribution of honours is considered important in establishing this new role (as are royal philanthropy and ceremony, considered in the next section). Their scope and frequency was extended, with fourteen new or enlarged orders of chivalry under Victoria, and the introduction in 1888 of 'New Year honours' and 'birthday honours'.[61] Although the system reinforced the class hierarchy through its numerous gradations, honours came to be accepted by members of the working class because, argues McKibbin, 'for most of the recipients no class was involved; they were a class-neutral representation of the idea of the nation'.[62] Moreover in 1917, with the creation of the Order of the British Empire, the Palace established an 'all ranks' list, with awards going to workers. However, it is worth remembering that honours could spark sectional resentments or be accepted in bad faith. Harrison sensibly adds the qualifications that the monarchy's 'healing role' has not been crucial in any areas of potential division in society, and 'it can help to unify only if it works with the grain of opinion'.[63] In other words, the monarchy can reflect and entrench integration, but not cause it.

One reason why the monarchy's class-reconciling role has been limited may be because of its 'less publicized role' as head of the establishment, inextricably bound to the aristocracy.[64] This was a favoured theme for Victorian and Edwardian republicans,[65] and in some senses the link continued to evolve. In the late nineteenth century there was a congruence of interest between the court and an increasingly Conservative aristocracy, as the number of peers increased and court appointments were used as 'a fertile source of political patronage'.[66] The post-war disappearance of European monarchies meant that the Royal Family had to turn to British aristocrats for marriage partners, and in contrast to his grandmother's criticisms of the native aristocracy or his father's cosmopolitanism,[67] George V epitomized the Norfolk squirearchy. Moreover, in the appointment of courtiers, '"Old Corruption" did not merely linger: it positively

[60] Harrison, *Transformation*, pp. 334–5.
[61] Ibid., p. 334; Ford and Harrison, *Hundred Years*, p. 263.
[62] McKibbin, *Ideologies*, pp. 19–20.   [63] Harrison, *Transformation*, p. 337.
[64] K. Martin, *The Crown and the Establishment* (Harmondsworth, 1963), p. 81.
[65] A. Taylor, *Down with the Crown* (London, 1999), p. 199; Taylor, '"Pig-sticking princes": royal hunting, moral outrage, and the republican opposition to animal abuse in nineteenth- and early twentieth-century Britain', *History* 84 (2004), 30–48.
[66] H. C. G. Matthew, 'Public life and politics', in Matthew (ed.), *The Nineteenth Century, 1815–1901* (Oxford, 2000), p. 123.
[67] Longford, *Victoria*, p. 441; D. Thompson, *Queen Victoria: Gender and Power* (London, 1990), p. 41; K. Urbach, 'Diplomatic history since the cultural turn', *Historical Journal* 46 (2003), 991.

thrived', numbers growing with the multiplication of junior royal households. Cannadine judges that 'most of these courtiers were obscurantist
and reactionary in the extreme', with a hierarchical and 'thoroughly Tory'
vision of society they shared with George V.[68] McKibbin sees these attitudes continuing in the reigns of Edward VIII and George VI, dismissing
the former's embracing of American glamour as a 'trivial revolt'.[69]

Harrison, on the other hand, has argued that from the early years of
Victoria's reign the monarchy remained distanced from the aristocracy,
which explains why in the twentieth century 'the first was left standing
amidst the ruins of the second'. Victoria embraced some middle-class values, and 'London society' was continually diluted and extended by the
admission of successive groups of newcomers.[70] So for Beatrice Webb,
'society' in the last quarter of the nineteenth century was 'a shifting mass
of miscellaneous and uncertain membership . . . a body that could be
defined, not by its circumference, which could not be traced, but by its
centre or centres' – the court, the cabinet, the racing set and 'a mysterious
group of millionaire financiers'.[71] The fact of dilution is undeniable, but
its consequences are debatable. The aristocracy remained part of 'society', and plutocracy is no more 'classless' than democracy. Monarchy was
left standing because the political system shielded it with a thoroughness
it was not prepared to extend to the aristocracy.

Historians have also assessed how well royal education has prepared
monarchs for their political and ceremonial role. Peter Gordon and Dennis Lawton judge that 'no previous monarch had been so systematically educated on British lines as Victoria', yet in contrast no subsequent monarch (or current heir) has been anywhere near adequately
educated.[72] McKibbin argues that the most striking feature of the education of George V, Edward VIII and George VI was its 'aimlessness' and
narrowness, leaving them with 'the cultural and educational attitudes

---

[68] D. Cannadine, *The Decline and Fall of the British Aristocracy* (New Haven, 1990), pp. 244–
5, 249, 304–7.

[69] McKibbin, *Classes*, pp. 4–6. Against the claims in Rhodes James, *Spirit Undaunted*,
pp. 277, 285–6, that George VI was a 'progressive liberal' at ease with the Labour
government, see *The Duff Cooper Diaries, 1915–1951*, ed. J. J. Norwich (London, 2005),
p. 453, for the King's 'most outspoken' criticism of his ministers: 'he seems to hate and
despise them'.

[70] Harrison, *Transformation*, pp. 332–4. See also N. W. Ellenberger, 'The transformation
of London "society" at the end of Victoria's reign: evidence from the court presentation
records', *Albion* 22 (1990), 633–53.

[71] B. Webb, *My Apprenticeship* (1926; Cambridge, 1979), pp. 47–53.

[72] P. Gordon and D. Lawton, *Royal Education* (London, 1999), though see Matthew
'George V' for a more positive assessment of George V's own education and that of
his sons. Princesses Elizabeth and Margaret, however, were especially badly served: S.
Bradford, *Elizabeth* (London, 1996), pp. 40–1, and idem., 'Princess Margaret Rose',
ODNBO.

of landed-gentry-with-military-connections'.[73] What these authors also recognize, however, is the difficulty in deciding what is an appropriate royal education. The royal role is also about temperament, as Edward VIII's short reign demonstrated.[74] What historians should also consider is the impact of the 'normal', daily course of royal life on the monarchy. There is no single adequate work on this,[75] though glimpses of the extraordinary nature of his life are offered by biographies and memoirs.[76] Just as Jeffrey Auerbach has argued that 'imperial boredom', monotony, and melancholy pervaded the lives of British imperial administrators,[77] so the monarchy should be explored in terms of 'royal boredom' in the face of the restrictions of royal life. One response was typified by George V: over-compensation through obsessive concern with the accuracy of the game book or of dress.[78] Another was Edward VIII's selective and superficial revolt against 'my father's slowly turning wheel of habit, leading him year after year in unchanging rotation from one Royal residence to another and from one Royal pursuit to another'.[79]

II

Bagehot's *The English Constitution* has had an enduring influence on writing about the British monarchy, and several approaches to its significance can be found. In royal biographies, it has automatically been treated as authoritative. Some historians have been interested in whether it was an accurate account of the monarchy's role in the 1860s, or only became so later: most commonly it is judged incorrect for the 1860s because Bagehot lacked 'inside political knowledge' and underestimated the importance of party government, but correct for George V's reign.[80] Prochaska has dismissed Bagehot as turning 'some fine, misleading phrases, which have besotted monarchists and constitutional writers ever since', but lacking genuine insight into the extent of the 'efficient' role of the monarchy in civil society through royal philanthropy. Bagehot as a political journalist was 'little attuned to social issues or the problems of the poor'.[81] Marxist

[73] McKibbin, *Classes*, pp. 3–4.
[74] Ziegler, *Edward VIII*, p. 386, judges that failure to take advice was 'at the heart of the Duke's problems'.
[75] Several books describe the royal household's structure, but give little sense of how it works on a daily basis: e.g. J. Glasheen, *The Secret People of the Palaces* (London, 1998); B. Hoey, *All the Queen's Men* (London, 1992).
[76] E.g. *Louisa: Lady in Waiting*, ed. E. Longford (London, 1979); Lord E. Pelham-Clinton, *Life at the Court of Queen Victoria, 1861–1901*, ed. B. St. John Nevill (Stroud, 1997).
[77] J. Auerbach, 'Imperial boredom', *Common Knowledge* 11 (2005), 284–6.
[78] Rose, *George V*, p. 40; Matthew, 'George V'.
[79] Duke of Windsor, *King's Story*, p. 283.   [80] Harrison, *Transformation*, p. 52.
[81] F. Prochaska, *Royal Bounty* (New Haven, 1995), p. 101.

historians believe that his book is best regarded as giving 'the middle classes an apologia for the aristocratic parts of the Constitution in the best of bourgeois terms', or a 'self-congratulatory myth' of a modern 'disguised republic', which provided the middle class with 'an alibi for not bothering to think farther' about the monarchy.[82] Conservative historians have interpreted Bagehot's condescending view that the common people were 'stupid' as meaning that he believed they had 'a certain sane common sense'.[83] In another approach he is an early political scientist formulating a rudimentary but testable notion of the popular 'deference' which underpinned the political system.[84] In contrast Richard Crossman stood Bagehot's view of deference on its head, suggesting that 'the secret of our political stability is the deferential attitude of our rulers'.[85] More recently, several writers have sought evidence in various periods for Bagehot's view that the 'immense majority' of Victoria's subjects 'will say she rules by "God's grace"'.[86]

Most of these approaches assume that some parts of Bagehot's analysis of the monarchy are relevant for the present day, and that the scholar's task is to identify which ones. None is primarily interested in contextualizing it in relation to Bagehot's other writings and Victorian public debates. By contrast, this has been the objective of intellectual historians and the editors of two recent editions of *The English Constitution*. These have argued that it must be relocated within the parliamentary reform debates from the later 1850s, and that it is best understood as a comparative study of parliamentary and presidential government.[87] Bagehot's rejection of the theories of mixed government, separation of powers and unconstitutional royal power, and emphasis on the monarchy's ceremonial role presented

---

[82] E. P. Thompson, 'The peculiarities of the English', *The Poverty of Theory and Other Essays* (London, 1978), p. 54; Nairn, *The Enchanted Glass*, pp. 361–5.

[83] N. St. John-Stevas (ed.) *Walter Bagehot* (London, 1959) p. 49; G. Himmelfarb, *Victorian Minds* (London, 1968), pp. 230–1; and in a more sophisticated form, S. Collini, D. Winch and J. Burrow, *That Noble Science of Politics* (Cambridge, 1983), p. 170.

[84] A. Briggs, *Victorian People* (Harmondsworth, 1965), pp. 99–100; J. G. Blumler, J. R. Brown, A. J. Ewbank and T. J. Nossiter, 'Attitudes to the monarchy: their structure and development during a ceremonial occasion', *Political Studies* 19 (1971), 149–71; R. Rose and D. Kavanagh, 'The monarchy in contemporary political culture', in R. Rose (ed.), *Studies in British Politics* (London, 1976), pp. 16–41.

[85] R. H. S. Crossman, 'Introduction', in W. Bagehot, *The English Constitution* (London, 1963), p. 33.

[86] W. Bagehot, *The English Constitution*, ed. M. Taylor (Oxford, 2001), p. 40; Craig, 'Crowned republic?', 169; B. Pimlott, *The Queen* (London, 2001), pp. 646–7, who argued that 'the persistence of the belief in the special access of Monarchs and by extension other royals to divine grace, alluded to by Bagehot, may indeed point in the direction in which we should be looking'.

[87] M. Taylor 'Introduction' to Bagehot, *The English Constitution*, pp. ix, xv. xx; P. Smith, 'Introduction' to W. Bagehot, *The English Constitution* (Cambridge, 2001), p. vii; H. S. Jones, *Victorian Political Thought* (Basingstoke, 2000), pp. 67–8.

'nothing . . . to astonish anyone familiar with the existing literature on the subject'.[88]

More original were Bagehot's views on the tension between social cohesion and national progress. Such progress was only possible where government was 'government by discussion', and parliamentary government was more effective than presidential government in harnessing intelligence and promoting tolerance – the hallmarks of government by discussion.[89] But parliamentary government was only compatible with certain 'national characters', which are the product of natural selection and the force of imitation.[90] Even then, a progressive community with the appropriate national character might be unstable because of the survival among the majority of the population of elements of 'the unstable nature of their barbarous ancestors'.[91] Bagehot therefore needed an explanation of 'how rational government by an élite could command the allegiance of masses supposedly incapable of rational political understanding', and found it in the deference of the masses to monarchical rule.[92] Yet Paul Smith has noted that Bagehot's assertion that the masses believe that the monarch really rules had no firmer basis than what could be gleaned from speaking to servants, and that it is 'not clear how far he really believes this picture of popular innocence' – especially since he systematically undermined the idea that the practical working of government still required a monarch.[93]

For Bagehot, the popularity of the monarchy was closely connected with its political role. Despite reservations about 'a timeless but ultimately futile discussion of whether the British . . . have ever really loved their monarchy',[94] most historians of the institution have considered part of their task to be explanation of its popular hold. Even so, there is surprisingly little research on 'what the monarchy has meant to the public at different times',[95] and even on the extent of royal popularity. The point is disputed for the pre-1870s period, and such claims as that after 1918 the

---

[88] Smith, 'Introduction', pp. xiii–xv.

[89] W. Bagehot, *Physics and Politics* (London, 1896 edn.), pp. 41, 64, 158.

[90] Collini, Winch and Burrow, *Noble Science*, pp. 164–70; D. M. Craig, 'Democracy and national character', *History of European Ideas* 29 (2003), 499–501.

[91] Bagehot, *Physics and Politics*, p. 154.

[92] Smith, 'Introduction', pp. xx–xxi; Taylor, 'Introduction', pp. xxi–xxv; Bagehot, *English Constitution*, pp. 34, 37, 46, 65, 185.

[93] Smith, 'Introduction', pp. xxi, xxvi; Bagehot, *English Constitution*, p. 44.

[94] M. Taylor, 'Republics versus empires: Charles Dilke's republicanism reconsidered', in D. Nash and A. Taylor (eds.), *Republicanism in Victorian Society* (Stroud, 2000), p. 25.

[95] Craig, 'Crowned republic?', 184. The most useful studies are H. Jennings and C. Madge (eds.), *May the Twelfth* (London, 1937); P. Ziegler, *Crown and People* (Newton Abbot, 1979); and M. Billig, *Talking of the Royal Family* (London, 1992). See also *Mass-Observation at the Movies*, ed. J. Richards and D. Sheridan (London, 1987) for popular reactions to newsreels featuring royalty during the Second World War.

monarchy's 'hold on the popular imagination was much strengthened' remain matters of judgement.[96]

In addressing this issue, constitutional historians have tended to invert Bagehot. Where he saw parliamentary government deriving support and legitimacy from popular deference towards the monarchy, they consider the late Victorian monarchy's prestige to stem from its association with parliamentary government and with liberalism. Even so, Bogdanor returns to Bagehot in maintaining that the electorate needs 'the reassurance of a visible presence'.[97] Other historians have used sociological, psychological or anthropological theories. Edward Shils's and Michael Young's famous 1953 article on 'the meaning of the coronation' is most widely cited. While accepting that all societies have a clash of interests and beliefs, they argue that societies are nevertheless kept 'generally peaceful and coherent' by agreements on shared moral values; and that Britain had 'a degree of moral unity equalled by no other large national state', principally because of the 'assimilation of the working class into the moral consensus'. For them, the coronation is the ceremonial occasion for the affirmation of these moral values and for 'the Queen's promise to abide by the moral standards of society', such that through the mass media monarch and people were 'brought into a great nation-wide communion', with the characteristics of a religious ritual. Other, more frequent, royal events similarly affirm moral values: for example, the monarch's Christmas broadcast helps generate devotion to the monarch 'for the virtue which he expresses in his family life', which is in turn an expression of 'devotion to one's own family, because the values embodied in each are the same'.[98]

Critics of Shils and Young point to their excessive functionalism and neglect of issues of power.[99] But, like Shils and Young, they accept that the monarchy is a dominant national institution, and broadly endorse Frank Parkin's theory of deviance: the 'normal' condition of dominant institutions is to enjoy popular support among all classes, unless individuals participate in normative sub-systems which act as 'barriers to the dominant values'.[100] On this understanding, explanation should be concerned

---

[96] McKibbin, *Ideologies*, p. 7.   [97] Bogdanor, *Monarchy*, pp. 40, 303.

[98] E. Shils and M. Young, 'The meaning of the Coronation', *The Sociological Review* 1 (1953), 63–81.

[99] N. Birnbaum, 'Monarchs and sociologists' *Sociological Review* 3 (1955), 5–23; S. Lukes, 'Political ritual and social integration', *Essays in Social Theory* (London, 1977), pp. 52–73. McKibbin, *Classes*, p. 13, endorses aspects of Shils's and Young's argument, but argues that there were 'always tacitly assumed that there were areas of British life where it could not expect its moral and emotional authority to be effective'.

[100] F. Parkin, 'Working-class Conservatives: a theory of political deviance', *British Journal of Sociology* 18 (1967), 282.

less with the monarchy's popularity than with its periods of unpopularity. Psychological theories indicate the same conclusion.[101] On balance, the call to integrate sociological and anthropological theories into research on the monarchy has not met with a positive response,[102] and with changing intellectual fashions, most historians probably find them 'rather crude and elitist'.[103] Instead, except for the impact of literary criticism on feminist studies of the monarchy, historians eschew theory (aside from noting its existence) and concentrate on recovering the specific historical context. This often produces thorough research into different aspects of royal public events and activities. But mostly these studies adopt an elite perspective, using sources left by Palace officials and other organizers, and usually assume that the popular reaction was what these had planned for and expected.

Many explanations of royal popularity still follow Cannadine's 1983 essay. He outlined ten aspects needing investigation: the monarch's political power; his or her character and reputation; the nation's economic and social structure; the national self-image; the type, extent and attitude of the media; the state of technology and fashion; the condition of the capital city where most royal ceremonials took place; the organisers' attitudes; the nature of the ceremonial as actually performed, and commercial exploitation of the occasion.[104] This remains a valuable research agenda, and several areas remain little studied. More contentious is how Cannadine interpreted developments in these areas. He focused his interpretation on the increasing elaboration, frequency and impact of royal ceremonies, and found especial significance in the period from the 1870s to 1914 – 'a time when old ceremonials were staged with an expertise and appeal which had been lacking before, and when new rituals were self-consciously invented to accentuate this development'.[105]

Cannadine's essay should be considered in conjunction with his co-authored study of the Diamond Jubilee in Cambridge, and his book on the development of class in modern Britain. The planning of the 1897 celebrations in Cambridge exposed tensions between the university, the

---

[101] E.g. E. Jones, 'The psychology of constitutional monarchy', *New Statesman and Nation*, 1 Feb. 1936, 141–2, arguing that in a constitutional monarchy, a Freudian desire for, yet horror of, parricide is reconciled by veneration of the monarch and periodic removal of the prime minister.

[102] As noted by D. Cannadine, 'Divine rites of kings', in D. Cannadine and S. Price (eds.), *Rituals of Royalty* (Cambridge, 1987), pp. 2–4, 12–9, though for acknowledgement of the difficulties see E. Hammerton and D. Cannadine, 'Conflict and consensus on a ceremonial occasion: the Diamond Jubilee in Cambridge in 1897', *Historical Journal* 24 (1981), 143–4. Perhaps the most successful use of sociological theory is the use of Ernest Gellner's theory of nationalism in Nairn, *Enchanted Glass*.

[103] Craig, 'Crowned republic?', 184.

[104] Cannadine, 'Context', pp. 106–7.   [105] Ibid., pp. 108, 120.

middle-class town elite and the local working class; but the celebrations themselves demonstrated a large degree of consensus around a social order in which 'the empire, the university, the mayor, the volunteers and the church were all accorded star billing'.[106] Cannadine's book on class argues that, of the possible forms it might take, the idea of class as denoting a hierarchical society 'has had the widest, most powerful and most abiding appeal', partly because 'Britain retains intact an elaborate, formal system of rank and precedence, culminating in the monarchy itself'. The proliferation of royal ceremonials from the 1790s onwards renewed and reinforced this vision, because the latter 'put hierarchy on display with unprecedented vividness and immediacy'.[107]

These three works together indicate why Cannadine believes grand ceremonies can account for royal popularity. Essentially he endorses the Shils and Young view of a reaffirmation of values, albeit those associated with hierarchy and, as the Cambridge study suggests, those which are dominant rather than general. This is plausible, and the case is strengthened by understanding that relatively infrequent grand national ceremonies were 'reproduced in miniature' in the localities, in comings-of-age on country estates, formal openings of new town halls, and the processions, anniversaries and festivals of friendly societies, chapels and volunteer brigades.[108] Yet Cannadine does not systematically consider the meaning of ritual for its audience. This remains the least satisfactory aspect of his work, especially since he appears sometimes to endorse the vague Bagehotian idea of the emotional draw of the 'theatrical show'.[109] Cannadine does wonder whether in Cambridge in 1897 many workers were not 'hostile or indifferent, and merely regarded the celebrations as an excuse to have a good time', but assumes that the context makes this seem 'intrinsically unlikely'.[110] The problem is that a top-down approach means that an audience's reaction is left to plausible speculation or plain guesswork.

William Kuhn has criticized Cannadine's notion of the 1870s to 1914 as the heyday of 'invented tradition'.[111] First, he challenges a facile view that practices could simply be made up at will. By 1900 'continuities may have outweighed inventions', and he demonstrates how ceremony organizers placed great importance on precedent and accuracy: the more accurate notion would be 'renovation of tradition'.[112] Peter Hinchliff has

---

[106] Hammerton and Cannadine, 'Conflict', 115–43.
[107] D. Cannadine, *Class in Britain* (New Haven, 1998), pp. 22–3, 124–5.
[108] Ford and Harrison, *Hundred Years*, p. 261; and see Cannadine, 'Context', p. 138, and Cannadine, *Class*, pp. 124–5.
[109] Cannadine, 'Context', p. 516.
[110] Hammerton and Cannadine, 'Conflict', p. 143 n. 136.
[111] Cannadine, 'Context', p. 108.
[112] W. M. Kuhn, *Democratic Royalism* (London, 1996), pp. 4, 72, 151.

similarly shown that at Edward VII's coronation, 'a more traditional pattern began to be re-established', based on detailed scholarship of rituals reaching back to the Middle Ages.[113] Moreover, it is important to distinguish between different types of royal ceremonies. The 1887 Golden Jubilee, for which the only precedent was that of 1809, and the 1935 Silver Jubilee, for which there was no precedent, left greater room for innovation than more frequent or fundamental royal occasions.[114] Second, Kuhn shows that ministers played an important part in planning royal ceremonies; that the '*apparent* separation of ceremony from politics was itself the object of intense and feverish political activity'; and that Victoria herself was sceptical about the probity and value of public spectacles.[115] Third, against Cannadine's cynical 'bread and circuses' view, Kuhn argues that the monarchy was also 'the possession, sometimes the obsession, of educated men and women', and that often these, as much as the masses, were the intended audience. Lord Esher in particular intended the ceremonies he orchestrated 'for a more select audience than those imagined by Bagehot'.[116] Nonetheless, the effect of royal ceremonies on the people could hardly not be a critical consideration. Consequently they were gradually made 'representative': for the public thanksgiving for the Prince of Wales's recovery in 1872, seats were allocated for nonconformist and labour leaders, and by 1937 four ordinary workpeople were personally invited by George VI to the coronation service.[117] Moreover, the interest of politicians in grand ceremonial occasions may well have been because they themselves expected benefits, in terms of approval among the electorate.[118]

A second front raises doubts about Cannadine's view that royal ceremony before the 1870s was so infrequent and 'ineptly managed' that it had little popular impact. In contrast, Colley has argued that the growth of newspapers, civic pride, and voluntary and loyalist organizations under

---

[113] P. Hinchliff, 'Frederick Temple, Randall Davidson and the coronation of Edward VII', *Journal of Ecclesiastical History* 48 (1997), 71–95, though see 97–8 for the invention of one ritual, the retention of consecrated oil for subsequent coronations.

[114] The only type of royal ritual to receive systematic research is funerals: see J. Wolffe, *Great Deaths* (Oxford, 2000), and 'Royalty and public grief in Britain: an historical perspective, 1817–1997', in T. Walter (ed.), *The Mourning for Diana* (Oxford, 1999), pp. 53–64. Of course Princess Diana's death and funeral produced an outpouring of commentary: see e.g. M. Merck (ed.), *After Diana: Irreverent Elegies* (London, 1987); J. Richards, S. Wilson and L. Woodhead (eds.), *Diana: The Making of a Media Saint* (London, 1999).

[115] W. M. Kuhn, 'Ceremony and politics: The British monarchy, 1871–1872', *Journal of British Studies* 26 (1987), 133–62.

[116] Ibid., 162; Kuhn, *Democratic Royalism*. p. 72.

[117] Ford and Harrison, *Hundred Years*, p. 262; Jennings and Madge, *May the Twelfth*, p. 6.

[118] For the 1870s, see Prochaska, *Royal Bounty*, pp. 110–1; and for the 1935 Jubilee, McKibbin, *Classes*, p. 8.

George III meant that 'the efficacy of royal celebration was increased and assured by the active collaboration of a multiplicity of individuals and interest groups far removed from the inner circle of Britain's socio-political elite'. By 1820 it was 'axiomatic that royal celebration should ideally involve all political affiliations, all religious groupings and all parts of Great Britain', and should seem to be national and not sectional celebration'.[119] Against Cannadine's further suggestion that George IV's and William IV's political partisanship 'made grand royal ceremonial unacceptable, then renewed royal unpopularity made it impossible', there is Colley's evidence of many 'ostentatiously bi-partisan' local committees organising coronation ceremonies in 1821, 1831 and 1837, and the popular success of George IV's official visits to Dublin and Edinburgh.[120] Studies of Victoria's and Albert's provincial visits in the 1840s and 1850s demonstrate that they had 'learned how to provide crowd-pleasing spectacles for [their] provincial subjects', by 'a potent combination of splendour, modernity and homeliness that was in tune with middle class expectations of a national monarchy' – indeed they had little choice because town councils, railway companies and newspapers often made the Queen's wishes for a private visit impossible.[121] What meaning did the cheering crowds attach to these occasions? John Plunkett argues that they were public displays of 'Victoria's reliance on the approval of her subjects, a celebration of the inclusivity and participation of the People in the political nation', and were 'invested with the discourse of popular constitutionalism'. Yet even this remains guesswork, as the 'assimilation of the monarchy into individual subjectivities' is still unexplored.[122]

For recent times, there is growing interest in how the ceremonial monarchy has been affected by the 'decline in formality' and increased social diversity and heterogeneity of norms. It has been noted that in many respects it became less formal, two key changes being a filmed documentary of the Royal Family's lifestyle in 1969 and the Queen's 'walkabouts' from the 1970s.[123] 'Ancient' ceremonies have been altered, and the monarchy has enjoyed some recent ceremonial successes. However, for some historians it still remains a Victorian 'great-power monarchy', which exists awkwardly in contemporary society and cannot match the

---

[119] L. Colley, 'The apotheosis of George III: loyalty, royalty and the British nation, 1760–1820', *Past and Present* 102 (1984), 112; Colley, *Britons*, pp. 217–36.

[120] Cannadine, 'Context', p. 109; Colley, *Britons*, p. 231.

[121] A. Tyrrell and Y. Ward, '"God bless her little majesty": the popularising of monarchy in the 1840s', *National Identities* 2 (2000), 109–24; Prochaska, *Royal Bounty*, pp. 81–99; J. Plunkett, *Queen Victoria: First Media Monarch* (Oxford, 2003), ch. 1.

[122] Ibid., pp. 14, 17, and cf. p. 8.

[123] Harrison, *Transformation*, p. 326; Pimlott, *The Queen*, pp. 379–88, 397, 447; Ziegler, *Crown and People*, p. 183.

scale and impact of previous royal occasions. Crucially, it no longer has the earlier web of institutional supports, especially the countless local civic ceremonies to mark every royal birth or wedding, nor the force of 'a potent and evocative constitutional symbolism' which underpinned earlier ceremonial successes.[124]

Another set of explanations for royal popularity predicts a brighter future for the monarchy. Prochaska argues that it has remained relevant, and thwarted republicanism and socialism because it created a new role as a focus for civil society through its patronage of charities and its 'highly visible, public-spirited social service'.[125] Although royal philanthropy was often motivated by fear of political disorder, by the mid-nineteenth century the monarchy had become 'a force for liberal values', and by its encouragement of voluntary organizations, was fostering 'democratic aspirations among the lower classes'. Indeed its civic activities meant that it could (though it did not) 'make claims to a hybrid form of republican virtue'.[126] Consequently, royal charitable work has generated little political or media criticism, even though at times it was deployed as 'a bastion of individualism against collectivism' – notably under the Attlee Labour government.[127] In the 1990s, nearly 3,500 organisations had royal patrons, and there was 'no sign that the royal family is being deserted by its charitable allies'.[128] Indeed, some historians believe that the decline of socialism presents the monarchy with new opportunities to extend its charitable work, and 'is likely to sustain royal popularity'.[129]

Prochaska identifies two further reasons why royal philanthropy has created royal popularity. First, from Prince Albert's time it brought the monarchy into close contact with large numbers of the working and middle classes. This was true even during Victoria's 'seclusion' after Albert's death, when her refusal to undertake public ceremonial duties is supposed to have damaged the monarchy – because she continued most of her charitable activities and was everywhere greeted by 'large enthusiastic crowds'. Second, the monarchy always encouraged the belief that individuals, however humble, had a claim on its services, and through civic and charitable associations and the honours system, 'the royal culture of

---

[124] Cannadine, in *Times Literary Supplement*, 3 Nov. 1995; Plunkett, *First Media Monarch*, pp. 245–7.

[125] Prochaska, *Royal Bounty*, passim; Prochaska, *Republic of Britain*, p. xviii.

[126] Prochaska, *Royal Bounty*, pp. 81–86, 98–9, 150, 176, 206; Prochaska, 'George V and republicanism, 1917–1919', *Twentieth Century British History* 10 (1999), 27–51.

[127] Prochaska, *Royal Bounty*, pp. 206, 275, 127–33, 232–8. This does not mean that there was no basis for criticism: see D. Cannadine, 'Social workers', *London Review of Books*, 5 Oct. 1995, for the comment that growing royal giving coexisted with growing royal taking, as tax exemptions and civil list savings increased.

[128] Prochaska, *Royal Bounty*, pp. 274–5.

[129] F. Prochaska, 'The monarchy and charity', *ODNBO*; Harrison, *Transformation*, p. 381; V. Bogdanor, *Power and the People* (London, 1997), pp. 188–93.

hierarchical condescension and the mass culture of social aspiration successfully merged'. Where Cannadine assumed in a Bagehotian way that the royal appeal to the masses was substantially emotional, Prochaska declares that people were 'not as dim as Bagehot gave them credit for being'. The crowds who cheered royal patrons understood that they performed a necessary role and supported useful, ameliorative schemes.[130] Yet Prochaska as much as Cannadine has an elite perspective, with no attempt to examine the sources which could give a detailed impression of the views of ordinary participants in charitable visits. Nevertheless, Prochaska's contribution is not just important in itself, but prompts thought about other, still unresearched, aspects of the 'efficient' public royal role, for example the relationship between monarchy and sport, especially football.[131]

Both Prochaska and Cannadine have emphasized the 'feminisation of the monarchy'. The former argued that the availability of dutiful female royal patrons has been essential for the welfare monarchy, and noted that since the 1830s the sovereign was more often a queen than a king, while the latter asserted that in the modern Royal Family 'kings reigned, but matriarchy ruled', and that 'George VI seems to have been the ultimate castrated male'.[132] Only very recently have feminist and other historians begun systematic study of the connections between royal gender, the royal role and royal popularity, though mainly for Victoria's reign.[133]

The pioneering work was Dorothy Thompson's *Queen Victoria: Gender and Power* (1990). She wondered whether a female monarch appeared to English subjects 'more amenable to constitutional control' and less 'political' in an age when public politics was exclusively a male preserve, and suggested that non-English and colonial subjects found a female, matriarchal, monarch more acceptable than a king. She also noted George Eliot's remark that the Queen 'calls forth a chivalrous feeling', and argued that her public 'seclusion' after 1861 was not universally condemned because it was understood that she would continue many important female tasks, such as advising daughters.[134] Reynolds similarly argued that Victoria 'shared the ideal of the private, domestic woman

---

[130] Prochaska, *Royal Bounty*, pp. 87–91, 100–2, 110–1, 150–1, 178, 204, 238.

[131] See suggestive comments in R. Holt, *Sport and the British* (Oxford, 1992), and by George Lansbury in Nairn, *Enchanted Glass*, p. 341. Kings and princes were often presented as sportsmen.

[132] Prochaska, *Royal Bounty*, p. 280; D. Cannadine, *History in Our Times* (London, 1998), p. 66; Cannadine, 'Biography', 303. See also the comment in Ford and Harrison, *Hundred Years*, p. 267, that people could identify with the monarchy because a 'figure resembling the Queen presided over many Victorian families'.

[133] The other main exception is contemporary comment on Princess Diana: see e.g. B. Campbell, *Diana, Princess of Wales: How Sexual Politics Shook The Monarchy* (London, 1998).

[134] Thompson, *Queen Victoria*, pp. xvi, 138–9.

and the public, political man', that her court's domesticity disguised her actual role in government, and that the public came to regard her reluctance to appear in public as 'suitably womanly' and her eventual appearances as 'courageous acts'.[135]

The most suggestive work has been by Margaret Homans and Adrienne Munich, who share the view that 'Victoria was central to the ideological and cultural signifying system of her age'.[136] Exploring the paradox of a female monarch in an age when women were expected to 'obey', Homans argued that Victoria's role as a wife 'subdued anxieties about female rule', made her a model for the middle class, and facilitated the shift to a symbolic monarchy, since although women were not active political participants a wife was expected to exercise 'influence', display status, and be 'available for idealization'. Her public seclusion after 1861 enacted the withdrawal of the constitutional monarch from a role in government, and if absent in person she was nevertheless ubiquitous in popular literature.[137] For Munich her 'inspired performances' of 'the age's significant cultural codes' enabled people to imagine they were doing the Queen's work, whether in explorations, imperial wars, or even having portraits made of their pets.[138] Both authors have been criticized for lack of historical rigour, in their bold readings of texts characteristic of some literary and cultural studies without paying any attention to the reception of those texts, and Homans for an insistence on Victoria's active agency in fashioning the monarchy which expresses feminist priorities, unwarranted by the evidence.[139] Moreover, insistence on Victoria's agency once again reflects the top-down approach to investigations of royal popularity. Although the greater female support for monarchy is sometimes noted, this has not received detailed historical explanation.[140] Nor are there studies of areas of specific female interest, such as royal weddings or fashion.[141]

Modern royal masculinity remains almost wholly unstudied, either in terms of how kings and princes imagined themselves, or how their male

---

[135] Reynolds, *Aristocratic Women*, pp. 189–90, 209.

[136] M. Homans and A. Munich, 'Introduction', in Homans and Munich (eds.), *Remaking Queen Victoria* (Cambridge, 1997), p. 2.

[137] M. Homans, *Royal Representations* (Chicago, 1998), pp. 2, 101, ch. 2 ; M. Homans, '"To the Queen's private apartments": royal family portraiture and the construction of Victoria's sovereign obedience', *Victorian Studies* 37 (1993), 1–41.

[138] Homans and Munich, 'Introduction', p. 5; A. Munich, *Queen Victoria's Secrets* (New York, 1996), p. 278.

[139] Arnstein, *Queen Victoria*, p. 10; R. Altick, 'Performing queen', *Times Literary Supplement*, 14 May 1999; K. Israel review, *Social History* 25 (2000), 59–60.

[140] Though for a social psychologist's views, see Billig, *Talking*, ch. 7.

[141] For suggestive material see E. Allen, 'Culinary exhibition: Victorian wedding cakes and royal spectacle', *Victorian Studies* 45 (2003), 457–84; N. Arch and J. Marschner, *The Royal Wedding Dresses* (London, 1990); V. Mendes and A. de la Haye, *Twentieth Century Fashion* (London, 1999); L. Ebbetts and T. Graham, *The Royal Style Wars* (London, 1988).

personae appealed to their male and female subjects.[142] Other historians
have found explanations for royal popularity less in monarch's gender
than in identification with the Royal Family, established through royal
portraiture and probably more powerfully through reports of sentimental and trivial details, which simultaneously offer escape into 'a fairy-tale
world' and a familiar image of a middle-class family. Williams has charted
the Victorian evolution of this identification, noting the enormous coverage of the Princess Royal's wedding in 1858.[143]

Ceremony, charity and family as sources of royal popularity all
depended on the media for their projection, and the various media have
been prominent in cultural studies of the monarchy. For Plunkett, the
Victorian growth of mass print and visual media was chiefly responsible for the 'almost limitless plasticity' of the Queen's public image.
Newspapers had an enormous and constant appetite for royal stories,
which generated a fusion between deferential and disrespectful strands
of reportage.[144] Yet it is astonishing how long it took for the disrespectful
strand to become really prominent – perhaps not until the 1980s – and
even then a 'bad' story could generate sympathy or reaffirm the Queen's
integrity in upholding the monarchy's ideals.[145] Visual media were consistently supportive: royal *cartes de visite* widely circulated an intimate and
flattering image of royalty in the Victorian era, while between the wars the
British Board of Film Censors forbade any depiction or reference to the
Royal Family in feature films.[146] With the institution of the Christmas
Day broadcast in 1932, George V was the first monarch able to speak
directly to his subjects, equating 'the family audience, the royal family,
the nation as family' at a uniquely propitious moment in the calendar.[147]

Historians have noted a connection between television and the construction of a less formal monarchy in the 1960s, but it is in other

---

[142] Useful indications are M. Francis, 'The domestication of the male: recent research on
nineteenth- and twentieth-century British masculinity', *Historical Journal* 45 (2002),
637–52, and – again on the important issue of fashion, on which Edwards VII and VIII
made notable contributions – B. Shannon, 'Re-fashioning men: fashion, masculinity,
and the cultivation of the male consumer in Britain, 1860–1914', *Victorian Studies* 46
(2004), 597–630.

[143] Williams, *Contentious Crown*, pp. 192, 203, 205, and see S. Schama, 'The domestication
of majesty: royal family portraiture, 1500–1850', *Journal of Interdisciplinary History* 17
(1986), 155–8, 183. The reality was, of course, very different: see e.g. Cannadine, 'Last
Hanoverian sovereign?', pp. 146–51.

[144] Plunkett, *First Media Monarch*, pp. 2, 7, 98, 238–43.

[145] See Billig, *Talking*, ch. 6.

[146] J. Plunkett, 'Celebrity and community: the poetics of the *carte-de-visite*', *Journal of
Victorian Culture* 8 (2003), 55–77; A. Schwarzenbach, 'Royal photographs: emotions
for the people', *Contemporary European History* 13 (2004), 255–80; J. Richards, *The Age
of the Dream Palace* (London, 1984), pp. 117–8, 264–5, 269.

[147] P. Scannell and D. Cardiff, *A Social History of Broadcasting*, vol. 1 (Oxford, 1991),
pp. 280–1.

disciplines that television's ability to fashion royal popularity has been investigated. Dayan and Katz argued that such ceremonies as royal weddings are 'characterized by a *norm of viewing* in which people tell each other that it is mandatory to view', and '*integrate* societies in a collective heartbeat and evoke a *renewal of loyalty* to the society and its legitimate authority'.[148] Moreover, both the BBC and commercial television still accord respect and exercise discretion in their reportage of the monarchy.

Television also developed new genres, notably the soap operas, which now attract the largest audiences, often much larger than audiences for royal events.[149] A number of writers have claimed that the popular national and international appeal of the monarchy now lies in the fact that it is a 'full-blown Soap Monarchy'.[150] British soap operas began on radio in the late 1940s, but it was not until the 1980s rumours about the failing marriage of the Prince of Wales that the parallels struck home. In 1984, Ros Coward observed that popular assimilation of the Royal Family with soap-opera conventions meant that it was not regarded as a political institution, but considered only in terms of human behaviour, human emotions and family choices, and that the effect was to reinforce traditional values and define women in terms of sexual attraction.[151] As soap operas generate tremendous loyalty among their predominantly female audience, so a 'soap monarchy' may partly explain why the contemporary monarchy has greater appeal among women. Television has also been a force shaping modern celebrity culture, and younger members of the Royal Family – above all Princess Diana – have come to be treated in the media as celebrity 'stars'.

This tendency to equate monarchy with soap opera or celebrity has been challenged on the grounds that it misses the true distinctiveness of monarchy. For Nairn, this distinctiveness lay in its possession of 'the "glamour" . . . of persons and symbols ordinary in appearance but quite

---

[148] D. Dayan and E. Katz, 'Defining media events', in H. Tumber (ed.), *News* (Oxford, 1999), pp. 51, 54–5; and Dayan and Katz, 'Electronic ceremonies: television performs a royal wedding', *Media Events* (Cambridge, Mass., 1992), pp. 16–32.

[149] *Coronation Street* and *EastEnders* were the top two programmes in term of ratings in 2005, and the wedding of Prince Charles to Camilla Parker Bowles in April 2005 attracted 7 million viewers compared to 13 million for the wedding of Ken and Deirdre in *Coronation Street*: *Guardian*, 11 Apr. 2005, 9 Jan. 2006. See also D. Self, *Television Drama* (London, 1984), p. 32.

[150] R. W. Johnson, 'Tom Nairn and the monarchy', *Heroes and Villains* (Hemel Hempstead, 1990), p. 156; D. Cannadine, *The Pleasures of the Past* (London, 1990), p. 9.

[151] R. Coward, 'The royals', *Female Desire* (London, 1984), p. 171. For some rather different emphases, see C. Geraghty, *Women and Soap Opera* (Cambridge, 1991), pp. 54–62, 82–97, 117.

super-ordinary in significance'.[152] For Rosalind Brunt, it is the institution which comes closest in modern times to possessing 'charisma'.[153] Michael Billig, seeking to reconstruct 'common-sense thinking' from interviews, argued that the monarchy's fame is 'completely unlike that of any other celebrity in the modern world' for two reasons. First, entertainment celebrities are not considered to 'embody a national heritage and the future continuity of a nation'. Second, no other figures are guaranteed a lifetime of celebrity from birth, and this permanence of royal fame means that 'our' lives run in parallel to theirs in a reassuring continuity.[154]

A feature that the contemporary monarchy shares with celebrity culture is marketing. The range of royal memorabilia has long been astonishing in variety and volume. From the early 1840s royal visits were exploited by souvenir manufacturers, and grand royal ceremonies could provoke fierce competition among businesses and housing districts.[155] Not only were goods used to sell royalty; royalty was used to sell goods. Thomas Richards has argued that the use of Victoria's image 'both legitimated consumption for women by offering them the Queen's stamp of approval, and lured even more women into department stores by leading them to believe that there they, too, would be treated like royalty'.[156] The use of the contemporary monarchy for advertising is more discreet and controlled through the granting of royal warrants, and membership of the Royal Warrant Holders' Association.[157] Nonetheless, marketing was and is an expression of what might be called 'banal monarchism' – the ways in which a positive view of the monarchy is insinuated into the everyday lives of its subjects. By contrast, the amount of anti-monarchist memorabilia is negligible, and has no everyday impact. The 'royalness' of material culture and its impact is another area that requires much further research.[158]

'Banal monarchism' is a deliberate echo of Billig's notion of 'banal nationalism', meaning how nationalism is made 'the endemic condition' of people's daily lives, for example by the newspapers' trope of addressing

---

[152] Nairn, *Enchanted Glass*, p. 27, 45, 214.

[153] R. Brunt, 'A "divine gift to inspire"?: popular cultural representation, nationhood and the British monarchy', in D. Strinati and S. Wagg (eds.), *Come On Down?* (London, 1992), pp. 285–301.

[154] Billig, *Talking*, pp. 19, 220–3.

[155] Tyrrell and Ward, 'God bless', 115; Jennings and Madge, *May the Twelfth*, pp. 11, 24–6, 82, 300–1.

[156] T. Richards, *The Commodity Culture of Victorian England* (Stanford, 1990), p. 102.

[157] For royal warrants, www.royal.gov.uk.

[158] E.g. K. Jeffrey, 'Crown, communication and the colonial post: stamps, the monarchy and the British Empire', *Journal of Imperial and Commonwealth History* 34 (2006), 45–70.

'*this* country' or '*the* nation'.[159] A recognition that the monarchy some-how embodies national identity is more or less ubiquitous in the historical literature, but it is too often assumed to be self-evident, unproblematic and 'eternal'. Not only does this infringe the usual historical insistence upon attention to context; it also concedes, unexamined, what is perhaps the central monarchist claim – that in some metaphorical or even real sense the monarchy is the nation. This is not to reject the claim: Billig's analysis of his interviewees' language showed how closely they equated monarchy and nation, and it is evident that certain royal events can trigger moments of deep reflection about national identity.[160] But the equation is complex and certainly not complete. It has sometimes been questioned, as with criticisms of Albert in the mid-1850s and of 'a German on the throne' during the First World War. Less remarked has been evidence of an indifference to the symbol of monarchy at times of national crisis, such as Vera Brittain's 1941 meditation on the word 'England', as meaning not its Royal Family but 'the fields and lanes of its lovely countryside'.[161] Also, what could be regarded as an English monarchy serving as the unifying symbol of a multi-national state, has had the potential to create nationalist tensions.[162] That this potential has hardly ever been realized has been ascribed variously to such material factors as railways, commerce or educational institutions which 'blended' the nationalities, to the closeness of English intellectuals to the 'Ukanian monarchy' and state, and to the monarchy's and the state's sensitivity towards national sensibilities on grand ceremonial occasions'.[163] More recent examinations of the nature of English national identity have concluded that it did not impede the growth of British national identity. Hugh Kearney

[159] M. Billig, *Banal Nationalism* (London, 1995).
[160] Billig, *Talking*, p. 33, 38–9; and see e.g. J. Wolffe, 'Judging the nation: early nineteenth-century British evangelicals and divine retribution', in K. Cooper and J. Gregory (eds.), *Retribution, Repentance and Reconciliation* (Woodbridge, 2004), pp. 198–9, 293–5 (the deaths of Princess Charlotte in 1817 and Prince Albert in 1861), and J. McGuigan, 'British identity and "the people's princess"', *Sociological Review* 48 (2000), 1 (the death of Princess Diana).
[161] V. Brittain, *England's Hour* (London, 1941; 1981), pp. 195–6. See also Ziegler, *Crown and People*, ch. 3; Richards and Sheridan, *Mass-Observation at the Movies*, pp. 185, 213, 399, 414.
[162] E.g. M. Cragoe, 'Two princes: manipulating monarchy in mid-Victorian Wales' (unpublished paper), describing nationalists' difficulties in erecting a monument to Prince Llewellyn and loyalists' success in erecting one to Prince Albert in the 1860s.
[163] K. Robbins, 'An imperial and multinational polity: the "scene from the centre", 1832–1922', in A. Grant and K. Stringer (ed.), *Uniting the Kingdom?* (London, 1995), p. 251; Nairn, *Enchanted Glass*, pp. 183–4; J. Loughlin, 'Allegiance and illusion: Queen Victoria's Irish visit of 1849', *History* 87 (2002), 491–513; S. Pašeta, 'Nationalist responses to two royal visits to Ireland, 1900 and 1903', *Irish Historical Studies* 31 (1999), 488–504; J. S. Ellis, 'Reconciling the Celt: British national identity, empire, and the 1911 Investiture of the Prince of Wales', *Journal of British Studies* 37 (1998), 391–418.

notes the compatibility of an often ethnic 'Englishness' with a historically inclusive civic British identity, and Krishnan Kumar suggests that English nationalism appeared only towards the end of the nineteenth century, and even then took 'cultural, not political form'.[164]

A further debate has been whether a monarchical national identity has subsumed class identity. For Nairn, the forging during the French wars of 1793–1815 of a 'Royal-conservative' nationalism was a 'virtually total triumph'. It shaped a conformist, corporatist, insular and consolatory consciousness of 'class' as confined within a hierarchical culture, which enabled the state 'to bury the political and ideological dimension of class-struggle virtually without a contest'.[165] For Colley, because national mobilization was connected with popular participation, the British ruling classes were nervous about resorting to it, with the effect that much of the growing sense of nation was 'spontaneously generated from below' by social groups who used it as a strategy to advance their sectional interests.[166] For both Colley and Nairn, then, class and nation were not antithetical but two sides of the same processes – but for Colley, class consciousness was normally oppositional to some degree.

Historians have detected variations of the equation between monarchy and nation. Williams found that the identification of monarchy with 'national greatness and national cohesion' increased from the 1870s.[167] Kearney considered that the First World War created a civic, non-sectarian, common feeling of 'Britishness', turning partly around the monarchy.[168] More controversially, Nairn has argued that by the 1990s an 'unstoppable slide' in the monarchy's popularity indicated that its 'glamour' had vanished, and that a royal sense of nationhood had been abandoned.[169] A more common view is that by the 1990s, any coherent notion of national identity had become more difficult because of the unprecedented social diversity created particularly by Caribbean and Asian immigration since 1948 – though in such views, the implications for the monarchy have rarely been noted.[170]

Given the centrality in the literature of the relationship between the monarchy and national identity, it is surprising that no historian has yet

---

[164] H. Kearney, 'The importance of being British', *Political Quarterly* 71 (2000), 15–25; K. Kumar, *The Making of English National Identity* (Cambridge, 2003), pp. x, xii, 181–3.

[165] Nairn, *Enchanted Glass*, pp. 134–6, 184–5, 231, 265, 321–2.

[166] L. Colley, 'Whose nation?: class and national consciousness in Britain, 1750–1830', *Past and Present*, No. 113 (1995), 97–117.

[167] Williams, *Contentious Crown*, pp. 153–5.

[168] Kearney, 'The importance of being British', 21.

[169] Nairn, *Enchanted Glass*, pp. x, xx, xxviii; idem., *After Britain* (London, 2001), pp. 52–3.

[170] J. Harris, 'Tradition and transformation', in K. Burk (ed.), *The British Isles since 1945* (New York, 2002), p. 122; R. Weight, *Patriots* (London, 2002), pp. 73–3; Kearney, 'Importance of being British', 23–4; Kumar, *Making of English National Identity*, pp. 239–72.

followed Nairn in making this their main focus. The closest is perhaps Richard Weight's *Patriots*. He charts the decline since 1940 in the significance of the 'four main stays' of British national identity – monarchy, Protestantism, democracy and the empire. He sees the English subsuming their identity in the idea of Britain, and thereby treating the other nationalities with a 'myopia and complacency' which proved fatal to national unity. Although the monarchy accommodated national sensibilities in its ceremonies, it was powerless to counteract government 'thoughtlessness, lack of tact and disregard of sentiment' in Scotland and Wales. Crucially, when by the early 1990s the monarchy 'was virtually all that was left of Britishness', it entered a great period of crisis which left it useless for promoting a British identity.[171] The argument is contentious, and other writers have emphasized the persistence of the structural underpinnings of British identity and the New Labour project to promote a new kind of Britishness, while the popular response in Scotland and Wales as well as England to the Queen's Golden Jubilee in 2002 suggested a more effective British institution.

For Kumar, the reason why English nationalism has remained inhibited, is that the English have been empire-builders and so subscribed to an 'imperial' or 'missionary' nationalism reaching beyond nations; and other historians have long stressed the ubiquity of empire in the life of the nation since the 1880s.[172] More recently the impact of the expansion and loss of the empire on royal identity has been examined. So the 1870s is regarded as marking 'a new emphasis on the Crown as symbol of imperial unity', with a female monarch well placed to benefit from the images of motherhood and womanliness associated with empire. Victoria's jubilees and funeral had at their heart military processions which highlighted imperial might.[173] And where the 1876 Royal Titles Act had provoked criticism, the 1901 Royal Titles Act making Edward VII King of Britain, Ireland 'and the British Dominions beyond the Seas' had cross-party support.

Cannadine's *Ornamentalism* challenged imperial historians' assumptions about the character of the empire. He argued that it should be regarded as a complex social rather than racial hierarchy, which sought to replicate British social structures – a social vision dramatized and

---

[171] Weight, *Patriots*, pp. 10–2, 212–6, 279–81, 681–4, 726–7, 730.

[172] Kumar, *The Making of English National Identity*, pp. 32–4, 188–90; and see e.g. J. M. Mackenzie, *Propaganda and Empire* (Manchester, 1984); J. M. MacKenzie (ed.), *Imperialism and Popular Culture* (Manchester, 1986); F. Driver and D. Gilbert (eds.), *Imperial Cities* (Manchester, 1999). But for a contrary view see B. Porter, '"Empire, what empire?"', *Victorian Studies* 46 (2004), 258–61; B. Porter, *The Absent-minded Imperialists* (Oxford, 2004).

[173] P. Ward, *Britishness since 1870* (London, 2004), ch. 1, and see Williams, *Contentious Crown*, pp. 155, 173, 175–7; Thompson, *Queen Victoria*, p. 130; Matthew, 'Public life and politics', p. 124.

inculcated by royal tours, royal governor-generals, proconsular pomp and honours, and in India the royal durbars of 1877, 1903 and 1911.[174] It has been criticized by some for its elite perspective and its romanticizing of a bloody and racist enterprise.[175] Others have suggested that British understandings of kingship and royal occasions or visits were manipulated by indigenous rulers and elites to increase their own authority, while Jon Lonsdale has demonstrated that Africans had a constitutional rather than 'ornamental' attitude towards the imperial monarchy: they looked to it for protection against local colonial excess, and expected a reciprocal relation of benefits between wealthy patrons and loyal clients.[176] As for the Commonwealth, most studies have been constitutional rather than political histories. Philip Murphy, however, has suggested that the monarchy might have been an obstacle to the development of closer relations between Britain and her former colonies, for the Queen was regarded as being susceptible to political or personal 'embarrassment', which might undermine British prestige in the territory concerned and tarnish the monarch's image in Britain.[177]

Murphy's reminder that the monarchy's imperial and post-imperial identity had an influence on its popularity in Britain prompts two further observations. Once again, the adoption of an elite perspective means there has been almost no attempt to investigate how ordinary people responded to imperial greatness and its decline. One female diarist noted on Jubilee Day 1887, that 'it was rather a proud thought to feel all these potentates were our subjects, & had come in a way to do homage'.[178] How common was this sentiment? Was it based on a sense of racial superiority? Did it persist until the end of empire, and what replaced it after the end of empire?[179] Second, as Matthew commented: why did the 'great turning point' in Britain's world role represented by creation of the welfare state

[174] D. Cannadine, *Ornamentalism* (London, 2001), pp. xix, 8–9, 45–54, 65–9, 85–100, 114–8.

[175] E.g. S. Rosenberg, '"The justice of Queen Victoria": Boer oppression, and the emergence of a national identity in Lesotho', *National Identities* 3 (2001), 133–53; M. Davis, *Late Victorian Holocausts* (2001), part I.

[176] See A. Clarkson, 'Pomp, circumstance, and wild Arabs: the 1912 royal visit to Sudan', J. Lonsdale, 'Ornamental constitutionalism in Africa: Kenyatta and the two queens', and J. Willis, 'A portrait for the Mukama: monarchy and Empire in colonial Bunyoro, Uganda', all in *Journal of Imperial and Commonwealth History* 34 (2006), 71–85, 87–103, 105–122.

[177] P. Murphy, 'Breaking the bad news: plans for the announcement to the Empire of the death of Elizabeth II and the proclamation of her successor, 1952–67', ibid., 139–54; idem., 'The African queen? Republicanism and defensive decolonization in British tropical Africa, 1958–64', *Twentieth Century British History* 14 (2003), 243–63.

[178] Z. Shonfield (ed.), *The Precariously Privileged* (Oxford, 1987), p. 148.

[179] For some speculations, see 'Introduction' to B. Schwarz (ed.), *The Expansion of England* (London, 1996), pp. 1–8; S. Howe, 'Internal decolonization? British politics since Thatcher as post-colonial trauma', *Twentieth Century British History* 14 (2003), 286–304.

and abandonment of the title 'emperor' in 1947 not bring about 'some fundamental reconsideration of the role of the monarchy'.[180]

One reason why monarchs tend to resist change may lie in the significance of their coronation. It both represents a quasi-ordination and consecration[181] and displays and legitimates the social hierarchy,[182] so monarchs – with the notable exception of Edward VIII – are likely to feel a sacred obligation to defend their patrimony, including its Anglican basis. The nineteenth-century state endorsed the power of prayer, royal ceremony was seen by some as essentially religious and, more pervasively, as John Wolffe has commented, 'at the time of Britain's zenith as a great power in the late nineteenth and early twentieth centuries, claims to God's especial favour were extensively made.'[183] By the 1930s, the Church of England was 'increasingly becoming a sector in society rather than pervading and guiding society as a whole';[184] and despite signs of renewed prominence in the 1950s, its loss of wider moral authority over society continued after the Second World War, making it 'the private pursuit of a minority'.[185]

However, there is poll evidence that in 1964 around 30 per cent believed that the Queen had been chosen by God, and some 35 per cent in the mid-1950s; and Ziegler guesses that the figure must have been around 50 per cent before 1939.[186] Wolffe finds much evidence of the vigour of 'civil religion' – 'the use of religious forms and language in public life', still often 'founded on the conviction that direct contact is being made with God, or at least with something transcendent'. The monarchy is central to this practice, and in re-examining familiar royal duties and ceremonies, he has emphasized a religious dimension neglected by other historians. The implication is that religious ritual satisfied that residual, diffuse Christianity of the majority of the population. Even so, Wolffe considers that television – by replacing local church attendance with viewing in homes – has weakened the religious impact of grand ceremonies.[187]

Wolffe sees supernatural beliefs as instances of 'common religion', and McKibbin has argued that the inter-war monarchy 'developed a

---

[180] H. C. G. Matthew, 'George VI', *ODNBO*.

[181] See esp. I. Bradley, *God Save the Queen* (London, 2002), ch. 4; C. Longley, *Chosen People* (London, 2003), ch. 2.

[182] D. Cannadine, *Class in Britain* (New Haven, 1998), pp. 85, 155.

[183] F. M. Turner, 'Rainfall, plagues, and the Prince of Wales', *Journal of British Studies* 13 (1974), 60; Kuhn, 'Ceremony and politics', 155–6; J. Wolffe, 'The religions of the silent majority', in G. Parsons (ed.), *The Growth of Religious Diversity, Vol. I* (London, 1993), p. 325.

[184] G. I. T. Machin, 'Marriage and the churches in the 1930s: royal abdication and divorce reform, 1936–7', *Journal of Ecclesiastical History* 42 (1991), 81.

[185] Weight, *Patriots*, pp. 12, 223–6, 727.   [186] Ziegler, *Crown and People*, p. 36.

[187] Wolffe, 'Religions of the silent majority', pp. 309–10, 317, 321–6, 342.

quasi-magical character' and that as life became more dominated by 'rational' procedures, 'arguably the magic became yet more acceptable to the public'.[188] Yet the argument that the popularity of the monarchy is explained as much or more by its hold on common religion as on civil religion, is unconvincing. Such magical beliefs about royalty can still be found in tabloid newspapers, but the tone is a mixture of earnestness and knowingness.[189] The inter-war tone was less familiar, but no less knowing.

III

Monarchy has seemed impregnable in Britain: it has been acceptable to the political establishment and popular with the people. Consequently many historians of the monarchy have never given republicans more than a passing reference. From the 1960s there were a few specialist studies of republican movements,[190] but their history tended to be of interest mainly to committed republicans.[191] Then in the 1990s, the growing difficulties of the monarchy combined with studies of classical republicanism among political philosophers and intellectual historians, created a strong revival of interest. These historiographical origins have produced two broad approaches.

The first is typified by Antony Taylor, who regards the notion of 'anti-monarchism' as more satisfactory than the term 'republicanism'. In Britain 'republican' has been a 'detached cerebral form' of thought, and one 'more helpful to the defenders of monarchy than to its opponents', because of associations with violence and continental influences. Moreover, except in 1848 and in the aftermath of the Paris Commune, it was hardly present in radical discourses. 'Anti-monarchism', on the other hand, was firmly based in a native British tradition and drew inspiration from the example of Cromwell and the radical critique of 'Old Corruption'. Far from this critique seeming outdated and irrelevant after the government reforms from the 1830s to the 1870s, it acquired new relevance when for the first time it could be applied exclusively to the monarchy.

---

[188] McKibbin, *Classes and Cultures*, pp. 14–5.
[189] The death of the Queen Mother saw a spate of such stories, e.g. *Sun*, 3 Apr. 2002.
[190] E.g. N. J. Gossman, 'Republicanism in nineteenth-century England', *International Review of Social History* 7 (1962), 46–60; R. Harrison, *Before the Socialists* (London, 1965), ch. 5; D. Tribe, *President Charles Bradlaugh M. P.* (London, 1971); E. Royle, *Radical Politics, 1790–1900* (London, 1971), and *Radicals, Secularists and Republicans* (Manchester, 1980); F. A. D'Arcy, 'Charles Bradlaugh and the English republican movement, 1868–1878', *Historical Journal* 25 (1982), 367–83.
[191] E.g. E. Wilson, *The Myth of British Monarchy* (London, 1989); S. Haseler, *The End of the House of Windsor* (London, 1993).

Taylor's aim is to rehabilitate this submerged current of popular opposition, by taking sensational coverage of royal scandal, extravagance and
imperial ambition as serious and effective in conveying 'the hollowness
and moral bankruptcy of the Crown'. Most radicals rejected violence,
and expected the monarchy simply to fade away in the face of popular
education and social advancement. But it remained a stance detached
from the Liberal party, expressing a refusal to accept the compromises of
the existing party system. Even so, Taylor believes that anti-monarchism
'had a very real meaning for many subjects of the throne', although he is
unable to give an estimate of the numbers.[192]

The second approach is that of Eugenio Biagini and Miles Taylor.
Biagini is interested in 'cerebral elements' – the influence of classical
republican notions of participatory citizenship, civic virtue and concern
for the common good, notions not regarded as incompatible with a virtuous constitutional monarch. He argues that both Liberal thinkers and
Liberal party followers subscribed to these notions in the 1860s and early
1870s. Working- and middle-class enthusiasm for this form of republicanism was evident in their participation in the Volunteer movement, which
enshrined the right of the people to bear arms and 'represented a great
democratic symbol, in contrast with the standing army and its aristocratic
ethos'.[193] Biagini does not, though, consider how Liberals reacted to the
attacks on Victoria in 1871–2, when her neglect of constitutional duties
and alleged appropriation of public money demonstrated a disregard for
the common good. Taylor has, however, examined the ideas of the principal Liberal critic in those years, Sir Charles Dilke. Conventionally his
attacks on the cost of the monarchy – an enduring preoccupation of anti-
monarchists – is treated simply as 'political opportunism', in order to
appeal to working-class audiences. Taylor criticizes a concentration on
anti-monarchism, arguing for a move beyond 'the fixation with monarchy' to 'recover the broader context of the discourse of republicanism'.
In the case of Dilke, this means understanding his view that inevitable
laws of social evolution would spread republican governments throughout
the world, unless arrested by imperial governments' greed, corruption,
creation of bureaucracy and disregard for laws. This, he believed, had

---

[192] Taylor, *Down*; A. Taylor and L. Trainor, 'Monarchism and anti-monarchism: Anglo-
Australian comparisons, c. 1870–1901', *Social History* 24 (1999), 158–73; A. Taylor,
'Medium and messages: republicanism's traditions and preoccupations', and '"The
nauseating cult of the Crown": republicanism, anti-monarchism and post-Chartist politics, 1870–5', in Nash and Taylor, *Republicanism*, pp. 1–11, 51–70; idem., 'Republicanism reappraised: anti-monarchism and the English radical tradition, 1850–1872',
in J. Vernon (ed.), *Re-reading the Constitution* (Cambridge, 1996), pp. 154–78.

[193] E. F. Biagini, 'Neo-roman liberalism: "republican" values and British liberalism,
c. 1860–1875', *History of European Ideas* 29 (2003), 55–72.

happened in Napoleon III's France, and in 1871 he feared the British imperial system would do the same. His republicanism therefore 'arose out of his dislike of imperialism', and his objection to monarchy from its centrality in the British imperial system.[194]

A difficulty is that the term 'republicanism' describes a wide range of beliefs; it had a 'protean nature', allowing individuals to change their position 'depending on personal whim or changed political circumstances'.[195] Without the discipline of forming a party and fighting elections, anti-monarchists had little incentive to systematize their thought; Biagini's vision of a seemingly uniformly lofty Liberal rank and file perhaps stretches credibility; and there may have been some distance between what Dilke intended to argue, and how his audience received his arguments. It is plausible that an amalgam of 'anti-monarchical' and 'republican' elements characterized the beliefs of many individuals. Even anti-monarchists could be surprisingly sympathetic to certain royal persons, just as republicans could respect a virtuous monarch. Plunkett, moreover, draws attention to a broader set of cultural and commercial considerations which could produce a similar outcome: *Reynolds's Newspaper*, for example, was in principle anti-royalist, yet indulged in a similar style of reporting the Royal Family in personal terms to that of other newspapers – which helps explain why it achieved a large circulation.[196]

As well as producing novel accounts of the early 1870s 'republican moment', recent scholarship has also moved backwards to re-examine Chartism, and forwards to re-examine labour and socialist politics up to 1914. Engels thought that the 'English Chartist is politically a republican' – a view that Antony Taylor strongly and Williams more equivocally re-assert.[197] Paul Pickering, however, has argued that most Chartists were loyal to the monarchy, either because they believed the Queen had the power to help them secure the Charter, or because they understood that she did not.[198] This view would fit more readily with a recent emphasis on the success of the monarchy's 'civic publicness' and 'royal populism' in the 1840s; or it may be that civic leaders felt it their civic duty to greet royal visitors, irrespective of their private beliefs.[199]

---

[194] Taylor, 'Republics versus empires', 25, 30–4.
[195] Prochaska, *Republic of Britain*, p. xvi.   [196] Plunkett, *First Media Monarch*, p. 62.
[197] *The Condition of the Working Class in England in 1844*, in K. Marx and F. Engels, *On Britain* (Moscow, 1962), p. 265; Taylor, *Down*, ch. 2; Williams, *Contentious Crown*, pp. 16–17.
[198] P. A. Pickering, '"The hearts of the millions": Chartism and popular monarchism in the 1840s', *History* 88 (2003), 227–48.
[199] See Prochaska, *The Republic of Britain*, p. 74, for the case of a Chartist mayor in this position.

Pioneering labour historians detected instances of socialism in republican movements in the 1870s, and anti-monarchism in socialist bodies in the 1890s;[200] they judged Keir Hardie's republicanism as 'unfruitful and even damaging to the party';[201] and they explained the Labour party's acceptance of the monarchy after 1918, by its recognition of the institution's value and a calculation of the practical impossibility of removing or reforming it. More recently Antony Taylor has argued that anti-monarchism influenced Labour pioneers in the 1880s in the context of broader opposition to the aristocracy, land monopoly and hereditary power, but that by 1914 'the oppositional nature of anti-monarchism had driven it outside a Labourism now poised to reap the benefits of power'.[202] Neville Kirk's examination of the socialist press broadly supports this view: although principled anti-monarchism continued and developed between 1901 and 1911, it co-existed with widespread *de facto* acceptance of the monarchy and 'in significant but limited, uneven and contested ways, actual support for it'.[203] Mark Bevir, however, argues that the Democratic Federation had a continuing debt to the democratic ideal of 'republican radicals' rather than to an anti-monarchism which not all of them endorsed, and that it was the Labour Party's reliance on ethical socialism and Fabianism which led to its 'uncritical stance towards the state'.[204] Future research on the Edwardian period might usefully also consider the republicanism of the suffragettes. They 'sustained a fierce dislike of royal power and authority' and provoked particular opprobrium from George V and Queen Mary.[205]

There has not yet been thorough published research on the Labour party's attitude towards the monarchy after 1914. Prochaska considers that many Labour MPs were 'theoretical' republicans – favouring abolition of the monarchy in principle, but as practical politicians seeing little advantage in taking up the issue.[206] In contrast, Nairn has sketched a bitter and provocative analysis of Labour's thraldom to 'Royal-distributive

---

[200] E.g. H. Pelling, *The Origins of the Labour Party, 1880–1900* (Oxford, 1965), p. 5; C. Tsuzuki, *H. M. Hyndman and British Socialism* (Oxford, 1961), p. 127.

[201] K. O. Morgan, *Keir Hardie, Radical and Socialist* (London, 1975), pp. 71–3; I. McLean, *Keir Hardie* (London, 1975), pp. 47–9.

[202] Taylor, *Down*, pp. 112, 204.

[203] N. Kirk, 'The conditions of royal rule: Australian and British socialist and labour attitudes to the monarchy, 1901–11', *Social History* 30 (2005), 78–83, 87.

[204] M. Bevir, 'Republicanism, socialism, and democracy: the origins of the radical left', in Nash and Taylor, *Republicanism*, pp. 73–89.

[205] Taylor, *Down*, pp. 204–7; Harrison, *Peaceable Kingdom*, pp. 54–8; Pope-Hennessy, *Queen Mary*, pp. 467–9.

[206] Prochaska, *Republic of Britain*, pp. xvi–xvii. For useful comments on Labour observations on the monarchy from the 1880s to 1924, see P. Ward, *Red Flag and Union Jack* (Woodbridge, 1998).

Socialism', where the 'Old Regime' resolved the issues of democracy and national identity by creating 'an anti-egalitarian, Royal-family identity'. In comparison, the essence of republicanism and of modern socialism is a 'deep social image of democracy', and confidence about the 'uncrowned democratic dignity and initiative' of the people.[207] It is worth noting that the monarchy's relative unpopularity in the 1990s did not create a powerful anti-monarchist movement, but only sporadic, scurrilous spasms of anger.[208] Despite speculation that the 'New Labour' government's constitutional ambitions might change the monarchy, Blair has proved as staunchly monarchist as every previous Labour Prime Minister.[209]

By 2000, the political system as a whole was seen as dysfunctional in a post-industrial society in which 'deference and rigid hierarchy and static social relations' were no longer taken for granted.[210] This stimulated revived interest in classical republicanism among a few left-wing politicians and intellectuals. David Marquand has produced an incisive analysis of the British political crisis as 'the product of a long-standing contradiction between the promise of democracy and the reality of essentially monarchical power'. The political system is 'predemocratic' in that the executive, to which the Crown's prerogative powers had over centuries been transferred, is not subject to effective parliamentary control of Parliament. Low election turnouts show that the system's legitimacy is draining away, and the only solution is that 'the monarchical culture of government at the centre should be replaced with a republican one'. There are similarities between Marquand's and Nairn's view, yet strikingly for Marquand, reforming the government's 'monarchical culture' appears to entail no reform of the monarchy itself.[211]

As well as examining the ideas of republicans, historians also need to study the ideas of monarchists – the articulate, committed ideologues of the institution. It is generally assumed that the meaning of monarchy lies in how it acts, rather than in what it says and what is said and written for it. Only Nairn has rather impressionistically dissected its component claims. As Prochaska has written, 'compared to republican clubs, the

---

[207] Nairn, *Enchanted Glass*, pp. 13, 156, 186–9.

[208] Tony Benn's 1992 bill to create a socialist commonwealth, with the Queen replaced by a president elected by MPs, never even came to a vote: Prochaska, *Republic of Britain*, p. 211.

[209] *Guardian*, 4, 7 March 1996, 21 Nov. 1997; A. Seldon, *Blair* (London, 2004), p. 287.

[210] Power Inquiry, *Power to the People* (York, 2006), pp. 18–19, 104–5.

[211] D. Marquand, 'Monarchy, state and dystopia', *Political Quarterly* 76 (2005), 333–6; D. Marquand, *Decline of the Public* (Cambridge, 2004), pp. 5–6, and see similarly W. Hutton, *The State We're In* (London, 1995); A. Gamble and T. Wright, 'The future of the monarchy', *Political Quarterly* 74 (2003), 1–3. There have, however, been a few recent proposals for the reform of the monarchy, notably the Fabian Society, *The Future of the Monarchy* (London, 2003).

Constitutional Monarchy Association and the Monarchist League are long lived. And if history is any guide, pure monarchists are, if anything, more inflexible and belligerent than pure republicans, and they might not go quietly'.[212] If so, it is important to understand not just the ceremonies and the personalities which can inspire such intransigence, but also the ideas. Such a study would chart the origins, evolution and propagation of core monarchist notions. Many have been discussed already in this chapter. Other, more commonplace views are Ivor Jennings's that the 'personification of the State has some psychological effects', such that it is 'easier to put aside our private interests in order to serve the Queen than it is to put them aside in order to serve the State'; Dermot Morrah's view that the Queen is 'the embodiment of the life of the people, so that what is done for her is done for all'; and Arthur Bryant's view that 'the only kind of state in which Englishmen could be happy was that of a constitutional monarchy'.[213] The most important has been that the country can be both a democracy and a monarchy. The propagation and reception of monarchist ideas has hardly been studied in any depth; but it should start with a recognition of early socialization into a favourable view of the monarchy.[214]

History is an accumulative discipline, so a future agenda in part consists of more, different, and better research in the areas outlined in this chapter. But one theme has emerged more insistently than others – the incompleteness of a top-down approach. To recover precisely what ordinary people thought about the monarchy at a particular moment in time will no doubt be difficult and often impossible, and the results will more often than not be anecdotal and fragmentary. But historians still need to try, if their claims about public opinion are not to be as tendentious as those of republicans and monarchists themselves.

---

[212] Prochaska, *Republic of Britain*, p. 226.

[213] I. Jennings, *The Queen's Government* (Harmondsworth, 1954), p. 32; D. Morrah, *The Crown* (London, 1953), p. 32; A. Bryant, *A Thousand Years of British Monarchy* (London, 1975), p. 94.

[214] For suggestions see e.g. V. Chancellor, *History for their Masters* (Bath, 1970), ; S. Heathorn, *For Home, Country, and Race* (Toronto, 2000), pp. 78–84; D. Garratt and H. Piper, 'Citizenship education and the monarchy: examining the contradictions', *British Journal of Educational Studies* 51 (2003), 128–48; O. Stevens, *Children Talking Politics* (Oxford, 1982), pp. 21–102, 138–43, 146–7.

Part I

2 Whig monarchy, Whig nation: Crown, politics and representativeness 1800–2000*

Jonathan Parry

This essay advocates what one might call a Whig interpretation of the survival of the British monarchy – as distinct from a 'Tory' view which has held the upper hand in the historiography. The monarchy's most fervent admirers and its most passionate republican critics have both tended to explain its attraction in terms of the power of deference, of mystique and of ceremonial – either antiquated or invented. So have a number of historians. They have emphasized the visual splendour and irrational appeal of royalty, its ability to project a dignified, majestic and ethereal fairytale image. At an academic level, these arguments have been stimulated by insights from other disciplines, such as anthropology, and from postmodernism.[1] What follows does not seek to refute these interdisciplinary approaches, which have injected a welcome sophistication into the literature on the subject. The royal family's ability to offer a good show and to radiate a remote but intriguing glamour has certainly contributed significantly to its continuing popularity. In all ages, monarchy necessarily involves performance; successful sovereigns are icons. But they are iconic

---

* I would like to thank: Patrick Higgins, Julian Hoppit, Paul Readman and Gareth Stedman Jones for reading a version of this chapter; Joanna Lewis, Norman McCord, Miles Taylor and the contributors to this volume for their contributions, particularly at the conference from which this book derives; Sutherland Forsyth and Richard Williams, for general discussion; and *Demos*, for originally commissioning me to write a short essay along these lines, which was published in their collection for the 2002 Jubilee, *Monarchies: What Are Kings and Queens For?*

[1] See, e.g., newspaper reactions to the death of Queen Elizabeth the Queen Mother in March 2002. In the *Sunday Telegraph* (the newspaper in which Peregrine Worsthorne had habitually stressed the importance of mystique for the preservation of monarchy), Andrew Roberts praised the pomp and anachronism of royal ceremony (7 & 14 April 2002). Meanwhile in the *Observer* (31 March) and a number of articles in the *Guardian*, Anthony Holden and Jonathan Freedland emphasized the monarchy's outdatedness. See also Freedland's *Bring Home the Revolution* (London, 1998). For academic emphasis on the developing ceremonial and pageantry of monarchy, see David Cannadine, 'The context, performance, and meaning of ritual: the British monarchy and the "invention of tradition", c. 1820–1977', in E. Hobsbawm and T. Ranger (eds.), *The Invention of Tradition* (Cambridge, 1983), pp. 101–64. W. M. Kuhn, *Democratic Royalism* (Basingstoke, 1996) criticised Cannadine in various ways but still emphasized ceremonial: 'it was the ceremonies that won over people of different political stripes and class loyalties' (p. 10).

at a number of levels, and beneath the surface image lies a broader and deeper political and constitutional context, since the monarchy is, after all, a political institution and a matter of political debate. My aim is to situate the monarchy within that political context. This involves asking questions which are slightly different from those asked either by those who concentrate on monarchical ceremonial, or by those who have examined the issue of the monarchy's real political power.[2]

By 'Whig interpretation', I mean one in which the value of monarchy is understood primarily in terms of its role and symbolism within the representative constitutional system that was the legacy of post-1688 Whiggism. The primary function of the monarchy over the last two hundred years has been to help legitimize the authority of a parliamentary regime in various ways: by strengthening respect for its laws, by encouraging loyal service to it, and by giving the impression that it operates relatively fairly. That fairness is suggested partly by the monarch's apparent personal powerlessness in the face of parliamentary sovereignty, but partly also by the way that his or her presence and activities have historically limited the power and status of party politicians – and thus have continued to give some credence to the traditional Whig notion of the balanced constitution.

This essay takes a very brief and general view of its subject over the last two centuries. However, it focuses more on the history of monarchy in the nineteenth century, complementing the essay in this volume on the first half of the twentieth century by Philip Williamson. It argues that the nineteenth-century Liberal political elite was concerned to maintain monarchy as one aspect of a 'Whiggish' vision of the constitution and of national identity. This was part of a broader strategy of legitimizing state institutions, which was made easier in the course of the nineteenth century by the extension of the political nation and the increased sense of government accountability to the people. In the first two-thirds of the century, the Whig strategy had to cope with a Radical assault on 'Old Corruption' which included significant criticism of the monarchy. The timing and severity of the attacks followed much the same pattern as in the case of some other potentially contentious and costly structures – such as the Church Establishment, the colonial system and the army. The Second Reform Act of 1867 appeared to usher in a final crisis for most of these institutions, and a few difficult years followed. But then it became apparent that the extension of the franchise had instead

---

[2] For the latter in the nineteenth century, see, e.g. F. Hardie, *The Political Influence of the British Monarchy 1868–1952* (London, 1970); G. H. L. Le May, *The Victorian Constitution* (London, 1979); W. L. Arnstein, *Queen Victoria* (Basingstoke, 2003).

reduced the attractiveness of the old allegations that they were exclusive and extravagant, and instead allowed the 'national' aspects of their appeal to be celebrated more unequivocally. Therefore the years 1868–72 offer a significant pointer to why not only royalty, but also other elements of the 'Establishment', continued to prosper. Despite a challenge, the Whiggish approach was upheld: a strictly constitutional monarchy as an essential badge of British distinctness and political stability.

In other words, the survival of the monarchy is best understood when it is seen in the context of broader political debate. And the main reason for the survival of all the 'Establishment' institutions through the nineteenth century was general popular acceptance of the political order after 1867, which allowed a slow shift in political debate away from constitutional and old-style fiscal issues towards social and labour ones. The monarchy's fortunes did *not* improve primarily because of any major change of image achieved by the actions of the royal family itself. Indeed the range of attitudes to the royal family remained as diverse, and familiar, as before.

The final sections of this essay briefly consider some of the ways in which this 'Whiggish' notion of monarchy has persisted, and remained widely attractive, since the mid-nineteenth century. They also argue that though significant elements of modern monarchy are 'magical', they are neither particularly irrational nor incompatible with the 'Whiggish' model. In a post-modern age, we are more tolerant of deviations from strict rationality than were mid-Victorian intellectuals like Walter Bagehot, whose somewhat condescending and literal distinction between the 'efficient' and 'dignified' parts of the constitution has been so influential on subsequent discussion.[3] Pomp and ceremony can often be appealing and uplifting. But people are not stupid, and the potency of ethereal patriotic images and symbols depends on the attractiveness of the mundane elements of which they are very obviously composed.

I

We need first to understand the ambivalence of the leading eighteenth- and nineteenth-century Whig and Liberal politicians towards the monarchy. In the seventeenth and eighteenth centuries, Crown power had been the most central issue in British politics. The Bill of Rights of 1689 had prevented the monarch from imposing taxes without parliamentary

---

[3] Bagehot concluded that the monarchy's main purpose was to overawe the 'ignorant' classes who could not grasp the reality of Parliamentary government. The implication was that Britain, far from being a constitutional model for other countries, was rather backward, but that it would evolve out of its current irrationality as popular enlightenment grew: W. Bagehot, *The English Constitution*, ed. M. Taylor (Oxford, 2001), pp. 193, 199.

consent, and from interfering in elections, dismissing judges or maintaining a standing army. Even so, allegations of excessive monarchical influence continued for generations. At various times in the eighteenth and nineteenth centuries, both political parties suggested that the Court's political pretensions were 'un-English'.

In particular, the most fundamental principle of the Whig party, as it developed from the 1780s, was that, unchecked, the exercise of Crown and Court influence had the potential to damage political liberty and good government. The main reason for the Whigs' early commitment to the idea of party was that a virtuous common bond between politicians was necessary in order to resist the natural tendency of monarchs to restrict the independence of Parliament and the liberties of the people. Between 1760 and 1830, many Reformers argued that the Crown – the King and his ministers combined – exercised too much power, especially over taxation and patronage. The result of this criticism was the 1832 Reform Act, but though William IV reluctantly agreed to support it, he did not seem to understand its effects on his prerogative. He sacked his Whig ministers in 1834, only to watch as electorate and Parliament voted them back a few months later.[4] This was a crucial moment in the decline of royal power. Even so, Whig-Liberal opinion continued to be wary about its revival, and about the power at Court of unaccountable royal advisers – so much so that until 1867 Victoria was refused permission to have her own private secretary, on the ground that she needed no guides other than her ministers.

Between the 1840s and 1870s, there still seemed to be a political threat from the Court in one field in particular, that of foreign policy. High political factionalism, resulting from the fragmentation of both political parties in the crisis over the Corn Laws and religious policy in 1845–7, played into the hands of Prince Albert, who quite rightly saw party as an obstacle to the reassertion of royal power. Albert added the balcony to Buckingham Palace, between 1846 and 1851, so that the royal family could better receive the acclamation of the people – part of his plan to enhance the monarchy's claim to be a significant political player, an embodiment of national will overriding the petty partisanship of politicians.[5] His strategy owed a great deal to his German upbringing and advisers. He became unpopular in the media on account of his connections with foreign Courts and his policy differences with Lord Palmerston, whom he felt was too unsympathetic to other powers, particularly in central Europe.[6]

[4] N. Gash, *Reaction and Reconstruction in English Politics 1832–1852* (Oxford, 1965), ch. 1.
[5] On the plans for the balcony, see E. Healey, *The Queen's House* (London, 1997), pp. 157–63.
[6] R. Williams, *The Contentious Crown* (Aldershot, 1997), pp. 99–102, 161–3.

Though Lord John Russell's removal of Palmerston from the Foreign Office in 1851 was seen by Palmerston's promoters as the action of a Prime Minister too loyal to an unpatriotic Crown, this was unfair. Palmerston's problem was that his undiplomatic behaviour towards all the other powers had alarmed a quietist and economy-minded liberal cabinet as well as the Court, making his position politically untenable. As befitted a hereditary Whig, Russell was hardly less hostile to Albert's foreign policy meddling than Palmerston.[7] When he in turn became Foreign Secretary under Palmerston in 1859, and the Queen repeatedly objected to the two men's Italian policy, Russell complained that 'we might as well live under a despotism'.[8] One reason for Russell and Palmerston's determination to pursue an assertive policy over Italy in 1859–60, and for the Liberals' anxiety to resuscitate party vigour in the 1860s, was to check continuing royal lobbying on foreign policy questions. The future Lord Kimberley, a Liberal minister, interpreted the Palmerston government's embarrassing policy failure over Schleswig-Holstein in 1864 as conclusive proof that executive government had lost the capacity either to educate and lead the public mind, or to discipline the Queen's 'Continental Advisers' who 'don't act on English principles of policy'. He argued that a stronger party system would allow a more decisive and liberal foreign policy, independent of both the Court and the insular quietists in the Commons.[9] The reassertion of a vigorous policy-based Liberalism under Russell and Gladstone in the mid-1860s aimed at reasserting professional representative politicians' control over the system. The passage of a further Reform Act in 1867 then decisively strengthened two-party politics and reduced the scope for Crown intervention.

Defence of the power of party and Parliament remained a key theme for the Victorian Liberal party. It came together to win a great victory at the general election of 1880 on the ticket of hostility to 'Beaconsfield-ism', Disraeli's apparently 'un-English' political system, which seemed to include a revival of monarchical power. Gladstone detected interference by the Queen in foreign policy, a 'corruption . . . due to Lord Beaconsfield'.[10] The publication of Albert's biography in stages between 1875 and

[7] When Queen Victoria asked him whether he really thought that a subject was justified in disobeying his sovereign, he replied that, 'speaking to a sovereign of the House of Hanover', he could only say that he did: G. W. E. Russell, *Prime Ministers and Some* (London, 1918), p. 22.

[8] Granville to Argyll, 31 Aug. 1859, in Lord E. Fitzmaurice, *The Life of Granville George Leveson Gower, second Earl Granville 1815–1891* (2 vols., London, 1905), I, pp. 356–7.

[9] *The Journal of John Wodehouse, first Earl of Kimberley for 1862–1902*, ed. A. Hawkins and J. Powell (London, 1997), pp. 99, 126, 130–1, 136, 197.

[10] R. Shannon, *Gladstone: Heroic Minister 1865–1898* (London, 1999), pp. 220–1. See J. P. Parry, 'The impact of Napoleon III on British politics 1852–1880', *Transactions of the Royal Historical Society*, 6 ser., 11 (2001), 172–3.

1880, under her patronage, seemed to Liberal critics to set out a disturbing model of royal assertiveness.[11] On constitutional and image grounds, Liberals objected to the Royal Titles Act of 1876, which gave the Queen the alien title of Empress, in relation to India. At the root of criticism of the Crown was the widely held view, 'partly known, partly suspected', that the Queen had encouraged Disraeli to risk war with Russia, against the wishes of many in his cabinet.[12] Her displays of partisanship notoriously included a visit to his house at Hughenden in December 1877, as the Eastern crisis raged.

In counterpoint to this alarm about sectional Crown influence, the Whig-Liberal tradition emphasized the need for state accountability to the people through Parliament, and for active popular involvement in politics. Many nineteenth-century politicians subscribed to ideas of political participation and public virtue that were drawn from the classical republics and can be called civic republicanism.[13] The Liberal ideal was that power should lie with the people's representatives in Parliament, checking Crown tyranny, upholding the public interest (the *res publica*) against sectional interests, and protecting the freedoms of self-governing local communities. Britain was a 'crown'd republic', in Tennyson's words, guided by representative men both at Westminster and in town halls: Manchester and Birmingham were seen as the modern equivalents of those great Renaissance republics, Venice and Florence.[14] In 1867 Frederic Harrison argued that 'England is an aristocratic republic', and Bagehot that it was a 'disguised' one.[15] The ambiguity of the republican concept made many Liberals reluctant to use it, as we shall see. Nonetheless, by the mid-nineteenth century, and especially after the extension of the franchise in 1867, they had no real doubt that the constitution was fundamentally sound and that the royal family could not step too far out of line, at least in domestic matters. In the early 1870s, Kimberley, no toady to the Queen, observed that the 'total absence of intrigue on her part against particular Ministries' was a major reason why she was respected.[16] Even

[11] See 'Verax' [H. Dunckley], *The Crown and the Cabinet* (Manchester, 1878).

[12] *The Diaries of Edward Henry Stanley, 15th Earl of Derby (1826–93), between 1878 and 1893*, ed. J. Vincent (Oxford, 2003), pp. 10, 35, 88, 103, 176; H. Dunckley, 'The progress of personal rule', *Nineteenth Century*, 4 (1878), 800–1; J. Chamberlain (ed.), *The Radical Programme* (London, 1885), pp. 39–40.

[13] For a distinction between civic and constitutional republicanism, see B. Worden, 'Republicanism, regicide and republic: the English experience', in M. van Gelderen and Q. Skinner (eds.), *Republicanism* (2 vols., Cambridge, 2002), vol. I, pp. 309–10.

[14] Tennyson's phrase appeared in the epilogue (1872) to his *Idylls of the King*, dedicated to the Queen.

[15] F. Harrison, 'Our Venetian constitution', *Fortnightly Review* 3 (1867), 278; Bagehot, *English Constitution*, p. 193.

[16] E. Drus (ed.), 'John, first Earl of Kimberley: a journal of events during the Gladstone ministry, 1868–74', *Camden Miscellany* 21 (London, 1958), 26.

the foreign policy disputes discussed above attracted more publicity than their innate significance deserved, because politicians exploited them for advantage. Palmerston benefited from his clashes with Albert between 1848 and 1853, because his behaviour appealed to many Whig and Radical libertarians.

Moreover, already in the eighteenth century there had been a broad and basic satisfaction in the propertied classes about the relationship between Crown and Parliament. The balances in the constitution were generally felt to keep abuses of power from any quarter to a minimum.[17] Occasional episodes revealed that the latent powers of the King remained substantial, and that ministries were vulnerable without his support until well after 1800. But they also revealed that kings could not ignore political realities: George III needed Pitt the Younger at least as much as Pitt the Younger needed George III. At the level of day-to-day management, George II was undoubtedly correct in 1744 to reflect that 'Ministers are the Kings in this country'.[18] The expansion of the state bureaucracy under George III strengthened his ministers' power more than it strengthened his own. British political legitimacy rested on notions of divine providence rather than divine right: the sovereign should govern in accordance with the will of Parliament because the British people and British constitution were marked out by God for a great destiny. In 1762, Oliver Goldsmith remarked that 'an Englishman is taught to love the King as his friend, but to acknowledge no other master than the laws which himself has contributed to enact'.[19]

There was, then, a deep-rooted sentiment that monarchical influence was a vested interest that the British constitution must continue to check. However, it would be misleading to suggest that, at any time after the reign of George III, it was regarded as a *particular* evil; it was probably less threatening than several other vested interests that excited criticism in the second quarter of the nineteenth century. Moreover, the governing classes were keen to present the modern state as well-managed and *dis*interested, and the three Reform Acts of 1832, 1867 and 1884–5, and the repeal of the Corn Laws in 1846 and the escape from revolution in 1848 all contributed to their success in doing that, in the eyes of most of the political nation.[20] It was a crucial element of the Whig constitutional model that, though in principle the monarch could still be a threat to the

---

[17] H. T. Dickinson, *Liberty and Property* (London, 1977); J. A. W. Gunn, *Beyond Liberty and Property* (Kingston-upon-Thames, 1983).

[18] J. Cannon and R. Griffiths, *The Oxford Illustrated History of the British Monarchy* (Oxford, 1988), p. 473.

[19] O. Goldsmith, *The Citizen of the World* (London, 1969), p. 33.

[20] Historians of Victorian politics have recently tended to argue this. I have developed the arguments at greater length in *The Politics of Patriotism* (Cambridge, 2006).

constitution, in practice his or her personal biases could be checked by the power of Parliament. In that case, the monarch became something much more attractive: a personification of the legitimate authority, representativeness and inclusiveness of the government – that is, of the Crown as an institution.

II

Nineteenth-century Parliamentarians generally tried hard to uphold the institution of monarchy, fundamentally in order to bolster the authority and legitimacy of the state. Debates about the constitution were not just about protecting English freedoms, but also about winning widespread popular respect for the rule of law. As the most visible representation of the law, and of the long continuity and legitimacy of the state, the constitutional monarch was the readiest point of identification with Britain's unique regime. One Victorian Whig argued that people 'require a personal embodiment and not merely an abstract office as a permanent focus for their love and reverence'.[21] The coronation service was designed to strengthen and sanctify Crown authority by suggesting its derivation from God.[22] Both Tories and Whigs continued to appreciate the value of the royal imprimatur in legitimizing government acts. Indeed the advocates of potentially radical change – such as parliamentary reform in 1830–2 – found monarchical support especially valuable.

One characteristic of Whiggism until the mid-nineteenth century was attachment to patronage politics as a way of guaranteeing the virtue of public servants and the representation of a reassuringly wide variety of interests (particularly important, for example, in Catholic Ireland). In a late defence of this idea of civil service appointment, in 1854, Russell argued that the alternative, recruitment by open competition, was 'republicanism' – because the Crown's responsible ministers were no longer to control the nomination of state servants.[23] By the 1870s, open competition was the norm, reflecting the mid-Victorian state's commitment to a more meritocratic, examination-based notion of disinterestedness, based on the claim that the public service was open to all. But Russell's comment illuminates the wider Whig belief that the maintenance of top-down authority, and of politicians' political and moral *responsibility* for national affairs, was as crucial a benefit of the representative English constitution as the attainment of consent from below. In the Whig model of the constitution, the close links between executive and Parliament forced MPs to

[21] E. Ashley, *A Monarchy and a Republic* (London, 1873), p. 17.
[22] See I. Bradley, *God Save the Queen* (London, 2002), esp. ch. 4.
[23] J. Morley, *The life of William Ewart Gladstone* (3 vols., London, 1903), vol. I, p. 511.

take some responsibility for the maintenance of legitimate authority, while they were simultaneously accountable to their constituents and obliged to consider their grievances. In a republic, by contrast, delegates were answerable only to voters, and could be swayed more directly by their passions. Yet republican regimes were also potentially tyrannical because they made a claim to absolutism, in the name of the people.[24]

Suspicion of the extremist tendencies of republicanism was founded on horror at the descent of the French revolutionary republic into terrible bloodshed, and then into dictatorship in the 1790s and 1800s. These events cast a very long shadow over all European politics in the first half of the nineteenth century. George III became widely identified as the father of the nation, and a symbol of stability and morality, as a point of contrast with the successive French experiments of 1789–1815. It was at this point that *God Save the King* became generally used as the national anthem in place of the more libertarian *Rule Britannia*.[25] Thereafter the French seemed unable to avoid a perpetual destabilizing oscillation between autocracy and bloody republican uprisings, until the 1870s. Between 1848 and 1851, for example, the republican experiment again failed. Meanwhile the collapse of the American Union in civil war between 1861 and 1865 seemed another example of the inability of republican systems to maintain national unity and civilized values. It was widely argued that they encouraged feebleness in public morals and in constitutional relations. The prevalence of materialism, the low level of political education, and the lack of an altruistic patriotism in the United States could be attributed to the absence of propertied political leadership and of Church Establishments. The federal system seemed to encourage gridlock between branches of the constitution which could all claim popular legitimacy, justifying resistance and eventual revolt. The impeachment of President Johnson, after the war, ensured that criticisms of the system continued. Such a constitution could only be maintained by a 'wise, calm and generous temper' – but the North had behaved with typical American arrogance in suppressing the constitutional rights of the South.[26]

---

[24] Earl Grey, *Parliamentary Government Considered with reference to Reform* (London, 1864 edn.), p. 27; H. Reeve, 'Earl Grey on parliamentary government', *Edinburgh Review*, 108 (July 1858), 277–8, 281–2; P. Guedalla, *The Queen and Mr Gladstone 1880–1898* (London, 1933), p. 120.

[25] L. Colley, 'The apotheosis of George III: loyalty, royalty and the British nation 1760–1820', *Past and Present*, 102 (1984), 103–4.

[26] H. Reeve, 'The disunion of America', *Edinburgh Review*, 114 (1861), 560–4, 577–8; Bagehot, *English Constitution*, pp. 14–25; Ashley, *Monarchy and Republic*, pp. 7–15. More generally, see D. A. Campbell, *English Public Opinion and the American Civil War* (Woodbridge, 2003).

In the years after 1848, when the Chartist threat had been seen off in Britain, the contrasts with less successful regimes seemed as striking as in the 1790s. Most mid-Victorian commentators were sure that the links between the various parts of the British constitution had facilitated political stability and strengthened moral leadership. The Great Exhibition of 1851 appeared to demonstrate both the reality of class harmony and the extent of Britain's global greatness. There was much comment about the lack of social unrest among the six million who came during the five and a half months that 'the people's palace' was open, and what this said about the national polity and character.[27] At the mass opening ceremony, the Queen moved around unprotected in what the Turin Embassy called 'an inspiration to liberalism'.[28] *Punch* saw it as

a magnificent lesson for foreigners – and especially for the Prussian princes, who cannot stir abroad without an armed escort – to see how securely and confidently a young female Sovereign and her family could walk in the closest possible contact, near enough to be touched by almost everyone, with five-and-twenty thousand people, selected from no class. . . . Here was a splendid example of that real freedom on the one hand, and perfect security on the other, which are the result of our constitutional monarchy, and which all the despotism and republicanism of the world cannot obtain elsewhere, let them go on as long as they may, executing each other in the name of order, or cutting each other's throats in the name of liberty.[29]

After the opening ceremony, Russell told the Queen that 'No republic of the Old or New World has done anything so splendid or so useful'.[30]

In fact, the Whig model of the constitution placed as much stress on the quality of governing class leadership as on the mechanics of political relationships. A key element of Victorian Whig-Liberal governance was the projection of exemplary political and moral values, in order to encourage respect for law and decency among the political nation, and responsible and accountable behaviour by the elite – which seemed necessary if the latter were to maintain their position. For example, Russell blamed the 1789 Revolution on the decadence and selfishness of the *ancien régime* French aristocracy. By the constitutional, social and educational reforms of the 1830s, and by reforming the Established Church, he hoped to ensure that such weaknesses did not infect British political life.[31] The

---

[27] J. Auerbach, *The Great Exhibition of 1851* (New Haven, 1999), pp. 158, 166–7.

[28] C. R. Fay, *Palace of Industry, 1851* (Cambridge, 1951), p. 25.

[29] 'Punch's own report of the opening of the Great Exhibition', *Punch*, 20 (1851), 190.

[30] Fay, *Palace of Industry*, p. 70.

[31] See Lord John Russell, *The Causes of the French Revolution* (1832), pp. 80–1, R. Brent, *Liberal Anglican Politics* (Oxford, 1987), pp. 56–7, and J. P. Parry, 'Past and future in the later career of Lord John Russell', in T.C.W. Blanning and D. Cannadine (eds.), *History and biography* (Cambridge, 1996), pp. 142–72.

tone of the Court would obviously play a crucial part in maintaining the quality of social and moral leadership, because of the personal visibility and iconic status of the monarch. George III had been associated with a pure family life, moderate habits and generous philanthropy, especially to religious charities and the support of the poor and sick.[32] Victoria, like him, was celebrated in the middle-class press both for philanthropy and for the purity of her family life. Through her charitable work, she was projected as the guardian of the ill, the downtrodden, and the animal kingdom.[33] She took her duties as the defender of the Protestant faith very seriously.[34] She was well aware that the royal family must set a positive example rather than the extravagant, foppish and exclusive tone which had been the legacy of George III's male children. In 1868 she sanctioned the publication of her bathetic *Highland Journal*, setting before her readers the example of a wholesome life of picnics and piety.[35] One reason for this was to offer a good model to the upper classes, a substitute for the high-profile projection of royal family life that had been possible during Albert's lifetime, and a different tone from that associated with her own scapegrace elder son.

The governing classes saw constitutional monarchy as not just a defining symbol of the legitimate and beneficial authority of the state, but also a symbol of Britain's power abroad. This was clear in relation to both Europe and the empire. Foreign secretaries – particularly Palmerston and Russell – urged constitutional monarchy as an ideal for Europe because it best secured authority, liberty and progress. Both men presented it to domestic audiences as England's trademark, the spread of which would assist her prestige and psychological dominance in Europe. They viewed the battle over European forms of government as the equivalent of military warfare. Every gain for autocracy was a gain for Austria, Russia or the 'Holy Alliance'; every republican regime might become a vehicle for propagating the ideas of the French Revolution. Palmerston considered that 'large republics seem to be essentially and inherently aggressive'.[36] Either way, internal and external stability was unlikely. Victories for constitutional monarchies, on the other hand, demonstrated that Europe was following the Providential path to a higher civilization – to England's

---

[32] G. Ditchfield, *George III* (Basingstoke, 2002), pp. 88–9, 143.

[33] E. Longford, *Victoria R. I.* (London, 2000 edn.), pp. 378–9, 405, 443; F. Prochaska, *Royal Bounty* (New Haven, 1995), pp. 91–4, 111, 115.

[34] W. L. Arnstein, 'Queen Victoria and religion', in G. Malmgreen (ed.), *Religion in the Lives of English Women 1760–1930* (London, 1986), pp. 88–128.

[35] Queen Victoria, *Leaves from the Journal of Our Life in the Highlands, from 1848 to 1861*, ed. A. Helps (London, 1868).

[36] Palmerston to Normanby, 28 Feb. 1848, in E. Ashley, *The Life of Henry John Temple, Viscount Palmerston 1846–1865* (2 vols., London, 1876), vol. I, p. 81.

advantage. However, the slow pace of these victories demonstrated all the more clearly the superiority of the British talent for self-government: in 1858 Earl Grey noted that it was only in (British-protected) Belgium and Piedmont that governments of this stable, progressive type had yet been successfully established.[37]

Royal personages were particularly valuable embodiments of the sense of national pride and distinctness, and, as the century progressed, imperial pride as well. The sailor suit made on board the Royal Yacht for the infant Prince of Wales in 1846 sparked one of the greatest and most enduring fashion crazes of all time – not least because it coincided with the first of the major Victorian invasion panics about the aggressive intentions of the French navy. The settler colonies were generally seen as particularly striking examples of the 'English' capacity for self-government under the law, in contrast to the failures of the continent; there too, therefore, a royal presence could underline the uniqueness of the British constitutional model. From 1860, the Queen's sons undertook a number of tours of Australia, Canada and South Africa, and one of them (the Duke of Connaught) and one of her sons-in-law (the Marquess of Lorne) served as Governors-General of Canada. These visits were designed to strengthen loyalty to the Crown, all the more important in view of the vigorous meritocracy of those societies, and to provide a solid testimony to the benefits of British rule as against the republican alternatives in the United States and elsewhere. For example, one important concern of Derby, as Colonial Secretary negotiating a settlement with the Transvaal in 1884, was to maintain British suzerainty over the whole of South Africa, which for him was synonymous with the prevention of a Boer republican ascendancy.[38] In 1873, Evelyn Ashley argued that the monarchy was the great bond that kept an increasingly self-governing empire together.[39]

III

However, at times in the nineteenth century there was a Radical political challenge to the position of monarchy, which should also be understood as part of a broader strategy. Between 1800 and 1870 the main aim of parliamentary Radicals was to attack what is now often known as 'Old Corruption', that is to say, those aspects of the elite political system that could be accused of directing taxpayer revenues to the specific benefit of particular individuals, groups and classes. In Radical eyes, such people

[37] Grey, *Parliamentary Government*, p. 15.
[38] See the entry for 15th Earl of Derby, *Oxford Dictionary of National Biography* (p. 196).
[39] Ashley, *Monarchy and Republic*, pp. 19–20.

milked their position for their own benefit and offered the public no value in return. More broadly, Radicals had an instinctive suspicion of state power, tending to regard it as unaccountable, potentially oppressive of popular liberties, and biased in favour of privileged sections rather than the national interest. As a very visible symbol of this elitist state, the Crown, and specifically the person of the monarch, naturally featured prominently in this critique. So did recipients of state patronage at home and in the colonies, and office-holders in the Church Establishment and the military. At the most basic level, the history of Liberal politics in the nineteenth century was the story of the compromises made between this Radical movement and the Whiggish constitutional ideas discussed above. Many elite Whigs sympathized with the Radical criticism of state illiberality and extravagance, as was evident from their joint attacks on Toryism before 1830. Economy and accountability were key themes in Whig as well as Radical politics. But the Whig concern with the legitimate authority of state and Church also led to tensions between them, which were particularly intense at times of enhanced Radical fervour – such as in the economic depressions and social anxiety of the late 1810s and the dozen years after 1838.

At these times especially, there was enormous scope for Radical criticism of the extravagance of the monarchy. In the 1810s and early 1820s, this was all the greater because it was so easy to satirize George IV's private vices and appetites, both in themselves and as a symbol of the selfish excess of an *ancien régime*. In the late 1830s, Radicals and Tories joined in criticism of the close alliance between the new Queen and Melbourne's Whig government, which bore fruit in the successful manoeuvre to reduce the parliamentary grant to Albert on his marriage in 1840. Radicals were critical enough of workshy *British* aristocrats' ability to siphon taxpayers' money off for their personal benefit. The argument that the grant to Albert's entourage would be going to immigrant *Saxe-Coburg* princelings and retainers made it an even more irresistible target. In 1843, *Punch* remarked that the bells rung to celebrate the birth of the latest royal child were in fact ringing the changes '£.s.d.'[40]

However, this rhetoric was merely an element of a much more general campaign against the extravagance and elitism of the political establishment. Even in the 1810s and 1820s, and certainly in the post-Reform Act era, those who pointed to the power of vested interests in the state had many targets to choose from: the Corn Laws, the Church, official sinecures, excessive military and diplomatic expenditure, and the

---

[40] Williams, *Contentious Crown*, pp. 14, 17–18; D. Thompson, *Queen Victoria* (London, 2001 edn.), pp. 25, 33–6.

'aristocratic' tone of government, whether Tory or Whig. So this was a general Radical critique. Moreover, it was severely blunted by the changes to the image of the state that stemmed from the events of 1846 at home and 1848 on the continent. The repeal of the Corn Laws was the single most important demonstration that official policy was no longer determined by the sectional interests of the landed classes. Then a number of developments suggested that the British polity was essentially fair-minded and disinterested, certainly compared to that of her continental rivals: the concerted and successful attack on 'unEnglish' and 'aristocratic' approaches to government between 1848 and 1850, the collapse of the Chartist threat after 1848, and the booming economy of the 1850s and 1860s.[41] In the 1850s, though specific groups of Radicals continued to point to particular examples of vested interest influence in politics, it was not possible to generate anything like the amount of indignation, and anything like the coalition of opinion, against them as had been directed against the electoral system in 1829–31 or the tariff system in the 1840s. Free trade, expenditure cuts, and the removal of many sinecures in Church and State progressively softened the virulence of the 'Old Corruption' critique. Moreover Victoria, unlike her predecessors, kept her spending within the agreed terms of the civil list.[42]

On the other hand, there was a general assumption in the 1850s and 1860s that the direction of political movement would continue to be towards the parliamentary Radical ideal: towards more rigorous Commons control over official expenditure, a further attack on patronage and 'interest' politics, and a vigorous utilitarian questioning of the merit of traditional institutions. The logic of liberal representative politics seemed to be to move ever more decisively away from the *ancien régime* state, in which a coalition of vested interests at Court, in the military and in the civil, diplomatic and colonial service had obliged the taxpayer to maintain them and to uphold their sectional benefits. Thus when a major piece of further electoral reform was passed in 1867, which gave more parliamentary influence to the provincial leaders of middle-class and artisanal Radicalism, the consensus was that this would lead to renewed calls for economy and institutional scrutiny. Gladstone's government won a large majority at the election of autumn 1868 on the twin policies of Church disestablishment in Ireland (seen by British Nonconformists as a prelude to disestablishment on the mainland) and expenditure cuts. Spending on the army and navy was reduced from £27.1 million to £21.1 million between 1867–8 and 1870–1, with a particular focus on the reduction

---

[41] I have discussed these themes further in *Politics of Patriotism*, chs. 1 and 4.
[42] As was pointed out by e.g. *Nonconformist*, 8 Feb. 1871, p. 133.

of the colonial defence burden. The Liberals' expectation was for these self-governing institutions to bear the cost of their own defence, in a self-conscious rejection of the pre-1850 system of imperial economic and military protection.

So, when Radical criticism of the cost and utility of the monarchy revived between 1868 and 1871, that too should be seen as part of a general movement. There were specific catalysts of this criticism, particularly the seclusion of the widowed Queen and the playboy lifestyle of the Prince of Wales, whose denial of adultery in the witness-box in the Mordaunt divorce trial in 1870 was not universally believed. But these were given much greater significance by the wider political mood of economy and inquiry. In 1870–1 Radical MPs such as G. O. Trevelyan pushed forward the argument that the links between the Court and the army – exemplified by the position of the Queen's cousin, the Duke of Cambridge, as Commander-in-Chief – operated as a major obstacle to the rationalization of the military. A number of Radicals argued that the logic of the franchise extension of 1867, by which power passed to 'the people', was that they should truly govern themselves, in a republican system.[43] There was much criticism when in 1871 the Queen requested parliamentary grants to support two of her children, as Prince Arthur came of age and Princess Louise married. A well-publicized anonymous tract, called *What does she do with it?* (perhaps written by Trevelyan), alleged that the Queen had consistently saved money for her private use from her annual civil list entitlement, and should use that money to support her children. Fifty-one Radical MPs voted to reduce the annuity proposed for Prince Arthur in July 1871. In November, to a popular audience in Newcastle, Sir Charles Dilke criticized the cost of the monarchy and the 'political corruption' that hung around it, implied that Victoria exercised considerable power, and claimed that a move towards a republic was a matter of 'education and time'.[44] Under the influence of the Paris Commune, Mazzini and the dynamism of post-war America, a number of artisanal republican clubs were founded in the early 1870s, eighty-five in all by 1874, and the movement was supported by Bradlaugh and other high-profile Radical figures.

Yet the threat from constitutional republicanism was exaggerated. In Parliament, most Radical opponents of the grants merely wanted to show that the reformed Commons could pressure the monarchy to be more accountable and more 'national', performing a service commensurate with its cost. George Dixon, who proposed reducing Arthur's annuity, saw

[43] See e.g. Williams, *Contentious Crown*, p. 41.   [44] *Times*, 9 Nov. 1871, p. 6.

it as an anti-republican move to reassure the taxpayer.[45] Thomas Wright remarked that working-class republicanism would be better named 'Utilitarianism', since its preoccupation was with reducing the cost and unaccountability of the Court. To the extent that it had objectives beyond that, it was usually a shorthand all-purpose cry for the better representation of working-class interests in politics.[46]

Thus the debates of 1871 showed the limits to the criticism of monarchy. In early 1872, a motion by Dilke to inquire into the Queen's expenditure, with a view to establishing whether her civil list income was excessive, was seized on by his opponents as an attempt to promote the republican agenda; it got two votes in Parliament. As one Radical writer, J. M. Ludlow, put it in 1870, in the modern, rational age there was less instinctive devotion and loyalty to monarchy, but a great deal of considered and genuine 'respectful friendship' to the sovereign.[47] Most provincial Nonconformists were great admirers of the monarchy, not least from pride at their ancestors' role in the replacement of the Stuarts by the Hanoverians. From that perspective, the glorious Cromwellian period, when Dissenting principles had held sway in England, was attractive not so much because of its republicanism but because it was an essential precursor to the current system of exemplary constitutional governance. To Nonconformists, and many other middle-class Victorians, the modern monarchy was not just constitutionally but also morally representative, because they identified it with pure family values that reflected and promoted the best of their own class's morality.[48] This moral image of the royal family was one that the more respectable elements of the middle-class press were particularly assiduous in developing. It is presumably that image that Ludlow felt encouraged the sentiment of 'respectful friendship'. At the time of her Golden Jubilee of 1887, her girlish remark on realising that she would become Queen, 'I will be good', was widely quoted and became a Jubilee song.[49]

---

[45] *Hansard's Parliamentary Debates*, Third Series, 208, cc. 584–5, 31 July 1871.

[46] T. Wright, 'English republicanism', *Fraser's Magazine*, 3 (1871), 757, 759; D. Craig, 'The crowned republic? Monarchy and anti-monarchy in Britain 1760–1901', *Historical Journal*, 46 (2003), 183.

[47] J. M. Ludlow, 'Europe and the war', *Contemporary Review*, 15 (1870), 659–60.

[48] In mid-Victorian northern town halls – such as Rochdale and Leeds – Cromwell was portrayed in a line of English rulers, as a symbol of the nation's civic republicanism. After Albert's death, Victoria's prolonged mourning was defended by the Nonconformist politician John Bright as an example of domestic piety and a mark of her humanitarianism: G. M. Trevelyan, *The life of John Bright* (London, 1914), pp. 398–9. For the loyalty of Nonconformist Wales, on account of Victoria's religious and moral values, see J. Davies, 'Victoria and Victorian Wales', in G. H. Jenkins and J. B. Smith (eds.), *Politics and Society in Wales 1840–1922* (Cardiff, 1988), p. 15.

[49] J. L. Lant, *Insubstantial Pageant* (New York, 1979), p. 169; Williams, *Contentious Crown*, p. 215.

One catalyst of pro-monarchist sentiment in 1872 was the service of Thanksgiving for the Prince of Wales's escape from typhoid in December 1871, which sparked popular and press enthusiasm. But it is not plausible to suggest that either the illness of the Prince of Wales, or the wise guidance of Gladstone and other royal image-makers around this time, caused a change in the nation's view of monarchy.[50] Rather, the debate of 1871–2 about the royal family paralleled a much broader debate about what kind of political nation Britain was. The Thanksgiving service gave the media the chance to underline the merits of existing constitutional arrangements and their superiority to French republicanism – particularly after the bloody end to the Paris Commune – and Russian autocracy.[51] The reaction against liberal-left republican inclinations was part of a more general propertied and middle-class anxiety about the power of mass working-class movements under the post-1867 franchise. Crucially, it was easier to rally opinion behind the monarchy now that the inclination of, and opportunity for, the Queen to obstruct the political process seemed smaller than ever. The Radical George Potter suggested that republicanism would remain largely a theoretical movement as long as the monarchy remained of good character, and the Crown and its ministers remained impartial between classes.[52] The impulse behind the movement had always been a feeling that the governing elite in general was unrepresentative. After the large extension of the franchise in 1867, this was more difficult to argue, and so republicans turned their attention to more significant examples of privilege and inequity. The Social Democratic Federation of 1884 absorbed the energies of many working-class republicans, and was interested primarily in social questions, though also in the further extension of democracy and the abolition of the Lords.[53]

To put it another way, the events of the early 1870s showed the limits to traditional British Radicalism, reaching far beyond the specific status of the monarchy. The Church of England was never disestablished, though 1871–3 saw the apogee of the campaign for it, reflected in well supported parliamentary motions. Initial pressure for it from the Liberation Society was countered by the Church Defence Institution and a

---

[50] F. Harcourt, 'Gladstone, monarchism and the "new" imperialism', *Journal of Imperial and Commonwealth History*, 14 (1985), and Kuhn, *Democratic Royalism*, both emphasize the second in particular.

[51] Williams, *Contentious Crown*, pp. 171–2 (*Times, Sunday Times, Illustrated London News, Daily Telegraph*).

[52] Potter, *Nonconformist*, 19 April 1871, pp. 372–3; Mundella, *Hansard*, 210, c. 312, 19 March 1872.

[53] M. Bevir, 'Republicanism, socialism, and democracy in Britain: the origins of the Radical left', *Journal of Social History*, 34 (2000), 351–68.

powerful Conservative revival.[54] The Radical demand for cuts in colonial expenditure similarly led to a reaction in favour of the imperial connection. The Colonial Institute, later the Royal Empire Society, was founded in 1869 specifically to resist pressure from Radical MPs to erode the links between metropolis and empire, and in the 1870s both Liberal and Conservative governments saw the merit of a renewed focus on imperial themes. Generally, government expenditure cuts were reversed: after significant reductions in 1869–71, spending rose inexorably under governments of both parties, and was up by 50 per cent by 1895. Gladstone was defeated in 1874 when he campaigned on the abolition of the income tax: it was no longer such a sensitive issue. The introduction of competitive examinations across almost the whole civil service in 1870 was the final victory for Radicals in the battle against 'Old Corruption' and political patronage.[55] The abolition of the purchase of commissions, more effective co-operation between regular soldiers and the volunteers, increasing regimental territorialization, and growing international rivalry all contributed to the process by which the cost of the army became accepted as a worthwhile charge on the state, rather than a subsidy for an aristocratic bolthole and arm of domestic repression.

After 1867, in other words, the long-standing Radical critique of the vested-interest state finally lost its bite, as a result of franchise extension, the revival of the party system, and yet more evidence of the state's fiscal fairness between classes and interest groups. The decline of this persistent rhetorical tradition benefited institutions like the monarchy, the army and the colonies in two ways. First, they were no longer so clearly in the political firing line. Radicals slowly became more preoccupied with issues of using the power of the state for the benefit of working people, whether through social reform, trade union issues or questions of redistributive taxation. The effect was not to destroy criticism of the monarchy, which continued along very similar lines as before, but instead to make it less significant politically. As the *Radical Programme* observed in 1885, 'so long as the functions of royalty are recognized as being ornamental and consultative . . . Radicals have something else to do than to break butterflies on wheels'.[56] Second, the greater willingness to celebrate the inclusiveness of the political system made it less controversial to express pride in institutional symbols of British political stability, liberty and success, of

[54] J. P. Parry, 'Nonconformity, clericalism and "Englishness": the United Kingdom', in C. Clark and W. Kaiser (eds.), *Culture Wars* (Cambridge, 2003), pp. 152–81.

[55] H. J. Hanham, 'Political patronage at the Treasury 1870–1912', *Historical Journal*, 3 (1960), 75–84. I have written about the themes of this paragraph in more detail in *Politics of Patriotism*.

[56] *Radical Programme*, p. 40.

which the monarchy was the most visible. Moreover, the growing international tension after 1870, which made foreign policy themes so central politically, encouraged politicians and commentators repeatedly to invoke patriotic arguments and comparisons with other nations. And propertied and middle-class people particularly continued to emphasize the religious and moral leadership which they associated with royalty, which they hoped would set a good example to the rising democracy. In all these ways, the crisis of 1870–2 strengthened the Whig view of the constitution, featuring a dignified monarchy validating the rule of law and moralizing a parliamentary regime, just as it also strengthened the Whig idea of a broad, relatively undogmatic national Church Establishment fulfilling a similarly exemplary function.

IV

If we accept that it was the political context, much more than royal behaviour itself, that determined the monarchy's fortunes, this makes it easier to explain continuing criticism of it. The most striking thing about attitudes to the royal family, whether favourable or unfavourable, is how venerable and indeed ossified they are. In particular, every generation of republicans, setting up as cutting-edge Radical thinkers fearlessly challenging convention, fails to realize that its arguments are extremely traditional. The republican view is based on sentiments that have come naturally to many Englishmen for hundreds of years: admiration for the principle of popular self-government, and belief that it suits the national character; dislike of symbols of privilege at the head of the state; a revulsion at the moral tone associated with certain selfish, money-grubbing and lazy royals; hostility to the cost of subsidizing this system; a distaste for the 'sycophancy and snobbery' that hovers around the throne.[57] As H. G. Wells wrote in 1926, while the monarchy endures, 'the old army system remains, Society remains, the militant tradition remains'.[58] Some have always claimed that the royal family of the day is more aristocratic (and foreign) than national, more decadent than exemplary. For centuries, princely indolence, extravagance, arrogance and ill-treatment of women have been pilloried with relish. In the 1810s and 1820s, George IV was satirized more viciously than any present-day royal, while his discarded wife Caroline – seen as a weak and wronged woman – was championed as strongly as the Princess of Wales in the

---

[57] For the quotation, see ibid, p. 39. For anti-monarchical sentiment generally in the nineteenth century, see A. Taylor, *'Down with the Crown'* (London, 1999).
[58] K. Rose, *King George V* (London, 1983), p. 396.

1990s.[59] Criticism of the lifestyle of Victoria's Prince of Wales did not abate after he recovered from illness in 1871, nor did parliamentary criticism of his mother's financial requests. When, in 1889, the Commons considered the issue of the grants to be paid to his children in adulthood, at one stage 134 MPs opposed the allocations.[60] During rationing in and after the Second World War, there was considerable popular criticism of the royal family's conspicuous and privileged consumption patterns, and of the cost of Princess Elizabeth's wedding.[61] Increasing visibility and accountability in the matter of royal expenditure, the waiving of monarchical tax privileges, and some curbing of royal extravagance, have helped to marginalize such criticism during Elizabeth II's reign.[62] But it can never disappear entirely. By its nature, a royal family will be a target for accusations of privilege and cosseting. Indeed, perhaps it is even necessary in a modern democracy that some royals should be identified by the media as arrogant spendthrifts, partly in order to sell newspapers, but also as a contrast, in order to define and publicize public-spirited behaviour by others – royals and non-royals. Moreover, it has been an important clause in the unwritten contract between monarchy and people since 1688 that the Crown is held, not just on sufferance, but as a legitimate object of popular rebuke, gossip and prurience, a symbol of a free political society.

In the face of these arguments, the monarchy has survived partly because, as noted above, the odds are stacked in its favour, since the enormous effort of changing the constitution is generally perceived greatly to outweigh the practical benefits of doing so. But it is also the case that the various elements of the 'Whig' model – the monarchy's association with national identity, with constitutional balance and liberty, and with exemplary public values – continue to be widely attractive, to the political elite and to the wider public. Here too, what is striking is the way that ancient arguments have endured.

Firstly, the royal family has provided a symbol of national unity in times of crisis, has played a major role in commemorations of military valour, and has benefited from these associations. Wars and international tensions, and the perceived extremism of foreign regimes, have all encouraged a rallying of sentiment around the monarchy. Increasing identification with the Crown in the late nineteenth century was bound up with

---

[59] T. W. Laqueur, 'The Queen Caroline affair: politics as art in the reign of George IV', *Journal of Modern History*, 54 (1982), 417–66.

[60] Williams, *Contentious Crown*, pp. 61–2.

[61] I. Zweiniger-Bargielowska, 'Royal rations', *History Today*, 43:12 (1993), 13–15.

[62] On the financing of the monarchy, see V. Bogdanor, *The Monarchy and the Constitution* (Oxford, 1995), pp. 183–96.

the growing nationalism generated by European imperial rivalries. The First World War and the Russian Revolution then strengthened this tendency – though stalemate in war also stimulated a brief but alarming revival of antipathy to the 'German' connections of the family, prompting a rebranding of the monarchy in 1917 in specifically British terms.[63] And it was the royal family's status as the homely antithesis of Hitlerian militarism, shrillness, savagery and decadence that did most for its image during the Second World War.[64] Even fifty years later, in the VE-Day commemorations of 1995, the reappearance of the surviving members of the 'family at war' on the Buckingham Palace balcony had great emotional resonance. At times of threat, the British state has been represented by a fallible, often unremarkable, largely powerless and speechless human being. Such a person has been a fitting standard-bearer for a regime that has consistently rejected the heroic rhetoric of Utopian dictatorships. While Russia bowed down to Communism and Germany goose-stepped into Nazism, George VI stammered for England.

This association with anti-Utopian politics has not been merely symbolic. The monarchy has helped to preserve the British system from the possibility of absolutism. It is not just Kings and Queens whose potentially overbearing ambitions have been checked by the British constitution. It remains 'balanced', in the sense that the monarchy has helped to limit the pretensions of the political class. Taking the twentieth century as a whole, it was probably true that that class remained less grand and less insulated from criticism than its equivalent in France or Germany. There are several reasons for this, not all connected with royalty. Nonetheless, the deep-rooted distinction between partisan Prime Minister and impartial monarch underlines the message that beyond the feverish but often trivial warfare of day-to-day politics there is a shared focal point of communal identification, symbolizing the nation itself, to which the most powerful politicians must, literally, bow. In 1885, Earl Cowper, in reflecting on the British escape from the peril of the continent, Caesarism, maintained that the Crown was a 'chief bulwark . . . of our liberty' by drawing to itself 'much of the popular enthusiasm which would otherwise be accumulated upon the favourite of the moment'.[65] And the monarchy has retained substantial constitutional powers which are hardly exercised but which, in the hands of active politicians, would be of immense potential significance.

At the same time, the monarchy has strengthened the polity, not least because its aura of traditionalism has helped to dignify contentious

---

[63] Rose, *George V*, pp. 174–5.
[64] B. Pimlott, *The Queen* (London, 1997 edn.), pp. 56–77.
[65] Earl Cowper, 'Caesarism', *Nineteenth Century*, 17 (1885), 10.

decisions and to disguise and legitimize significant changes – including the emergence of the Labour party and the challenges to national sovereignty since 1973. In the eighteenth and nineteenth centuries, the majesty of monarchy also helped to hide the puny powers of the central state. However, the more common criticism at the beginning of the twenty-first century is that the centralization of power in Whitehall since the 1960s has given the executive excessive authority – which can then be exacerbated by use of the royal prerogative.

The royal family has also associated itself with institutions and values of civil society which are essentially independent of the state. In the process, it has added greatly to its own base of support. By continuous and extensive patronage of charitable organizations, it has publicized the idea of social service and given lustre to hundreds of voluntary bodies – from the Citizens' Advice Bureaux to freemasonry. This has won it a large constituency of admirers, not least upper- and middle-class women, for whom such institutions offered a social purpose long before most career paths were open to them. They have felt their labours validated by royal approval, garden parties and investitures. Meanwhile, many male members of the royal family have been connected with voluntary ventures which have taught values of self-help, with the often subconscious message that dependence on the state is to be abhorred. From the Duke of York's boys' camps of the 1920s to the Duke of Edinburgh's Award Scheme and the Prince's Trust, they have emphasized confidence-building, courage and enterprise.[66] The other principal association of royals has been with the armed services, as figurehead and inspiration. The monarchy's military connections have contributed to the process by which the army and navy have remained at the same time unusually independent from those who actually exercise political power, and yet immensely loyal to a resolutely constitutional regime. Indeed Victoria and George V both supported army commanders – the Duke of Cambridge and General Haig – in key battles with politicians, though not necessarily to wise effect.[67]

Social service has to be a key theme of modern monarchy, because it is by far the best card with which to counter the equally unavoidable allegations of royal selfishness, privilege and extravagance. To earn respect, monarchs need to be seen to sacrifice personal desires and freedoms in the cause of national duty. Indeed it is this sacrifice – rather than anything more elaborate and mystical – which has been the central theme of

[66] Prochaska, *Royal Bounty*, passim, esp. pp. 191, 253.
[67] H. Strachan, *The Politics of the British Army* (Oxford, 1997), ch. 3; K. Martin, *The Crown and the Establishment* (London, 1962), pp. 96–101.

the coronations of George VI and of Elizabeth II. Both were projected as flawed human beings, overcoming private desires in favour of community commitment, just as Christ represents humanity struggling to find a personal relationship with God. The sacrifices made by each – the stammering, painfully shy and reluctant King, atoning for his brother's shirking of duty, and the young Queen who had hardly had a private adult life – were easier to comprehend than the arcane rites of the service. Certainly public service, along with Christianity, decency, mutual respect and tolerance, are among the values that the monarchy has promoted most assiduously in the course of the twentieth century – as described by Philip Williamson below for the interwar period.

V

Another element that has often been said to heighten the appeal of monarchy has been its splendour and visibility. It is certainly true that the role of ceremonial revived from the 1880s, reflecting a desire to project the monarch to a larger political nation, and to encourage respect for social hierarchy. The stage on which most large-scale royal events took place was redesigned to better effect between 1906 and 1913: the Mall was widened, Buckingham Palace refronted and the Victoria Monument built.[68] Edward VII had been personally attracted to the idea of a stylish, visible monarchy, ever since his admiring visits to Napoleon III's Paris as a youth. And aristocrats and plutocrats liked the snob value of participating in royal displays, or of rubbing shoulders with a glamorous King. One of the benefits of ceremonial is that its multiple meanings appeal to different people for different reasons, so it would be unwise to adopt a one-dimensional explanation of its attraction. However there is no incompatibility between the emergence of this more visible and stage-managed monarchy and the themes of this essay.

This is, firstly, because much of the enhanced presentation of monarchy was itself political, designed to strengthen particular government objectives. The splendour of Edward VII's coronation should be seen in the light of concerns with national vigour and efficiency after the Boer War, and anxiety to boost Edward's own profile. Moreover, military spectacle played a large part in ceremonial elsewhere in Europe at the same time, and elements of British society felt the need to issue a reminder of the might of the British state and armed forces.[69] The Unionist government of the day was also anxious to use royal events to improve popular

---

[68] Cannadine, 'Context, performance and meaning', p. 128.
[69] This anxiety can be traced from the 1880s: Lant, *Insubstantial Pageant*, pp. 154–5.

understanding of and sympathy for the empire – as was apparent in 1897, when Joseph Chamberlain planned the Diamond Jubilee as a demonstration of imperial unity. Similarly, an ostensibly 'National' government, facing an election in 1935, found attractions in identifying itself with the above-party aura cultivated for George V's Silver Jubilee.[70] A major reason for the revival of the ceremony of Investiture of the Prince of Wales in 1911 was the Liberal government's desire to empathize with Welsh identity and political demands.[71]

However, as Walter Arnstein has reminded us in one particular context, there were strict limits to the amount, and grandeur, of British Crown ceremonial.[72] Victoria disliked it: in the 1860s and 1870s she rejected pageantry and extravagance as 'unsuitable to the present day', in favour of 'hard work and domestic purity'.[73] Even at the Jubilee of 1887 she refused to wear her Crown and robes or to ride in the state coach. The *Spectator* noted that 'it was a friend of all who was welcomed, rather than a great Sovereign'.[74] Ten years later, that redoubtable German lady, the Grand Duchess of Mecklenburg-Strelitz, was appalled at the lack of decorum on Jubilee Day: 'after 60 years Reign, to thank God in the Street!!!'[75] The most applauded aspect of the day was the Queen's drive to the working-class districts south of the Thames. Here there was little pomp, just an iconic woman on show to her people. In armistice week in 1918, George V drove round the East End every day.[76] Moreover, though a grandiose imperial monarchy was projected to Indians and Africans in the early twentieth century, there was much less emphasis on it at home.[77] George V preferred an ordinary, 'bowler-hat' style of kingship; he rode around the British Empire Exhibition of 1924 on a toy train. He attended the FA Cup Final and inaugurated the Royal Command Performance.[78] His second son, President of the Industrial Welfare Society, inspected so many factories and mines that his family called him 'the foreman'.[79]

---

[70] R. McKibbin, *Classes and Cultures* (Oxford, 1998), p. 8.

[71] J. S. Ellis, 'Reconciling the Celt: British national identity, empire, and the 1911 Investiture of the Prince of Wales', *Journal of British Studies*, 37 (1998), 391–418.

[72] W. L. Arnstein, 'Queen Victoria opens Parliament: the disinvention of tradition', *Historical Research*, 63 (1990), 178–94.

[73] P. Guedalla, *The Queen and Mr Gladstone 1845–1879* (London, 1933), p. 370; Longford, *Victoria*, p. 349.

[74] Lant, *Insubstantial Pageant*, ch 6; Williams, *Contentious Crown*, p. 215.

[75] J. Pope-Hennessy, *Queen Mary 1867–1953* (London, 1959), p. 335.

[76] F. Prochaska, *The Republic of Britain 1760–2000* (London, 2000), p. 173.

[77] The romantic imperialist Alan Lennox-Boyd made this distinction between the domestic and the imperial monarchy in 1934: P. Murphy, *Alan Lennox-Boyd* (London, 1999), p. 41.

[78] D. Farson, *Marie Lloyd and Music Hall* (London, 1972), pp. 88–97.

[79] S. Bradford, *King George VI* (London, 1989), pp. 79–80.

Moreover, most of the celebration of royal Jubilees and weddings has taken place at a local level, reflecting the decentralized nature of the polity and the importance of voluntary activity. This has continued a trend begun by Victoria and Albert's tours to provincial towns in the 1840s and 1850s, when local committees were invariably determined to demonstrate their loyalty and hospitality in displays of civic pride. When the Queen opened Leeds Town Hall in 1858, the *Leeds Mercury* saw this as a sanctioning of 'Municipal self-government'.[80] On the occasion of the 1887 Jubilee, many towns and villages set up funds for improvements to commemorate the Queen's reign, and held municipal parades of local voluntary bodies. There were innumerable fêtes and parties, offering popular enjoyment laced with civic piety.[81] Hardly any of these events required royal participation; instead, they were occasions for urban leaders and philanthropists to demonstrate their status and public spirit by funding hospitals, drinking fountains and other civic benefits. In the same way, minorities used royal celebrations to demonstrate their own integration into society. In 1863, for example, the *Jewish Chronicle* expressed the enthusiasm of 'loyal Jewish subjects' at the Prince of Wales's wedding, seeing this as an opportunity to celebrate a regime that had given them constitutional rights.[82] It was possible for local versions of royal celebrations to reflect different agendas and develop different identities because the image of royalty itself on these occasions was not particularly dominant or overbearing. Indeed it was often little more than an empty vessel into which a choice of coloured liquids could be poured. However it is doubtful if this effect could have been achieved had Victoria not already been so strongly identified with philanthropy and voluntary institutions, and to some degree with support for religious minorities. At the beginning of her reign, for example, she took pleasure in bestowing the first Jewish knighthood on Moses Montefiore.[83]

Perhaps most importantly, royal celebrations offer people a holiday and festival atmosphere in which routine is suspended, and a carnival can be enjoyed – again, often with comparatively little overt reference

---

[80] J. Plunkett, *Queen Victoria* (Oxford, 2003), pp. 41–4; Williams, *Contentious Crown*, p. 196.

[81] Lant, *Insubstantial Pageant*, p. 174. There is a useful discussion of the multifaceted meanings of local Jubilee celebrations in E. Hammerton and D. Cannadine, 'Conflict and consensus on a ceremonial occasion: the Diamond Jubilee in Cambridge in 1897', *Historical Journal*, 24 (1981), 111–46.

[82] Williams, *Contentious Crown*, p. 181.

[83] Longford, *Victoria*, p. 78. At this period, she also followed her Whig government's agenda by warmly greeting the Irish Catholic leader O'Connell, though her enthusiasm for Ireland was rather patchy in later years: Victoria to King Leopold, 22 Feb. 1838, in A. C. Benson and Viscount Esher (eds.), *The Letters of Queen Victoria . . . between the Years 1837 and 1861* (3 vols., London, 1908), vol. I, p. 106.

to the individual royals in question.[84] Where royalty does feature more prominently, the suspension of reality is more marked, because the projection of a wedding or coronation on such a large stage allows a collective expression of ideals and hopes for our elegant, smiling 'friends'. It is in this sense that it is legitimate to associate royal events with 'fairy-tale' and 'magic' – words that were used as far back as the 1887 Jubilee.[85] Royal appearances offer a mixture of the magical and the mundane, not particularly because of the ceremonial involved, but because media attention romanticizes human stories with which millions can in any case identify: hence Bagehot's famous dictum that a 'princely marriage is the brilliant edition of a universal fact, and, as such, it rivets mankind'.[86] The ceremonies can easily appear inclusive and representative. In 1858, on the marriage of Princess Victoria, the *Illustrated London News* observed that 'every one feels just as if there was to be a wedding in his own family and means to make it a festivity'; in 1871, the *Daily Telegraph* said the same about Princess Louise's wedding.[87] Widespread popular interest in the activities of royal women and children, particularly, is entirely predictable. There had been enormous demand for memorial prints and commemorative pottery after the death of Princess Charlotte in 1817.[88] The *Illustrated London News* could be relied upon to give its readers tearjerking accounts of the death of Princess Alice in 1878 – seventeen years to the day after her father! – after catching diphtheria by smothering her desperately ill infant son with motherly love.[89]

It remains the case that royal weddings, Jubilees and funerals tend to occupy an enchanted space, a parallel universe to the humdrum normality of workday life – all the more alluring because it is one which much of the nation can briefly enter. At the end of the disruption to routine caused by the lying-in-state of George VI in 1952, Harold Macmillan entered in his diary, 'le roman est fini; l'histoire commence'.[90] To a lesser extent, the same effect occurs with more run-of-the-mill royal visits, which still project glossiness, general cheerfulness and lack of content. This distance from the normal reminds us that though there are brief periods when the

---

[84] See McKibbin, *Classes and Cultures*, pp. 10–2.

[85] Williams, *Contentious Crown*, p. 253 (*Daily News, Spectator, Pall Mall Gazette*).

[86] Bagehot, *English Constitution*, p. 41. See, e.g. R. Brunt, 'The family firm restored: newsreel coverage of the British monarchy 1936–45', in C. Gledhill and G. Swanson (eds.), *Nationalising Femininity* (Manchester, 1996), p. 145, and J. Williamson, *Consuming Passions* (London, 1986), pp. 75–6.

[87] *Illustrated London News*, 23 Jan. 1858, p. 73; Williams, *Contentious Crown*, p. 207.

[88] S. C. Behrendt, *Royal Mourning and Regency Culture* (Basingstoke, 1997), ch. 6.

[89] *Illustrated London News*, 21 Dec. 1878, esp. p. 574–5.

[90] *The Macmillan Diaries: the Cabinet Years 1950–1957*, ed. P. Catterall (London, 2004 edn.), p. 144.

monarchy captures the centre-stage, because it is to some extent nationally representative, for the vast majority of the time it does *not* in fact feature largely in the popular imagination. In 2001–2, as in 1976–7 and in 1886–7, most of the public seemed uninterested in an impending Jubilee only months before its successful realization.[91] Most people, most of the time since 1800, have not thought very much about the royal family, since there has been little to suggest that the monarch has much power. In a liberal parliamentary state, the action is rightly elsewhere.

Royalty may well not have occupied a larger place in people's thoughts at the time of Queen Victoria's death than at the Queen Mother's in 2002. Arnold Bennett thought that the crowd at the former's funeral were not 'deeply moved', but 'serene and cheerful'.[92] When George VI died, football and rugby matches went ahead; George Wigg remarked that the large crowds at them were the result of many using the king's death as an excuse to miss work.[93] Mass-Observation reported widespread indifference to royal broadcasts even during the Second World War.[94] No doubt it is true that automatic signs of outward respect for the monarchy have declined, as part of a general waning of deference and the emergence of a self-consciously illusionless media. But it is not clear that its real popularity is much greater, or smaller, than it has been for a long time, and it seems to be able to generate more press coverage than ever. The recent explosion of media interest in it has tended to give an exaggerated impression of popular concern on the subject. Vox pop broadcasting and internet culture has unearthed and published a range of individual opinions that have always existed, and has given them all a rather ponderous significance. It has made fervent expressions of support for the monarchy, and of opposition to it, seem more widespread than they probably are.

VI

That the monarchy remains in place is due neither to popular irrationality on the one hand, nor, *mainly*, to the actions of its own leading figures, or to specific images that may from time to time have been 'constructed' for it. It is certainly not because of the attractiveness of ceremonial for its own sake. The primary cause, instead, is general acquiescence in the political order, and patriotic identification with the nation-state and its symbols.

---

[91] On the 'very straggling and weak movement' of 1887, see Lant, *Insubstantial Pageant*, ch. 5, esp. p. 138, and T. Richards, *The Commodity Culture of Victorian Britain* (London, 1991), pp. 74, 77–8. On the 1977 Jubilee, see Pimlott, *The Queen*, pp. 443–53.

[92] J. Gardiner, *The Victorians* (London, 2002), p. 146.

[93] *The Backbench Diaries of Richard Crossman*, ed. J. Morgan (London, 1981), p. 71.

[94] Zweiniger-Bargielowska, 'Royal rations', 13.

Republican sentiment has been effective when it has been able to point to the bias and exclusivity of the rulers of the state as a whole. From the mid-nineteenth century, this sentiment has usually been marginalized in favour of a general confidence in the representativeness of the state. The decline of monarchical power has been one reason, but only one, for that increased confidence, but the institution of monarchy has certainly benefited from it. Moreover, the perception that the sovereign does not exercise political power has ensured that s/he occupies a role quite distinct from partisan politicians, making it easier for him or her to appear to embody the national interest at times of crisis. Many people have found that embodiment reassuring in various ways and at various times, while those whom it leaves cold have not cared enough to agitate vigorously for a republican agenda. In addition, the continuation of widely held republican sentiment, in the broadest sense of the world, has forced the royal family to behave in ways which minimize the criticisms of privilege, indolence, extravagance and unrepresentativeness that it still inevitably attracts from many quarters. Relentless media scrutiny and a long tradition of irreverent satire have intensified that process.

Because monarchy has not played the prime role in its own survival, it is not necessary to argue that it has ever appeared attractively representative. In some contexts it can appear so, particularly at times of crisis. But more generally its task is not to appear offensively unrepresentative, and the best way of doing that is to be bland, even dull, and to allow different groups to see in it what they wish to be seen. It was the middle-class press, rather than Victoria and Albert, who were most anxious to portray the royal couple as exponents of bourgeois family values; it was the civic dignitaries of the northern towns who read most into their visits of the 1840s and 1850s. Such images and visits validated the values of those who celebrated them, even while Victoria's military patronage suggested a very different image and appealed to a different constituency of support. Successful monarchies operate at a multitude of levels, but usually without committing too exclusively to any one image. Blandness and dutifulness make possible a fairly flexible and adaptable appeal – and of course the monarchy has, throughout the period, adapted to changes in social expectations to some degree, in ways too numerous and subtle to discuss in a general essay. Too much charisma, on the other hand, would be awkward, not least because it implies a Caesarist approach which constitutional monarchy needs to avoid.

As long as it can avoid major scandal and obvious unrepresentativeness, there is no reason to think that monarchy will not continue, within the parameters that have served it well for the best part of two centuries. The two major threats to it are, firstly, that the political elite might decide that it no longer serves its purposes, or, secondly, that the public might no longer see merit in the values that it expresses and the activities that it supports. The former would require a minority view on the left to become a majority one, perhaps because of a progressive loss of interest in identifiably national constitutional traditions, and a move towards a more continental-style political culture. The second might possibly require an erosion of 'respectable' public values and a falling-away from interest in the kinds of social service with which the royal family is willing to associate. (However it should be said that true republicans would bitterly resent the implication that committed voluntary service is impossible without encouragement and validation from a social establishment.) There are those who say that either or both of these developments are quite likely in the next few years: that politicians, or the public, are progressively less familiar with historic ideas of nation and community. The fact is, however, that Robespierres and Cassandras have been saying *that* for two hundred years as well. As Adam Smith remarked, there is a great deal of ruin in a nation.

The feminization of the monarchy
1780–1910: royal masculinity and
female empowerment*

Clarissa Campbell Orr

The idea of a feminized monarchy, together with much of the agenda for
researching the modern monarchy as an institution rather than as a series
of biographies, has been suggested with great verve by David Cannadine
in a number of articles and reviews. In his review of Sarah Bradford's
biography of the king, he described George VI as 'the ideal man to take
on the emasculated job of being a constitutional monarch in twentieth-
century Britain'. Furthermore, as he was 'supported and sustained by
three generations of firm and formidable Windsor women, George VI
seems to have been the ultimate castrated male in the British royal family;
kings reigned, but matriarchy ruled'.[1] Commenting on Princess Diana's
funeral in 1997, he observed that 'the twentieth century has been an
unprecedentedly constraining time for British royal men, even as it has
provided unprecedented opportunities for British royal women'.[2]

Cannadine has also accepted the argument of Frank Prochaska's influential study of royal philanthropy, that by identifying itself with the charitable initiatives of the voluntary sector, the monarchy, from the reign
of George III, both positioned itself above politics and assimilated to
itself the domestic, Christian, respectable dimension of the middle classes
in an age of evangelical revival and revolutionary threat. Reviewing this
book Cannadine noted how Queen Adelaide's benefactions 'refigured
those connections between matriarchy, domesticity, kindness and charity
which have been so marked a feature of the British monarchy from Queen

* I am grateful to the Central Fund for Sabbaticals at APU, Cambridge Campus, during
 which this chapter was written, and to Séan Lang, Alison Ainley and Rohan McWilliam
 for taking over my teaching and administrative responsibilities so cheerfully. I would like to
 thank Naomi Tadmor, Alistair Davies, and the members of the History Work in Progress
 Seminar at Sussex University, for their hospitality and comments on an earlier version of
 this paper, and similarly Andrej Olechnowicz, Jon Parry, Karina Urbach, Michèle Cohen,
 Rohan McWilliam, Yvonne Ward, Philip Mansel, Jonathan Petropoulis, and Andrew
 Hanham, for their immensely helpful discussions and suggestions for its improvement.
 Its remaining shortcomings are all my own.
[1] D. Cannadine, *History in Our Time* (London, 1998), p. 65.   [2] Ibid., p. 83.

Victoria via Queen Alexandra, Queen Mary and the Queen Mother, to Queen Elizabeth and the Princess of Wales'.[3] He suggested that during the nineteenth century, the welfare monarchy was combined with a family monarchy, a ceremonial monarchy and an imperial monarchy, to enable the institution to adapt and survive to modern times. In his most recent analysis, Cannadine has reiterated the idea that 'it might be that constitutional monarchy is in fact emasculated monarchy, and thus a feminized version of an essentially male institution. For constitutional monarchy is what results when the sovereign is deprived of those historic male functions of god, governor and general, and this in turn has led – perhaps by default, perhaps by design? – to a greater stress on family, domesticity, maternity and glamour.'[4]

These are compelling suggestions, although it may be that the domestication of the monarchy is not quite the same as the emasculation of it. Cannadine has also made some powerful suggestions as to how we should consider the chronology of royal development, and therefore the timing of any process of feminization. Of course, there are several overlapping chronologies possible, depending on what feature is being analyzed. In his seminal article in *The Invention of Tradition*, he traced the evolution of royal ritual into four phases: the fifty years between 1820 and 1870 when ritual was ineptly organized in a still pre-industrial society; from 1877 to 1914, the heyday of successful invented tradition when Imperial monarchy and synchronized ritual was perfected; from 1918 to 1953, when the prestige of this monarchy lingered in contrast to the destruction of the Austrian, Russian German (and Ottoman) empires; and a fourth era, between Elizabeth II's coronation and her silver jubilee, when Empire had declined and the age of TV monarchy began.[5] As this essay will explore below, the dismissal of the Regency era as an age of incoherent ritual prevented Cannadine from appreciating that the incoherence reveals much about the conflicting elements of modern monarchy which first became evident then.

In a later article, he switched the focus from the invention of tradition to the political character of the monarchy, and emphasized the need to 'explode the widespread myth of the Victorian monarchy's premature modernity'. He traced its continuities with the Hanoverian monarchy,

---

[3] Ibid., p. 27. Diana, Princess of Wales was still alive when Cannadine's review of F. Prochaska, *Royal Bounty: The Making of a Welfare Monarchy* (New Haven and London, 1995) appeared.

[4] D. Cannadine, 'From biography to history: writing the modern British monarchy', *Historical Research* 77 (2004), 303.

[5] D. Cannadine, 'The context, performance and meaning of ritual: the British monarchy and the "invention of tradition" c. 1820–1977', E. Hobsbawm and T. Ranger (eds.), *The Invention of Tradition* (Cambridge, 1983).

suggesting that Victoria and Albert both wanted a powerful, benevolent monarchy *above* politics – in eighteenth-century terms, a patriot monarchy – which nonetheless retained constitutional guarantees, and insisted on the executive, decision-making power of the monarchy. He suggested that Edward VII, George V and George VI were conservative and impatient with democracy; and that Edward VII' s surrender of some personal power was a negation, not the fulfilment, of Albert's ideal of constitutional monarchy. Victoria, however, needed a myth of domestic monarchy in order to disguise the fact that the monarchy had changed in the later part of her reign. And as 'mad' George III's domestic monarchy was not an acceptable precedent, she had to establish her own myth of domesticity.[6] If the Victorian monarchy was feminized, it was in the sense of becoming a domesticated monarchy, not in Cannadine's other sense of an emasculated, constitutional monarchy, because the latter did not arrive until the twentieth century. The Victorian monarchy combined domesticity, executive influence and imperial grandeur.

This essay responds to some of these ideas about feminization and chronology. It suggests that the important era to consider for the roots of the monarchy's modernity is the Regency – defined as the era of George, Prince of Wales from before the formal Regency in 1811 until his death as George IV in 1830. In this era are to be found some key themes that recurred in the Edwardian era – including Edward VII's heyday as Prince of Wales after the institution of the imperial monarchy in 1877. These themes are: the Prince of Wales as a feminized monarch in waiting; the tension between militarism and domesticity; the monarch's link with fashion, exemplified by the dandy in a commercial society; and the gender politics of *ancien régime* monarchy. These all have a bearing on the ways in which the monarchy might be considered to be either emasculated or, less drastically, as domesticated. Furthermore, does this feminized monarchy (as for convenience it can be called for the present) have any links to feminism? If royal persons are atypical men and women,[7] how is the history of gender – the changing construction of femininity and masculinity – reflected in, or even constituted by, the monarchy? Does feminization entail female empowerment, or feminism *avant la lettre*? Are women better at incorporating elements of masculinity into their official personas than are men at incorporating elements of femininity?

[6] D. Cannadine, 'The last Hanoverian sovereign? the Victorian monarchy in historical perspective 1688–1988', in A. L. O. Beier, D. Cannadine and J. Rosenheim (eds.), *The First Modern* Society (New York, 1989).

[7] Cannadine, 'From biography to history', 302.

I

Britain's modern monarchy dates from the Regency era because at this time several important trends can be discerned: a re-positioning of the monarchy above politics into the realm of philanthropy and national patriotism; the equation of monarchy with domesticity by George III and Queen Charlotte, but also, through their eldest son, its alignment with celebrity culture and an intrusive media; and within this commercialized public sphere, the commodification of the monarchy, whereby royal and aristocratic lives became the stuff of newspaper scandal and sentimentalization. Britain was not a fully industrialized society, but it was certainly a consumer one. Royal gossip sold newspapers, while its tastes could be mimicked in cheaper versions of consumer goods for the quality. The monarchy's equivocal relationship with fashion had begun.[8]

At first glance there can be no more absurd figure than the Prince of Wales who became Regent. His self-indulgent corpulence made it easy for Charles Lamb to ridicule him as the Prince of Whales.[9] Yet George IV's conception of monarchy warrants analysis precisely because his successes as well as his failures tell us much about the dilemma of modern monarchy, and because it is in his lifetime that debates about the role of women articulated in the revolutionary 1790s were linked to royal behaviour and attitudes. He is fascinating because he did not know whether to look back to a partly imagined *ancien régime*, or forward to the modern commercial society – the nation of shopkeepers in Napoleon's phrase – that Britain had become.

When George died in 1830, Talleyrand, that great aristocratic survivor of the French Revolution, commented that 'Kings nowadays are always seeking popularity, a pointless pursuit. King George IV was *un grand seigneur*. There are no others left'.[10] Did Talleyrand mean to imply that George IV had no grasp of the constitutional arrangements of Britain – that, unlike his father, he had not imbibed the lessons of 1688? George III fully believed that Britain's polity had been providentially determined and protected, and that he must preserve the constitutional arrangements of 1688. Yet for all his identification with both constitutional and domestic propriety, George III was always aware that kings must play their part. His coronation coach, celebrating British victory in the Seven Years' War, was designed, Jonathan Marsden has argued, to be a kind of moving,

---

[8] J. Marsden (ed.), *The Wisdom of George III* (London, 2005), pp. 1–2. Josiah Wedgwood's appointment as Potter to Queen Charlotte is the most obvious example of the link between royal taste and commercial society.

[9] My discussion is greatly indebted to S. Parissien, *George IV* (London, 2001).

[10] Cited in C. Hibbert, *George IV* (Harmondsworth, 1976), p. 787.

rococo baldaquin, allowing maximum visibility of the young monarch.[11] The King and Queen were both assiduous in holding drawing rooms and levées, and keeping the mechanisms of court life in good working order. But this was not the same as identifying the court with mere fashion: it had to be inclusive, so risked being dull. However, the King was remarkably good at living the part of a royal figurehead. He dressed in military style in the Windsor uniform he had designed; he rallied troops personally to quell the Gordon riots; when a lunatic shot at him in Drury Lane theatre, he had the presence of mind to step to the front of the balcony to display himself as unhurt, as well as the compassion to recognize his assailant was mentally deranged, not a political assassin.[12] His consort Charlotte knew how to dress in her courtly diamonds when state occasions required, even if her natural tastes were more bluestocking, less showy.[13] In private at Kew or Windsor, the family lived in a genteel family-oriented aristocratic style favoured by many of the British peerage and some of their continental counterparts – such as Maria Theresa in Vienna at Schönbrunn, the Scandinavians and the lesser German courts – even if their architectural setting was less splendid than either fellow-rulers or some of their subjects.[14] For what George, as a conscientious executive monarch, knew, was the danger of an extended royal family seeming to be a drag on the public purse. He made the mistake of not negotiating a larger settlement at the start of his reign, and was always short of money for his family; this is why he never built the new palace at Kew which Chambers had designed for him. It was Soane's palace for the Bank of England that Parliament agreed to finance – a celebration of the public credit which facilitated the post-1688 monarchy.[15]

The Prince of Wales in contrast seems to have imbibed no lessons on financial probity nor on the blend of public magnificence and private modesty that was beginning to be the preferred royal style in an age of evangelical revival. His father had written boyhood essays on the post-1688 revolution settlement, and understood its terms.[16] There is

[11] J. Marsden, 'George III's state coach in context', in Marsden, *Wisdom*.

[12] C. Hibbert, *George III* (London, 1998); G. M. Ditchfield, *George III* (London, 2002); S. Llewellyn, 'George III and the Windsor Uniform', *Court Historian* 1 (1996), n.p.

[13] M. Pointon, 'Intriguing jewellery: royal bodies and luxurious consumption', *Textual Practice* 11 (1997), 493–516; J. Rudoe, 'Queen Charlotte's jewellery: reconstructing a lost collection', in Marsden, *Wisdom*; *Diary and Letters of Madame D'Arblay*, ed. C. Barrett, 6 vols. (London, 1904), vol. 2, pp. 56–7, 88.

[14] M. Winterbottom, 'Dining with George III and Queen Charlotte', and J. Marsden, 'Introduction', in Marsden, *Wisdom*.

[15] D. Watkin, *The Architect King* (London, 2004); J. Harris and M. Snodin (eds.), *Sir William Chambers* (New Haven, 1996); M. Richardson and M. A. Stevenson (eds.), *John Soane, Architect* (London, 1999).

[16] J. Brooke, *King George III* (London, 1972); Ditchfield, *George III*.

no record that Prince George did exactly the same, but it is known that the king impressed on his two eldest sons, George and Frederick – one of whom was his heir and the other, as Prince-Bishop of Osnabrück, a sovereign prince in his own right – that 'princes not being obliged to labour with their hands, were to labour with their heads, for the good of their people.'[17]

The Prince of Wales seems to have decided, though, that a prince needed to *display* himself to his people, not *think* about their welfare, and it is not clear how far he internalized the nuances of the nature of Britain's parliamentary monarchy. When his father urged economy on him during the recession after the War of American Independence, when he was in the full flood of enthusiasm for building Carlton House, he protested to a friend that 'it would be improper' for him as heir 'to live with less degree of magnificence than I have hitherto have done'.[18] This concept of magnificence seems more like a Renaissance idea of princely behaviour than an enlightened one. During the 1788 Regency crisis, he sought unrestricted powers – partly in order to appoint his Whig friends to office – and in 1812 relished the transition to an unrestricted Regency so that he could pursue his building projects. His concern to display monarchy in magnificent style suggests a French type of representational, *ancien régime* monarchy, not surprising in this most Francophile prince.

Certainly 'Prinny' admired *all* the French Bourbons. They had been the most successful exemplars of princely magnificence; French taste was still dominant throughout Europe. The costumes designed for George's lavish coronation in 1821 were modelled on a mix of English Jacobethan and the style of Henri IV, the first Bourbon.[19] George's remodelling of Buckingham Palace was an attempt to replicate the Palace of Versailles; all his life the prince was interested in pictures or furniture associated with the supreme exponent of impressive monarchy – Louis XIV – whose sunflower motif was utilized at the Brighton Pavilion.[20] He was similarly obsessed with memorabilia and decorative arts from the reigns of Louis XV and XVI.[21] Yet George's connoisseurship of Bourbon paraphernalia was not just self-indulgence: it was an essay in outflanking the upstart Napoleon. The elaborate Gothic conservatory added to Carlton House contained stained-glass pictures of all the kings and princes of Wales since 1066, stressing the long line of kingly legitimacy.

[17] As recalled by the poet James Beattie from a conversation with their tutor, Bishop Markham: M. Forbes, *Beattie and his Friends*, (Altrincham, 1990), p. 85.

[18] Parissien, *George IV*, p. 125.

[19] V. Cumming, 'Pantomime and pageantry: the coronation of George IV', in C. Fox (ed.), *London World City 1800–1840* (London, 1992), pp. 39–50.

[20] Parissien, *George IV*, pp. 195–6.   [21] Ibid., pp. 197–8.

Similarly, to underline the principle of legitimacy, the Prince always treated Louis XVIII as a king during his exile in England.[22] The fête in 1811 to celebrate the inauguration of the Regency was held officially in his honour.

George's keen dynastic sense was also reflected in the fête in August 1814 for the people, held in three London parks, whose pretext was the celebration of the centenary of the Hanoverian succession. Hanoverian arms were also prominent in the costumes for his visit to Scotland in 1822. He was fascinated by the House of Brunswick's genealogy, and founded the Guelphic order to reward the German legion officers at Waterloo and civilian contributions to Hanover, as well as to commemorate the medieval ancestry of the family – another way of underlining ancient prescriptive rights in an era when Napoleon had occupied Hanover, swept away the old Holy Roman Empire, and redrawn the political and dynastic map from Madrid to Warsaw.[23] George also visited Hanover in 1821, marking its restoration to his family as well as its elevation to a kingdom. The visits to Ireland and Scotland suggest the aim of representing monarchy, of performing acts of kingship, throughout all the component kingdoms of a typically composite, *ancien régime* type of monarchy. Parissien noted that it was 400 years since the sovereign had visited Ireland *peacefully*.[24] The Scottish visit, stage-managed by Walter Scott, was the first visit of a monarch since George's favourite king, Charles I – his model as a collector and patron of the arts – had been crowned in Edinburgh in 1631.[25] The visit also enabled the Hanoverian monarchy finally to lay the ghost of Jacobitism, to convert it into sentimental romanticism, and re-invent themselves as a Scottish dynasty.[26]

Even in his leisure, the prince projected an image of kingly power. The chinoiseries of the Royal Pavilion at Brighton suggested an ancient, immovable and autocratic regime: an image of stability in a time of flux. Its Indian exterior, in the words of a jaundiced Whig MP, deploying language imbued with Montesquieu's contrasts between oriental 'despotism', and monarchy based on the principle of honour, 'resembles more the pomp and magnificence of a Persian satrap seated in all the splendour of oriental

---

[22] P. Mansel, *Louis XVIII* (London, 1981).

[23] N. H. Nicholas, *History of the Royal Order of the Guelphs* (London 1814); A. Hanham, 'Regency knights: the Royal Guelphic Order' (Unpublished lecture, Burlington House, 28 Apr. 2004). I am indebted to the author for showing me a copy of his lecture.

[24] Parissien, *George IV*, p. 317. For Victorian attempts to have a member of the royal family resident in Ireland or appointed as viceroy, see J. H. Murphy, '"Mock court": the Lord Lieutenancy of Ireland 1767–1922', *Court Historian* 9 (2004).

[25] Parissien, *George IV*, p. 318, and ch. 16.

[26] H. Trevor-Roper, 'The invention of tradition: the Highland tradition of Scotland', in Hobsbawm and Ranger, *Invention of Tradition*.

state than the sober dignity of a British prince, seated in the bosom of his subjects'.[27]

It was all too easy for caricaturists like Gillray or Cruikshank to give a visual character to criticism of the indolent and self-indulgent prince. One caricature depicted the prince being winched on to his horse – which actually did happen – dressed in Chinese robes – which was an amusing exaggeration. Thus ridicule helped puncture the apparent pretensions to continental absolutism. The fêtes in London could be quite popular, but they were not sufficient for the prince to achieve sustained respect, which fluctuated and finally declined altogether in his last reclusive years. After Waterloo, the contrast between his lavish banquets in Brighton, some conceived by the great French chef Carême, and the hardship of recession, was pursued relentlessly by the radical press. But what, to pursue counter-factual history, if George had been less disreputable, less fat, less easy to ridicule? He was certainly able to bring off these entertainments in terms of charm and exquisite manners. Nathaniel Wraxall commented:

Louis XIV himself could hardly have eclipsed the son of George III in a ballroom, or when doing the honours of his palace surrounded by the pomp and attributes of royal state.[28]

He was also a natural actor, as Brummell observed.[29] He might have created a more successful image of royal poise and dignity: an asset in an age of royal restoration. Instead, the Austrian Ambassador noted with dismay that the king's publicly displayed affection for Lady Conyngham at the coronation was a '"curious sight" when "the dignity of sovereignty" was attacked on all sides'.[30] George oscillated between *ancien régime* politesse and self-absorbed hedonism.

II

One aspect of George's absurdity is that he could not convincingly cut a dash as a military monarch in an age of warfare. The *raison d'être* of most eighteenth- and nineteenth-century monarchy was still to be a warrior

---

[27] J. Dinkel, *The Royal Pavilion, Brighton* (London 1983), pp. 13, 49. India should, I suggest, be understood as Britain's off-stage theatre of baroque power. Eighteenth-century parliamentary monarchy in Britain was not lavish, but away from the British Isles, the East India Company's servants could conduct visits to rajahs riding on bejewelled elephants, satirized in the famous cartoon of Charles James Fox as 'Carlo Khan': see D. Cannadine, *Ornamentalism* (London, 2002).

[28] Cited in Hibbert, *George IV*, p. 61.   [29] Ibid., p. 68.

[30] Cited in M. J. Levy, *The Mistresses of George IV* (London, 1996), p. 155.

king, served by a noble officer elite.[31] The Austrian, Prussian and Russian monarchies were all military monarchies; and it has been argued that the monarchy collapsed in France partly because it failed to inspire confidence as a military monarchy with a convincing foreign policy.[32] Even Britain's parliamentary monarchy had its military dimension: William III, architect of the Glorious Revolution, was a military monarch, while George I and George II fought in battle. The Treaty of Vienna had seen Britain at a new zenith of imperial acquisition and European reputation. Yet George had had nothing to do with this in person. Instead of a military career, his father had decreed that he should become a domesticated – we might say a feminized – male.

During the eighteenth century it was becoming a convention that the heir to the British throne should not be risked on active military duty. This was related to the English sensitivity about standing armies, and the perception of James II as a military king whose tyranny had had to be curbed in 1688. The role of commander-in-chief was devolved on to the second son: in George III's reign, Frederick, Duke of York. Yet the young George had been given guns at five to bolster his timidity, and yearned for a military role, especially once war with France began in 1793. He imagined himself as another Black Prince.[33] With the exception of the asthmatic Augustus, all the other brothers were in the services, in various parts of the Empire – Canada, Gibraltar, Hanover, the West Indies.

George III insisted however that his heir should stay in Britain; and the most he could be was Colonel of the 10th Light Dragoons, whose duties included escorting the royal family between Kew, Windsor and London. Once they were stationed in Brighton, George created an elaborate military camp with his own sumptuous tent, and concentrated on wine, gambling, and designing uniforms and militaria. Gradually the regiment was transformed into a new Hussar-type cavalry, with more new uniforms to match.[34] Thus, because of the risk of killing the heir to the throne on active service, he was reduced to the role of spectator; the most obvious badge of late Georgian masculinity, active military service, was denied him.

Meanwhile, his debts had mounted, so that by 1795 he was forced to contemplate an official, dynastic marriage which would eclipse his illegal marriage to the Catholic Mrs Fitzherbert (another echo of the

---

[31] J. Tosh, 'The Old Adam and the New Man: emerging themes in the history of English masculinities 1750–1850', in T. Hitchcock and M. Cohen (eds.), *English Masculinities 1660–1800* (Harlow 1999), esp. p. 222.

[32] P. Mansel, *Dressed to Rule* (London, 2005), ch. 2; T. C. Blanning, *The Origins of the French Revolutionary Wars* (London, 1986).

[33] Parissien *George IV*, p. 104.   [34] J. Mollo, *The Prince's Dolls* (London, 1997).

ancien régime: she was compared to James II's Catholic bride, Mary of Modena).[35] George III insisted to his son:

There cannot be a doubt that the English do view with a jealous eye any decided predilection in those on or naturaly [sic] to mount the Throne to military pursuits, and I certainly feel the force of that opinion as strongly as anyone . . . My younger sons can have no other situation in the State but what arises from the military lines they have been placed in. You are born to a more difficult one, and which I shall be most happy if I find you seriously turn your thoughts to . . . May the Princess Caroline's character prove so pleasing to you that your mind may be engrossed with domestic felicity . . . and . . . a numerous progeny may be the result of this union.[36]

George III had had a very retired upbringing at the hands of a mother who wanted to insulate him from the influences of a dissolute aristocracy; he had then been fortunate to find in his arranged marriage a compatible partner, and he delighted in his young children. He clearly could not imagine that the recipe that had suited him should not suit his son and heir also; and Evangelical influences meant that some of the English aristocracy were already adopting moderation and domesticity too, prefiguring the new respectability and paternalism of the early Victorian era.[37] To an extent, then, the enforced military passivity of George, Prince of Wales conforms to Cannadine's suggestion that constitutional monarchies – or more accurately for the nineteenth century, parliamentary monarchies – tend toward emasculating the military role of the sovereign or his heir.

Yet domesticity did not suit the Prince of Wales, whose gender politics were decidedly of the *ancien régime* sort. His amours included actresses, milliners, and older married women – a throwback to the Stuarts (though not dissimilar from his grandfather Frederick).[38] He was never entirely faithful to Mrs Fitzherbert. What is different about the context of the Prince's love affairs and disastrous marriage, is the new debate on gender and female rights that emerged in the 1790s. In 1799, Mary Robinson, his first serious mistress, who had given up her career on the stage for him and was now a poet and novelist, published her *Letter to the Women of England*. A friend now of Mary Wollstonecraft and William Godwin, she passionately defended the right of women to voice their side of the story when they had been wronged by the double standard – even to fight

[35] Parissien, *George IV*, pp. 66–7, 205.
[36] *The Later Correspondence of George III*, ed. A. Aspinall, 5 vols. (Cambridge, 1962–70), vol. 2, (8 Apr. 1795).
[37] J. Schneid Lewis, *In the Family Way* (New Brunswick, 1986); A. Stott, *Hannah More, The First Victorian* (Oxford 2003); D. Roberts, *Paternalism in Early Victorian England* (London, 1977).
[38] Parissien, *George IV*, p. 85.

duels to defend their reputations. She argued their need for a university education and their right to stand for Parliament, while celebrating the history of women's accomplishments, especially in the writing profession. The behaviour of royalty and the modern debate on gender are therefore linked in this important decade for the birth of modern rights discourse. For Robinson, the critique of aristocratic misogyny was also a specific criticism of royalty.[39]

In marrying George, Caroline was marrying someone with essentially nothing much to do. As he had once said to his father, rebuking him for his late rising, he had nothing really to get up for. He was a man due to occupy eventually the most significant role available in the public sphere; yet he lived mostly as an aristocratic gentleman in the private sphere of pleasure (which was, nonetheless, publicly reported in the scandal sheets and prints). The conventions of parliamentary monarchy were still fluid in his father's reign, and it was not yet clear that the king as well as the heir should be above politics. Nonetheless, he spoke little in the House of Lords, confining his early support for the Whigs during the controversial 1784 election mainly to hospitality and entertainment. As we have seen, he did not have a military role. And he did not, like peers who were inactive in politics, become a model landowner in the countryside, developing new agricultural methods alongside cultural patronage. Instead he was identified with a geography of pleasure, at Brighton, where his presence helped the resort to flourish. Caroline may have been an ill-mannered and ill-educated hoyden, but she was used to men who had a more significant purpose in life: her father and eldest brother were among the most noted generals of the age. She scornfully considered her husband would have made 'an excellent tailor, shoemaker or hairdresser but nothing else', and that 'it would have been better if she had been the prince and he the man to wear the petticoats'.[40]

Several commentators noticed an effeminate quality about the Prince's behaviour. This is not a sexual description, implying homosexuality or bisexuality, so much as a moral and cultural category. In classical thought,

---

[39] P. Byrne, *Perdita* (London, 2004); M. Robinson, *A Letter to the Women of England* and *The Natural Daughter*, ed. S. M. Selzer (Peterborough, Canada, 2003). I have argued elsewhere that Mary Astell, 'the first feminist', also needs to be understood in a royal context and Mary Wollstonecraft in an aristocratic one: see C. Campbell Orr, 'Introduction', in C. Campbell Orr (ed.), *Queenship in Britain 1660–1837* (Manchester, 2002), and Campbell Orr, 'Aristocratic feminism, the learned governess, and the republic of letters', in S. Knott and B. Taylor (eds.), *Women, Gender and Enlightenment* (London, 2004). For a succinct and penetrating discussion of the relationship between 1790s feminism and the widening sphere for eighteenth-century women, see A. Clark, 'Women in Eighteenth-Century British Politics', in ibid.

[40] Cited in Cumming, 'Pantomime and pageantry'.

the Greeks contrasted the manly Spartans with the effeminate Persians. Orientalism was associated with luxury and a culturally feminine pre-occupation with ease and personal adornment. Worries about political misconduct or failure in the eighteenth century were often expressed in the language of effeminacy, suggesting that an effete and francophile aristocracy was the root cause of national failure.[41]

Even the Duchess of Devonshire, George's friend, thought 'he looks too much like a woman in man's clothes'.[42] It was reported that he began to blubber when told that Brummell did not like the cut of his coat.[43] Perdita's critique of aristocratic masculinity in the 1790s – and she had the prince and his set in mind – contrasted 'those shadows of mankind who exhibit the effeminacy of women, united with the mischievous foolery of monkies', with the many women who performed domestic tasks of great physical drudgery, or carried heavy loads to market.[44] In 1811, when the Regent might have formed a Whig ministry, Lord Grey doubted that the Prince 'will have nerves to take the manly and decisive measures which alone can enable him to conduct the government with effect'.[45] In 1821, Byron's poem *Sardanopolis* depicted an oriental king who first appears dressed as a woman – an allusion to the Regent's love of women and the arts.[46] Princess Lieven, the Russian ambassador's wife, described the atmosphere of the Pavilion in the 1820s in terms of decadent classical luxury:

I do not believe that since the days of Heliogobalus, there have been such magnificence and such luxury. There is something effeminate in it which is disgusting . . . One spends the evening half lying on cushions; the lights are dazzling; there are perfumes, music, liqueurs.[47]

Criticisms of the Regent's combination of unmanliness and petty despotism came to a crescendo in popular criticism of his behaviour to his wife. The arranged marriage was a complete failure. The fastidious prince found her viscerally repellent, and his reactions exemplified both male tyranny and effeminate passion. To his family and in public opinion he was most to blame for the estrangement, for the extent to which

---

[41] See e.g. K. Wilson, *The Sense of the People* (Cambridge, 1995), pp. 178–205; Tosh, 'The Old Adam'; M. Cohen, 'Manliness, effeminacy and the French: gender and the construction of national character in eighteenth-century England', in Hitchcock and Cohen, *English Masculinities*; M. Cohen, *Fashioning Masculinity* (London, 1996).
[42] Cumming, 'Pantomime and pageantry', p. 49.
[43] V. Murray, *High Society in the Regency Period 1788–1830* (London, 1999), p. 30.
[44] Robinson, *Letter*, pp. 48–9.   [45] Hibbert, *George IV*, p. 359.
[46] M. Butler, 'Hidden metropolis: London in sentimental and romantic writing', in Fox (ed.), *London*, pp. 187–198.
[47] Murray, *High Society*, p. 122.

he tried to regulate access to their daughter, and the undignified way he tried to obtain evidence of her misconduct by arranging for the 'Delicate Investigation' to be carried out.[48] Even when her flamboyant conduct abroad became the stuff of gossip throughout Europe, the Whigs found it useful to take up her cause, and she became a popular heroine when she returned to the country in 1820 to claim her right to be queen. George's attempt to divorce her by a special Bill of Pains and Penalties, was seen by radicals as an attempt to manipulate the constitution. Her rights were championed as a means of criticizing the now reactionary George and his Tory ministers, and the evidence against her prepared for the Bill of Pains and Penalties contained in the famous green bag became a topic of amused ridicule, with the caricaturists again having a field day. Anna Clark's recent review of this episode places it in the context of a series of sexual scandals centred on public figures and the monarchy, which raised constitutional issues through colourful human stories of peccadilloes in high places, beginning with the alleged affair of the Dowager Princess of Wales, George III's mother, with the Earl of Bute, and her malign petticoat influence, and including the scandal caused by the Regent's brother, the Duke of York, whose mistress Mary Anne Clark sold army commissions. The investigation into this revealed a web of corrupt patronage in the Church and the East India Company, as well as the army. As well as being politically manipulative, the royal family could also be portrayed as absurd and unnatural, when some of the elderly daughters of George III finally married, and some of their brothers ditched long-term mistresses in order to marry legally and beget an heir to the throne after Charlotte, Princess of Wales, had died in childbirth in 1817.[49]

When the Regent was not seen as feminized, he was often described as infantilized, because of his petulant selfishness as well as his matronly

---

[48] F. Fraser, *The Unruly Queen* (London, 1996); Fraser, *Princesses* (London, 2004); S. David, *Prince of Pleasure* (London, 1999); Parissien, *George IV*, ch. 10; Hibbert, *George IV*.

[49] A. Clark, *Scandal* (Princeton, 2004); Clark, *The Struggle for the Breeches* (London, 1995); T. Lacquer, 'The Queen Caroline affair: politics as art in the reign of George IV', *Journal of Modern History* 54 (1982), 417–66; D. Thompson, 'Queen Victoria, the monarchy and gender', in *Outsiders* (London, 1993); D. Wahrman, '"Middle-class" domesticity goes public: gender, class and politics from Queen Caroline to Queen Victoria', *Journal of British Studies* (1993), 32, pp. 396–432; T. Hunt, 'Morality and monarchy in the Queen Caroline Affair', Albion 23 (1991), 697–722; Hunt, '"The Prince of Whales": caricature, charivari and the politics of morality', in M. Shirley and T. Larsen (eds.), *Splendidly Victorian* (Aldershot, 2001); J. Fulcher, 'The loyalist response to the Queen Caroline agitation', *Journal of British Studies* 34 (1995), 481–502; E. A. Smith, *A Queen on Trial* (Stroud, 1994); M. Girouard, *The Return to Camelot* (London, 1981); N. Rogers, *Crowds, Culture and Politics in Georgian Britain* (Oxford, 1998). For the outpouring of popular grief on the death of Charlotte Princess of Wales, see S. C. Behrendt, *Royal Mourning and Regency Culture* (London, 1997).

mistresses. One of the most frequent ways he was caricatured, was as a Great Babe.[50] Contrastingly, although he liked children, he was not very involved with his own daughter, and when she ran away in 1814 from Warwick House because of conflicts over her desire to have her own household, he was described through another prism of distorted masculinity, as the despotic father (a topos of debate since the publication of Richardson's *Clarissa* in 1750). Seizing the chance to capitalize on another example of royal dysfunctionality, Lord Brougham asked whether 'anything as barbarous as the Regent's treatment of his daughter could be found outside Turkey'.[51] Effeminate, infantile, despotic – the prince was hard to categorize as manly to his contemporaries.

III

Cannadine has argued that in the context of the 1820s, apart from the personal failings of George IV, it would not have been possible to elevate the monarchy above party to perform a dignified ceremonial role, since a fully constitutional monarchy had not yet evolved. I would add to this a third consideration: George's desire to be a leader of fashion as well as a Grand Seigneur. These were inconsistent goals. Although grand monarchies can also function as arbiters of elegance and taste, and the social functions of a court can give an opportunity for fashions in costume and ornament to be displayed, it is not necessarily desirable for the sovereign to become a fashion icon.

Fashion is impermanent, fickle, throwaway; it cannot suggest the stability and dignity of a permanent institution, subtly modulating tradition. To suggest permanence was even more important after the French Revolution and the defeat of the 'Corsican corporal'. Yet George never grew beyond his youthful dandyism. Just as Louis XVI did not know whether he wanted to be an *ancien régime* or an enlightened king, so George did not know whether he wanted to be an efficient and ceremonial part of England's parliamentary *ancien régime* or a modern celebrity.

The dandy was a new social type, made possible by the advanced commercialization of Britain. Prince Pückler-Muskau made some acute observations in 1826 of the way the status hierarchies in Britain had been superseded by this new category of fashion, to which old or new money might aspire. He believed that as the 'Kings of England live like private men' (he was writing when George IV had become extremely reclusive), the rich aristocracy had to give a focus to society. As this wealth was both old and new:

---

[50] Parissien, *George IV*, pp. 349–50.   [51] Hibbert, *George IV*, p. 357.

by a tacit convention – not nobility, not wealth, but an entirely new power was placed on the throne, as supreme and absolute sovereign – Fashion: a goddess who in England alone, reigns in person . . . with despotic and inexorable sway . . . the present King, for instance, is a very fashionable man . . . his father was not in the least degree so . . . our pattern 'dandy' has not the least independence, even in his bad qualities: he is the trembling slave of fashion.[52]

Dandyism is essentially about being part of a coterie; a contemporary synonym was an 'exclusive'. Who was in and who was out was regulated by an arcane set of decisions about the successful cut of a coat, or the opening of one's snuff-box. These standards could be created and destroyed by a word. When the Prince and Beau Brummell fell out, this was apparent when Brummell asked Lord Alvanley, who was accompanying George, 'Who is your fat friend?' In a single phrase the prince's glamour was pricked like a burst balloon; he was a social failure with an awkward body, not a trend-setter.[53]

The dandy was closely related to the Regency beau or buck, a lineal descendant of Richardson's Lovelace, who routinely swept women off their feet or eloped with an heiress, regarded servant girls as fair game, and as well as perfecting an elegant attire, also liked to dress as ordinary coachmen and drive as fast as possible. There were many dandies who were also cavalry officers. The Prince of Wales's regiment, the 10th Light Dragoons, was full of them. Its aim was to transform itself into the new kind of Hussar regiment with its dashing braided uniform and half-slung cloak. Perdita Robinson fingered this military dandy in her *Letter* when she scathingly described one confessing 'that he had changed his regiments three times, because the regimentals were *unbecoming*!'[54]

Pückler-Muskau was surely right to discern that for the sovereign to go on trying to play the role of man of fashion, undermined his dignity. He was in danger of becoming just another celebrity, as we would say today. Yet the Regent's link to dandyism is important precisely because of this new conjunction of fashion and celebrity, as another aristocracy to set against the titled aristocracy, in an age of economic dynamism and social fluidity. An aspect of this new aristocracy is the social mixing that the pursuit of fashion encouraged. Anyone, from a cook to a peer's son to a *nouveau riche* officer could become an 'exclusive', or help to achieve exclusivity. The Prince's parties were criticized by his Chief Equerry because this search for one kind of exclusiveness made him not exclusive enough: the guests 'were of all ranks and in no respect select'.[55]

---

[52] *Regency Visitor: the English Tour of Prince Pückler-Muskau described in his Letters 1826–1828*, ed. E. M. Butler (London, 1957), pp. 333–5, 337–8.

[53] E. Moers, *The Dandy* (London, 1960); see also Murray, *Regency Society*.

[54] Robinson, *Letter*, p. 48.   [55] Cited in Parissien, *George IV*, p. 249.

Finally, the obsession with fashion was another reason why the Regent was never content with his aesthetic achievements. No sooner had Carlton House been created as a model of restrained French classicism, than it was being redecorated in a bewildering succession of styles – from Chinese to Gothick. The Royal Pavilion started as an elegant villa, acquired some Chinese décor, then its Hindoo exterior, and internally a final apotheosis of Chinoiserie and assorted oriental and European motifs. The prince's knowledge as a connoisseur and patron could not be extinguished, but he was never able to move beyond a momentary enthusiasm to achieve a kind of timelessness. He was just the most conspicuous consumer (and debtor) of his time. The monarchy between 1812 and 1830 was able only with partial success to represent either dignified ceremony, long lineage and royal splendour, or domestic respectability, piety and financial probity. But the tensions suggested real choices which would have to be made in successive reigns for the monarchy to remain acceptable, or even popular.

IV

William IV's reign marks a turning point for the monarchy in two ways. First, he acquiesced in the passing of the Reform Act of 1832, which marks the political end of Britain's *ancien régime*, and inaugurated the shift from parliamentary to constitutional monarchy. Secondly, William's consort Adelaide of Saxe-Meiningen, after being identified popularly as a Tory resister to reform, successfully transformed herself into a philanthropic paragon. She also gave her excitable and possibly porphyric husband a respectable domestic life, after his long liaison with the actress Dorothy Jordan – which had been admittedly domestic, but unrespectable. The British monarchy can be interpreted as feminized in this reign, both in the sense of being more limited in its political scope, and becoming more domestic.[56]

History is not linear, however, and it is doubtful that Queen Victoria saw herself as continuing this trend towards constitutional monarchy. The Bedchamber Crisis is seen as a turning point, when she was meant to bow to the majority party in the Commons in choosing her household; yet her continuing political influence was a daily reality for her ministers. Sir William Harcourt remarked of her behaviour when Lord Rosebery was

---

[56] For the end of the political *ancien régime* see J. S. Lewis, *Sacred to Female Patriotism* (London, 2003), and J. C. D. Clark, *English Society 1688–1832* (Cambridge, 2002); for Queen Adelaide, A. W. Purdue, 'Queen Adelaide', in Campbell Orr, *Queenship in Britain;* F. K. Prochaska, *Royal Bounty* (London, 1995).

Prime Minister: 'The spirit of George III survives in his descendant.'[57]
Her executive role was examined as early as Frank Hardie's 1935 book
and has been given a cogent reappraisal in Walter Arnstein's magiste-
rial, succinct study, which underlines the active role she took in foreign
policy. The importance of her court and her courtiers was suggested by
K. D. Reynolds and is further explored by Michael Bentley in this volume.[58] The sovereign after 1837 was female, but, to adapt Arnstein's
insistence on paradox, she was not necessarily a 'feminized' constitutional monarch. How did the three factors discussed in relation to the
Regency monarchy – the urge toward grandeur, the tensions between the
heir's domesticity and his militarism, the role of fashion versus respectable
dullness – play themselves out in her reign, including its 'Edwardian' era?

The move toward grandeur outlined by Cannadine is still a fruitful concept, though it needs some modification: first because the monarchy was
able to create its theatrical and spectacular display of ceremonial power
even before it had become fully constitutional, and secondly because, as
Arnstein has argued, there was a certain degree of ceremonial ritual before
the imperial era.[59] When Disraeli re-invented the monarchy as an imperial spectacle in the 1877 Jubilee year, this also revived the sovereign's
own popularity, badly injured by her reclusive habits on being widowed.
The titular change to Empress as well as Queen effectively integrated
the oriental, quasi-baroque splendour that had always been a characteristic of Indian princely rule into a metropolitan context, as well as giving
it legitimate expression on Indian soil in the form of the imperial durbars. In 1911, George V and Queen Mary presided over one in person
to great acclaim; they would also adapt graciously to the limited role of
twentieth-century monarchy, making friends with Labour politicians and
trade union leaders, and continuing the welfare aspect of the throne.[60]

But although the evolution toward this dual monarchical role of ceremonial splendour and constitutional limitation began in Victoria's reign,
its Imperial splendour had little to do with her. Queen Victoria may
have had a low opinion of her heir, but Bagehot's 'unemployed youth'
should nonetheless be seen as far more successful than his Regency predecessor as king-in-waiting in reconciling the variables of patient waiting,

[57] W. L. Arnstein, *Queen Victoria* (London, 2003), p. 186; D. Cannadine, 'The last Hanoverian sovereign?'

[58] F. Hardie, *The Political influence of Queen Victoria* (London, 1935); Arnstein, *Queen
Victoria*; K. D. Reynolds, *Aristocratic Women and Political Society in Victorian Britain*
(Oxford 1998).

[59] W. L. Arnstein, 'Queen Victoria opens parliament: the disinvention of tradition', *Historical Research* 63 (1990), 178–94.

[60] J. Pope-Hennessy, *Queen Mary* (London, 1956); F. Prochaska, 'Queen Mary', *Oxford
Dictionary of National Biography* (Oxford, 2004); Cannadine, *Ornamentalism*, ch. 8.

respectable domesticity, and ceremonial propriety versus dandy fashion-
ability, new money, and private self-indulgence. Queen Victoria knew
the country 'could never bear to have George IV as Prince of Wales
over again',[61] yet she excluded her own eldest son from access to official papers until 1891. However, Edward was briefly in the Grenadier
Guards, so could wear military dress with a little authenticity. Furthermore, as the late Victorian, Imperial monarchy became adept at projecting its grandeur in ceremonies and rituals from London to Bombay, South
Africa to Singapore, Edward could always be counted on to play his role
well in public. His well-conducted visits to Canada and America in 1860
and India in 1875 were pointers to the future. He made a considerable
input into the successful arrangements and extensive entertainment of
the two Jubilees, royal events ever more precisely and solemnly choreographed, with none of the mixture of pantomime and spectacle that had
characterized George IV's uneven efforts at public splendour.[62] Edward
and his suitable and beautiful consort Alexandra also conducted court
presentations and other routine royal rituals successfully for Victoria at
St James's.

Nor was it the case that it was only he liable to cause his mother
embarrassment; the reverse was also true. Edward was alert to the danger that his mother's reclusiveness presented to the monarchy, and also
to the disrepute her fulsome tributes to John Brown in her second journal from the Highlands could create. She ignored his advice to publish it
privately.[63] As he grew older, and his nephews and nieces intermarried
into the third generation of European royalty, he even projected a certain
kind of amiable royal gravitas as the 'uncle of Europe'.[64]

V

As a female sovereign, Victoria escaped the dilemma of giving up the
male warrior-role for domestic felicity: there was no anomaly in a queen
regnant who did not lead troops into battle. Her predecessor, Queen
Anne, had a consort, George of Denmark, who was Lord High Admiral,
while on land the military role devolved on the Duke of Marlborough.
But a military role for Victoria's consort did not evolve. Albert declined

[61] Aronson, The King in Love (London, 1988), p. 131.
[62] Cannadine, 'Invention'; Ornamentalism.
[63] For instance, in 1871 Vicky, the Princess Royal mobilized her siblings to write to their
mother, urging her to consider public opinion about her seclusion. For Edward's advice
on publication: Aronson, King in Love, pp. 68–9; also P. Jullian, Edward and the Edwar-
dians (London, 1967), pp. 62–3.
[64] G. Brook-Shepherd, Uncle of Europe (London, 1975); T. Aronson, The Grandmama of
Europe (London, 1973).

the role of commander-in-chief when it was suggested, partly because he lacked relevant experience, but also because he was too busy with the role as adviser he had already carved out for himself, not to mention his cultural and educational projects, such as sitting on the Royal Commission to determine the decoration of the Houses of Parliament, being a reforming Chancellor of Cambridge University, and encouraging the Great Exhibition. This rejection of soldiering was surely all the more acceptable because it was in tune with the declining premium on military masculinity in the 1840s and 50s.[65] Instead, as Arnstein has shown, it was the queen who carved out a role for herself as warrior queen.[66]

If the queen was slow to reign rather than to rule and was never neutral in her political views, especially on foreign affairs, she did elevate the monarchy above party in this military capacity. She was proud of being a soldier's daughter, and reviewed troops regularly during the years when she would not open Parliament. She managed to combine both 'male' and 'female' roles in her military enthusiasm. She commiserated with war widows, sent off her troops and welcomed them back in person, and sent them chocolates at the front; but she also urged her ministers to take on Russia in 1854–6 and again in 1877, enjoyed her jingoistic tour round London in 1900 after the relief of Ladysmith, welcomed better news from the Boer War on her deathbed, and was given a military funeral. She therefore set the precedent in the twentieth century for royal females – whether queens consort, queens regnant, or Princesses royal, to be honorary colonels of regiments. The reminiscences of Princess Mary Louise, granddaughter of Queen Victoria, vividly evoke this continuity of royal women "performing" masculinity, by a page of illustration showing Queens Victoria and Elizabeth II, mounted on horseback in almost identical uniform, reviewing troops.[67]

If it was not appropriate for Victoria's husband to perform a military role, and she could incorporate masculine elements into her own position, the queen also had other royal men who could assist her, notably her cousin, George, Duke of Cambridge, and her second and third sons, Alfred, Duke of Edinburgh, and Arthur, Duke of Connaught. They did not all eschew a dashing, dandified persona in order to manage the equation of military prowess with middle-class respectability. George, a few weeks younger than Victoria, was a child of the Romantic age, and the offspring of a suitable dynastic liaison that was also a love-match. Like his parents, he was determined to marry for love, and left the country

[65] Tosh, 'The Old Adam', pp. 233–6.
[66] W. L. Arnstein, 'The warrior queen: reflections on Victoria and her world', *Albion* 30 (1998), 1–28.
[67] Princess Marie Louise, *My Memories of Six Reigns* (Harmondsworth, 1959), illustrations 23 A and B.

soon after his cousin's succession, in order to avoid being manoeuvred into an arranged marriage with her. He married an actress, Louisa Fairbrother, against the terms of the 1772 Royal Marriages Act. She led a private but respected existence in her London house, where her guests numbered literary luminaries and politicians, including Gladstone. There were three FitzGeorge sons, who were eventually introduced to, and cordially liked by, their maternal grandmother, Augusta, Dowager Duchess of Cambridge. Cambridge's biographer sees this cultivated, elegantly mannered, musical family as a living link with the *douceur de vie* of the *ancien régime*, which 'rejecting most of the vices of the Regency period, retained something of its gaiety.'[68] One enduring 'vice' was George's long-term attachment to another Louisa, the daughter of a Yorkshire baronet, whom he met at Almack's through Adolphus Fitzclarence. This cousin, one of William IV's sons, combined a successful naval career with being a theatrical enthusiast, co-founder of the Garrick Club, and something of a dandy.[69] Elements of raffish Regency masculinity thus continued to exist near the throne; Cambridge and his sons, who were either in the army or navy, were among the cronies of Edward, Prince of Wales.[70]

Victoria's military role was also represented by the royal sons Alfred and Arthur (the latter named after the hero of Waterloo), who successfully pursued respectively a naval and military career, and then served in various imperial posts in India, South Africa and Canada. The queen did not approve of Alfred, however, because she deplored his morals – which, as a young man, were typical of the fast aristocratic set of the Prince of Wales's circle, involving wine, actresses, and obliging married women.[71] Arthur by contrast was the apple of his mother's eye, the son who had turned out completely right, whom she wished the self-indulgent Bertie resembled, and whose military heroism thrilled her. His family life – he married a Prussian princess – was unproblematic; his share in royal philanthropy was to help found the Red Cross.[72]

Not all of Victoria's masculine relatives were suitable for consolidating a link between monarchy and domestic felicity in the manner inaugurated by George III. Yet famously the most important man in her life, Albert, Prince Consort, enabled her to achieve precisely this link. At home, Victoria liked to defer, and to be depicted as deferring, to Albert as paterfamilias, friend and counsellor; and this helped quell his anxieties over

[68] G. St Aubyn, *The Royal George* (London, 1964), p. 277.
[69] C. Tomalin, *Mrs. Jordan's Profession* (London, 1995), p. 313.
[70] See photograph, dated 1889, in R. Hough, *Edward and Alexandra* (London, 1992), between pp. 166–7.
[71] *Darling Loosy: Letters to Princess Louise 1856–1939*, ed. E. Longford (London, 1991), p. 250; also *Dearest Affie*, ed. J. van der Kiste and B. Jordaan (London, 1984).
[72] Arnstein, 'Warrior queen'; *Victoria*, p. 160. See also N. Frankland, *Witness to a Century* (London, 1993).

the inherent emasculation of being a prince consort. His reinvention as a Scottish laird, and emphasis on his own descent from Anglo-Saxon warriors, both helped to project his masculinity.[73] Albert was nothing if not 'respectable' in the familial role which the evangelical revival had created for men, in order to wean them away from the male camaraderie of the club and the pub. It is often overlooked that in creating 'the angel in the house' role for women, Victorian domestic ideology also aimed to Christianize, domesticate and sentimentalize men. The mid-Victorian male was allowed to shed a manly tear and to look to an effeminized Christ as a role model. Thus Albert, in reaction to his raffish Coburg relatives, and in contrast to the Regency pattern of absentee fatherhood and polygamous amours still followed by many of the aristocracy, aligned the monarchy once more with a pattern of virtuous domesticity exemplified by George III and Queen Charlotte.[74] Albert's enthusiasm for family life also concealed the fact that the 'grandmother of Europe' was not very maternal, preferring children to babies, but also dominating her adult daughters and sons. Adrienne Munich has suggested that the pantomime dames and strong females in Gilbert and Sullivan opera represent a collective fear of the dominant dowager she became.[75] Victoria's extravagant grief over Albert's death created and endorsed an entire cult of Victorian widowhood, though the exact character of her subsequent friendships with both John Brown and the Munshi, Abdul Karim, her Indian secretary, is far from clear.[76] But it had been Albert who had helped to 'feminize' the monarchy, i.e. to associate it with domesticity, even if, as Cannadine has rightly suggested, his political ideals for a liberal monarchy were not the same as modern, constitutional ones.

VI

What of the problematic link established by George IV between the monarchy and fashion? Victoria was not a fashion icon. Having become the widow of Windsor, she stuck with her 'uniform', even refusing to exchange her bonnet for a tiara for the jubilees. There were elements of the dandy in Edward, but not on the same scale as George, Prince of Wales.

---

[73] A. Munich, Queen Victoria's Secrets (New York, 1997), ch. 2.

[74] L. Davidoff and C. Hall, Family Fortunes (London, 1987); M. Roper and J. Tosh (eds.), Manful Assertions (London, 1991); C. Christ, 'Victorian masculinity and the angel in the house', in M. Vicinus (ed.), A Widening Sphere (London, 1978); M. Girouard, 'Victorian values and the upper classes', in T. C. Smout (ed.), Victorian Values (Oxford, 1992); A. Clark, Struggle; Tosh, 'The Old Adam'; B. Hilton, 'Manliness, masculinity and the mid-Victorian temperament', in L. Goldman (ed.), The Blind Victorian (Cambridge, 1989).

[75] Munich, Queen Victoria's Secrets, ch. 5.

[76] A. Lambert, Unquiet Souls (London, 1984); T. Aronson, Heart of a Queen (London, 1991).

As he matured, his style moved beyond fashion to represent quintessential English style and correctness. Indian princes emulated him; he was deferred to as an expert on the intricacies of dress codes for mourning, wearing decorations, and the nuances of formal and informal dress.[77] Although known behind his back as Tum-Tum, Edward was never as obese as the corseted George IV. He never needed to be winched on to his horse.

He was not as extraordinarily extravagant as George, though the old landed families kept aloof from his association with the new money of Jewish financiers and 'randlords'. But at least his financier friends helped him arrange his investments or lent him money, which precluded his needing parliamentary subventions.[78] Nor was he an outstanding collector and connoisseur; his country house at Sandringham was not an exotic hybrid fantasy building filled with exquisite and sometimes extraordinary treasures, but a Jacobethan retreat for organized large-scale shooting not dissimilar from the country residences of plutocrats, complete with his wife's cluttered memorabilia and Fabergé knick-knacks. The Wales's family was cheerfully unintellectual, as Mary of Cambridge found somewhat to her dismay when she married Edward's second son, George.[79] In fact Edward's sporting enthusiasm for shooting, racing and golf, meant that he fitted better into English landed society and its country pursuits than George IV had ever been able to do. He was always the urban sophisticate; but Edward's rural routines made him seem satisfyingly English. He was never more popular than when his horse Persimmon won the Derby in 1896.[80] His style of masculinity might have been the opposite of his father's prim respectability, but it was a style which went down well in much of nineteenth-century Britain. As Mark Girouard has observed, the expansive, debonair, promiscuous aristocrat had his working-class counterpart in the Jack the Lad boxing promoter or race-course fixer. The Victorian working classes were divided between the 'rough' and the 'respectable' – who along with their middle and upper middle-class counterparts, would have been more offended at Edward's morals than the former.[81] Nor was he an hysterical hypochondriac, as George IV had been, so his near-fatal bout of typhoid fever in 1871 evoked genuine sympathy and helped defuse republican sentiment.

Of course, Edward sometimes came very close to damaging scandal on occasions, which was meat and drink to the radical press. The Tranby

---

[77] Jullian, *Edward*, pp. 72–3, 180.
[78] A. Allfrey, *Edward VIII and his Jewish Court* (London, 1991).
[79] J. Mordaunt Crook, *The Rise of the Nouveaux Riches* (London, 2000); the Wales's philistinism is best documented in Pope-Hennessy, *Queen Mary*.
[80] Aronson, *King in Love*, pp. 168–9; also Jullian, *Edward*, p. 147.
[81] See references in note 75.

Croft affair which implicated Edward in a country house scandal where a guest cheated at baccarat was a decidedly unsavoury element. After this he gave up baccarat for bridge. He had to testify in court during the Mordaunt divorce case, and was also implicated by association in the scandal created by Lady Aylesford's affair with his friend Lord Randolph Churchill.[82] But his marriage to Alexandra of Denmark was infinitely more successful than that between Caroline of Brunswick and George, Prince of Wales; she was able to combine an eternally youthful beauty with devoted motherhood. In time, her 'look' became fixed, beyond fashion, into her own personal, regal style.[83] At the start of their marriage she was even able to keep up with his life as the centre of the metropolitan fast set, and although she did not – as many of her female aristocratic contemporaries did – have her own love affairs, she managed to condone the Edwardian double standard regarding her husband's infidelities for most of the time, though she found Daisy, Countess of Warwick, particularly irksome. (Her consolation was the devoted platonic love of Oliver Montagu.)[84] They also had five children, which again, unlike Prinny, made Edward's official domestic arrangements seem quite normal, and he shared with Alexandra a devotion to their family. It was these children who paid the price for his philandering, as Alexandra doted on them, perpetuated their childhood with her sentimentality, and maintained that none of her daughters really wanted to marry.[85]

Like many aristocratic couples, they could lead very separate lives in their various residences without this signalling they were estranged; and when Alexandra felt especially pained by his mistresses, she could plausibly extend her own vacations with her family in Denmark, or cruise in the Mediterranean to visit her brother, the King of Greece. She was pointedly absent for Edward's fiftieth birthday, for instance. That this accommodation of her husband's philandering was possible was also due to the fact that Edward always treated Alexandra publicly with the utmost respect, and on public occasions they could still appear to be a handsome, dignified royal couple. This was a code of behaviour that Louis XV would have recognized. Indeed, it seems appropriate that many of the interiors of the country houses which Edward frequented, including Sandringham and the homes of the new plutocrats he favoured, had rooms decorated in an eclectic eighteenth-century French style – 'tous les Louis', which evoked the sophisticated hedonism associated with all things French, and also an elegant *politesse*. Edward's French biographer

---

[82] Both summarized in Hough, *Edward and Alexandra*, and Aronson, *King in Love*.
[83] Aronson, *King in Love*.   [84] Ibid. and Hough, *Edward and Alexandra*.
[85] Alexandra's 'babying' of her grown children is best documented in Pope-Hennessy, *Queen Mary*.

Philippe Jullian has commented on the affinity of the Edwardian era with the France of the Second Empire, 'dominated as it was by financiers and beautiful women'.[86] The royal geography of pleasure could be displaced beyond England to the resorts and spas of the Continent, where he often went incognito. Finally, Edward's three chief mistresses were all the 'New Woman' kind of females, as Aronson has observed, who benefited from rather than were exploited by their position: they did not write feminist tracts.[87]

VII

Edward, Prince of Wales's sexual morality was not a named target in the feminist debates of his era – Votes for Women, Chastity for Men – which meant the monarchy was not directly implicated in Edwardian feminist discourse.[88] The same cannot be said about the redefinition of masculinity in the 1880s, when homosexual activity was criminalized and a new identity of being 'earnest' emerged. This new discourse came very close to the throne in the person of Edward's languid and far from conventionally masculine eldest son, the Duke of Clarence. His preoccupation with the niceties of uniform made even his own father nickname him 'Collars and Cuffs'. Here indeed was an effeminate male, though probably a bisexual rather than a homosexual one, raised in an atmosphere of girlish femininity, doted on by his mother and three sisters, and very much a part of the new wave of aesthetic dandyism that emerged by the 1890s. Aronson has shown how closely connected he was through his associates to the upper-class homosexual sub-culture that revolved around male brothels like the one in Cleveland Street, and has explored the evidence for the cover-up of Lord Arthur Somerset's connection with the case. Somerset was superintendent of the Prince of Wales's stables, and therefore able to introduce Eddy into the metropolitan circles he frequented. By 1889, when Somerset fled to France to avoid prosecution, and (as he claimed in private) to protect the throne, rumours were circulating in the American and Continental press that the young prince had been at the brothel. Though this cannot be conclusively proved, it seems likely. However, the radical MP Labouchere was unable to make headway in the House of Commons when he claimed there had been a conspiracy to prevent various prosecutions. The Prime Minister Lord Salisbury quietly made it clear that charges against Somerset should not be pursued, and

[86] Jullian, *Edward*, p. 229; see also pp. 50–51 for his friendship with Ferdinand de Rothschild and his eighteenth-century collection at Waddesdon, and ch. 6, p. 182 for the comparison with Louis XIV.
[87] Aronson, *King in Love*.   [88] L. Bland, *Banishing the Beast* (London, 1995).

the establishment closed ranks.[89] There has also been speculation that Eddy's uncle by marriage, the Marquis of Lorne, husband of Princess Louise, was homosexual. Elizabeth Longford and Jehanne Wake have reviewed the case for and against, which rests largely on his associations, and concluded that it is unlikely that any ambivalent inclinations he may have had were overtly expressed.[90]

More obvious examples of effeminized royal males who were nonetheless heterosexual are the hapless sons-in-law of Queen Victoria, Prince Christian of Schleswig-Holstein (husband of Princess Helena) and Prince Henry of Battenberg (husband of Princess Beatrice). Their marriages were permitted on condition that they lived in England with their mother-in-law. They may have brought a greater degree of informality and masculine teasing into the widow's household, but Prince Henry found being military governor of the Isle of Wight so Ruritanian that he begged to serve in the Ashante Wars, where he died of fever.[91] Another emasculated bridegroom was Prince Francis of Teck, husband of the queen's cousin Mary Adelaide of Cambridge, who on his marriage resigned his commission in the Austro-Hungarian army to live in Richmond, where his only occupation was to garden, obsessively rearrange the décor of White Lodge, and fret over his succession claims to the Kingdom of Württemberg.[92]

The gender politics of the 1880s and 1890s, in which New Women challenged the sexual morality of men, and the authority of parents, did not impinge on the monarchy. Rather, the gender politics of masculinity, with the emergence of modern homosexual identity, overshadowed the institution with bizarre rumours of vice and complicity in high places. Victoria's daughters Helena and Beatrice rebelled against her matriarchal repression to the extent of getting married, but in return had to live with their husbands in the queen's homes. Edward's daughters and daughter-in-law were New Women only insofar as they smoked, though Princess Maud was a bit sporty and rode a bicycle, and Princess Mary had the intellectual seriousness and philanthropic concerns of New Women, such as Mrs Humphry Wards's heroine Marcella in the eponymous novel. Her biographer observed that she would have made a good factory inspector or museum curator, had she needed to work – not impossible careers for New Women. She also had a certain independence of spirit, never

---

[89] T. Aronson, *Prince Eddy and the Homosexual Underworld* (London, 1994). According to Aronson, the further identification of Prince Eddy with the Jack the Ripper murders, made in various forms since the 1970s, can be shown to be implausible.

[90] *Darling Loosy*, pp. 51–4; J. Wake, *Queen Victoria's Unconventional Daughter* (London, 1988).

[91] D. Duff, *Hessian Tapestry* (London, 1967), provides vignettes of the two sons-in-law, as does Aronson, *Underworld*.

[92] Pope-Hennessy, *Queen Mary*.

minding fulfilling social engagements on her own when married to George V, or making cultural visits while he was occupied with sport, but this was combined with an utter devotion to family, and a sense of partnership in sustaining the monarchy alongside her husband.[93]

But are there any other ways in which the debate on woman's role during Victoria's reign was connected to royal women? Did they engage with the 'woman question'? It has become a commonplace to quote the Queen's protest against 'the mad, wicked folly of woman's rights' as expressed in private to Theodore Martin, in reaction to the aristocratic feminist, Lady Amberley, speaking in public in 1870 on woman's suffrage. Lady Amberley, her sister Rosalind Howard, Countess of Carlisle, and their mother the educational reformer Lady Henrietta Stanley, co-foundress of Girton College, represent only one end of the wide spectrum of Victorian feminism – and are a useful reminder to historians of feminism, who usually concentrate on middle- and working-class activists, that the contribution of aristocratic women was significant.[94] In fact much of mid-Victorian feminism grew out of an adaptation of the late eighteenth- and early nineteenth-century moral activism of women as philanthropists and patriots, campaigning against the Corn Laws or slavery, arguing the case for better education for themselves in order to equip them better for motherhood, and engaging in all kinds of charity work. The mission to the poor and distressed was extended more specifically to women's missions to other women.[95] Much of this activism was 'womanist' rather than feminist insofar as it did not challenge legal restrictions on property ownership in marriage or demand the franchise. When women were enabled to sit on School Boards and take part in local government after 1870, they often interpreted this in womanist terms – an extension to their charitable role in 'mothering the parish'.[96] Even the Langham Place group, which first began the agitation on married women's property rights, also concentrated on a range of 'middle of the spectrum' issues, such as female emigration, access to higher education, and women's entry to the professions – including the 'female' ones of teaching and nursing, as well as the more controversial ones of painting and medicine.[97] Thus

---

[93] Ibid.   [94] See references in note 39.

[95] See L. Colley, *Britons* (London, 1990), pp. 273–87; F. Prochaska, *Women and Philanthropy in Nineteenth-century England* (Oxford, 1980); A. Tyrrell, '"Women's mission" and pressure-group politics in Britain 1825–1860', *Bulletin of the John Rylands Library* 63 (1980), 194–230; C. Midgley, *Women against Slavery* (London, 1992).

[96] P. Hollis, 'Women in council: separate spheres, public space', in J. Rendall (ed.), *Equal or Different?* (Oxford, 1987).

[97] C. A. Lacey (ed.), *Barbara Bodichon and the Langham Place Group* (London, 1987), P. Hirsch, *Barbara Bodichon* (London, 1998); C. Campbell Orr (ed.), *Women in the Victorian Art World* (Manchester, 1995); D. Cherry, *Painting Women* (London, 1993); M. Diamond, 'Maria Rye: the primrose path', in C. Campbell Orr (ed.), *Wollstonecraft's Daughters* (Manchester, 1996).

Queen Victoria deplored women attending medical school, but accepted dedication of a volume of verse printed by the Victoria Press, a project by the Langham Place activist Emily Faithfull to train women in the printing trades.[98]

The monarchy is connected to these women's issues in two main ways. First, as already suggested, insofar as it was shifting its role from George III's reign toward patronage of charitable causes, it was already part of a feminization process, which tried to make the Crown apolitical, as well as harnessing it to the Evangelical morality whose aim was to curb the excesses of masculine violence and exploitation, and empowered women as the guardians and shapers of the nation's manners and morals. Various royals became patrons of societies and organizations dedicated to a range of improving causes, from maternity provision, education, and housing to care of the infirm and disabled. These activities empowered the nineteenth-century woman and legitimated activity outside the immediate family, without challenging social hierarchy or legal restrictions. Prochaska has shown how Queen Adelaide accelerated the pace for this evolution of the institution into the 'welfare monarchy,' and Arnstein has argued that Victoria's philanthropy – she was patron of 150 institutions – has been neglected by historians and biographers.[99] The tradition has been continued by all the royal consorts subsequently, as they moved through the cycle of Princess of Wales to Consort to Queen Dowager, up to its recent charismatic exponent the late Princess Diana, as well as by successive princesses royal and the daughters and granddaughters of Queen Victoria. Nor is charity a female prerogative – all the royal males have their charities too; both sexes participate in the feminization of the monarchy in this sense.

The royal example of female philanthropic activism was undoubtedly encouraging to the respectable middle classes. John Ruskin connected royalty symbolically with female agency in his essay in *Sesame and Lilies*, 'Of Queens' Gardens', in which he urged women to be 'no more housewives, but queens'. Feminist historians have found Ruskin's essay problematic: it seemed to endorse the 'sentimental priesthood' of women so scathingly criticized by the rational egalitarians, J. S. Mill and Harriet Taylor. Revisionist readings of this text have permitted a more sympathetic understanding of Ruskin's advocacy, arguing that he was writing 'across gender' to encourage a more humane response to the dehumanization of industrial society that men and women could both display, and invoking a mythic conception of woman-power. As Adrienne Munich concludes, '"Of Queens' Gardens" attempts to ennoble a process

---

[98] Munich, *Queen Victoria*, pp. 63, 218.   [99] Prochaska, *Royal Bounty*.

consolidated during Queen Victoria's reign of bringing the queen to the level of the middle classes while it exhorted the middle class woman to aspire to the level of queens'.[100] For elite women, this activism was a continuation of a familiar role, spiced perhaps by the Victorian fashion for neo-chivalric queenly women.[101]

Secondly, the Victorian monarchy was directly connected to the process by which woman's empowerment through philanthropy became feminist activism. This occurred via several of Victoria's children, most notably Princess Louise, Prince Leopold, and – abroad in Hesse-Darmstadt – Princess Alice. Again a common link in all three cases was the friendship and influence of Ruskin, who from the 1870s was enlarging the scope of his work beyond the morality of art to include social, economic and environmental issues. Ruskin corresponded with Princess Alice about her watercolour painting and encouraged her nursing projects. She also took advice from Florence Nightingale over the nurses' training school she founded in 1867, which became important during the Franco-Prussian War.[102] Prince Leopold met Ruskin when he was at Oxford, where Ruskin was giving the Slade Lectures on Art. Through him Leopold became interested in the University Extension Movement, and the demand for green spaces in cities: as President of the Kyrle Society which campaigned for parks for the urban poor, he once shared a platform with William Morris. Leopold also admired Josephine Butler's support for women's education, but thought her campaigns on behalf of prostitutes were not a subject for ladies. He wrote to his sister Louise commending Mrs Butler's educational projects, not knowing she had already become her supporter.[103]

Victoria's fourth son Leopold presents the most interesting example of royal masculinity. His haemophilia seemed to outline for him a future of invalidism and chronic dependence on his mother, who wished him to play roles similar to her daughters before they succeeded in marrying – to stay at home and assist her secretarially, or, in an echo of his father, to become a foreign-affairs adviser. The role of saintly invalid child and ailing, gentlemanly adult was one beloved of Victorian fiction and sentiment; it was one he could easily have allowed himself to play. At

---

[100] Munich, *Queen Victoria's Secrets*, pp. 21–2; S. Aronofsky Weltman, '"Be no more housewives, but queens": Queen Victoria and Ruskin's domestic mythology', in A. Munich and M. Homans (eds.), *Remaking Queen Victoria* (Cambridge, 1997); D. Birch, 'Ruskin's womanly mind', *Essay in Criticism* 38 (1988), 308–24; D. Sodenstrom, 'Millett vs. Ruskin', *Victorian Studies* 20 (1977), 283–97.

[101] Girouard, *Return to Camelot*; Reynolds, *Aristocratic Women*.

[102] Duff, *Hessian Tapestry*; K. D. Reynolds, 'Princess Alice', *Oxford Dictionary of National Biography* (Oxford, 2004).

[103] C. Zeepvat, *Prince Leopold* (Stroud, 1998), p. 103.

nineteen he wrote ruefully to his secretary, Robert Collins, 'you ought to call me "Pamela" . . . on account of my purity of mind and body'.[104] Nevertheless, he successfully rebelled against all his social restriction, winning the battle to attend Oxford, to engage in public causes to do with education, music, the disabled, and the environment, and eventually to marry. He even obtained the essential badge of late nineteenth-century princely masculinity – the right to wear a proper military uniform – when he was made honorary colonel of the 3rd Battalion Seaforth Highlanders.[105] Although his mother had limited his exposure to the fast set among the aristocracy, he had even managed to acquire some sexual experience – possibly with the help of the debonair Crown Prince Rudolf of Austria, and he was a friend of Lillie Langtry before she met the Prince of Wales.

Princess Louise exemplified the combination of artistic talent with progressive social ideas that was characteristic of the Bohemian circles in which she moved. It needs to be remembered that the profession in which Victorian women first made their mark was art; Louise, a talented sculptress, was typical of a second generation of artistic women, after the Pre-Raphaelites, who received formal training, recognition and exhibition of their work. Louise's attendance at the National Art Training School in Kensington to study modelling was limited by her social duties, but it helped her advance beyond genteel amateurism. Her support for female education is shown most clearly in her role as president of the Women's Educational Union, which organised non-denominational, meritocratic secondary schools for girls through the Girls Public Day School Trust. She also helped Elizabeth Garrett Anderson raise funds for her hospital for women.[106] In another area where women were following 'artistic' careers, Queen Victoria accepted patronage of the Arts and Crafts influenced Royal School of Needlework and her daughter, Princess Helena, was an active supporter.

VIII

Royal approval for the widening opportunities for women continued in the twentieth century. A considerable number of royal women became actively associated with the newly respectable nursing profession, as patrons but also as qualified practitioners. Princess Helena founded the Princess Christian Nursing Home at Windsor; her daughters Marie Louise and Helena Victoria continued her work. Edward's daughter

---

[104] Ibid., p. 131
[105] Ibid., pp. 102, 136–7, 161 and illustration of him in his uniform opposite title page.
[106] Wake, *Queen Victoria's Unconventional Daughter*, pp. 169–172; 98; for her Bohemian friends, *Darling Loosy*, p. 235, and C. Dakers, *Clouds* (London, 1993).

Louise, Duchess of Fife, was a state-registered nurse who worked professionally in two world wars. Others, like Mary Adelaide of Cambridge, Victoria's cousin, and her daughter May, the future Queen Mary, were patrons of hospitals and nursing homes. The latter's daughter, Mary, Princess Royal, was a VAD probationer at Great Ormond Street from 1918 to 1920, and passed the advanced nursing qualification with Honours. She told her mother she considered nursing to be her true vocation.[107] In such ways these royal women contributed to the right of women to enter the professions as well as linking the royal family to the everyday world.

Cannadine is surely right to see this identification of monarchy with philanthropy as part of the connection between 'matriarchy, domesticity and kindness' that makes its twentieth-century version both feminized and constitutional. Biological accident has also played a part in giving the twentieth-century monarchy a feminine face, both in the longevity of Queens Consort Mary and Elizabeth, compared with their respective husbands George V and VI, and in George VI's and Elizabeth's producing daughters, not sons. But does this add up to emasculation?[108] Another way to interpret this would be to see the prominence, strength and longevity of these women as representative of many ordinary women's experience in a century of two world wars, as a result of which single women and war widows soon outnumbered men. It is also emblematic of the co-dependency of those surviving men on the women who 'held the fort' at home, or on those upper-class young women who joined up. As an honorary 2nd subaltern at the ATS Motor Training Transport near Windsor, Princess Elizabeth turned out to have an uncanny genius for spotting mechanical faults in the heavy vehicles she drove.[109] Moreover, George VI had been a serving naval officer well before being forced to assume the mantle of king after his brother's abdication; arguably his profession, and then his recognition of duty, was more 'manly' than the behaviour of Edward VIII. The latter's abject devotion to Mrs Simpson and rumoured sexual inadequacy made him seem effeminized by comparison, and he never fathered children.

Monarchy is a peculiarly self-reflexive institution. Not only do some of its structures repeat themselves – the problem of what an heir is to do before acceding or the ambiguity of a female sovereign – but its members

---

[107] G. K. S. Hamilton-Edwards, 'Mary, Princess Royal'; J. van der Kiste, 'Princess Helena'; H. E. Worton, 'Princess Helena Victoria'; K. Rose, 'Princess Mary Louise'; K. D. Reynolds, 'Louise, Duchess of Fife', *Oxford DNB*.

[108] Cannadine, *History in Our Time*, p. 65.

[109] L. Wieff, *Queen of Tomorrow* (London, 1944 and 1949); personal communication from Miss Ruth Doggett, 12 August 2005.

are like their predecessors in the unpredictable ways of all families, and also deeply conscious of their predecessors more than most families, given that it is an hereditary 'business'. Queen Mary gave the present Prince of Wales a christening cup given originally by George III to a godson in 1780, 'so that I gave a present from my gt-grandfather, to my great-grandson 168 years later', as she recorded in her diary.[110] Royal women guard and transmit reminiscences, just as so many ordinary women do.

Edward VIII identified with the Prince Regent, a predecessor who put private pleasure before public responsibility. The 1920s and 1930s saw rehabilitations of George IV by a succession of biographers, at the same time as taste-makers close to the throne like Cecil Beaton and Osbert Sitwell, rediscovered the Regency period and the Regent's supreme connoisseurship.[111] It seems appropriate that Edward abdicated while resident at Fort Belvedere, one of the buildings created in Windsor Great Park in the Regent's last reclusive years.

A continuing connection between monarchy and homosocial, if not homosexual, culture, has been explored by William Kuhn and Yvonne Ward, who show to what extent the monarchy's royal image, or subsequent historical analysis, has been the creation of gay men such as Lord Esher, Arthur Benson, Lytton Strachey, Cecil Beaton, James Pope-Hennessy, and Harold Nicolson.[112] Yet royal masculinity is still strongly identified with the 'manliness' of military service, even in post-war peacetime Britain. When Prince Edward left the Marines it was widely rumoured (as if it mattered in the age of Gay Pride) that he was homosexual; the public still seems rather to prefer royal men to be heterosexuals in uniform. At the same time, they also like caring royal men; it seems likely that royal men as well as royal women will find their position to be publicly acceptable, the more they continue with their part in the 'welfare monarchy'.

Despite his philanthropy, the public has remained divided over the type of royal masculinity shown by the present Prince of Wales. As with the Regent and Caroline, his unfortunate first marriage raised all

---

[110] Pope-Hennessy, *Queen Mary*, pp. 81–90, for her sense of dynastic history; p. 616, for diary entry. Although Queen Mary could not have been more unlike the bright young things of the 1930s who admired the Regency for its wit and fast living, she encouraged the restoration of the Royal Pavilion at Brighton, and gave back items to the Royal Collection to furnish it, in line with her interest in the Royal Collection and previous royal collectors: Dinkel, *The Royal Pavilion*.

[111] Parissien, *George IV*, pp. 379, 419, fn. 15; Dinkel, *The Royal Pavilion*, p. 45.

[112] W. Kuhn, *Democratic Royalism* (London, 1996); Y. Ward, 'Editing Queen Victoria: how men of letters constructed the young Queen' (PhD thesis, La Trobe University, Melbourne, 2004). I am indebted to Yvonne Ward for a copy of her thesis and for invaluable discussions.

kinds of feminist issues; but unlike Queen Alexandra, Diana, Princess of Wales refused to accept royal adultery, thereby challenging the Edwardian sexual politics of the royal family. Like Edward VIII's passion for Mrs Simpson, Charles's passion for Camilla Parker Bowles was seen as pathetically dependent. She is a descendant of Edward, Prince of Wales's mistress Alice Keppel, whose tact and ability to soothe the royal temperament she has evidently inherited; but the Prince of Wales has not perfected his predecessor's debonair charm and philistine bonhomie. Instead his sporty, polo-playing persona and archaic dependence on an entourage of servants sits uncomfortably in the public mind with his conversations with his plants, his conservationist agenda, and his religious ecumenism, which might otherwise have endeared him to the hippie generation with its environmental concerns and New Age eclecticism. However, his civil marriage to Camilla, now Duchess of Cornwall, in an age of blended families and serial marriages, has made him more like many British couples, and may have halted his unpopularity.

His cousin David Linley, whose ancestors include the late Victorian artist Linley Sanbourne and the 1930s theatre designer Oliver Messel, has been more successful at broadening the range of royal masculinity, by perpetuating the connections with Haut Bohemia begun by Princess Louise and continued by George VI's brother George and sister-in-law Marina, and his own parents, Princess Margaret and Anthony Armstrong-Jones. Educated at that monument to Edwardian Arts and Crafts progressive education, Bryanston, he is a successful designer-maker of luxurious bespoke furniture. Meanwhile Charles's sister the Princess Royal has been an Olympic standard horsewoman, survived divorce, remarriage and unpopularity, plodded on with her charities, notably Save the Children, and marched in uniform trousers as an honorary colonel behind her grandmother's funeral cortège, thus neatly displaying the ability of royal women to be both warriors and nurturers.[113] Perhaps it is the case then that in a constitutional – feminized – monarchy, royal women are better than royal men in combining elements of 'feminine' as well as 'masculine' role-playing demanded of modern royal persons: as Elizabeth II has demonstrated for over half a century.

[113] Unlike her forebears, Princesses Sophia, Amelia and Augusta, daughters of George III who fell in love with equerries in the Windsor entourage but could not officially marry them, Princess Anne has been able to marry Commander Tim Lawrence, whom she met when he was an equerry at Buckingham Palace when she was married to her first husband, Captain Mark Phillips.

4   Crown, spectacle and identity: the British monarchy and Ireland under the Union 1800–1922

James Loughlin

The monarchy's relationship with Ireland under the Union began and ended badly. George III's refusal to endorse the promised Catholic emancipation that was supposed to accompany the Irish Act of Union reinforced the moral illegitimacy it immediately assumed for nationalists, creating a deep sense of betrayal that prepared the agitational ground for Daniel O'Connell's political career and with it the Irish constitutional tradition. And yet, when southern Ireland disengaged from the Union in 1922 in the guise of the Irish Free State, it was to the accompaniment of a bloody civil war with a focus on an oath of allegiance to the King. In fact, Catholic Ireland's relationship with the monarchy was multifaceted, combining elements of opposition, attachment and indifference depending on context, and explicable neither in terms of undiluted allegiance nor in those of rejection. In surveying its dimensions, account should be taken not only of Irish royal visits but also of the public arena in which contact was made, the institutions of the British state in Ireland, and Ireland's evolving socio-economic and political development. To this end, the essay is divided into the following sections: the Irish Viceroyalty; the problems posed for the monarchy with reference to the symbolic embodiment of Britain and Ireland; the political impact of major royal visits to Ireland; the difficulties of building upon the great outpourings of loyalty that royal visits appeared to generate; and the role of monarchy in the early twentieth century, as cultural nationalism developed and the struggle for independence brought the Union to an end.

I

While the Irish Act of Union completed the constitutional development of the United Kingdom as a state, it did not create a unified economic, public and political arena. Ireland was, and would remain throughout the Union period, economically underdeveloped compared to Britain; its sectarian divisions would remain entrenched, becoming exacerbated in Ulster as

108

popular nationalism developed; while the centralized administration – the Viceroyalty – was unique within the Kingdom, creating the impression of constitutional membership combined with colonial status. It is the obvious place to begin an assessment of the monarchy's relationship with Ireland.

Originating as a system of English control in the reign of Henry VI, the problematic Anglo-Irish relationship ensured its survival despite Ireland's inclusion in the expanded British state after 1800.[1] In fact, the Viceroyalty mirrored to a significant extent the political system in Britain. The Viceroy[2] was literally a *substitute* for the monarch, as distinct from representative. The office entailed a court and the forms pertaining to a court, enhanced in 1783 when George III instituted the Order of Saint Patrick to accompany the Orders of the Thistle and the Rose. The Chief Secretary was the Irish 'Prime Minister'. Moreover, just as the monarchy in Britain sat at the apex of a hierarchical social order, so in Ireland the Viceroyalty was supported by the landed aristocracy whose great houses provided staging points for Viceroys on their tours of the Irish countryside. More generally, the viceregal court functioned as a cohesive force in the Irish non-nationalist – though not necessarily non-Catholic – world, setting a standard and pattern of social culture and manners.[3] It was a British world whose landscape, certainly in the urban thoroughfares of Dublin, was signified through naming and monuments. Dublin's synecdochal representation of loyal Ireland was marked topographically by street names, hospitals, bridges, monuments – contentiously in the case of the equestrian statue of William III in College Green – and the great monuments to the British national heroes, Nelson in Sackville (later O'Connell) Street, and Wellington in Phoenix Park.[4] Furthermore, just as royalty massively developed its charity work in the nineteenth century to create what Prochaska has described as a 'welfare monarchy',[5] so a similar development can also be observed in regard to

---

[1] For accounts, see V. Crossman, 'Chief secretary', in S. J. Connolly (ed.), *The Oxford Companion to Irish History* (Oxford, 2002), pp. 85–6; H. Morgan, and S. Connolly, 'Lord deputy', 'Lord lieutenant', ibid., pp. 343–4; K. Flanagan, 'The Chief secretary's office 1853–1914', *Irish Historical Studies* 24 (1984), 197–225.

[2] Officially known as 'Lord Lieutenant', 'Viceroy' is more appropriate. The usage is illustrated in C. O'Mahony, *The Viceroys of Ireland* (London, 1912).

[3] For the history of the Order, see P. Galloway, *The Most Illustrious Order of St. Patrick 1783–1983* (Chichester, 1983); 'The Court of Dublin Castle', in R. B. McDowell, *Historical Essays 1938–2001* (Dublin, 2003), p. 8.

[4] Ibid., p. 2; P. Murphy, 'The politics of the street monument', *Irish Arts Review* 10 (1994), 202–4; Y. Whelan, *Reinventing Modern Dublin* (Dublin, 2003), chs. 2 and 3.

[5] F. Prochaska, *Royal Bounty* (London, 1995).

the Viceroyalty.[6] However, the differences between the monarchy and its Irish manifestation were more significant than the similarities.

While it is generally true that the Chief Secretary came to take on the actual burden of Irish administration and with it a seat in the Cabinet,[7] that process was not irreversible. A combination of political crisis and personal authority could see the Chief Secretary sidelined as the Viceroy took the Cabinet seat and combined the responsibilities of the former with his own, as happened under the Spencer Viceroyalty from 1882–5.[8] In this context, for nationalists, Spencer merely embodied a system wherein coercive apparatus and state symbolism were inextricable and where an elevated 'royal' arena above political conflict did not exist. While the great royal palaces in Britain could be seen increasingly during the nineteenth century as symbolic of the separation between the constitutionally representative and the politically functional (Westminster) as the monarchy lost its direct political influence, this was not the case in Ireland. Dublin Castle housed both the throne room and the offices dealing with the suppression of rebellion, agrarian crime and popular agitation. In 1893, C. P. Trevelyan, an ADC to the Viceroy, Lord Houghton, appointed under Gladstone's second Home Rule government, thought it indicative of the Irish administration's role that while 'the figure of justice' stood above the gates of Dublin Castle, it was 'looking inward with *her back turned to the people*.'[9]

The incongruous juxtaposition of royal symbolism and coercive function was not lost on visitors. The American pressman, George Smalley, thought it 'strange that this third-rate barracks should really be Dublin Castle' and that in these 'paltry circumstances . . . the state and splendour of a Viceregal establishment have to be kept up.'[10] Nor did the Castle's location in the city enhance its regal authenticity.

If a traditional function of royal magnificence has been to symbolize the physical well-being of the land and people of which the monarch is the embodiment,[11] then Dublin Castle's position in one of the most deprived and poverty-ridden areas of the city represented an abysmal failure to facilitate that function. The Irish novelist, George Moore, who came from a landowning family, gave expression to a personal grievance against Castle officials thus: 'The Castle arises like an upas tree amid

---

[6] For the period up to 1830, see E. Brynn, *Crown and Castle* (Dublin, 1978), pp. 101–9; and for the latter period of the Union, M. Keane, *Ishbel* (Newtownards, 1999).

[7] Crossman, 'Chief secretary', pp. 85–6.

[8] See J. Loughlin, 'Nationality and loyalty: Parnellism, monarchy and the construction of Irish identity 1880–85', in D. G. Boyce and Alan O'Day (eds.), *Ireland in Transition 1867–1921* (London, 2004), pp. 35–56.

[9] Trevelyan, quoted in A. J. A. Morris, *C. P. Trevelyan 1870–1958* (Belfast, 1977), p. 14.

[10] 'Dublin Castle', in G. Smalley, *London Letters* (London, 1890), II, pp. 140–1.

[11] See A. M. Hocart, *Kings and Councillors*, ed. R. Needham (1936; London, 1970), p. 202; L. Mair, *Primitive Government* (Harmondsworth, 1962), p. 220.

ruins and death; the filth of the surrounding districts is extreme'.[12] The
exercise of viceregal pretensions amid some of the worst slum areas of
any city in the empire spoke metaphorical volumes about the relationship
between the viceregal system and the mass of the ruled.

After a hundred years from the enactment of the Union, a period which
saw the British state in Ireland gradually assume a position of equidis-
tance between the island's divided peoples, with Catholic emancipation
in 1829, disestablishment of the Anglican Church in 1869, elected local
government in 1898, regional development policies for the impoverished
west of Ireland, and the fundamental agrarian problem well on its way to
resolution with the passage of the Wyndham Act in 1903,[13] the viceregal
system remained as contentious in nationalist Ireland as it had been at
the beginning. The author and journalist, R. B. O'Brien, spelt out why
this was so in a pamphlet addressed to the Viceroy:

> You are a 'constitutional' ruler in a country whose constitution has
> been destroyed. You represent a monarchy which rests on a
> Parliamentary title. But your office has survived Parliamentary
> institutions in Ireland. The English monarchy is the embodiment of
> English nationality; the Irish Viceroyalty is the very negation of Irish
> national sentiment. Were you the representative of an absolutist
> sovereign your position would be consistent and might be strong. As
> the representative of a constitutional king it is inconsistent and
> hopelessly weak . . . A constitutional sovereign draws his strength
> from the people, but the people are not behind you.[14]

Individually respected and popular Viceroys can be identified.[15] But these
were overshadowed by a greater number of unpopular office-holders:
twenty-seven of the thirty-seven Viceroyalties between 1800 and 1909
were, according to one estimate, 'out of sympathy' with 'Irish national
feeling'.[16] Moreover, scandals in Dublin Castle, especially the insider
theft of the 'Irish Crown Jewels' – the insignia of the Order of Saint
Patrick – in July 1907,[17] added ridicule to the institution's negative
popular image.

The Viceroyalty's lack of popular support and alienation from national
traditions made its assumption of the forms and procedures of monarchy
a tempting subject of ridicule. George Moore wrote:

[12] G. Moore, *Parnell and His Island* (London, 1887), p. 20.
[13] For general surveys of developments under the Union, see K. T. Hoppen, *Ireland since
1800* (London, 1999); D. G. Boyce, *Nineteenth Century Ireland* (Dublin, 1990).
[14] R. B. O'Brien, *England's Title in Ireland* (London, 1905), pp. 3–4.
[15] E.g. Wellesley, Carlisle, Anglesey (at times), Mulgrave and Aberdeen: O'Mahoney,
Viceroys of Ireland.
[16] R. B. O'Brien, *Dublin Castle and the Irish People* (London, 1909), pp. 16–17.
[17] See F. Bamford and V. Bankes, *Vicious Circle* (London, 1965). The jewels were never
recovered.

> it is there [Dublin Castle] that the Viceroy holds his mock court
> . . . it is certain that when a man not a king is forced to mimic
> royalty as far as possible, that everything that is grotesque in the
> original becomes in imitation a caricature. . . . Underlings, hirelings
> of all sorts, swarm about this mock court like flies about a
> putrefying carcass.[18]

In fact, those appointed to the viceregal office often expressed wonder and disbelief at the transformation in public attitudes to their persons which the post entailed, and also at the duties they were expected to perform,[19] while the absurdities of the office only seemed enhanced by the seriousness with which they were performed.[20] Furthermore, it was plain that the source of the Viceroy's authority resided, not in royal origins, but in the elected government that had appointed him and whose departure from office terminated his own. Lack of regal authenticity meant that viceregal ritual did not function on a national plane above party politics, but was itself an arena for conflict. Both its form, and public reaction to it, were only too likely to be shaped by political considerations.[21] At best, the Irish Viceroyalty was a very pale and imperfect reflection of its parent, and had little to offer the latter by way of instruction – though this did not deter the outspoken Viceroy, Lord Anglesey, from giving some brutally frank advice on the practice of kingship to the rather eccentric Duke of Clarence, about to assume the throne as William IV.[22] It only added to the system's weaknesses that its abolition was a recurring issue in the nineteenth century.[23]

And yet, for all their criticism of the viceregal system, nationalist attitudes to it were far from wholly straightforward: symbolically, as O'Connell had recognized,[24] it set Ireland apart as a separate constitutional entity. Suggestions for its abolition were often based on the belief

---

[18] Moore, *Parnell and His Island*, pp. 20–4. Moore was almost matched in his contempt of the Viceroyalty by Thackeray, 'The Irish Sketchbook [1843]', in W. M. Thackeray, *Sketchbooks* (London, 1902), pp. 577–8.

[19] *The Journal of John Wodehouse, Earl of Kimberley for 1862–1902*, ed. A. Hawkins and J. Powell (Cambridge, 1997), p. 144; *Earl Cowper by His Wife* (London, 1913), p. 363; A Native, *Recollections of Dublin Castle and Dublin Society* (London, 1902), p. 6.

[20] Ibid., pp. 2–6.

[21] See, for example, Lord and Lady Aberdeen, '*We Twa*' (London, 1925), I, pp. 264–8. Unionists, of course, boycotted the viceregal functions of Home Rule Viceroys. See L. O'Broin, *The Chief Secretary: Augustine Birrell in Ireland* (London, 1965), pp. 124–5.

[22] Marquis of Anglesey, *One Leg: The Life and Letters of Henry William Paget, First Marquis of Anglesey 1768–1854* (London, 1961), pp. 226–31.

[23] In the late 1840s, Lord Clarendon was convinced that he was the last holder of the office. See 'Clarendon to Henry Reeve, 17 Dec. 1848' in H. Maxwell, *The Life and Letters of George William Frederick, Fourth Earl of Clarendon* (London, 1913), I, pp 292–4.

[24] W. J. O'Neill Daunt to the editor, *Nation*, 7 Jul. 1883.

that this would consolidate the Union.[25] In the early 1880s, opinion for and against the Viceroyalty within the broad nationalist family tended to reflect class distinctions. Those supporting its retention tended to be influenced by O'Connellite elitist preferences for a non-agrarian nationalist movement led by Ireland's social betters. Opponents came mainly from a younger, more democratic group of Parnellite MPs, at war with the Spencer Viceroyalty.[26] But the attitude of this group seems to have been driven largely by the passions of the moment. Parnell raised no objections when the Viceroyalty was retained as part of Gladstone's Home Rule scheme in 1886. Indeed, the scheme resolved the issue of what the nationalist community's attitude to the Viceroyalty should be. In 1889 the radical nationalist *Nation* declared:

> The existence of the Viceroy is inconsistent with the theory of the Incorporation . . . and the abolition of the office will be resisted by all Nationalists. The office has been put to scandalous uses, but its abuse is no proof that it cannot be turned to account for the good of both England and Ireland.[27]

So while the institution merited criticism when abused by coercive regimes, it nevertheless signified Ireland as a separate nationality, and under Home Rule would register as an authentic element of the country's constitutional life: it would be a mechanism for the expression of national identity through monarchical forms and ritual. From 1800 to 1885, however, Westminster anxieties about Ireland rendered the idea unacceptable.

II

British concerns extended further than simply securing Ireland's place in the United Kingdom. From the 1798 rebellion to the Chartist movement in the 1840s, all significant popular agitations in Britain came with fears of either Irish stimulation or actual Irish involvement. Queen Victoria remained anxious throughout her reign about the destabilizing effects in Britain of Irish agitation,[28] a fear that also motivated Unionist governments in their reformist schemes for Ireland in the period

---

[25] This was the only constitutional change for Ireland which Queen Victoria (sometimes) found acceptable. Ireland would then be governed in the same way as her beloved Scotland: S. Lee, *Queen Victoria* (London, 1904), pp. 157–8.
[26] Loughlin, 'Nationality and Loyalty', pp. 42–3.   [27] *Nation*, 18 May 1889.
[28] See, for instance, Queen to Lord Hartington, 12 Dec. 1880, RA VIC/D29/200, Windsor Castle. Material from the Royal Archives is used with the permission of Her Majesty Queen Elizabeth II.

1887–1905.[29] To concede Irish self-government seemed likely only to exacerbate Britain's internal state security, encourage enemies abroad, and suggest imperial weakness.

The rejection of Irish autonomy was buttressed by an ethnocentric frame of reference which defined Irish 'character' as emotional and unsuited to independence, unlike solid 'Anglo-Saxons' whose guiding hand Ireland was much in need of.[30] The Celtic Irish were, though, inclined to monarchical loyalty, which could be exploited for this purpose,[31] a view expounded by the middle-class *Illustrated London News* as received wisdom: 'governed very much by their imagination. . . . They are essentially Monarchical. They have instincts of reverence for the Throne. Their tendency is to adhere to a common centre, if only it . . . will admit of being embraced by their affections.'[32]

As a 'common centre' the monarchy had developed significantly, ever since the crises of the state and the patriotism they stimulated during the long Napoleonic wars began the process of setting the monarchy on a plane of national allegiance above the political fray,[33] with the ability to give meaning to everyday life. The process was given ideological underpinning in Edmund Burke's *Reflections on the Revolution in France* (1790) with its 'organic' integration of monarchy and people, and culminated in the role which the royal family with Victoria at its head came to perform as a model of middle-class values.[34] That role demonstrated its national patriotic utility in the effectiveness with which the illness of the Prince of Wales in 1872 – a royal instance of a common everyday experience – undermined the English republican movement.[35] In this context, it should be noted that addressing the realm of everyday experience was exactly how the monarchy was intended to combat Irish nationalism.

[29] L. P. Curtis Jr, *Coercion and Conciliation in Ireland 1880–1892* (New Jersey, 1963), pp. 406–8; A. Gailey, *Ireland and the Death of Kindness* (Cork, 1987), p. 3.

[30] The first substantial study of the subject, and still the most penetrating, is L. P. Curtis Jr, *Anglo-Saxons and Celts* (Bridgeport, Conn., 1968).

[31] Queen Victoria regarded W. S. Trench's Anglo-Saxonist *Realities of Irish Life* (London, 1869) – the publishing sensation of the year – as an authoritative source on Ireland: *Your Dear Letter: the Private Correspondence of Queen Victoria and the Crown Princess of Prussia 1865–1871*, ed. R. Fulford (London, 1971), p. 229.

[32] *Illustrated London News*, 5 Aug. 1871.

[33] See L. Colley, 'The apotheosis of George III: loyalty, royalty and the British nation', *Past and Present* 102 (1984), 94–129.

[34] For a lively discussion of this aspect of Victoria's persona, see A. Munich, *Queen Victoria's Secrets* (New York, 1996), p. 130, chs. 6–8. However, as Cannadine has persuasively argued, Victoria sought to remain above party politics but *governmentally* active: see D. Cannadine, 'The last Hanoverian sovereign? the Victorian monarchy in historical perspective 1688–1988' in A. L. O. Beier, D. Cannadine and J. M. Rosenheim (eds.), *The First Modern Society* (Cambridge, 1989), pp. 139–41.

[35] E. Longford, *Victoria R.I.* (London, 1964), pp. 389–91. For discussions of anti-monarchical sentiment, see A. Taylor, *'Down with the Crown'* (London, 1999); R. Williams, *The Contentious Crown* (Aldershot, 1997).

Burke, however, had made a clear distinction between Britain and Ireland, and never intended his arguments to apply to the latter. For instance, while his defence of the Protestant constitution had an obvious appeal for opponents of Catholic emancipation,[36] Burke rejected the coronation oath argument on which opposition to it was largely based.[37] More generally, while in Britain dynastic and constitutional amendments were framed in the context of traditions and a culture that legitimized those changes, in Ireland the Protestant elite's tendency to keep alive the memory of conquest and expropriation on which their power was based, together with the enforcement of the penal laws, ensured that a trans-sectarian, state-supportive, culture did not develop.[38] Whereas the traditions of Britain acted as a cement for the constitutional order, those of Ireland were subversive of it. Ireland was not simply another region of the United Kingdom like Wales and Scotland, whose local patriotic traditions were being overlaid in the early nineteenth century by a British cultural palimpsest acting to secure the state. And while the kingdom included Britain and Ireland, the monarchy's ability to symbolize or embody both islands had significant limitations.

The Glorious Revolution created a foundation myth of the modern British monarchy, a Protestant monarchy framed in opposition to those of Catholic Europe. Any departure from that model was bound to be difficult. In this context it should be noted that not only was George IV opposed to Catholic emancipation on the same grounds as George III, but despite using the coronation of the Catholic James II as a model for his own,[39] Catholic Ireland had no symbolic representation in his coronation ceremony.[40] The inability of the monarchy to conciliate Catholic Ireland during the early years of the Union left a crucially important space for O'Connell's mobilization of Ireland's nationalist traditions. O'Connell would define the constitutional tradition in the period of the Union, together with an agenda for self-government that, in an amended form, would endure until Sinn Fein decisively displaced constitutionalism at the general election of 1918.

O'Connell belongs to a category of leaders defined as 'dominant figures of society' possessed of charisma derived from 'the inherent sacredness of

---

[36] See e.g. Lord Chancellor Eldon, in H. Twiss, *The Public and Private Life of Lord Chancellor Eldon* (London, 1844), II, p. 550.

[37] Burke to Langrishe, 3 Jan. 1792. in E. Burke, *Letters, Speeches and Tracts on Irish Affairs*, ed. M. Arnold (London, 1881), p. 226.

[38] L. Gibbons, *Edmund Burke and Ireland* (Cambridge, 2003), p. 164 and *passim*.

[39] R. Fulford, *George IV* (London, 1935), p. 225.

[40] See Lords of the Committee of Council appointed to Consider of His Majesty's Coronation to George IV, 16 July 1821, *The Letters of King George IV*, ed. A. Aspinall (Cambridge, 1938), III, p. 446. Duke of Buckingham and Chandos, *Memoirs of the Court of George IV* (London, 1859), I, p. 181.

central authority'[41] – in fact, figures possessed of 'royal' authority. Others can be identified in Britain and Ireland during the Union period, such as Wellington, the great hero of Waterloo, Parnell, the Home Rule leader in the 1880s, and Sir Edward Carson.[42] Wellington's 'central authority' was demonstrated by his insistence on forcing through, against the King's will, Catholic emancipation to avert rebellion in Ireland. It was brilliantly caught in a political cartoon drawing on the ancient notion of the monarch as the centre of the universe, but with the royal presence of George IV obliterated by the Duke (Fig. 4.1). Nevertheless, unlike O'Connell, the authority of Wellington and Carson was exercised to preserve the constitutional *status quo* – in the latter's case to the point of civil war.

O'Connell's regal charismatic presence was widely subscribed to; for example, in forms of political ceremonial, popular addresses, anecdotes and, not least, the inclination of the Orange press to present him as someone who, in a self-governing Ireland, would not be a subject of, but a 'balance' to, the sovereign.[43] It was a regality *Punch* was quick to ridicule (Fig. 4.2).[44] In fact, in the Irish folk tradition the Anglo-Irish relationship was metaphorically reconfigured in a story of O'Connell, possessed of great sexual prowess, having Queen Victoria as a mistress.[45]

By the late 1820s, O'Connell had virtually come to personify Ireland in folk myth; he has a much larger presence than other nationalist leaders such as Wolfe Tone, Thomas Davis or Parnell,[46] and accompanied the Young Pretender, Charles Edward Stuart, and Napoleon as saviours of Ireland.[47] Yet while O'Connell was adept at exploiting Irish historical grievances and traditions to serve the cause of Repeal, he was careful to situate his arguments historically within the ideological carapace of the Glorious Revolution; and politically in the context of British concerns about Napoleonic France – which coincided with his own – at a time when British identity itself was assuming the shape it would take during the Union period. The Ireland O'Connell was publicly arguing for was one that accepted the monarch as a hegemonic source of allegiance, and, by implication, identity. He stressed the loyalty of the Catholic Irish to William III and his Hanoverian successors, rejection of James II and

[41] C. Geertz, 'Centers, Kings and charisma: reflections on the symbolics of power', in J. Ben-David and T. N. Clark (eds.), *Culture and Its Creators* (Chicago, 1975), p. 171.

[42] Loughlin, 'Nationality and loyalty', pp. 35–7; A. Gailey, 'King Carson: an essay on the invention of leadership', *Irish Historical Studies* 30 (1996), 66–87.

[43] W. J. O'Neill Daunt, *Personal Recollections of O'Connell* (London, 1848), I, pp. 69, 98–9, 108, 130–1; II, pp. 152–3.

[44] 'King O'Connell at Tara', *Punch* (1843).

[45] See D. Ó Muirithe, 'O'Connell in the Irish folk tradition', in K. B. Nowlan and M. R. O'Connell (eds.), *Daniel O'Connell* (Belfast, 1984), p. 59.

[46] R. Uí Ógain, *Immortal Dan* (Dublin, 1996), p. 1.   [47] Ibid., p. 87.

Figure 4.1. *Eclipse of the King.* © Copyright the Trustees of the British Museum.

the Jacobite tradition,[48] and also accepted Ireland's place in a culturally and commercially British world. O'Connell's primary concern was not cultural identity but constitutional autonomy. In a self-governing Ireland the King would not be an English King but an 'Irish King', in an Irish constitution, together with 'an Irish House of Lords and an Irish House of Commons'.[49]

---

[48] O'Connell's speeches, 1800, 1810, 1812–13, in *The Life and Speeches of Daniel O'Connell*, ed. J. O'Connell (Dublin, 1846), I, pp. 31, 153, 266, 343–4; O'Connell in the Commons, 4 Mar. 1831, in M. F.Cusack, *The Speeches and Public Letters of the Liberator* (Dublin, 1875), I, p. 106.

[49] O'Connell speaking on repeal, 18 Sep. 1810, in *Life and Speeches of O'Connell*, I, p. 55.

KING O'CONNELL AT TARA.

Figure 4.2. 'King O'Connell at Tara'. From Punch, 1843.

It would be wrong to conclude that O'Connell's speeches consisted only of loyal utterances. Indeed, the need to address the very different sensibilities of British opinion and those of native Catholic Irishmen provoked the jibe in Parliament that there must be another Mr O'Connell speaking outside the House.[50] Moreover, when it became clear that Queen Victoria had no sympathy with the Repeal demand, O'Connell's personal attitude towards her was far from friendly.[51] Nevertheless, he had a profound influence on the constitutional tradition's attitude to monarchy. The notion of loyalty to the throne in a symbiotic relationship with Irish self-government would be its central thread: effusively so with the first leader of the Home Rule movement, Isaac Butt;[52] reluctantly at first for Parnellites until Gladstone's conversion to Home

[50] R. B. McDowell, *Public Opinion and Government Policy in Ireland 1801–1846* (London, 1952), p. 121.
[51] J. Loughlin, 'Allegiance and illusion: Queen Victoria's Irish visit of 1849', *History* 87 (2002), 494.
[52] J. Loughlin, 'Isaac Butt', in Connolly, *Irish History*, p. 69; D. Thornley, *Isaac Butt and Home Rule* (London, 1964).

Rule;[53] and especially so for the last leader of the movement, the pro-imperial John Redmond.[54] Certainly in the nationalist critique of British rule in Ireland under the Union it was generally the case that no explicit attack was made on the person of the sovereign,[55] a position encouraged by the progressive disengagement of the monarch from the corridors of political power.[56]

Nevertheless, O'Connell's attempt to eliminate, or at least neutralize, the politically damaging effects of the chasm Burke had identified between Irish and British traditions had only limited success. Arguably, his own national prominence inhibited monarchical allegiance, but certainly the recurring problems of land and poverty in Ireland acted as a stimulus to the energizing of bitter historical memories,[57] leaving later nationalists open to the same charge of political duplicity that faced O'Connell.[58] Also, the rise of Catholic nationalism, in turn, helped reinforce Ireland's internal sectarian divisions.

III

It is against a background of recurring economic crises, sectarian division and political disaffection that the monarchy's *active* role in Anglo-Irish relations has to be assessed. That role had its origins in George IV's visit to Ireland in 1821, shortly after his coronation on 19 July, and, among other things, is noteworthy as marking the beginning of the royal tours that became characteristic of the modern British monarchy. In the Irish context it appeared to effect a remarkable harmony between Ireland's bitterly divided ethno-religious factions, demonstrated in a collective outpouring of unbounded allegiance to the throne. The visit appeared to defy rational explanation. The Irish Catholic peer, Lord Cloncurry, recorded that 'a strange madness seemed at that juncture to seize people of all ranks in Ireland', madness he admitted to having shared himself.[59] Countess

[53] J. Loughlin, *Gladstone, Home Rule and the Ulster Question 1882–93* (Dublin, 1986), ch. 4.

[54] P. Bew, *John Redmond* (Dundalk, 1997).

[55] See e.g. R. B. O'Brien, *A Hundred Years of Irish History*, intro. John Redmond (London, n.d. [1902]). Parnell, however, attacked Queen Victoria's famine contributions in the 1840s during a fund-raising tour of North America in 1880: Loughlin, 'Nationality and loyalty', p. 36.

[56] As the *Nation* (14 Oct. 1871) put it: 'the royal prerogative . . . is now the very deadest of dead letters.' But see F. Hardie, *The Political Influence of Queen Victoria* (Oxford, 1937).

[57] Loughlin, *Gladstone*, pp. 33–4.

[58] The Ulster Orange Leader, Colonel Saunderson, for example, delighted in exposing the contradictions of nationalist arguments in his pamphlet, *Two Irelands, or Loyalty Versus Treason* (Dublin, 1884).

[59] Lord Cloncurry, *Personal Recollections* (Dublin, 1849), p. 277.

Glengall described a mood in Dublin close to hysteria: 'Bedlam broke loose would be tame and rational to the madness of this whole nation.'[60] The architectural historian, Maurice Craig, has suggested its source in the loss of Ireland's native parliament and sense of national cohesion: 'an era of individuals, of occurrences apparently isolated and apparently without meaning . . . How else but in isolation can we regard the fantastic scenes at the visit of George IV in 1821.'[61]

The success of the visit can be explained, partially at least, by reference to a number of background factors. The scene-setting was congenial. In April 1821, a Catholic relief bill had passed in the Commons, and, though rejected by the Lords, it was a positive signal encouraging Catholic support for the forthcoming royal visit; especially by the presentation of non-contentious addresses of welcome from Catholic prelates[62] whose Church had abandoned the Stuart cause in the 1760s and embraced conciliation of the Hanoverian regime.[63] Also, a 'Letter' addressed to 'the People of Ireland', quite likely inspired by the Dublin Castle authorities, disassociated the King from any responsibility for the defeat of the recent Catholic relief bill.[64] Moreover, against a background of increasing economic hardship,[65] the proclamation of the visit provided a welcome stimulus to trade, from the letting of houses to the engagement of services and manufacturing – the latter apparently given a special stimulus by a request from the King that all his subjects approach him in Irish-made attire[66] – and no less a stimulus to personal ambition with an inevitable scramble for honours.[67] In sum, the visit and the enthusiasm it engendered can be seen as driven by its own self-sustaining socioeconomic dynamic. A further factor was that while George IV was publicly reviled in England,[68] in an Irish context he could be read much more positively.

[60] Countess Glengall to Mrs F. Taylor, 27 Aug. 1821, in *Creevy*, ed. J. Gore (London, 1949), pp. 218–9.

[61] M. Craig, *Dublin 1660–1860* (Dublin, 1952), p. 307.

[62] Sir J. Parnell to D. Scully, 19 Apr. 1821, in D. Scully, *The Catholic Question in Ireland and England*, ed. B. McDermot (Dublin, 1988), p. 648.

[63] M. Buschkühl, *Great Britain and the Holy See 1746–1870* (Dublin, 1982), chs. 1–3.

[64] Anon, *The King's Visit to Ireland, in a Letter Addressed to the People of Ireland* (Dublin, 1821), *passim*.

[65] Gearoid Ó Tuathaigh, *Ireland Before the Famine 1798–1848* (Dublin, 1972), pp. 137–8.

[66] *Dublin Evening Post*, 19 Jul. 1821; S. H. Burke, *Ireland Sixty Years Ago: Being an Account of a Visit to Ireland by H. M. King George IV in the Year 1821* (London, 1885), p. 29. For a sense of the volume of activity the visit generated, see the materials relevant to Queen Victoria's first visit to Ireland in 1849 (HO45/2522, National Archives).

[67] S. Lynam, *Humanity Dick Martin, 'King of Connemara'* (Dublin, 1989), p. 200.

[68] J. H. Plumb, *The First Four Georges* (London, 1966), p. 151: 'Few monarchies have struggled under the weight of such . . . self-indulgent vulgarity.'

It was noted that he was the first monarch to come to Ireland in a spirit
of conciliation, and had a reformist history. But most importantly, the
King was known as the 'secret' husband of Mrs Fitzherbert, a Roman
Catholic. Accordingly, the expectations of many Catholics, especially
prelates with powerful influence among the laity, were high, and gave
a lead through their participation in the events of the visit.[69] No less
important was the enthusiastic participation of O'Connell, who defined
the visit's success in terms of the elevation of Ireland's Catholic community to a position of equality with Protestants through the agency of the
King's favour.[70] For his part, the King, whose ability to 'work' a public
gathering was considerable,[71] responded equally well to the enthusiasm
of the Dublin populace. He was especially solicitous of Catholic clerical and lay sensibilities,[72] and made significant charitable donations.[73]
Moreover, throughout the visit he had the company of his mistress, Lady
Conyngham of Slane Castle; while Dublin was unaffected by the controversy over his treatment of the late Queen that convulsed London,[74] and
showed no inclination to mourn her passing.[75] Unsurprisingly, he repeatedly compared 'the triumph of Dublin' with the 'horrors of London'.[76]

And yet merely a description of the events of the visit would hardly be
an adequate explanation of its success. In fact, George IV came to Ireland
with the prerequisites for mass adulation already in place, that is, royal
charisma derived from an integration of symbolism and power.[77] The
King was not just the central symbol of the constitutional order, but in
a pre-Bagehotian age – when the Crown still wielded significant political
authority – an authentic embodiment of the power the order possessed;
and the charisma generated was likely to be all the more effective if we
accept the view that it is most influential among those furthest away
from the centre of power[78] – indicated in the Irish context by 'the print
of his sacred feet cut in stone' at the point of the King's landing at

[69] W. J. Fitzpatrick, *The Life, Times and Correspondence of Dr Doyle* (Dublin, 1880), p. 181.

[70] Burke, *Ireland Sixty Years Ago*, pp. 28–9; T. C. Luby, *The Life and Times of Daniel O'Connell* (Glasgow, n.d.), p. 458; R. Dunlop, *Daniel O'Connell and the Revival of National Life in Ireland* (London, 1900), pp. 113–6.

[71] Anon, *A Brief Account of the Coronation of His Majesty George IV, 19 July 1821* (London, 1821).

[72] Major General Sir A. Barnard to Lady A. Barnard, 21 Aug. 1821, in *Barnard Letters 1778–1824*, ed. A. Powell (London, 1928), p. 297; Burke, *Ireland Sixty Years Ago*, p. 31; Cloncurry, *Personal recollections*, p. 278.

[73] Burke, *Ireland Sixty Years Ago*, p. 23. See also F. Prochaska, *Royal Bounty* (London, 1995), pp. 42–3.

[74] He sought to have her legally barred from assuming the throne as his Consort.

[75] W. H. Freemantle to Duke of Buckingham, 26 Aug. 1821, in Buckingham, *Memoirs of the Court of George IV*, I, p. 194.

[76] Diary entry, 17 Aug. 1821, in *The Croker Papers 1808–1857*, ed. B. Pool (1884; abridged edn., London, 1967), p. 61.

[77] Geertz, 'Centers, kings and charisma', p. 151.   [78] Ibid.

Howth.[79] Moreover, against a background of Catholic hopes, it can be argued that George IV came to this, the most troubled part of his kingdom, generating expectations derived from the properties traditionally associated with the kingly office, especially 'a source of justice and assistance to all members alike of a polity that in other contexts seems to be sharply divided.'[80] Thus, in the Irish context, the power of royal charisma lay in its ability to create, however temporarily, the social reality to validate the myth of national unity monarchy represented.

It would be difficult to ascribe the success of the visit to *ritual* effectiveness – as a mechanism of regulated contact intended to instil public awe and loyalty[81] – for the ritual of the Dublin visit provides ample evidence to support David Cannadine's argument on the incompetence of royal ritual in the early nineteenth century.[82] An elaborate procedure arranged for his intended port of Dunleary on 12 August, his birthday – from where he was to depart Ireland on 5 September – proved redundant when, to acknowledge the Queen's death just before he sailed for Ireland, he decided to disembark privately at Howth instead.[83] But he arrived drunk, threw himself into the midst of a harbour-side crowd, then proceeded to Phoenix Park accompanied by a boisterous, disorderly entourage.[84] The immediacy and unregulated nature of the contact between monarch and his Irish subjects accords with a condition anthropologists recognize as 'liminal';[85] a condition the King himself seemed to recognize when in a brief speech taking leave of his entourage, he declared: 'rank, station and honour are nothing; to feel that I live in the hearts of my Irish subjects, is to me the most exalted happiness.'[86] Moreover, when an alternative official entry to the city was arranged on 17 August, attended reportedly by a procession of 40,000 with 20,000 on horseback,[87] the King was again largely the instigator of popular reactions that led to the massive crowd assembled becoming almost uncontrollable, with the result that

---

[79] Glengall to Mrs F. Taylor, 27 Aug. 1821, in *Creevey*, pp. 218–9. The spot was later marked by a brass plate.

[80] Mair, *Primitive Government*, p. 229.

[81] For a discussion in regard to Queen Victoria's visit of 1849, see Loughlin, 'Allegiance and illusion', 507.

[82] D. Cannadine, 'The context, performance and meaning of ritual: the British monarchy and the "invention of tradition", c. 1820–1977', in E. Hobsbawm and T. Ranger (eds.), *The Invention of Tradition* (Cambridge, 1983), pp. 101–2.

[83] See George IV to Sir W. Knighton, 10 Aug. 1821, in *Memoirs of Sir William Knighton*, ed. Lady Knighton (London, 1838), I, pp. 144–8.

[84] W. H. Freemantle to the Duke of Buckingham, 26 Aug. 1821 in Buckingham, *Memoirs of the Court of George IV*, II, p. 194.

[85] See V. Turner, *Dramas, Fields and Metaphors* (London, 1974), pp. 273–4.

[86] Anon., *The Royal Visit, Containing a Full Circumstantial Account of Everything Connected with the King's Visit to Ireland* (Dublin, 1821), p. 14.

[87] Ibid., p. 43.

his carriage 'was at times so shaken that the noblemen who sat opposite his Majesty were under the necessity of supporting the arms of the King, to enable him to stand in an erect posture.'[88] Yet ritual disorder counted for little compared to the enthusiasm of the Dublin crowds, apparently expressing unadulterated loyalty. Such an impression was undoubtedly facilitated by the situational identity the city assumed for the visit.

All the usual, and divisive, architectural and sculptural signifiers of political allegiance in the metropolis were overshadowed by arches, banners and illustrations celebrating the King, his coronation, the general beneficence of the United Kingdom of Great Britain and Ireland, and the empire. Public buildings were illuminated and firework displays performed.[89] In sum, for the duration of the visit, Dublin was a celebratory symbolic context that transcended its usual, divisive identity, evident especially in the re-signifying of Dublin Castle, from the functional and symbolic centre of Ireland's coercion, to a location for the holding of events in which the country's political antagonisms dissolved in common expressions of loyal allegiance.

The royal visit of 1821 was of profound significance for the relationship of the monarchy to Ireland in the nineteenth century. As the first such event, it set a template for later visits and appeared to offer startling proof that the nationalist threat to the Union of Britain and Ireland could be successfully met. Certainly enough personal and anecdotal evidence emerged during the visit to support this view, leading the King to ascribe Ireland's formerly rebellious state to 'misrule'.[90]

Burke's 'organic' conception of the monarchy's relationship to state and society recognized no categories or forms of self that it could not inform and give meaning to. The royal visit, framed outside the party political sphere, appeared to demonstrate magnificently what was possible when the monarch and his people were brought into direct personal, 'authentic' contact. It gave powerful reinforcement to ideas that would underpin Westminster's Irish policy in the nineteenth century, especially the view that separatist movements did not represent the 'real' interests of ordinary people, who were naturally loyal to the Crown, and that the most effective means of eliciting loyal sentiment was to bring the Irish people more often into contact with royalty. George IV himself seemed to endorse this view when, in 1823, he declared that the only way to settle the question of Catholic rights and 'quiet' the country would be to hold a parliament in

---

[88] Burke, *Ireland Sixty Years Ago*, p. 15.   [89] Ibid., pp. 45–59.

[90] Ibid., p. 12; Sidmouth to Bathurst, 26 Aug. 1821, in Historical Manuscripts Commission, *Report on the Manuscripts of Earl Bathurst* (London, 1923), pp. 510–1; S. Leslie, *George IV* (London, 1930), pp. 138–9.

Ireland every three years,[91] which he, presumably, would have formally inaugurated.

As spectacle, the Irish visit could not compare with the great exhibition of national tartanry that seemed to convulse Scotland on the occasion of the King's visit in 1822.[92] But the Irish visit was politically more significant. The Scottish visit was confirmatory, a symbolic affirmation of Scotland's place in the United Kingdom and a wider developing British world. The Irish visit, however, was freighted with lessons on how to deal with one of the most serious problems facing the British state. A recurring remedy suggested for this problem in the nineteenth century was an Irish royal residence, which O'Connell strongly argued for in 1821.[93] What gave credibility to such thinking was how, at crucial points in the Union period, highly successful royal visits took place offering dramatic contrasts with recent rebellious activities.

George IV's visit of 1821 was replicated by Queen Victoria's enormously successful visit of August 1849.[94] Palmerston had assured the Prime Minister, Russell, that the Queen could rely on Irish 'character' to make it so.[95] Following the Young Ireland rising of 1848 and the devastation of the famine, the timing of the visit was not at first sight propitious. But an Irish visit had been mooted fruitlessly so many times since Victoria's accession that the feeling was that it had to take place now to avert the impression that the Queen was afraid to come. It is against this unpromising background that the remarkable outpouring of Irish loyalty, outdoing that of 1821, has to be seen. The fact that Victoria was in the early stage of a reign that would last over sixty years gave the 'lesson' of 1849 an enduring credibility, a reassuring experience and point of reference for future British administrations grappling with Irish disaffection. Again, the visit of 1849 was, unlike that of George IV in 1821, a visit by a royal *family* that was coming to be seen as the embodiment of British middle-class values. These values were respected in post-famine Ireland no less than in Britain, ensuring that the Queen rarely attracted personal abuse. In this context it is worth noting that Victoria proved as adept at exploiting mass emotions as George IV, but devoid of his display of intoxicated camaraderie. The visit of 1849 was a demonstration of the ritual effectiveness that would increasingly characterize royal performances in

---

[91] C. Wynn to Duke of Buckingham, 18 Dec. 1823, in Buckingham, *Memoirs of the Court of George IV*, II, p. 20.

[92] See J. Prebble, *The King's Jaunt* (London, 1988).

[93] *Freeman's Journal*, 31 Aug. 1821.

[94] See Loughlin, 'Allegiance and illusion', *passim*; J. Murphy, *Abject Loyalty* (Washington, 1999), ch. 3; W. Arnstein, *Queen Victoria* (Basingstoke, 2003), pp. 78–82.

[95] Palmerston to Russell, 5 Aug. 1849, in *The Later Correspondence of Lord John Russell*, ed. G. P. Gooch (London, 1925), I, p. 235.

the later nineteenth century, serving to affirm the utility of monarchy in dissolving Irish alienation from the British state as the experience of 1849 was repeated.

The Prince and Princess of Wales made a highly successful visit in 1868, following the Fenian rising of 1867.[96] Their return to Ireland in 1871 was significantly less so, and that of 1885 distinctly ill-timed, coming at the height of a Parnellite campaign against the Spencer Viceroyalty.[97] Nevertheless, in the longer term, 1885 could be seen as a reference point from which to chart the efficacy of nearly twenty years of Unionist reforms in Ireland. Intended to address the 'real' grievances of the Irish people, the reforms culminated in the Wyndham Act of 1903, which effectively solved the land question. It proved to be the perfect background to Edward VII's massively successful coronation tour of 1903, which Queen Victoria had signalled with her own congenial visit of 1900.[98] Only a variety of small groups associated with the emergent cultural/republican nationalism were intent on demonstrating irreconcilable opposition to the presence of a foreign Queen,[99] making the point that the visit could not marginalize Ireland's nationalist traditions.

The differences between Britain and Ireland regarding popular attitudes to monarchy (all the more striking given the great popular devotion to the monarch in the late nineteenth century Britain) were, ironically, actually facilitated by some of the Unionist reforms in Ireland. The concession of elected local government in 1898, for instance, resulted in the emergence of nationalist controlled councils all over Ireland. The vast majority of these, outside north-east Ulster, refused to participate in the celebrations marking the coronation of Edward VII in 1902.[100] Nevertheless, this apparent lack of loyalty provided a striking contrast to the success of the King's coronation tour of Ireland in August 1903.

The visit owed much of its success to the personality of the King, long regarded as more sympathetic to Ireland than his mother.[101] In fact, he was credited mistakenly with Home Rule sympathies, a mistake that almost certainly had its source in the often expressed support for Irish

---

[96] R. V. Comerford, *The Fenians in Context* (Dublin, 1998), pp. 153–5.
[97] Loughlin, 'Nationality and loyalty', pp. 40–56.
[98] *Irish Daily Independent*, 12, 27 Apr. 1900; *Irish Times*, 26 Apr. 1900. Sir H. Robinson, *Memories: Wise and Otherwise* (London, 1924), ch. 17; Lee, *Queen Victoria*, pp. 545–6; Arnstein, *Queen Victoria*, p. 192.
[99] See M. Gonne, *A Servant of the Queen* ed. A. N. Jeffares and A. M. White (1938; Chicago, 1995), pp. 269–70; S. Pašeta, 'Nationalist responses to two royal visits to Ireland 1900 and 1903', *Irish Historical Studies*, 31 (1999), 489–97.
[100] *The Times*, 24 Jun. 1902.
[101] See A. M. Sullivan, *Old Ireland: Reminiscences of an Irish K. C.* (London, 1927), p. 23.

autonomy of his wife, Queen Alexandra.[102] This impression could only have been lent verisimilitude by an Irish Viceroy, Lord Dudley, given to pro-nationalist sentiments.[103] Moreover, the Wyndham Land Act, which would effectively solve Ireland's long-running agrarian problem, was proceeding through its final parliamentary stages as the visit got under way. This was not entirely coincidental: the King had facilitated its passage and received credit for it in Ireland.[104] The visit was also attended by an unlikely fortuitous development.

As the royal yacht proceeded to Ireland, it became known that Pope Leo XIII had died. The King, though personally unaffected,[105] responded by implying that he was, making a number of very public gestures of acknowledgement.[106] In a period of greatly developing Catholic piety the King's actions resonated powerfully with Irish opinion, reflected in the comment of a little girl who said, 'I am so glad that we may love the King now because he spoke so nicely about the Pope.'[107] A radical nationalist intention to turn Catholics against the King by circulating the crudely anti-Catholic oath that formed part of his Declaration of Accession,[108] if it took place, clearly had little impact on public opinion. Opposition to the visit did result in the rejection of a proposal to offer the King an official welcome by Dublin Corporation, and none of the more than eighty addresses submitted to the King in southern Ireland came from a publicly elected assembly.[109] Rather, they came from professional, ecclesiastical, mercantile and scientific bodies.[110] But of course anti-Home Rule opinion in Britain was more inclined to find the authentic expression of Irish opinion in these institutions of civil society.[111]

But the success of the visit owed a great deal to the sure-footedness of the King. Having created a favourable context for it, he took care to devote himself to 'welfareist' activities of great concern to the everyday life of the Irish people.[112] Edward's conciliation of Irish Catholic sentiment led to

---

[102] Reginald, Viscount Esher, *Journals and Letters*, ed. M. V. Brett (London, 1934), I, p. 161 (4 Sep. 1892).

[103] Robinson, *Memories*, pp. 149–50.

[104] W. O'Brien, *An Olive Branch in Ireland and its History* (London, 1910), pp. 242–3; *Illustrated London News*, 25 Jul. 1903.

[105] See Wyndham to his sister Pamela, 25 Jul. 1903, in *Life and Letters of George Wyndham*, ed. J. W. Mackail and G. Wyndham (London, n.d.), II, p. 461.

[106] Elizabeth, Countess of Fingall, *Seventy Years Young* (New York, 1939), p. 284; *Illustrated London News*, 25 Jul. 1903; S. Lee, *King Edward VII* (London, 1927), II, pp. 161–3.

[107] Wyndham to Balfour, 26 July 1903, in *Life and Letters of George Wyndham*, II, p. 466.

[108] Gonne, *Servant of the Queen*, p. 323.

[109] Pašeta, 'Nationalist responses to two royal visits', 501.

[110] Earl of Meath, *Memories of the Twentieth Century* (London, 1924), p. 67.

[111] *Illustrated London News* (1 Aug. 1903) regarded the addresses as indicative of 'the spontaneous good-will of the Irish people'.

[112] See *Illustrated London News*, 1 Aug. 1903; Robinson, *Memories*, ch. 17.

privately expressed, disparaging remarks about 'Popish Ned' in Ulster,[113] but he was received enthusiastically in the North and credited with having 'stilled sectarian passions'.[114] By the time of the last important royal visit of the Union period, that of George V in 1911, Irish Catholicism had obtained further concessions.

In 1908, the great running sore of Irish higher education – the issue of a university the Catholic hierarchy could support – was removed with the establishment of the National University. And a highly significant gesture was made by George V, when he made clear his refusal to open Parliament unless the highly offensive anti-Catholic clauses of the Declaration of Accession were removed.[115] Moreover, as a monarchical acknowledgement – and appropriation – of Irish identity, the coronation is noteworthy for the fact that The O'Conor Don, a direct descendant of the last Irish High King, Rory O'Conor, carried the Standard of Ireland.[116]

The coronation visit to Ireland lasted only five days, from 8 to 12 July, and was in many ways a duplication of that of 1903. Dublin Corporation again refused an official welcome and radical nationalists sought, without much success, to disrupt royal events.[117] The nationalist leader, John Redmond, showed tolerance for the visit, if not enthusiasm, but again, as in 1903, it was the Catholic hierarchy that was to the fore in welcoming the royal party. Cardinal Logue greeted the King when he visited Maynooth, and the Catholic population in general gave the royal visitors an enthusiastic welcome on a par with, if not exceeding, that of 1903.[118]

The most significant difference between the two visits was the political context in which that of 1911 took place. A Liberal government was now in power, dependent on Irish Nationalist votes, and the power of the House of Lords to veto Commons legislation was about to be ended by the Parliament Act, leaving the path to the enactment of Home Rule open. It was a context that lent urgency to the claims of leading Unionist prints, the *Daily Telegraph* and the *Standard*, that popular enthusiasm for the King was an act of defiance against nationalist 'wire-pullers', led by clergy believed to have the power to determine the actions of the Catholic people.[119] Thus, in the final years of the Union, royal visits continued to validate opposition to Irish autonomy. However, while the need to build

[113] S. Leslie, *Long Shadows* (London, 1966), p. 130.   [114] *The Times*, 30 Jul. 1903.
[115] H. Nicolson, *King George V* (London, 1952), p. 162.
[116] M. Bence-Jones and H. M. Massingberd, *The British Aristocracy* (London, 1979), p. 148.
[117] See M. Ward, *Unmanageable Revolutionaries* (London, 1995), pp. 76–8.
[118] See *Freeman's Journal*, 13 Jul. 1911.
[119] Extensive reports from both papers were provided as examples of misrepresentation in *Freeman's Journal*.

upon the loyalty the visits appeared to elicit was recognized, it proved difficult to effect.

IV

The most popular means of doing so was through the establishment of a royal residence, but this proved problematic. First mooted during the royal visit of 1821, the proposal tended to run in tandem with the issue of abolition of the Viceroyalty, and with Balmoral as a model.[120] But Ireland was not Scotland. The latter was a largely contented part of the United Kingdom, and Balmoral could be both an unproblematic focus of loyalty and a congenial domestic residence. An Irish royal residence, on the other hand, was freighted with much greater expectations – to subvert separatist sentiment in a politically volatile environment.

In this context, the endemic nature of Ireland's socio-economic and political problems functioned to undermine the optimistic expectations that royal visits tended to generate. Like that of 1821, the visit of 1849 represented, essentially, a triumph of charismatic spectacle over political reality – the chasm between British and Irish national traditions was disguised, not dissolved. And for Queen Victoria, who defined allegiance to the throne in very personal terms, the re-emergence of republican and constitutional nationalism in Ireland thereafter was only too likely to be read as treachery.[121] By the early 1860s she had become disabused of the notion that royal visits, however successful, would be effective weapons in the struggle against Irish disaffection, and likewise unconvinced that a royal residence would be any better. Attempts to press the issue merely incurred royal displeasure,[122] though it remained a subject of debate until the end of the century.[123]

The Queen's fears were not without foundation. The issue of most concern in an agricultural country – land – took thirty-three years to be effectively addressed from 1870, and even then only under the pressure of agricultural crises and disorder that served to revive the memory of historical grievances dating from the land confiscations of the seventeenth century. The mid-Victorian period, which constitutes a historical 'gap' between the great national movements of O'Connell and Parnell, when

---

[120] *Punch* ridiculed the proposal in 1869 with a political cartoon entitled 'The Irish Balmoral', showing the Prince and Princess of Wales trekking across the barren west of Ireland on donkeys.

[121] Loughlin, 'Allegiance and illusion', 496.

[122] P. Magnus, *Gladstone* (London, 1954), ch. 9.

[123] J. G. S. McNeill, 'The Irish lord-lieutenancy and a royal residence', *Fortnightly Review* (Oct. 1897), 504–12.

'localism' characterized Irish politics,[124] and which opened with Queen Victoria's Irish visit of 1849, might have been more effectively exploited than it was. The visit of the Queen and Prince Albert in 1853 to open the Dublin Exhibition[125] and encourage the peaceful arts of industry was a useful initiative, but it was not associated with government action on the land question, agitation on which by a mobilizing tenantry was just beginning.[126] The only part of Ireland that was fiercely committed to the Crown and the Union by mid-century was Protestant north-east Ulster. However, monarchy did not shape the identity of loyalism, but rather was subsumed within its forms and practices; as such it served only to complicate the role Westminster hoped monarchy would play in Ireland as a whole.

Left to develop, the land issue impacted on Irish society in ways that further complicated government ambitions. The 'Romanization' of Catholic religious practice under the leadership of Archbishop Cullen from 1850 led to a great expansion of the lower clergy with strong links to the tenant-farmer class, and all too often sharing its political radicalism. During the height of land agitation in the late nineteenth century, their influence served to inhibit the natural tendency of many prelates to comply with viceregal wishes, and, accordingly, the legitimizing of Irish royal occasions.[127]

Again, the development of popular nationalism found expression in conflicts over the signifying of Dublin's urban space from the early 1860s that had negative royal effects. Queen Victoria's alienation from Ireland really started to take shape when nationalists opposed the erection of a statue of her beloved Prince Albert on College Green.[128] In this context, the politically unproblematic erection of Belfast's Albert memorial on a central site in the late 1860s was both a powerful structural signifier of a developing regional identity, and a useful overture for royal sympathy.

The controversy over Dublin's Albert statue signalled a campaign to assert a more distinctively nationalist presence in the cityscape, especially through the erection of the O'Connell monument in Sackville Street. Begun in 1865 and completed in 1882, at the height of the Parnellite agitation, it was an impressive monumental challenge to the symbolic

---

[124] The most important work to address the issue of localism is T. K. Hoppen, *Elections, Politics and Society in Ireland 1832–1885* (Oxford, 1984).

[125] J. Hone, 'Queen Victoria in Ireland', *History Today* 3 (1953), 501–10.

[126] F. S. L. Lyons, *Ireland Since the Famine* (London, 1973), pp. 115–22.

[127] See E. Larkin, *The Making of the Roman Catholic Church in Ireland 1850–1860* (Chapel Hill, N.C., 1980), pp. 3–95; D. Bowen, *The Protestant Crusade in Ireland 1800–70* (Dublin, 1978), pp. 230–1; T. Garvin, *The Evolution of Irish Nationalist Politics* (Dublin, 1981), pp. 55–7.

[128] E. Darby and N. Smith, *The Cult of the Prince Consort* (London, 1983), pp. 70–3.

British dominance of Dublin's central thoroughfare represented by Nelson's Pillar.[129]

These activities went together with the growth of popular democracy in the second half of the nineteenth century, ensuring that nationalist forces, riding on the back of – often violent – agrarian agitation, would find representation, and thus political influence, at Westminster in a way that made the addressing of their concerns urgent. Gladstone's conversion to Home Rule and the construction of his highly ambitious Home Rule scheme of 1886 was the outcome.

What is especially significant for our purposes is that Gladstone's guides in constructing his scheme were Burke's writings on Ireland – a 'magazine of wisdom'[130] – and O'Connell's professions of loyalty to the monarchy, which convinced him that nationality with loyalty could indeed be achieved through a properly constructed scheme. His would concede internal Irish self-government within the existing structures of the British state, thereby providing a mechanism for the growth of British patriotism with its focus on the sovereign to develop alongside local Irish nationality.[131] In this context, as we have seen, nationalist opinion came to regard the Irish Viceroyalty as the constitutional mechanism through which these separate strands of identity could be harmonized. But Gladstone's attempt to frame Irish allegiance to the monarchy through self-governing institutions provoked Conservatives into explicitly identifying the throne with Unionism, with the suggestion that Home Rule would damage irreparably the monarchic identity of the British state (Fig. 4.3).

The Unionist campaign did not prevent Gladstone's return to power in 1892, and the introduction of a second Home Rule bill; nevertheless, the collapse of the Parnellite movement over the O'Shea divorce scandal in 1891 undoubtedly diminished British support for the policy, and also created the space for a new cultural nationalism to develop. It was intensely preoccupied with the question of identity and what it meant to be Irish,[132] and addressed that issue, as we have seen, through opposition to the royal visits of 1900, 1903 and 1911. By the early years of the twentieth century, the opening that constitutional nationalism had provided for the state to shape Irish identity in a monarchical mode since the time of O'Connell began to close.

---

[129] For a discussion of nationalist monument building, see G. Owens, 'Nationalist monuments in Ireland c. 1870–1914: symbolism and ritual', in B. P. Kennedy and R. Gillespie (eds.), *Ireland: Art into History* (Dublin, 1994), pp. 103–17.

[130] Diary, 18 Dec. 1885, quoted in J. Morley, *The Life of Gladstone* (London, 1903), III, p. 211.

[131] See Loughlin, *Gladstone*, chs. 3 and 7.

[132] See S. Pašeta, *Before the Revolution* (Cork, 1999), ch. 9.

Figure 4.3. *The Royal Standard as Unionist Propaganda.* From *National Union Pamphlets,* c. 1890.

V

The Irish cultural debate of these years, transcending the unionist and nationalist communities, still had a place for the monarchy. One aspect was concerned about whether the Stone of Scone, which resided under the coronation chair in Westminster Abbey, was originally the coronation stone of the High Kings of Ireland, with implications for the credibility of historic links between the British royal family and the Celtic realms of the United Kingdom.[133] The monarchical dimension registered far more strongly, however, in Arthur Griffith's promotion of a dual monarchy, a proposal inspired by the example of Austria-Hungary.[134] In an Irish context, however, dual monarchy had its origins in O'Connell's idea of rendering the King 'Irish' through his taking the advice, and giving effect to, the legislative enactments of an Irish parliament. But whereas O'Connell was apparently happy, as his acceptance of the myth of the Glorious Revolution suggested, for Irish identity to be framed in a British monarchical mode, for Griffith the monarchical office was more significant as a constitutional mechanism. A controversial proposal, dual monarchy was intended to unite Ireland and more easily effect its disengagement from the Union than the outright promotion of a republic.

Debates about monarchy among cultural nationalists in the period up to 1914, however, were essentially subordinate disputes. John Redmond's Irish Parliamentary Party was still in control of nationalist Ireland, and the general elections of 1910, which left it holding the balance of power, allowed Redmond to force the Home Rule issue on to the parliamentary agenda, thereby providing an Irish focus – with an Ulster boiling point – for a much wider crisis of the British state that had developed over the Liberal government's social reforms and budgetary policy, and its curtailment of the powers of the House of Lords by the Parliament Act of 1911. Furious at their exclusion from power and with a party leader in Bonar Law with close Ulster Unionist connections, the Unionist leadership proceeded to push the political crisis to the point of civil war, including providing assistance in the acquisition of arms by the Ulster Volunteer Force.[135]

Reflecting this crisis of the state, an attempt was made to redefine the Unionist creed in line with current party practice. Lord Hugh Cecil argued that the government's interference with the powers of the Lords had disordered the estates of the realm, and that the time might be right for the monarch to take a more effective – 'national' – role in the nation's affairs;[136] while the eminent constitutional lawyer, A. V. Dicey, contradicted a lifetime's teaching by urging the intervention of the King in politics under any circumstances to prevent the implementation of Home Rule.[137] It was a role Queen Victoria and Prince Albert might

---

[133] T. W. Rolleston, *The Myths and Legends of the Celtic Race* (London, 1904), p. 105, claimed that it was, a claim rejected by William Bulfin, *Rambles in Eirinn* (Dublin, 1907), pp. 101–2.

[134] R. Davis, *Arthur Griffith and Non-Violent Sinn Fein* (Dublin, 1974), ch. 8.

[135] See J. Smith, *The Tories and Ireland 1910–1914* (Dublin, 2000), pp. 79–80.

[136] Lord H. Cecil, *Conservatism* (London, 1912), p. 226.

[137] R. Cosgrove, *The Rule of Law* (London, 1980), pp. 241, 249–51, 255.

have relished, but George V was too well-schooled in Bagehot to take on the task.[138] The onset of war at the end of July 1914 came as something of a relief.

The war provided the opportunity for Irish separatists to mount the *coup de théâtre* that was the 1916 rising, which, with the government's politically inept execution of the leaders, served to revive the Irish physical force tradition. It was a tradition whose efforts in 1848 and 1867 had, for our purposes, served only to provide dramatic points of contrast for the highly successful royal visits of the following years. The rising appeared also to effect a dramatic shift in the terms of debate about Irish self-government, away from accommodation with British constitutional forms and towards the goal of an independent republic. Certainly the rising set in train the sequence of events that would see the collapse of constitutional nationalism at the general election of 1918, and a war of independence that would deliver a far more advanced form of independence than Redmond could have hoped for in the pre-war period. Nevertheless, it did not displace consideration of solutions to the Irish question that included the monarchy.

In fact, the increasing radicalization of nationalist opinion in a crisis that seemed destined to settle Ireland's future, brought a focus and clarity to a debate over constitutional options that had not existed before. In this context, the monarchical dimension re-emerged in two distinct strands: Ireland having the status of an imperial dominion under the Crown; and a more influential proposal pushed by Arthur Griffith, of the revival of the Irish kingdom as it had existed before the Act of Union, but with its independence more effectively secured – deemed to have an Irish historical authenticity which the more recently created dominions lacked. The appeal of a monarchical constitutional option for nationalists was the possibility of maintaining the unity of Ulster and the rest of Ireland.[139] But Lloyd George put this option to Ulster Unionists in 1921 without success: British identity framed in terms of allegiance to the King could only be authentically experienced within the boundaries of the state of which he was the hegemonic emblem.[140] Imperial patriotism in this context was an imaginative construct lacking authentic cultural or constitutional underpinning.

Lloyd George's Ulster initiative, however, was part of a wider project, one that appropriated the abandoned O'Connellite tradition to oppose the demand for an Irish republic. Claiming that a republic had been

---

[138] On the influence of Bagehot on George V, see Nicolson, *King George V*, pp. 61–3.
[139] The issues are discussed in T. Hennessey, *Dividing Ireland* (London, 1998), ch. 5.
[140] See J. Loughlin, *Ulster Unionism and British National Identity since 1885* (London, 1995), p. 88.

explicitly disowned by 'the most famous national leaders in Irish history', Lloyd George quoted O'Connell on Ireland's 'undivided allegiance' to the monarch.[141] The argument made little impression on de Valera, while Ireland's monarchical identity as embodied in the Viceroyalty was already disintegrating.

Lacking the authenticity of the institution it aped, the state of the country during the last years of British rule made impossible any ritual representation of Ireland's membership of the United Kingdom. In fact, any public appearance by the Viceroy, Lord French, became difficult as arbitrary changes of venue and route were necessary to avoid a republican assassination gang. This group was no less conscious of his symbolic importance than the state authorities. *Where* he was to be killed was nearly as important as the act itself, the preferred site being the gates of Phoenix Park, to demonstrate emphatically Irish rejection of British rule.[142]

French avoided assassination, but proved incapable of meeting the challenge republicans posed. A man of limited political ability, wielding autocratic control of the Irish administration, he responded to this, the most serious crisis it had faced under the Union, with a bankrupt policy of economic regeneration to deal with Ireland's 'real' problems and the stern application of law and order to put down 'criminality'. It was a nineteenth-century Pavlovian response to the Irish question that had no hope of success. Castle government effectively ended in 1920.[143] Only then did Ireland get what might have made a significant difference to relations between the Viceroyalty and the nationalist people had it been conceded much earlier – a Catholic Viceroy.[144] Lord FitzAlan's role, however, was merely to formalize British withdrawal from southern Ireland.

That process effectively began when George V, in a speech inaugurating the opening of the Parliament of Northern Ireland in June 1921, set the stage for a truce between republicans and Crown forces which led to the negotiations that produced the Anglo-Irish Treaty of December 1921.[145] The treaty created the Irish Free State, an entity with dominion powers and the King as its constitutional head, and forced upon the Irish delegation under threat of the immediate resumption of hostilities.

---

[141] Lloyd George to Eamon de Valera, 26 Aug. 1921, in *The Round Table* (Dec. 1921), 45.

[142] D. Breen, *My Fight for Irish Freedom* (Dublin, 1950), chs 14 and 15.

[143] See E. O'Halpin, *The Decline of the Union* (Dublin, 1987), ch. 6.

[144] As the Viceroyalty was barred to Catholics by law, a special enabling bill was enacted to effect Lord FitzAlan's occupancy: see T. Jones, *Whitehall Diary, Vol. III* (London, 1971), p. 53.

[145] Nationalists in Belfast, however, saw it as confirmation of partition and their oppression by a local Protestant majority: see A. F. Parkinson, *Belfast's Unholy War* (Dublin, 2004), pp. 134–8.

But, as we have noted, it was an option unlikely to engender committed allegiance in Ireland. A diarist recorded the birth of Irish independence: 'We heard tonight Ireland is a Free State . . . Not a flag, not a bonfire, not a hurrah.'[146] Lacking popular support, the Free State was a constitutional form unlikely to endure once the republican leader, de Valera, came to power in 1932.[147]

VI

The significance of Ireland's relationship with the British monarchy under the Union is difficult to assess exactly. For nationalists, it was a means of reconciling Irish independence with the reality of British state power; for Westminster administrations, an agency for shaping Irish identity and allegiance to the Union. The monarchy's credibility in both respects depended more on expectation than evidence. The impressive demonstrations of popular loyalty that royal visits appeared to elicit were influential in shaping governmental beliefs that the Union could succeed, but lacked durability in the face of Ireland's endemic problems, nationalist traditions and the absence of a resident focus of loyalty. Yet the relationship between the monarch and the Irish people can be seen as merely presenting the most problematic scenario of a number that existed in the Union period.

Linda Colley's assessment of the mass adulation of George III in Britain during the heightened war patriotism of the Napoleonic era, for instance, cautions against a too ready acceptance of undiluted popular devotion to the monarchic order.[148] Likewise, it has been suggested that even British working-class devotion to the Queen-Empress in the late nineteenth century may have merely had a surface reality that disguised an internal system of values impervious to royal influence.[149] Even the great exhibition of Scottish loyal tartanry in 1822 has been subject to revisionist interpretation, with the suggestion that it be seen less as an affirmation of Scots loyalty to the British state than an assertion of national distinctiveness.[150]

In Ireland's case the depth of national alienation from the state allows for a greater degree of scepticism about the authenticity of displays of

---

[146] Celia Shaw diary, Dec. 1921, cited in M. Hopkinson, *Green Against Green* (Dublin, 1988), p. 35.
[147] See N. Mansergh, *The Unresolved Question* (London, 1991), pp. 276–8, for some pertinent comments.
[148] Colley, 'The apotheosis of George III', 122–9.
[149] P. S. Baker, 'The sociological and ideological role of the monarchy in Victorian Britain' (MA thesis, University of Lancaster, 1978), p. 5.
[150] See R. J. Finley, 'Caledonia or North Britain? Scottish identity in the eighteenth century', in D. Broun, *et al.* (eds.), *Image and Identity* (Edinburgh, 1998), p. 152.

popular loyalty, even as the great royal triumphs of 1821, 1849, 1868, 1903 and 1911 were taking place. As events lending credibility to the case for the Union they are testimony to the power, in the right circumstances, of royal ceremonial and enchantment. They also suggest at least the possibility of a different outcome to the Anglo-Irish relationship in the Union period, had Westminster's responses to Ireland's problems been more timely and enlightened.

Part II

5   Bagehot's republicanism*

David M. Craig

In March 1894, Joseph Tanner, a young Fellow of St John's College, Cambridge, was employed to instruct the Duke of York in naval and constitutional history. Walter Bagehot's *English Constitution*, which had recently become a recommended text for the Historical Tripos, was one of the books the Duke was advised to dip into. He made notes on the dignified functions of the monarchy and its remaining political powers, writing of its 'immense unexhausted *influence*' and concluding it was 'still a great political force' which offered a 'splendid career to an able monarch'.[1] For much of the twentieth century, Bagehot's pithy little book has been a staple for thinking about the monarchy. George VI, Elizabeth II and Prince Charles have all read it, or at least parts of it. Similarly when academics and journalists speculate about the nature of the monarchy, Bagehot is never far from view. In distinguishing between the 'efficient' and the 'dignified' parts of the constitution, it is thought that he detailed the political powers that remained to the monarchy, including the three famous rights to be consulted, to encourage and to warn, and went on to prescribe a new ceremonial role which was to have immense social and psychological importance in the twentieth century.[2] As an editorial in the *Observer* on the death of the Queen Mother in 2002 suggested, the monarchy added

* I am most grateful to Duncan Bell, Andrzej Olechnowicz, James Thompson and Philip Williamson for comments on an earlier draft of this essay.

[1] Printed in *The Collected Works of Walter Bagehot*, ed. Norman St John-Stevas, 15 vols. (London, 1965–86) [hereafter *CW*], XV, pp. 304–5.

[2] For the political role see F. Hardie, *The Political Influence of the British Monarchy 1868–1952* (London, 1970), pp. 9–10, 45–6, 73–4; R. H. S. Crossman, 'Introduction' to Walter Bagehot, *The English Constitution* (London, 1963), pp. 16–18; K. C. Wheare, 'Walter Bagehot', *Proceedings of the British Academy* 60 (1974), 188–92; N. St John-Stevas, 'The political genius of Walter Bagehot', *CW*, V, pp. 81–97; V. Bogdanor, *The Monarchy and the Constitution* (Oxford, 1995), esp. pp. 40–1, 69–74, 133; P. Hennessy, *The Hidden Wiring* (London, 1995), ch. 2. For the ceremonial role see D. Cannadine, 'The context, performance and meaning of ritual: the British monarchy and the "invention of tradition", c.1820–1977', in E. Hobsbawm and T. Ranger (eds.), *The Invention of Tradition* (Cambridge, 1983), esp. pp. 107, 119, 131; W. M. Kuhn, *Democratic Royalism* (Basingstoke, 1996), ch. 1; see also D. M. Craig, 'The crowned republic?: monarchy and anti-monarchy in Britain, 1760–1901', *Historical Journal* 46 (2003), 167–85.

'charisma and authority' to Parliament, and a 'legitimacy' and 'sense of continuity' that the state might otherwise lack.[3] While these authorities often diverge on the accuracy of Bagehot's views, there is little doubt that *The English Constitution* has been a buttress to the monarchy. This seems evident from its most famous passage: 'When there is a select committee on the Queen' – there is a hint of archness here – 'the charm of royalty will be gone. Its mystery is its life. We must not let in daylight upon magic.'[4] But Queen Victoria would not have been amused. George V once commented that she was 'quite displeased' when she heard he had been studying 'such a radical writer'.[5]

Bagehot might well have been amused by the posthumous reputation of his book. In his lifetime, *The English Constitution* did not make the dramatic impact that has sometimes been claimed. There were few reviews of the book, and all were short. He was better known as the banker and the economist, and accordingly appreciated by politicians. This was the man who advised Gladstone about the Bank Notes Issue Bill in 1865, and Stafford Northcote about Treasury Bills in 1877. *Lombard Street* was published in 1873 and had reached its sixth edition by 1875, but it took *The English Constitution* until 1891 to achieve the same distinction. Albert Dicey in 1881, Woodrow Wilson in 1895 and Leslie Stephen in 1900 all lamented that Bagehot was not as widely recognized as he deserved to be.[6] That said, *The English Constitution* steadily accumulated admirers in the last two decades of the nineteenth century, but unlike later commentators they were not particularly concerned with what it said about the monarchy, but with its overall account of the real workings of the constitution. R. H. Hutton's obituary in *The Economist* spoke of it as a 'valuable addition' to political science, while that of E. D. J. Wilson in the *Examiner* desired that it be mastered by every educated man in the country. Both James Bryce and Dicey praised the work highly, and felt that if Bagehot had lived longer, he might have rivalled Montesquieu or Tocqueville.[7] By 1916, Bryce could deliver an address in which he stated that anyone who had written on the British constitution was 'under an obligation for much that has become so familiar that perhaps the writer does not know

[3] *Observer*, 31 March 2002, p. 28.
[4] W. Bagehot, *The English Constitution*, ed. M. Taylor (Oxford, 2001), p. 55.
[5] As reported by Lord Riddell, 11 July 1914, *More Pages from my Diary: 1908–1914* (London, 1934), p. 218.
[6] A. V. Dicey, 'Bagehot's biographical studies', *The Nation* 32 (1881), cited in *CW*, XV, pp. 80–1; W. Wilson, 'A literary politician', *Atlantic Monthly* 76 (1895), 668; L. Stephen, 'Walter Bagehot', *National Review* 35 (1900), 936.
[7] R. H. Hutton, *Economist*, 31 March 1877; E. D. J. Wilson, *Examiner*, 31 March 1877, 41; J. Bryce to Mrs Barrington [1914] and 'Address', 24 March 1916; A. V. Dicey, 'Walter Bagehot', *Nation* 28 (1879), all reprinted in *CW*, XV, pp. 31, 43, 72, 74, 80.

it was to Walter Bagehot'.[8] It is this very familiarity – coupled with its famed irony – which has ensured that even as *The English Constitution* was increasingly mined for what it had to say about the monarchy, what Bagehot had actually argued was progressively obscured.[9]

This essay suggests that *The English Constitution* was not a blueprint for a rejuvenated monarchy, but in fact a defence of a particular form of republicanism. The first section discusses the widely held view that monarchy, aristocracy and deference were integral to workings of the British constitution. For this reason it could not be exported, and so new countries were advised to imitate the republicanism of the United States of America. Bagehot strongly opposed this line of thinking, arguing firstly that presidential government had many weaknesses, and secondly that critics of the British constitution had misunderstood it. The efficient part could, in theory, be exported, but the dignified part could not. The second section of this essay therefore focuses on Bagehot's comparison between royal and unroyal forms of cabinet government. His central argument was that even if a truly excellent monarch could be of *some* use in maintaining cabinet government, he or she was not absolutely *necessary*. In other words a non-presidential form of republicanism – cabinet government – was possible and potentially available to new polities. The final section explores Bagehot's belief that the emergence of the sort of 'national character' that could sustain cabinet government was very rare. In Britain, this process had been protracted and remained incomplete: only the most educated members of society understood that they effectively lived in a republic sustained by cabinet government. The mass of the population, by contrast, still firmly believed that they were ruled by the monarch. Until the spread of education enabled them to understand otherwise, the fiction of the monarchy was essential to ensure the disguise.

I

The English Constitution is not primarily about the monarchy. It was certainly not written to combat a republican threat, which barely existed

---

[8] Bryce, 'Address', *CW*, XV, p. 75.

[9] But for recent, and often excellent, discussions of Bagehot's wider significance, see D. Spring, 'Bagehot and deference', *American Historical Review* 81 (1976), 524–31; J. W. Burrow, 'Sense and circumstance: Bagehot and the nature of political understanding', in S. Collini, D. Winch and J. W. Burrow, *That Noble Science of Politics* (Cambridge, 1983), pp. 161–81; M. Francis and J. Morrow, *A History of Political Thought in the Nineteenth Century* (London, 1994), pp. 213–18; B. Harrison, *The Transformation of British Politics, 1860–1995* (Oxford, 1996), ch. 1; P. Smith, 'Introduction' to *The English Constitution* (Cambridge, 2001), pp. vii–xxvii; Taylor, 'Introduction' to *English Constitution*, pp. vii–xxix.

when Bagehot began writing in 1865. Even the brief 'republican moment' of the early 1870s hardly registered in the second edition of 1872 (though a series of articles in *The Economist* did deal with the question more fully). For educated liberals of this period, the question of the monarchy had effectively been solved, and it had been evident to them for some decades that they lived in a constitutional monarchy in which its political power had been safely constrained. For some commentators, even, the monarchy was of negligible importance. The idea that Britain was an 'aristocratic republic' was not restricted to foreign observers such as Louis Blanc and Hippolyte Taine.[10] For this reason, Bagehot's primary interest was the 'efficient' parts of the constitution, at the heart of which was the cabinet – 'a board of control' – chosen by the sovereign body, the House of Commons.[11] This fact, he announced, had been concealed by the old 'literary' theories of the balanced constitution and of the separation of powers. In destroying these theories, he claimed to have replaced them with the new idea of cabinet government. But this view cannot be taken seriously. As Angus Hawkins and others have observed, the idea that government was embedded in Parliament was by the end of the 1860s an almost tired formula.[12] There had been a steady stream of distinguished constitutional analyses in the 1850s and 1860s, including works by Earl Grey, John Stuart Mill, Erskine May and Lord Brougham. As well as Bagehot's own work, William Hearn's *The Government of England* and Alpheus Todd's *On Parliamentary Government in England* were published in 1867. With some justice a short piece in the *Contemporary Review* commented that 'Mr Bagehot's work is, fortunately, not of those whose chief claim to notice is their novelty, or this would be a late period for noticing it'.[13] Either Bagehot was not aware that he was repeating widely accepted formulae, or, as seems more likely, he thought his work went further in stripping away all the historical accumulations of the constitution in order to expose the importance of the simple form of government that lay beneath.[14]

The range of positions adopted on the constitution in the 1860s is evident if we compare Earl Grey's *Parliamentary Government* of 1858 and Lord Brougham's *British Constitution* of 1861. Bagehot's book bears

[10] Taylor, 'Introduction', xxiii; R. Williams, *The Contentious Crown* (Aldershot, 1997), pp. 92–107.

[11] Bagehot, *English Constitution*, ed. Taylor, p. 12.

[12] A. Hawkins, '"Parliamentary government" and Victorian political parties, c.1830-c.1880', *English Historical Review*, 104 (1989), 638–69. See also M. J. C. Vile, *Constitutionalism and the Separation of Powers* (Oxford, 1967), pp. 212–38; Smith, 'Introduction', xiv–xx.

[13] *The Contemporary Review* 9 (1868), 473.

[14] See Bagehot, 'The cabinet', *Fortnightly Review* 1 (1865), *CW*, V, p. 205 n. 6.

similarities to the former work, and is rightly seen as a firm rebuttal of the latter. Brougham's *Constitution* built on the deeply traditional view that each of the three pure forms of government was liable to degenerate unless mixed and balanced with the others. The logic of this argument was to give considerable power to the Crown. It controlled all appointments to office, could make war and peace, and chose how to spend the sums approved by Parliament. The powers and prerogatives of the Crown, however, were limited by the balancing powers of Lords and Commons, but not so far as to render the monarch redundant. A supportive ministry was 'likely to consult his opinion and wishes rather than bring matters to a collision with him. Many modifications of the measures of Parliament are likely to be adopted rather than come to a rupture with him.' Hence the monarch could 'exert a real influence'. 'This is the spirit of the Constitution', Brougham argued, 'which wills that the individual Monarch should not be a mere cipher, but a substantive part of the political system; and wills it as a check on the other branches of the system.'[15] Grey's *Parliamentary Government* took a very different approach. This work did much to popularize the view that the legislative and executive were fused, and that real power lay in the hands of ministers who were responsible to Parliament, and more particularly to the Commons. But Grey did not wish to relegate the monarchy to a walk-on part. It could and should dissolve Parliament when it had ceased to represent the nation, and could also act as a brake upon parliamentary government from time to time. 'The Crown, it is true, seldom refuses to act upon the advice deliberately pressed upon it by its servants . . . But the Sovereigns of this country nevertheless may, and generally have exercised much influence over the conduct of the Government, and in extreme cases the power of the Crown to refuse its consent to what is proposed by its servants, may be used with the greatest benefit to the Nation.'[16] Clearly Grey did not wish to go too far in diminishing the role of the monarch.

How, then, are we to understand what Bagehot was doing in writing *The English Constitution*? Was he merely repackaging *Parliamentary Government* in more stylish form? One important context for his work – as for Grey's – was the agitation for the extension of the franchise. When this had been proposed in 1859, he had written an essay on 'Parliamentary Reform' explaining his concern about ensuring a better representation of the working classes without swamping the other represented interests. This remained a basic theme in *The English Constitution*, which was written

---

[15] Lord Brougham, *The British Constitution* (London, 1861), p. 262.
[16] Earl Grey, *Parliamentary Government Considered with Reference to Reform* (London, 1858), p. 5.

at the time of growing interest in reform, and published as a book in the year of the Second Reform Act. But this is not the only – or even perhaps the most important – context in which this work should be understood. It needs also to be seen within an international perspective, and particularly as a contribution to debates about comparative government. This is evident from Bagehot's deep interest in French and American politics, to which he returned again and again between the 1850s and 1870s. To a lesser extent he was also interested in colonial issues, and particularly questions thrown up by the development of responsible government in the colonies.[17]

The conventional wisdom – shared by both Brougham and Grey – was to stress the peculiarities of the British constitution. It was a unique historical creation that was extremely difficult to export to other countries, and was unlikely to work when it was. Even British colonies in Australia and New Zealand were currently better off with a governor rather than experimenting with parliamentary government.[18] Continental observers agreed with the Whig idea that the constitution was the product of ages and adapted to the specific social conditions of the country. Taine's *Notes on England* had argued that this aristocratic republic had evolved slowly, and was only possible because of the inherited deference of the populace to the aristocrats who ruled for them.[19] The Duc de Persigny, until 1863 the loyal servant of Napoleon III, made much the same case, stressing that while England possessed excellent representative institutions, they only worked because of deference. Countries where the aristocracy lacked even influence were not therefore fitted for parliamentary government, and he concluded by stating that France under the rule of Napoleon III enjoyed the best form of government.[20] At first sight, Bagehot seems to have accepted this view. Miles Taylor has suggested that he wanted to 'disabuse his readers of the quaint notion that English-style parliamentary institutions could be exported to other countries, irrespective of national differences, differences of character, and differences of historical development'. Readers required a 'reminder of the difficulty and not

---

[17] For fuller accounts see Taylor, 'Introduction', xv–xx; M. Churchman, 'Walter Bagehot and the American civil war', *Dublin Review* 506 (1965), 377–93; N. St John-Stevas, 'Walter Bagehot and Napoleon III', *CW*, IV, pp. 15–24; D. Lowry, '"These colonies are practically democratic republics" (James Bryce): republicanism in the British colonies of settlement in the long nineteenth century' in D. Nash and A. Taylor (eds.), *Republicanism in Victorian Society* (Stroud, 2000), pp. 125–39; G. Varouxakis, *Victorian Political Thought on France and the French* (Basingstoke, 2002).

[18] Grey, *Parliamentary Government*, pp. 10–15, 198–219. See also M. Taylor, *The Decline of British Radicalism, 1847–1860* (Oxford, 1995), pp. 191–201.

[19] H. Taine, *Notes on England*, trans. E. Hyams (London, 1957), pp. 152–6, 160–7, 176–8.

[20] Bagehot, 'France or England', *Economist*, 5 Sept. 1863, *CW*, IV, pp. 89–90.

the ease with which parliamentary government could be exported from Westminster'.[21]

In fact, *The English Constitution* took a very different view from Taine and Persigny. The opening chapter – especially in its original *Fortnightly Review* form – made this transparent. Bagehot noted that foreign and colonial observers were deeply interested in how the English constitution worked, because they understood that sooner or later they would have to model new constitutions for themselves. 'They wish to see what parts are peculiar, insular, incapable of exportation – the produce of exceptional circumstances, the result of special and individual national characteristics; and, on the other hand, which parts are communicable, applicable, part of the general stock of useful political instruments.'[22] Too often, however, mistakes in constitution making had arisen because of a *mis*understanding of how the English model worked. The assumption was that the 'balanced union of three powers' had developed since the medieval period, and so 'the principal characteristics of the English Constitution are inapplicable where the materials for a monarchy or an aristocracy do not exist'. Likewise the 'mystic reverence' for and 'religious allegiance' to a monarchy had only evolved slowly, and certainly could not be artificially manufactured in a nation without it.[23] But rather than endorsing this view of the constitutional peculiarities of the English, Bagehot opposed it. It was 'superficial and erroneous' to suppose the English constitution was irrelevant to nations that lacked 'medieval materials' and in fact the 'experience of England is far more widely attainable, than this theory would lead us to suppose'.[24] A central purpose of *The English Constitution*, then, was to show that parliamentary government *could* be exported because beneath the 'very old and rather venerable' parts was something 'decidedly simple and rather modern'.[25]

There were good reasons to stress this. If it was widely agreed that Britain's constitution was inapplicable to most parts of the world, then it followed that new countries would have to emulate a rather different model. To radical and democratic critics in the 1850s and 60s, British institutions anyway had little to commend them in the abstract. The real source of inspiration to new nations, they suggested, was the United States and its republican presidential model. Indeed for many radicals this system represented the future of Britain once it had thrown off the chains of hereditary privilege.[26] A good instance of this thinking was the 'democrat'

---

[21] Taylor, 'Introduction', xv, xviii.

[22] Bagehot, 'The cabinet', *CW*, V, p. 204 n. 5.   [23] Bagehot, *English Constitution*, p. 6.

[24] Bagehot, 'The cabinet', *CW*, V, p. 205 n. 7.   [25] Bagehot, *English Constitution*, p. 10.

[26] E. Biagini, *Liberty, Retrenchment and Reform* (Cambridge, 1992), pp. 60–83.

historian, E. A. Freeman. In the early 1860s, he was thinking about what kind of constitutions would be best for new states, and had an enthusiastic interest in both Switzerland and America.[27] He was also attracted to presidential government, as he made clear in an article for the *National Review*, which Bagehot edited. There he complained that although in theory Britain possessed a separation of powers, in practice its executive powers were lodged in a cabinet appointed by the Commons. Whereas Bagehot praised this fusion, Freeman opposed it. In contrast to Britain, America's executive was elected by the people rather than the legislature, and served for a fixed term. For these reasons, presidential government was a 'far better, far more honest, far more stable' system than ministerial government.[28] The only reason the British system worked was because 'it is the natural and gradual growth of the circumstances of England'. Perhaps it could be transplanted to Europe, which still possessed the remnants of aristocracy and tradition, but it ought not to be attempted in the colonies of settlement. Indeed, ministerial government was the 'very last thing' to set up in a new commonwealth which lacked monarchy, aristocracy and respect for tradition. The 'absurdity' of a governor and a 'responsible ministry' in Australia and New Zealand was clear to Freeman, and he concluded that presidential government was better for such countries.[29]

Bagehot opposed all that Freeman praised. To show the advantages of cabinet government it was also necessary to show the disadvantages of presidential government, and so the United States was a target in many essays, and in *The English Constitution* particularly. Bagehot was opposed to both federalism – because it diluted sovereignty – and to the presidential system.[30] The advantage of a parliamentary system was that because it was made up of people with education, status and political knowledge, it was better suited to choosing the government. Furthermore, because

---

[27] Freeman – unlike Bagehot – was a firm advocate of federalism, and denied it was a cause of the American civil war: E. A. Freeman to G. Finlay, 4 April 1864 in W. R. W. Stephens (ed.), *The Life and Letters of Edward A. Freeman*, 2 vols. (London, 1895), I, p. 29. See J. W. Burrow, *A Liberal Descent* (Cambridge, 1981), chs. 7–8.

[28] E. A. Freeman, 'Presidential government' reprinted in his *Historical Essays*, 1st ser., (London, 1871), p. 396.

[29] Ibid. See also Freeman to G. Finlay, 7 January 1866 in Stephens (ed.), *Life and Letters*, I, p. 336.

[30] For federalism see Bagehot, 'The American constitution at the present crisis', *National Review* 13 (1861), *CW*, IV, p. 291 and Bagehot, *English Constitution*, pp. 155–7. For the presidential system see especially Bagehot, 'The defect of America: presidential and ministerial governments compared', *Economist*, 6 December 1862, *CW*, VI, pp. 161–4; Bagehot, 'Presidential and ministerial governments compared', *Economist*, 13 December 1862, *CW*, VI, pp. 165–7; Bagehot, 'The present crisis in America: the contrast between parliamentary and presidential Governments', *Economist*, 2 September 1865, *CW*, VI, pp. 172–5; Bagehot, *English Constitution*, pp. 14–25.

it chose from its own number, the very best tried and tested men led the executive. In presidential systems – particularly that of the United States – the president was elected by the people, who rarely had a full understanding of what they were doing, were prone to manipulation by professional electioneers, and had no means of knowing or testing the qualities of the candidate.[31] Worse, once elected, the president served for a fixed term 'however unfit, incompetent, and ignorant he may be', whereas a ministerial system could remove the executive whenever it wished.[32] Once in office, the president, unlike the prime minister, could not rely on the advice and guidance of the legislative body, and this strict separation between executive and legislature also meant that dangerous tensions and disagreements were likely to grow up between them.[33] Finally, presidential systems performed the educative functions of government less well. In Britain the legislative body was 'the great scene of debate, the great engine of popular instruction and political controversy', but in the United States, public opinion and political engagement were weak because the legislative body was not the seat of power.[34] It 'gives to the people less means of forming a good judgment upon their national affairs, and less means of obtruding their judgment on their rulers after it has been formed'.[35] But if presidential systems were so inferior to ministerial forms why did they continue to be regarded as a political ideal? Bagehot speculated that in part this was simply because of the imaginative hold the United States had on new nations, but it was also because of the widespread assumption that cabinet government required a king or his representative to choose the cabinet.[36] A central aim of *The English Constitution*, then, was to disprove this.

II

There are two chapters in *The English Constitution* entitled 'The Monarchy'. It is often forgotten that there is also a third – on the supposed checks and balances of the constitution – which completes the argument begun in the earlier two. The most influential of these chapters is the first, where Bagehot dealt with the 'dignified' functions of the monarchy, but it is important to begin with the second, where he concentrated on its 'efficient' role. There, it is usually assumed, he outlined what powers were

---

[31] Bagehot, 'The defect of America', *CW*, VI, pp. 162–3.
[32] Ibid., p. 163. In 'Presidential and ministerial governments compared' Bagehot also explained that the power of Congress over the President was weak, and that impeachment could only be used in exceptional circumstances. *CW*, VI, pp. 165–7.
[33] Bagehot, *English Constitution*, pp. 14–16.   [34] Ibid., p. 16.
[35] Bagehot, 'The present crisis in America', *CW*, VI, p. 175.
[36] Bagehot, 'The cabinet', *CW*, V, pp. 224–5 n. 17.

left to the monarchy, and defined the three famous royal 'rights'. But in fact this was not how he proceeded. He noted that the Queen had many powers which wavered between 'reality and desuetude', but assigned to the lawyer the task of describing those which were still current.[37] In other words the aim was *not* – as is commonly assumed – to list what powers Victoria might still lay claim to, but rather to compare what he called the royal and unroyal forms of cabinet government. This argument was suspended at the end of Chapter Four and only concluded in Chapter Eight on check and balances. Bagehot wanted the reader to imagine a simple form of cabinet government in which a single elected chamber directly appointed and dismissed its premier, 'just as the shareholders of a railway choose a director'.[38] By comparing this imaginary form with the British experience, it would be possible to see if a hereditary monarchy was essential to the workings of cabinet government. What role did it play during the birth, the duration, and the death of a ministry?

At the beginning of a new ministry, there was often no need for the monarch to play any role.[39] If Parliament was divided into 'two great parties' and the larger of these agreed upon its leader, then that man would become the prime minister. But in other cases, perhaps the monarch could provide a valuable service? Bagehot was thinking of situations when the Commons was divided into more than two parties, which enabled smaller groups to hold the balance of power, and when the majority party could not decide on a leader. He drew on recent examples in both cases, pointing out how in 1858 the Radicals had acted against the Liberals in keeping the Conservatives in power, and how in 1859 the Liberals – for a while – seemed uncertain whether Palmerston or Russell was their man. Surely in these situations it was better for the monarch to step in to appoint the best leader and the best government for the nation? But while Bagehot accepted that theoretically this was possible, he was at pains to show that unroyal cabinet government could work as well. Any party that could not agree on its leader nevertheless had a motive to settle upon the best man for the job for fear of damaging itself electorally. Similarly, even a divided Commons must realize that government had to go on, and eventually moderates of all groups would settle on the man most likely to carry support. Indeed, Bagehot felt that in such situations the Commons should not rely upon outside authorities to choose for it, because 'the responsibility of parliament should be felt by parliament'.[40]

---

[37] Bagehot, *English Constitution*, p. 54. This point was explored more fully in Bagehot, 'Introduction to the second edition', *CW*, V, pp. 182–90.

[38] Bagehot, *English Constitution*, p. 56.

[39] Ibid., pp. 57–63.   [40] Ibid., p. 62.

In other words, even in the supposedly politically weak and divided 1850s, cabinet government could emerge satisfactorily without the involvement of the monarch.

The same conclusion was reached about the role of a monarch at the termination of a ministry, which was examined in Chapter Eight. There needed to be a 'regulator' of unitary sovereignty, to ensure that when Parliament no longer adequately represented the nation it could be dissolved. This might occur for three reasons. Firstly, 'choosing chambers' could be prone to capriciousness, for instance in refusing to maintain ministers for a sustained period and so depriving the people of any real form of government. Secondly, it was easy for party organisations – always necessary to some degree in parliamentary government – to become overmighty, leading to the subjection of 'the whole nation to the rule of a section of the nation'. Finally, Parliament might embrace feelings, prejudices and desires which were opposed to the wishes and even the well-being of the nation. In all these cases it needed to be dissolved, and the nation asked whether or not it approved of its actions.[41] Was royalty essential to provide the regulator, Bagehot asked? In the case of a capricious Parliament, he felt the best person to deal with this was the prime minister himself. It was his government that was threatened, so he knew best if and when to appeal to the people for support. There was little chance that royal intervention would be better exercised. But the other two scenarios were less clear cut, and it seemed that the prime minister was not the best person to choose the timing of a dissolution. Even the most independent leader was still a partisan, and would be tempted to prolong the power of his party even if it was unpopular in the nation. Similarly, if he was chosen or supported by a self-serving Parliament, it was likely he would share some of its vices, or could use them to his advantage. What was needed was 'an extrinsic impartial and capable authority' who would 'restrain the covetousness as well as the factiousness of a choosing assembly'.[42] Some people thought colonial governors acted in such a fashion: they were often intelligent and usually not caught up in the vices of a colonial assembly. Bagehot disagreed, arguing that governors were unlikely to understand the issues at stake, had no great incentive to find the right moment to dissolve an assembly, and were viewed suspiciously as outsiders. The same was clearly true, then, of a hereditary monarch. Ultimately the best preventative against party zeal and self-seeking was public opinion. In a country where there was steady control over representatives, and a deep interest in politics, it was very difficult for MPs to ignore the people who

[41] Ibid., p. 162.   [42] Ibid., p. 164.

elected them. So in this case too, even if unroyal cabinet government was sometimes faced with difficult decisions, it was still perfectly feasible.

During the life of a ministry, also, the role assigned to the monarchy was not extensive. It is ironic that the royal rights to be consulted, to encourage, and to warn, have passed into twentieth-century constitutional lore. Bagehot, in fact, did not attach that much weight to them, and was merely glossing what the Queen thought to be her role, as articulated in a memorandum which Russell had read to the Commons in 1852.[43] Also, the language of rights has given this position a fixity which Bagehot most likely did not intend. He was not particularly impressed by theories of rights, and the idea that the monarch possessed them ran counter to his belief that the Commons was the sovereign body. For Bagehot, the monarch was best seen as a potentially useful counsellor to the premier. Their long experience might allow them to raise issues of which the elected premier was unaware, and the dignity of their position would ensure that their views were taken seriously. Over time, any useful suggestions a monarch proposed would be taken up by the ministry, but a wise monarch should expect no more. The disadvantage of the monarch's advisory role, however, was that because kings expected deference, and statesmen usually gave it, 'in a nearly balanced argument the king must always have the better, and in politics many most important arguments are nearly balanced'.[44] This was not entirely desirable. To make any difference, a monarch would have to be as able, and to work as hard as, the statesman, and given that statesmen were the most talented men of their generation, this was most unlikely. The suggestion seemed to be that in the vast majority of cases, the monarchy could add little or nothing to the business of government.

To drive this point home, Bagehot also considered the 'safety-valve' of the constitution, or the power to create peers, which was traditionally reserved to the monarch. In times of constitutional crisis, when a large number of peers might be needed to swamp the upper house, it seemed that the king or queen – rather than the prime minister – was most suited to hold this power. In theory, Bagehot agreed that 'an able and exterior' king would be useful, but he doubted whether the nation would be blessed with the right person at the right time.[45] The example of William IV

---

[43] Ibid., pp. 63–4. The memorandum was written on 12 August 1850, during the height of tension between the Court and Palmerston, and had been drafted by Baron Stockmar in March 1850. Stockmar's importance is discussed in G. H. L. Le May, *The Victorian Constitution* (London, 1979), pp. 61–75 and in D. Cannadine, 'The last Hanoverian sovereign?: Victorian monarchy in historical perspective, 1688–1988', in A. L. O. Beier, D. Cannadine and J. M. Rosenheim (eds.), *The First Modern Society* (Cambridge, 1989), pp. 139–46.

[44] Bagehot, *English Constitution*, p. 67.   [45] Ibid., p. 171.

during the Reform Bill crisis was not very salutary. Instead, he thought that the Commons itself should hold this power, and should only exercise it on a vote of three quarters of its members. This desire to shift powers from the Crown to the Commons was also evident in the introduction to the second edition of *The English Constitution*. There Bagehot focused on the Crown's ability to make treaties with foreign powers, and argued that this should become subject to parliamentary debate and approval. In effect control over foreign relations would be placed much more clearly within the control of the Commons.[46] As Vile has commented, Bagehot clearly went further than most of his contemporaries in claiming sovereignty for the Commons rather than for the King-in-Parliament. 'Bagehot, in fact, adopted a view of legislative sovereignty or supremacy more like that of the proponents of *gouvernment d'assemblée* than any earlier view of legislative supremacy in England; a fact which helps to explain why his ideas were so well received in extreme republican circles in the early years of the Third Republic.'[47]

Of course, Bagehot did not dismiss the role of the monarchy out of court, but the ironic tone of his comments is important. The reader was constantly reminded both of the failings of kings and queens before Victoria, and the difficulty of acquiring a truly excellent constitutional monarch. So for a monarch to choose a better premier than the Commons, he would have to be a man of 'singular discernment, of unprejudiced disposition, and great political knowledge'. He would have to 'play the part of that thoroughly intelligent but perfectly disinterested spectator who is so prominent in the works of certain moralists'. It seems likely that Bagehot had in mind the famed patriot king. But it would be a '*miracle*' if such a king existed, for they were as 'rare as genius'. Similarly, knowing when to dissolve Parliament was often beyond the competence of a hereditary king, usually a '*damaged* common man'.[48] He would have to know when Parliament was in the wrong, when the nation knew it to be wrong, and when exactly to choose dissolution. This required extensive knowledge of the world, and a man living in the privacy of the court was likely to be a 'poor judge of public opinion'.[49] Even if a hereditary monarchy could selectively breed to produce the required skills, the education and lifestyle of a prince were sure to smother them. The first two Georges were 'ignorant' of English affairs, while the third 'interfered unceasingly'. 'George IV and William IV gave no steady continuing guidance, and were unfit to give it'.[50] And although Bagehot praised both Victoria and Albert,

[46] Bagehot, 'Introduction to the second edition', *CW*, V, pp. 182–90.
[47] Vile, *Constitutionalism*, p. 227.
[48] Bagehot, *English Constitution*, pp. 59, 61, 166 (italics in original).
[49] Ibid., p. 167.   [50] Ibid., p. 69.

he was clear that no one should expect their heirs to be similarly talented and restrained.[51] So while in theory a monarch might be able to add something good to the workings of cabinet government, in practice it was much more likely they would do harm.

Bagehot's conclusion to his comparison between royal and unroyal cabinet government was that 'this royalty is not essential; that, upon an average, it is not even in a high degree useful'.[52] But as he noted in the second edition, he had 'great difficulty' in persuading readers of this fact, because the presidential model of republicanism seemed to transfix people's imaginations.[53] In 1863 he had insisted, in answer to the views of Persigny, that hereditary institutions in Britain could be swept away while still retaining the essence of cabinet government. It followed that 'The *true* British Constitution is adapted to the continent, though the apparent one is not; its simple essence would grow if it were cherished in any country in the same stage of civilization as, and with analogous economic conditions to, our own'.[54] But by the time of the second edition of the *English Constitution*, France had her own cabinet government. After Napoleon III was deposed in 1870, Louis Thiers was made *chef du pouvoir exécutif* in the following year. In all but name France had stumbled upon cabinet government. Thiers had been appointed by the National Assembly and could be removed by it, just as the English prime minister could be removed by Parliament. Bagehot could justly exclaim that 'No one can any longer doubt the possibility of a republic in which the executive and the legislative authorities were united and fixed; no one can assert such union to be the incommunicable attribute of a constitutional monarchy'.[55] Cabinet government was also applicable to the wider world, including Canada and even Australia. In the latter case, Bagehot responded to critics who thought it suffered from bad legislatures and unstable governments. He conceded that a presidential system might give the country more stability in the short term, but in the longer term cabinet government was better because it taught and improved the nation. It would be a mistake 'to abandon a government which may be excellent in the future when it is essentially wanted' in favour of 'a government which will never be better'.[56]

---

[51] Ibid., pp. 69–72. See also Bagehot, 'The gravity and difficulty of affairs in France', *Economist*, 7 Aug. 1869, *CW*, IV, p. 134.

[52] Bagehot, *English Constitution*, p. 176.

[53] Bagehot, 'Introduction to the second edition', *CW*, V, p. 190.

[54] Bagehot, 'France or England', *CW*, IV, p. 94 (italics in original).

[55] Bagehot, 'Introduction to the second edition', *CW*, V, p. 190.

[56] Bagehot, 'The prerequisites of cabinet government, and the peculiar form which they have assumed in England', *Fortnightly Review* 1 (1865), *CW*, V, p. 383, n. 70.

III

Why, then, did Bagehot devote a whole chapter to the dignified functions of the monarchy? To understand this it is important to recognize that while cabinet government was feasible in countries that lacked monarchies and aristocracies, Bagehot nevertheless insisted that there were important prerequisites for its successful operation. While France might have stumbled on cabinet government in 1871, it was unlikely to last there. In part this was because its institutional form was weaker than in Britain. Its 'premier' had no power to dissolve the assembly, which accordingly had no incentive to maintain any government. The 'cabinets' were filled with men from all parties, and so were weakened by the inevitable disagreements this created. But the other reason was that France lacked some of the necessary prerequisites of cabinet government. The assembly was tumultuous because its members were dogmatic, and were unwilling to listen and to compromise. Moreover, the nation had no liking for elective government and expected little good from it. In such an atmosphere it could not survive. So, cabinet government in France was a 'useful aid to our imaginations' but it would not endure.[57] It was necessary, Bagehot insisted, to know exactly what its prerequisites were. Any form of elective government required three features. First, the electors had to possess a reasonable level of trust in one another. Second, a calm national mind was needed in order to accept political change without undue distress. And third, a measure of rationality was needed to ensure the people knew that they were in fact electing their rulers. All three features only emerged in fairly developed civilizations.[58] Furthermore, cabinet government was a 'species' of the wider 'genus', and also required a long-lasting and competent legislature in order to elect and maintain an executive.[59] Taken together then, the conditions necessary for cabinet government ensured that it was rare. But it was rare not because it needed monarchies and aristocracies, but because it required 'the co-existence of several national characteristics which are not often found together in the world'.[60]

At this point, it is necessary to look more closely at the use Bagehot made of the idea of 'national character'. Recent accounts of this concept have demonstrated the widespread belief that it was possible to assess the different characteristics of nations, and their importance in making

---

[57] Bagehot, 'Introduction to the Second Edition', *CW*, V, p. 193.

[58] Bagehot, *English Constitution*, pp. 26–8. Even civilized nations did not fully demonstrate these three qualities, as a passage from the original essay on 'Prerequisites' in the *Fortnightly Review* made clear. See *CW*, V, p. 371 n. 59.

[59] Bagehot, *English Constitution*, pp. 26, 28–31.   [60] Ibid., p. 26.

certain kinds of government possible.[61] Tocqueville, famously, had shown how democracy in America was sustained by its social and religious *moeurs* – notions, opinions and habits – and had been sceptical about whether France could enjoy similar political forms.[62] Likewise, Bagehot argued in his 'Letters on the French coup d'état of 1851' that supposedly perfect forms of government could not be imposed on any nation, irrespective of its character. The French character was far too turbulent for elective government, and stood in marked contrast to the more sober characteristics ('stupidity' he called it) of the English. These youthful essays, however, avoided considering how national character emerged and evolved. Bagehot merely commented that its origins were mysterious, but that once established it was 'the least changeable thing' in the world.[63] This implied that only a few special nations would ever be fitted for parliamentary government. *The English Constitution* hinted otherwise, but it was only in *Physics and Politics* – which appeared initially as five essays in *The Fortnightly Review* between 1867 and 1872 – that Bagehot began to examine how progress occurred. *Physics and Politics* may indeed be regarded as a sequel or continuation of ideas mapped out in *The English Constitution*. While renowned as an early attempt to apply Darwin's ideas to society, it seems that Henry Maine's *Ancient Law* was a more influential model for thinking about social evolution. Like many works concerned with civilization in the 1870s, *Physics and Politics* explored the relationship between order and progress, and exemplified the growing appeal of the 'comparative method' to understanding politics.[64]

Before the emergence of political society, humans, Bagehot argued, were at the 'mercy of every impulse and blown by every passion'. They could take no material or mental comfort from the world around them: their minds were tormented by fear of it.[65] Whether intentional or not, pre-political humanity looked rather like the fearful creatures described by Hobbes. To survive and evolve humans needed law, because any form of polity gave a people a competitive advantage over those who lacked

---

[61] P. Mandler, '"Race" and "nation" in mid-Victorian Thought' in S. Collini, R. Whatmore and B. Young (eds.), *History, Religion, and Culture* (Cambridge, 2000), pp. 224–44; R. Romani, *National Character and Public Spirit in Britain and France, 1750–1914* (Cambridge, 2002); G. Varouxakis, *Mill on Nationality* (London, 2002); D. M. Craig, 'Democracy and "national character"', *History of European Ideas* 29 (2003), 493–501.

[62] Romani, *National Character*, pp. 148–56.

[63] Bagehot, 'Letters on the French coup d'etat of 1851', *Inquirer* (1852), *CW*, IV, p. 50. See also Varouxakis, *Victorian Political Thought*, pp. 115–22.

[64] See Spring, 'Bagehot and deference', 525–8; Burrow, 'Sense and circumstance'; J. W. Burrow, *Whigs and Liberals* (Oxford, 1988), pp. 67–72, 108–10; J. W. Burrow, 'Henry Maine and the mid-Victorian idea of progress', in A. Diamond (ed.), *The Victorian Achievement of Sir Henry Maine* (Cambridge, 1991), pp. 55–70; Francis and Morrow, *A History of Political Thought*, ch. 10.

[65] Bagehot, *Physics and Politics* (London, 1872), *CW*, VII, pp. 27, 49.

it. This was imposed on the weak by the strong, who elaborated binding rules to secure obedience. The soft-fibre of humanity was moulded into a 'cake of custom'. Rome and Sparta were good examples of such 'drilling' societies, where people obeyed authority and performed their duties, simply because that was what they did.[66] This early process of creating law also helped shape national character. Both were imposed and then protected by rulers in order to give society its corporate character, and hence an evolutionary edge.

The psychological model lying behind this was crucial to Bagehot's thinking. The mind imbibed ideas by unconscious imitation of what occurred around it (what Hume had called the 'contagion of manners'), and so those ideas which passed frequently before the mind were those that were believed. Once formed, however, the mind was not naturally receptive to new ideas, and people clung tenaciously to the customary ideas they had received. While difficult and slow, however, change was not impossible. Bagehot used the examples of changes in fashion and literature to show that a new idea or style might be developed by one or two people, and over time spread by unconscious imitation across a population.[67] The evolution of national character was to be understood in the same terms. This was important because once a firm polity had been shaped, then the next thing required for further progress was to break the cake of custom. This was in fact extremely difficult, because of the human tendency to reject innovation. For this reason most of the globe was still made up of stationary societies, which had barely developed since their foundation.[68] Only those countries that had allowed space for the 'variability' of ideas had developed. The key to European progress was – as many contemporaries believed – the growth of government by discussion because it was most suited to breaking down the cake of custom. In sections which were indebted to George Grote, Bagehot argued that in early Greece the king had held supreme power, but had utilized both a senate of counsellors and a 'listening assembly', where he tested whether the people would accept his ideas. This early stress on discussion gave a slight competitive advantage to such nations, and over time these assemblies gathered more power to themselves until in the classical world monarchy was completely overthrown.[69] '[O]ut of the *tentacula* of a monarchy' the Greeks and Romans had 'developed the organs of a republic'.[70]

---

[66] Ibid., p. 32. See also the original essay 'Prerequisites' from the *Fortnightly Review* in *CW*, V, pp. 369 n. 54, 371 n. 59.

[67] Bagehot, *Physics and Politics*, *CW*, VII, pp. 34–8, 70–3. [68] Ibid., pp. 102–5.

[69] For Grote see Bagehot, *English Constitution*, pp. 39–40, 179; Bagehot, *Physics and Politics*, *CW*, VII, pp. 32, 106–22 passim.

[70] Bagehot, *English Constitution*, p. 179.

The development of these polities was, Bagehot stressed, delicate. In the early stages, the members of free government must be limited to prevent the polity becoming unstable. Even in ancient Greece, the growth of reason that accompanied government by discussion did not extend very far down the social scale. Most of the citizens remained ignorant and superstitious.[71] So on the one hand, while discussion spread, it affected more people, broke down prejudice and promoted rationality; on the other hand, it was both a sluggish and irregular process. Even a civilized age inherited the human nature which was 'victorious in barbarous ages' and as such was 'not at all suited to civilised circumstances'.[72] While civilized societies counteracted the tendency towards unconscious imitation, in its 'uncivilized' parts the uneducated populace remained similar to the savage in their imitative abilities. By way of example, Bagehot claimed that if one sent a housemaid and a philosopher to a foreign country, the housemaid would pick up the language quicker than the philosopher because she had a greater propensity and need to imitate than her companion, who could retire into the inner life of the mind. In a familiar environment, however, the uneducated clung to their old habits, 'what throws them least out of the old path, and puzzles least their minds'.[73] *Physics and Politics* exemplifies the tensions between Bagehot the exponent of progress and Bagehot the supporter of custom. It was a book about the emergence of the age of discussion and the free-state, but it did not underestimate how slow and uneven the process was.

Once situated in this context, elements of *The English Constitution* – especially its historical digressions – come into sharper focus. England, like Greece and Rome, had also developed a republic from a monarchy. In the concluding chapter, Bagehot agreed with Freeman and Stubbs in arguing that the early Germanic tribes brought the vestiges of a free polity with them when they came to England. Unlike Greece and Rome, however, these vestiges had taken a long time to develop. Because England's population was more diffused and diverse than its classical predecessors, it needed the strong rule of monarchy for a longer time. 'The development of the English Constitution was of necessity slow, because a quick one would have exhausted the executive and killed the state.'[74] By the thirteenth century, however, the king had come to rely on a Great Council of the realm as advisers, and this eventually took the form of the Lords and Commons. Parliament was, however, but an expressive body. Bagehot then supplied a potted history (which he admitted was familiar) of Parliament from the time of Henry VIII to that of Victoria. The important

[71] Bagehot, *Physics and Politics*, *CW*, VII, p. 114.   [72] Ibid., p. 122.
[73] Ibid., pp. 75, 77.   [74] Bagehot, *English Constitution*, p. 180.

point was that by the mid-nineteenth century a free representative polity –
a republic – had been achieved: 'the appendages of a monarchy have been
converted into the essence of a republic'.[75] But the difference between
modern England and ancient Greece was that this transformation had
only occurred in fact, but not in appearance. In England there was still a
vast populace whose understanding lagged behind this reality. While the
higher classes had changed dramatically since the Middle Ages, Bagehot
insisted that 'the lower have varied little':

We have in a great community like England crowds of people scarcely more
civilised than the majority of two thousand years ago; we have others even more
numerous such, as the best people were a thousand years since. The lower orders,
the middle orders, are still, when tried by what is the standard of the educated
'ten thousand', narrow-minded, unintelligent, incurious.[76]

These people were the remnants of 'primitive barbarism'. They lacked
education and rationality, and still lived their lives according to inherited
custom. They had barely heard of Parliament, and certainly knew nothing
of the cabinet. In a famous phrase, Bagehot commented that if you asked
a cabman to take you to Downing Street he would not know where to go.[77]
According to its historical development, then, it appeared that England
lacked many of the prerequisites necessary for elective government, let
alone the more stringent features necessary for cabinet government.

The United States, and especially New England, did possess the prerequisites for cabinet government, for it was capable of electing a good
legislature. 'Where there is no honest poverty', Bagehot argued, 'where
education is diffused, and political intelligence is common, it is easy for
the mass of the people to elect a fair legislature.' If New England possessed cabinet government as a separate union it would be 'as renowned
in the world for political sagacity' as it now was for its happiness.[78] But the
people of old England lacked the social and educational competencies of
the new world. The mass of the uneducated could not, Bagehot claimed,
be told to choose their governors: 'they would go wild; their imaginations
would fancy unreal dangers, and the attempt at election would issue in
some forcible usurpation'.[79] In such nations – which included most in
existence – cabinet government was only possible if the nation was deferential. This concept has long attracted a great degree of interest, and
some historians have chosen to invoke Bagehot's argument as a convincing analysis of how mid-nineteenth century Britain actually worked.[80]

---

[75] Ibid., p. 186.   [76] Ibid., pp. 180, 8.
[77] Ibid., pp. 41, 35, 190.   [78] Ibid., p. 31   [79] Ibid., p. 27.
[80] See Spring, 'Bagehot and deference', passim. Also J. Roper, *Democracy and its Critics*
(London, 1989), pp. 152–6.

The important point here, however, was that the uneducated mass of the population delegated the power to choose its rulers to a selected and more educated elite. The advantage of this was enormous. 'It has the best people to elect a legislature, and therefore it may fairly be expected to choose a good legislature – a legislature competent to select a good administration.'[81] This deference could arise for two reasons, by custom or choice. In the latter case, the majority was persuaded of the benefits of deferring to an elite. Bagehot conceded that this, though, was difficult. 'In a future and better age of the world', however, it might be possible to obtain acquiescence to rule by the 'cultivated few'.[82]

In the case of England, deference operated primarily by custom, where the 'few rule by their hold, not over the reason of the multitude, but over their imaginations, and their habits'.[83] When examined closely, however, it appears that Bagehot had difficulties with his argument. As we have seen with Taine, it was common to argue that England enjoyed representative government because the population deferred to its aristocratic rulers. Bagehot's problem was that he wanted to say that the masses deferred to monarchs and aristocrats, but that these people were not the real rulers. In *The English Constitution*, he initially stated that the dominant opinion was now that of the middle class, the 'ordinary majority of educated men'. It was to this 'heavy sensible class' of urban and rural electors that the non-voting masses deferred. But in the next paragraph, Bagehot subtly changed approach and suggested that 'in fact' the mass of the people deferred to the '*theatrical show*' generated by the court and the aristocracy, but he did not explain why this created deference to ordinary educated men of the middle class.[84] For this reason, perhaps, Bagehot repackaged his argument in the introduction to the second edition. There he stated that the ordinary ten-pound householder deferred in both his opinion and his choice of MP to someone from the educated classes, because of the influence of rank and wealth. A voting nation of shopkeepers did not choose a Parliament of shopkeepers.[85] This approach, however, still had problems. Bagehot wanted to argue that the public consented to have an educated elite to represent it, because of the impression that courts and aristocracies made on its imagination. Moreover the 'ignorant' believed that these visibly fine people actually ruled, and so the 'real rulers are secreted in second-rate carriages; no one cares for them or asks about them, but they are obeyed implicitly and unconsciously by reason of the splendour of those who eclipsed and preceded them'.[86] What Bagehot found difficult was explaining how deference to those who

---

[81] Bagehot, *English Constitution*, p. 33.
[82] Ibid., p. 36.   [83] Ibid., p. 36.   [84] Ibid., pp. 33–4.
[85] Bagehot, 'Introduction to the second edition', *CW*, V, pp. 168–9.
[86] Bagehot, *English Constitution*, p. 35.

only appeared to rule actually produced real rulers. Whatever the case, without deference, cabinet government in Britain was impossible because the masses were not ready for it.

Once these points are accepted, it becomes easier to see what the real purposes of the monarchy's 'dignified' functions were. Bagehot was not prescribing a new role for the institution, but explaining its uses given the current nature of British society. And even the five arguments he supplied in the third chapter were not unequivocal. Take, for instance, the idea that the Crown was the head of morality. While George III and Victoria were exemplars of virtue, no other monarch since Anne had been, while George IV was if anything a model of vice.[87] The main reason why the monarchy was useful, was because it was a disguise which enabled the real rulers to be changed 'without heedless people knowing it'.[88] How was this possible? First, monarchy was strong government because it was easy to understand, and 'the mass of mankind . . . hardly anywhere in the world understand any other'.[89] Most people still firmly believed that the Queen really ruled them. Furthermore, ordinary men and women were much more interested in and attached to the personal lives of a royal family – 'nice and pretty events' – than in the political business of the nation. Bagehot summarized: 'royalty is a government in which the attention of the nation is concentrated on one person doing interesting actions'. In a republic, lots of people did dull things. 'Accordingly, so long as the human heart is strong and human reason weak, royalty will be strong because it appeals to diffused feeling, and republics weak because they appeal to the understanding.'[90] For very similar reasons, monarchy also strengthened government with religion. There was, Bagehot insisted, no good theological reason for this: after all, the duty of obedience applied to republics as much as monarchies. The real reason was historical. He was convinced that in the seventeenth and eighteenth centuries, the bulk of the populace thought the King governed by divine right. This was why the 'Glorious' Revolution was profoundly disturbing, why Jacobitism was genuinely popular, and why there was so little enthusiasm for the first two Georges. From the time of George III loyal sentiments returned and, Bagehot claimed, although all sound men laughed at the idea of divine right, 'the tenet still lives in ordinary minds', and so ordinary people thought Victoria 'has a divine right to the crown'.[91] The existence of the monarchy was essential, then, primarily because the mass of the population believed it underpinned the entire political and religious order.

[87] Ibid., pp. 45–9.   [88] Ibid., p. 51.   [89] Ibid., p. 38. Also, p. 28.   [90] Ibid., p. 41.
[91] Bagehot, 'Bolingbroke as a statesman', *National Review* 16 (1863), *CW*, III, pp. 49–50; Bagehot, *English Constitution*, pp. 41–4, 28; Bagehot, 'English republicanism', *Economist*, 15 April 1871, *CW*, V, p. 424.

The final reason why monarchy 'in a dignified capacity' was important was because it was the head of society. While Bagehot conceded that a monarchy was useful in preventing ambitious but 'base' men scrabbling for the 'highest post in conspicuous life', he did not attach much weight to this role.[92] It was a hangover from the medieval period, when the head of the polity and of society were one and the same. There was no obvious reason why this should be so, and indeed the qualities required to lead civil life were rather different from those esteemed in high society. In fact, if left to itself society did not need a single head, but would naturally create an aristocracy or elite – the 'upper ten thousand' – to lead it. Bagehot also considered the subject which has attracted so much comment: the visible and ceremonial functions of the monarchy. Here he was thinking primarily of court occasions such as presentations and attendances (rather than grand public pageantry) which were also leftovers – a 'sort of ritual' – of earlier centuries when the Court really mattered, socially and politically. But since Albert's death and Victoria's extended period of mourning, court occasions too had ceased with no discernible negative effect: 'everything went on as usual . . . The queen bee was taken away, but the hive went on'.[93] Bagehot noted the complaints of those who wanted to follow France and introduce a more splendid court in Britain, but he did not agree. 'We have voluntary show enough already in London; we do not wish to have it encouraged and intensified, but quieted and mitigated.' In the *Fortnightly Review* essay he added, 'If our Court were more theatrical than it is, our society would be worse than it is'.[94] Bagehot should not therefore be viewed as an 'inventor' of a ritualistic monarchy. Even in the early 1870s, during the brief popular resurgence of republicanism, he did not counsel a substantially increased ceremonial role for the monarchy.[95] In fact, he suggested, the jubilation that greeted the recovery of the Prince of Wales from typhoid at the end of 1871 showed that whatever mutterings there might be about the cost of the monarchy, there still existed a deep '*social* loyalty' to the throne, and that aristocracy and royalty were 'still thoroughly *popular* social ideas'.[96]

The monarchy was only useful because of the specific historical growth of Britain. For this reason, Bagehot had no time for those who thought monarchy should be introduced in societies unaccustomed to

---

[92] Bagehot, *English Constitution*, p. 46. See also Bagehot, 'The monarchy', *Fortnightly Review*, 1 (1865), *CW*, V, p. 238 n. 26.

[93] Bagehot, *English Constitution*, p. 49.

[94] Ibid., p. 50; Bagehot, 'The monarchy', *CW*, V, p. 239 n. 28.

[95] Although Bagehot, 'The cost of public dignity', *Economist*, 20 July 1867, *CW*, V, p. 413 had noted that the 'vulgar' were always pleased by 'state and show'.

[96] Bagehot, 'The illness of the prince of Wales', *Economist*, 16 December 1871, *CW*, V, p. 438.

it.[97] Nor was there any reason to assume that monarchy could or should last. The development of inductive science, and the growth of a business ethic, was producing a 'matter of factness' in the world, by which institutions were judged in instrumental terms. Already in America, Australia and New Zealand, people wanted all their institutions to be useful, and they could not be convinced that constitutional royalty was rational government.[98] Moreover, Bagehot thought that no one could feel enthusiasm for monarchy in the abstract, but only for an institution with deep roots which served useful functions. By contrast, he thought republicanism *was* admirable in the abstract.[99] His disagreements with the republican movement of the early 1870s were therefore founded not on opposition to republicanism per se, but on its current inapplicability to Britain. He opposed those activists such as Auberon Herbert and George Odger who tried to argue that social and especially economic improvement was contingent on introducing republican forms, and tut-tutted at people who would not believe that 'economic forces are nearly independent of forms of government'.[100] More importantly, however, he did not think the time was yet ripe. He was consequently scathing about people who advocated a penny-pinched monarchy, such as Charles Dilke.[101] This was the worst of both worlds: an illusion without the means of sustaining itself. Moreover, he was quite clear about the severe consequences of premature abolition of the monarchy. He repeatedly stated that the law was only obeyed – especially in the counties – because the masses assumed it emanated from the person of the Queen. Without her, its authority would vanish, and it would be necessary to introduce more troops, more police, and harsher laws to secure obedience.[102] Thus, 'the first end of republican institutions – the preservation of liberty – would have to be sacrificed to secure the first end of all institutions of government – the preservation of order'.[103] The Queen was the very sinew of the polity for the masses, and so her continued presence was essential to its survival. Without her, the government would 'fail and pass away'.[104] But this was not fixed in stone. Bagehot believed that as education spread and the population became more illuminated, it would be safe to dispense with the illusion that authority flowed from above. Scotland was already 'ripe for

[97] Bagehot, 'Mr. Bright on republicanism', *Economist*, 17 May 1873, *CW*, V, pp. 427–8.
[98] Bagehot, *English Constitution*, pp. 173–77.
[99] Bagehot, 'Mr Bright on republicanism', *CW*, V, p. 427.
[100] Bagehot, 'English republicanism', *CW*, V, p. 426.
[101] Bagehot, 'Sir Charles Dilke on the civil list', *Economist*, 10 January 1874, *CW*, V, p. 416.
[102] Bagehot, 'The residence of the Queen', *Economist*, 20 August 1870, *CW*, V, p. 421; Bagehot, 'English republicanism', *CW*, V, p. 424.
[103] Bagehot, 'English republicanism', *CW*, V, p. 425.
[104] Bagehot, *English Constitution*, p. 38.

republicanism', and England might be 'say fifty years hence'. Reverence for the monarchy would not be able to continue among a 'cultivated population', but by then, Bagehot claimed, a 'population capable of abstract ideas' would not need it.[105]

It seems that Victoria was right about Bagehot. The monarchy's main use was to prop up a fiction that was apparently necessary to secure obedience from an uneducated people. Cabinet government could work happily without a monarch, and was a form of government that *could* in due course be applied to societies lacking hereditary institutions. In Britain, in the meantime, as government's teaching functions worked more effectively, and as national education grew, the civilization of the masses would ensure that monarchy became redundant. There was, however, a tension at the heart of Bagehot's argument: supporting myths about the monarchy would tend to counteract the political education that would make republicanism more likely. This was a point developed by the positivist Frederic Harrison in an article on 'The Monarchy' in the *Fortnightly Review* in 1872. Although Bagehot was not mentioned by name, it is clear who Harrison had in mind. While he agreed that Britain was in effect a republic, he argued that its usefulness was impaired by hereditary institutions and values. 'We are told', he wrote, 'that monarchy is the theatric part of the constitution' and 'that the people must have a pageant'.[106] The problem, however, was that the language of monarchy undermined the promotion of republican values. 'The ennobling reality of loyalty to the nation is choked at every turn by the obsolete fiction of loyalty to a family – loyalty to a pageant – loyalty to a sinecure.'[107] In effect he was arguing that Bagehot should come clean, and promote the values he really believed. '[I]n the true republic, the nation is the visible ever-present and ultimate master: from the president to the meanest functionary, from the highest function of government down to every button on every policeman's coat, there is visibly, indelibly imprinted the nation, and duty to the nation, employment only to those worthy of the nation.'[108]

---

[105] Bagehot, 'English republicanism', *CW*, V, p. 425; Bagehot, 'Sir Charles Dilke', *CW*, V, p. 416; Bagehot, 'The thanksgiving', *The Economist*, 24 February 1872, *CW*, V, p. 440.
[106] F. Harrison, 'The monarchy', *Fortnightly Review* 1 (1872), 631. It was reprinted in his *Order and Progress* (1874).
[107] Ibid., p. 641.   [108] Ibid., p. 639.

6   Power and authority in the late Victorian and Edwardian court

Michael Bentley

'It is not easy', David Cannadine wrote in 1989, 'to make the study of Queen Victoria yield significant difficulties'.[1] It all depends where one starts. If the assumption is that monarchs were once powerful and now patently are not, that Victoria lost the personal command that her Court had once claimed to have and that thereafter 'the attenuation of royal power has continued inexorably',[2] then the Victorian 'Court' need hardly detain a political historian.[3] If, on the other hand, the crude notion of power as the ability to compel through the deployment of legitimate force were to become substituted by a more nuanced understanding of authority, conceived as an historically informed expectation of complaisance from social inferiors within a stratified society, then perhaps something remains to be said. One thing appears certain. Wherever one starts in this discussion, Bagehot got it wrong. In a sense he could do little other, granted his location in time and opinion, his commitment to a form of forensic liberalism, his immediate experience of Queen Victoria as Mrs Brown, his standing heir to a tradition of Whig certainty that had long since reversed the spin of Dunning's motion of 1780, and celebrated the palpable truth that the power of the Crown had diminished and ought to remain diminished. Dignified functions remained, of course. An opening here, an unveiling there, presiding with funereal *gravitas* on occasions of state: the Queen retained these simple pleasures. But her power had shrunk in the pages of *The English Constitution* to a shadow of that cast even by her seafaring uncle, just as his had dwindled after the profligacy of George IV and the ungovernable madness of his, George's, father. So the quotations leap from Bagehot's pages as though one had always known

---

[1] D. Cannadine, 'The last Hanoverian sovereign?' in A. L. Beier, D. Cannadine and J. M. Rosenheim (eds.), *The First Modern Society: Essays in English History in honour of Lawrence Stone* (Cambridge, 1989), pp. 127–65, at 127.
[2] Ibid., p. 127.
[3] The word 'court' confuses because of its legal connotation, but it seems right for the purpose here in implying a structure beyond the person of the monarch. It may seem cumbersome to capitalize it as 'Court' but that will at least obviate the confusion.

them. '[T]he functions of English royalty are for the most part latent . . . it acts as a *disguise*: it enables our real rulers to change without people knowing it . . .' There was the right to be consulted, the right to encourage, the right to warn.[4] Into this frame we can so easily slip other pictures of ineffectual foppery and all-too-effective fornication, compounding the irrelevance of the Victorian Court to serious matters of government with an image of resigned dissolution centred on Albert Edward, whose seeming lack of interest in matters of state visibly confirmed that power had moved elsewhere. Besides, evidence abounded that the world had turned on its axis. No monarch had thrown out a ministry, as eighteenth-century kings had enjoyed doing, since 1834. The Queen, if she did not shut up, manifestly had to put up with Gladstone until events in Parliament or at the hustings relieved her. She patently could not control either those elections or the parliamentary combinations that resulted from them. If any power remained to her, it presumably lay in her ability to rouse her relatives who ran, rather more autocratically than could she, most of Europe. Were this vestigial power real, on the other hand, then it was also dubious: a dark legacy from less enlightened days. The future could only promise its removal, together with all such vestiges, as British democracy conquered whatever foothills of resistance remained. Twentieth-century monarchs on this reading would be required, as George V boasted he had when Ramsay MacDonald kissed hands, to move with the times.

What is most alarming about this assumed model of progress is not so much its provenance as its permanence. For the twentieth century has had to cope with more than Bagehot. At the very time that Bagehot saw the beginning of the end, the beginning of a strain of constitutional history and constitutional law helped enshrine his conclusions. By the side of a radical intellectual *paparazzo*, one has to place figures such as William Stubbs, Samuel Rawson Gardiner, John Robert Seeley and Albert Venn Dicey: figures who constructed a past as a progression from royal to parliamentary or even democratic government, and whose current constitutional theory placed the taming of the monarchy at its centre. On that platform later writers built; and images of atrophied kings and queens in an Ensor or Jennings[5] look very close to what this late Victorian conventional wisdom had made plain. At one level, there is no arguing with that

---

[4] W. Bagehot, *The English Constitution* (1867) in F. Morgan (ed.), *Collected Works* (5 vols., Hartford, CT, 1889), vol. 4, pp. 87, 95, 112. Perhaps most radically: 'a republic has insinuated itself beneath the folds of a monarchy' (p. 91).

[5] Sir Robert Ensor discovered a constitutional monarch 'whose duty consists more in symbolizing power than in wielding it' and quoted Bagehot to explain why the power of Edward VII was less than Victoria's: *England 1870–1914* (Oxford, 1936), pp. 342–3. William Jennings, *The Law and the Constitution* (1933), p. 163, quoted Dicey on 'the residue of discretionary or arbitrary authority which at any given time there is legally

wisdom as soon as its assumptions have been granted. Once proclaim that law and constitutional convention contain the threshed grain of a social and political history within them, as Stubbs and Maitland united in proclaiming, and the Victorian Court retreats into cipher – victim of an initiative long since yielded to Parliament, product of a collapse of venal patronage, weighed down by the financial yoke of the civil list – and has little left but its palaces and pretensions. One of the benefits of thinking about a political history that does not start from there, on the other hand, is that other definitions of authority and power may become available. And the moment one begins to speak of royal power in the language of use rather than entitlement, of social reality rather than legal theory, then it becomes appropriate to ask questions about what Queen Victoria and her sons actually *did* rather than concentrate on what the constitutional handbooks imply that they ought to have been doing. In this respect, modern historians lag many years behind their medieval colleagues who have brought a more nuanced understanding to issues of royal power by locating it differently from where the constitutionalists put it.[6] Certainly the proliferation of rules in the nineteenth century helped confine that power. But the presence of rules can camouflage a no-less-present authority that is informally or non-formally exerted. Governance by rulers, this essay is going to argue, need not itself be rule-governed.

Where, then, should a search begin? To train the lens on front-page stories of political change will miss much of the thrust of this enquiry, though the well-known behaviour of the Queen in passing over Lord Spencer in favour of the imperialist Lord Rosebery as Gladstone's successor in 1894 is far too lightly dismissed by commentators in a suppressive *topos*: a flash in the pan, the exception that proves the rule. It may equally come into focus as exceptional only for its prominence and notoriety. We shall dwell

---

left in the hands of the Crown' and left aside power illegally left, though in *The Queen's Government* (London, 1953), p. 30, he enjoyed a post-coronation moment of relaxation: 'even the constitutional lawyer cannot ignore . . . emotion.' (p. 30).

[6] Some of the drift of this criticism will be found in T. N. Bisson, *Cultures of Power: Lordship, Status and Process in Twelfth-Century Europe* (Philadelphia, 1995); J. L. Nelson, *Politics and Ritual in Early Medieval Europe* (1986). I am grateful to Professor John Hudson for his help with this point. As late as 1959, at the modern end of the chronology, John Mackintosh remained convinced that 'Bagehot's great virtue [was] that he aske[d] the right sort of question'; and 'though [Queen Victoria and Prince Albert] did play a part . . . Bagehot was still correct in pointing out that it was not essential': J. P. Mackintosh, 'The early political influence of Queen Victoria', *Parliamentary Affairs* 12 (1959), 174–88. This essentialist notion strikes the present writer as confused. To try and imagine abstracting the monarchy from the nineteenth-century political structure is not a helpful thought-experiment: it reduces issues about authority and leadership to disposable items of 'prerogative' and thereby implies the continuous diminuendo that it ought rather to establish by argument. A refreshing early exception in the historiography is William M. Kuhn, 'Ceremony and politics: the British monarchy, 1871–2', *Journal of British Studies* 26 (1987), 133–62.

a little on the Home Rule crisis of 1886 and discover the Queen a player – indeed a party player – not merely a spectator. We shall discover Albert Edward as both prince and king with his cigar ash in every pie. More subtle among the various facets of royal power was the royal role as head of the Church of England. Unlike her great-grandson, Victoria had no use at all for defending faith: her commitment was to a particular under-standing of Anglicanism, and we shall find her determined to enforce her leadership over the heads of bishops and indeed prime ministers. Her son learned how to do that at his mother's knee. There is the hackneyed allegation of European conspiracy. We shall find little evidence for its success, though plenty for Victoria's ambitions and Edward's distaste: it is satisfying that the one province of power permitted to her by her lawyers should turn out to be also the most illusory. In a world (theirs and ours) fascinated by issues of 'social power', it will make sense too to consider whether the Court's undeniable power to coerce those groups who sought its gaze and favour, trickled over into the domain of political influence. Nods and hints, for the monarch thought it vulgar to wink, do not express themselves in the legal record, after all. Perhaps we should begin there, with the unwritten.

I

The social power of the Court is easily minimized by quoting the frequent irritation to which it gave rise among those who wished it otherwise. Had Peel understood the passion of peers and peers' wives about a possi-ble place in the Bedchamber, he might have stumbled less blindly into the famous crisis of 1839. Disraeli, who did understand it, later spent anguished hours smoothing the feathers of those excluded. Gladstone did not need to care about it since he was *persona non grata* within the Court in any case. And for Salisbury it was one of those Martian mys-teries that he took to exercise fellow members of his House; he may not have understood it, but he knew that others did and cared, and he tried to navigate between the rocks of aristocratic importunity and royal dis-pleasure. Creating peers in the first place formed one segment of this social power, of course. Prime ministers proposed, but Her Majesty fre-quently disposed. When Salisbury went to see her at the height of his power in 1896 in order to press a Farquarson of Braemar on her for a peerage, at the suggestion of the Duke of Devonshire, he had thought that his candidate's influence with the Dukedom of Fife would prove an advantage, granted the Queen's blood relationship with that family. Quite to the contrary and to his great surprise, he encountered 'a very strong objection'. 'The influence [Farquarson] possesses with the Fifes', he told

Devonshire, 'far from being a recommendation, was mentioned as an objection. There is some petty strain or other between the two "Courts" just at this moment.' Devonshire was told to wait, and Farquarson did not proceed.[7] For a face that fitted, on the other hand, social ambition could take great leaps with a peerage: letters in her own sloping hand, grander somehow for being indecipherable, with always a question or remark or moment of solace about one's spouse; integration, possibly, into the fast set of Albert Edward's playmates with endless agreeable shooting and dancing; a sense of having arrived. At the very pinnacle of society there lurked even the threat that the Queen might actually come and visit, as she did ruinously at Burghley in 1844 when the cost of refurbishing her temporary bedroom drew heavily on the Marquis of Exeter's resources. Happily she did this rarely. Not so the Prince of Wales, who visited himself on anyone rich enough to look after him properly, such as the long-suffering Duke of Richmond. Providing sufficient game for him to slaughter presented the easy part of the arrangement. He also required full luncheon when out on the moor, properly set on a table in a pitched tent and, Richmond reported in some amazement, beginning with hot soup and ending with liqueurs[8] – no small challenge when most proprietors could not achieve hot food inside their dining rooms.

Finding oneself 'in' or 'out', included or cut, mattered desperately to climbing politicians. Lord Charles Beresford, who had never been too stable in the first place, decided in 1891 that his wife had been gratuitously 'cut' by the Prince of Wales. He shot off letters to the Prince and entered into a long spat with Salisbury about his determination to exact an apology. At first Salisbury tried to help in a long letter of astonishing patience, telling Beresford that such things were of no objective importance, even if he were right that offence had been intended. But when Beresford persisted in his fury, Salisbury fed him to the wolves and abandoned him without compunction, for the Court had to be protected and the Queen's name kept out of such matters.[9] Similarly, when Albert Edward's personal life became too complicated for the Archbishop of Canterbury further to ignore, an entirely private round of letters between the Prince, Archbishop Benson and Salisbury ring-fenced the difficulty, and it became a matter of bloodless procedure turning on whether the Prince should go to Lambeth or write a letter or do neither. The determination to keep the Court out of

---

[7] Salisbury to Devonshire, 3 Dec. 1896, eighth Duke of Devonshire papers, MSS 340.2703, Chatsworth House.

[8] And, when Richmond tottered off to bed after supervising all this, his guests did not. 'I am told the hours are late, they sit up playing American Bowls': Richmond to Cairns, 16 Nov. 1873, Cairns MSS 30/51/2/ff. 139–40, National Archives.

[9] Salisbury to Beresford (transcript), 10 Aug. 1891, Christ Church [Oxford] MSS, E29.

politics privileged its position within that arena, and foreclosed avenues that politicians may have wished to pursue if left to themselves. When Salisbury sent a note to his new minister, Lord Randolph Churchill, in 1885, assuring him that he would not meet with 'inconvenient Court pressure', he had already checked that a green flag could be waved and was aware that he, the prime minister, was not holding it.[10]

Prime ministers saw the queen far more regularly than they would have wished, and the triply-underlined notes that flew from her pen could chase them all over the country (Disraeli got three in one day while out of London). Her vitality in the late 1860s and through the 1870s dissipates in retrospective images on film that was usually shot at the jubilee celebrations or during the Boer War, so that one tends unthinkingly to read back that persona into her post-purdah phase. When Disraeli enticed her back into the world, she was still in middle age and not at all the frail and frumpy woman of the late 1890s, or even the lame one lamenting the death of John Brown in the 1880s. 'What energy! What nerve! What muscle!', Beaconsfield wrote privately of her as late as 1879.[11] She continued to edge her writing paper with black borders three-quarters of an inch wide, reducing to half an inch in her later years; but her grief and occasional hysteria did not make her less demanding for information, or less ready to issue instructions in the form of advice. Nor was she content to deal only with the prime minister: individual ministers found out quickly that she expected them to write to her frequently about what they were doing. She demanded this especially from her foreign secretary; and Derby, for one, found himself in trouble for not obliging. Her complaint to Disraeli was speedily passed to his colleague with a gentle but unambiguous instruction to comply. Good boys could receive stars, and a very charming and full letter might arrive from Osborne or Balmoral expressing the Queen's gratitude to Mr X for keeping her informed and hoping that he would continue to write at any time, and that Lady X should be assured that the Queen remained anxious to hear better news of her. This strategy, as the old hands knew, was double-edged. Once the Queen decided that a man had the right ideas and a sympathetic attitude, he would find himself moved up the list in the dreaded rota to act as minister in attendance.

---

[10] Salisbury to Churchill, ?17 Aug. 1885, Churchill MSS 9248/7/unfol., Churchill College Archives, Cambridge.

[11] Beaconsfield to the Duke of Marlborough, 26 Nov. 1879, Marlborough MSS 9271/4/68. Professor Arnstein rightly reminds us that the talk of diminishing powers often ignores signal moments in the chronology: 'it was not in 1839 but in 1868 that she appointed a new Archbishop of Canterbury in the face of her prime ministers' preference. It was in 1885 that she triumphantly asserted her right to send telegrams directly to her generals without consulting the War Office first': W. L. Arnstein, 'Queen Victoria opens Parliament: the disinvention of tradition', Historical Research 61 (1990), 178–94 at 194.

This mechanism has not received its due prominence in accounts of royal authority, partly because of its very insidiousness as a rhythm in ministerial lives, partly because ministers felt unable in their memoirs and histories to say how much they detested it. But the requirement that the Queen should always have a minister with her when out of London placed an obligation on her prime ministers to work out a schedule of prefects. In theory, all ministers were liable for the summons. Salisbury could plead national duties and escape with a letter which often contained little guidance beyond platitude. 'Lord Salisbury with his humble duty respectfully submits to Your Majesty that there is nothing new or important going on in the political world either at home or abroad,' was one of his better effusions.[12] Others could hardly plead the same pressures. Granted the Queen's strong opinions about individuals, however, and the patent truth that some people lived closer to Balmoral or Osborne than others, the burden was borne disproportionately by particular individuals. On the Conservative side, the Duke of Richmond rendered years of loyal and sterling service when based in Gordon Castle: he plainly conceived an enormous affection for the Queen.[13] W. H. Smith crossed class lines with ease to become the apple of the Queen's eye until his death in 1890. Among the Unionists, Hartington made himself a cynosure when he saved England from Gladstone in 1886. True, for the more self-assured ministers, an evening of tedium with Her Majesty, pedestrian in everything but clearing her plate, would provoke more sarcasm than a sense of loyalty. Lord Randolph Churchill, made to attend at Windsor when he became a minister in 1885, dispatched to his mother a distinctly underwhelmed report of the occasion:

Windsor was deadly. After dinner the Queen talked for $\frac{1}{4}$ an hour to [Hicks] Beach, 10 mts to [Lord] G[eorge] Hamilton and 7 mts to me; then 3 mts more to Beach and, oh joy! took herself off to bed, then 20 mts more deadly work with the household, then a cigarette in the Smoking Room which was exactly $6\frac{3}{4}$ miles from my bedroom.[14]

Balmoral was far worse, of course, because one had to make what Salisbury called 'a weary journey to the Arctic part of Scotland',[15] after which everyone had to stay for so much longer than at Windsor or Osborne, while enduring a regime that hardly helped the Queen make friends. 'All the people in attendance are weary of Balmoral', Derby complained during a visit in 1874. 'There is nothing to do indoors, and they are never

---

[12] Salisbury to the Queen, 27 Mar. 1888, R[oyal] A[rchives, Windsor Castle] VIC/A66/101.
[13] E.g. 'I am very glad you found our gracious Mistress in good form': Richmond to Hardy, 30 Aug. 1877, Cranbrook MSS T501/257, Suffolk Record Office.
[14] Churchill to Duchess of Marlborough (copy), 5 Jul. 1885, Churchill MSS 9248/6.
[15] Salisbury to Devonshire, 30 Oct. 1900, Devonshire MSS 340.2841.

allowed to go out, even for half an hour, till 4 p.m. in case it should occur to the Queen that she might want any of them. They are naturally disgusted and talk of the great lady's selfishness.'[16] But Derby did not figure among nature's insecure personalities and was not the strongest of Victoriaphiles in the first place.[17] For a being such as Twitters Carnarvon, on the other hand, *not* receiving an invitation to Balmoral cut to the quick: it underlined his marginality in a Conservative party increasingly depressed by his going wrong over Ireland – 'he is so very green', Salisbury was to intone – after having already gone wrong over Russia. Quite plainly, Carnarvon felt miffed and excluded from an arena in which he supposed some authority to reside.[18]

Presumably Lord Hartington, now eighth Duke of Devonshire, felt the same in 1898 when he found himself obliged to respond to the Queen's eccentric command to join her in Nice. She would allow him freedom of movement, he was told, but she expected him to book into a Nice hotel for an indefinite period. It served as a reminder that the mountain occasionally came to Mahomet. Indeed no nation, apart from Ireland, seemed immune from the threat of a royal visit. Salisbury expressed his personal revulsion against most of the crowned heads of Europe hovering like dragonflies above the Côte d'Azur, after he misguidedly built a house there. The Indians had to tolerate incursions from the Prince of Wales and others. '[T]he presence of the Royal Princes from time to time in India,' Salisbury told his Indian secretary in 1885, 'in positions of authority, gives a reality to the monarchy, which with Oriental races is very desirable.'[19] The Irish case, meanwhile, gave rise to much indigestion among politicians over a protracted period as the Queen originally resisted and eventually, in 1897, forbade their clear plan to make her establish a royal residence there – a 'Royal Hotel', as they termed it, an Irish Balmoral from which she and her princes could create that allegiance and deference which she had accomplished in Scotland, and supply much needed reassurance to the Irish that they were taken seriously at Court. Which is the more significant to the historian of Court power: that those in positions of formal political power thought it important to move the Court occasionally to that contested country? Or that the Queen, encouraged by the horror of the Prince of Wales and Duke of York, flatly refused to

16 Derby diary 28 Aug. 1874, in *A Selection from the Diaries of Edward Henry Stanley, 15th Earl of Derby, (1826–93) between September 1869 and March 1878*, ed. J. Vincent (1994), p. 178.
17 'To manage, flatter, keep in good humour the Queen is in itself an occupation': Derby diary, 21 Jan. 1877, ibid., p. 369.
18 Richmond to Cairns, Cairns MSS 30/51/4/ff. 28–9: 'Hardy told me that Twitters [i.e. Carnarvon] was much disturbed at not being summoned to Balmoral'.
19 Salisbury to Churchill, ?18 Sept. 1885, Churchill MSS 9248/8/unfol.

let them?[20] Either way, the fate of this initiative does not sit well with an argument recommending royal impotence or the dispensability of royal authority.

Then consider those to whom this authority became of prime importance because they were prime ministers. Bagehot reviewed in his mind's eye the less evocative trio: Peel, Russell, Palmerston. He might have written differently after forty years' experience of Disraeli, Gladstone and Salisbury – all still to come when *The English Constitution* made its mark. Those early skirmishings turned not on Victoria but on Albert, to whom she referred petitioners: his authority and his enthusiasms entered and helped mould the sphere of the possible. After 1861, *a fortiori* after 1866, the world became different and so did her role within it, sometimes in ways known only to those behind doors that remained closed to Bagehot and his kind.[21] Now Gladstone, it should be admitted at once, is a problem, for one could use his continual defiance of the Queen's wishes as evidence for the Queen's having little but rage left among her weaponry from 1868. She could not prevent him from dallying with the devil – over the Irish Church in 1869 and above all over Irish nationalism in the 1880s – though she at least made it plain that Labouchere would not be welcome in the cabinet so long as he remained a republican. She could and did intrigue with the other side (in 1886 both other sides) to bring his plans to nought. She could also make him quite supremely miserable by treating him much worse than badly: appallingly, disgracefully, as Colin Matthew has lamented. A visit to Osborne in 1892, when he had become prime minister again, echoed the familiar theme. 'At the main interview', his diary records, 'the Queen was cautiously polite. In nothing helpful . . . Not one sympathetic word on any question however detached. After dinner a little unfrozen. [I] Read Englishman in Paris'.[22] More significantly, she could bamboozle him by refusing to discuss anything that mattered. A few months later in 1892 he was bidden to Windsor, and afterwards thoughtfully wrote down all the topics that the Queen had deigned to discuss with him. It is not the stuff of high strategy. 'The fogs of London & Windsor . . . The [poet] Laureateship . . . Condition of Lady Kimberley,

---

[20] Salisbury to Cadogan, 2 Nov. 1897, Cadogan MSS CAD/1226, House of Lords Record Office.

[21] 'To study the organs of State which exercise the executive and administrative functions is the most difficult task that a student of constitutional law has to perform. He is of necessity, without that acquaintance with what took place in Cabinet meetings or within government departments which could alone give him an intimate knowledge of the machine in operation': E. C. S. Wade and G. Godfrey Phillips, *Constitutional Law: an outline of the law and practice of the constitution* (1931, 8th edition, 1970), p. 170.

[22] Gladstone diary, 15 Aug. 1892, in *The Gladstone Diaries*, ed. H. C. G. Matthew (14 vols., Oxford, 1968–94), vol. 13, p. 59.

Has Mrs. Gladstone still a nephew who is master at Eton . . . Health of the Bishop of Rochester' and only finally the agricultural distress, which the Queen deemed the result of too many imports (the fault of foreigners), and the desirability of a royal commission to investigate it, which the Queen deemed otiose.[23] Gladstone did not enjoy these encounters, and his inability to avoid them says something for a persistent undertow of royal difficulty. His mistress could assuredly be overborne but the bearing took energy, patience and grit that most men expended on other problems. Easier, perhaps to jolly her along by taking a line of lesser resistance.

In turning to the Tory duumvirate, moreover, we see this ease visibly deepening. One of Disraeli's first acts on becoming prime minister for the second time in 1874 looked very much like a Court imposition. It was common knowledge that the Queen's personal vendetta against ritualists in the Church of England knew no bounds, and the ill-starred Public Worship Regulation Bill never threw off its putative origins as a royal retribution against them. That, and Disraeli's inspired elevation of the Queen to imperial status, gave the Court the friend who had been considered lacking. This important but familiar story masks a better one. For it was Queen Victoria who, toward the end of her life, observed that Lord Beaconsfield had been a great man but Lord Salisbury a greater; and the constitutional kitsch of the Beaconsfield era throws into rather subdued light a glow of warmth between the greater Tory presence of the nineteenth century's final quarter and his Queen. Like his Tudor ancestor, Lord Burghley, Robert Cecil, the third Marquis of Salisbury saw his personal understanding of and with the Queen to lie at the heart of what he wanted to achieve in politics. It was a love relationship. He took Gladstone's chalice in 1885 for her sake, not his own, and protecting her from the ravages of party life struck him ever after as an imperative. This did not mean that he found her always congenial: she was spoiled, frequently impossible, and he groaned about it quite as much as anyone else in the Court circle. It was he who famously designated her the fourth of his ministerial responsibilities, along with the premiership, the foreign office and Randolph Churchill. But he self-consciously matched his life with hers, his power alongside hers, and many years before her death in 1901 he had, Gwendolin Cecil remarked in a private letter, 'fixed upon [the event] in his mind as the period of his public life.'[24] Serving his Queen mattered to Salisbury not merely at a constitutional level but also at a devotional one and, as with his predecessor in the Conservative leadership, this devotion

---

[23] Ibid., 25 Nov. 1892, p. 153.

[24] Gwendolen Cecil to Lord Cross, 15 Jul. 1902, Cross MSS 51264, f. 148, British Library.

sometimes meant avoiding trouble by pre-empting it – not the behaviour of an individual monopolizing power. Even at the end, when he knew her so well, he dreaded having to negotiate his relinquishing of the Foreign Office to Lansdowne in 1900 while she, for her part, had lost nothing of her force in the matter of appointments, 'hostile to Balfour of Burleigh at the Admiralty, 'fill[ed] . . . with alarm' by the idea of Hicks Beach at the Home Office and more than ready to see the back of Cross and Ashbourne.[25]

Yet this very act of pre-emption removed controlling behaviour from the overt historical record. Only when a difference of view between Windsor and Downing Street became a patent rift, as over the Queen's disregard of Gladstone's advice as to who should succeed him in 1894, or her son's disregard of Campbell-Bannerman's advice in 1908, did evidence of royal power or weakness emerge in the newspapers or *Hansard* or political memoirs. For the rest one has to look for sidelights in the private correspondence and diaries of the period. It turns out that the Devonshire papers are especially rich in this respect for the late Victorian period, partly because Salisbury felt it necessary to consult Hartington assiduously in the days of uneasy understanding between Conservatives and Unionists after 1886, and particularly within the more formalized relationship from 1895. In attempting to form that third administration, Salisbury had to consult about sending Lansdowne, a Liberal Unionist, to the War Office and reported *en passant* that '[t]he Queen kick[ed] at Goschen for [the]Admiralty',[26] though he appears to have won her round. She then gave trouble in precisely the opposite direction when Salisbury did his best to get rid of the seventy-three-year-old Henry James, another Liberal Unionist, in the post-election reshuffle in 1900. 'The Queen is very much attached to James,' he complained to Devonshire, '& will not let him go'.[27] Nor did she. Another reason why Hartington mattered in this connexion, moreover, was that he had come so much to impress the Queen herself as a symbol of Raleigh-like solidarity in the face of Irish wickedness and Gladstonian evil. Her anger and sorrow at the murder of Hartington's brother in Phoenix Park in 1882 turned into a deeply felt gratitude when Hartington refused to swallow the pill of Home Rule at the end of 1885. Gladstone's heir-apparent spoke in strong terms against that policy in April 1886[28] and found the Duke of Cambridge declaring

[25] Akers-Douglas (from Balmoral) to Balfour, 17 Oct. 1900, Balfour MSS 49772, fo 18, British Library.
[26] Salisbury to Devonshire, 26 Jun. 1895, Devonshire MSS 340.2621.
[27] Salisbury to Devonshire, 6 Nov. 1900, ibid., 340.2846.
[28] The parliamentary speech of 9 April is not stressed in A. B. Cooke and J. Vincent, *The Governing Passion: Cabinet Government and Party Politics in Britain 1885–6* (Brighton, 1974), pp. 107–12.

himself 'Hartington's most sincere friend', while the Queen herself saw no point in remaining aloof from the party warfare dominating Parliament in the shadow of the first Home Rule Bill:

> As this is no party question [!], but one that concerns the safety, honour & welfare of her Dominions, the Queen wishes to express personally to Lord Hartington not only her admiration of his Speech on Friday Night but also to thank him for it.
> It shows that patriotism & loyalty go, as they always should, before Party.
> And she thinks with certainty now – that these dangerous and ill-judged measures for unhappy Ireland will be defeated.

She did not stop there. In August she pressed on Hartington his duty to form a coalition with Salisbury after the 'very satisfactory results of the Elections' and, when she failed to engineer that, she told Hartington that at the very least he must support the Conservative leader in all important questions. In December, when the departure of Churchill offered a chance for further reconstruction, she spent part of Christmas Day writing and underlining a letter to Hartington about his imperative duty to join the government in order to stop Gladstone coming back which could only, she said, be productive of 'most disastrous consequences'.[29] He did not come in and Gladstone did not come back, but she still took the trouble to write again in the New Year to commend the integrity of Hartington's behaviour and describe it, beautifully, in a Freudian mis-spelling, as 'partiotic.' Salisbury went out of his way to assure her, later in the year, that he had 'had a long talk' with Hartington and found him 'cordial & loyal'.[30]

Such correspondence leaves little room for the even-handedness implied in constitutional theory: the Queen and her Court took sides and fought corners. Their side and corner need not be Conservative; so perhaps in one respect they eschewed bias. One spectacular case in which it ran in an anti-Tory direction concerned an attempt by Gladstone's second government to push through a Deceased Wife's Sister Bill in 1883, one of nineteen such attempts before success in 1907. The thought seems arcane now, but the problem posed by biblical injunction against a man's

---

[29] Cambridge to Hartington, 10 Apr. 1886; Queen to Hartington, 11 Apr., 6 Aug., 25 Dec. 1886 and 5 Jan 1887: Devonshire MSS 340. Her mood had eased a little from its climacteric in December 1885 when she had told Salisbury: 'Mr Gladstone & Lord Granville are both utterly unfit, from age alone, to carry on the Government and to them the Queen will not resort. Whatever apparent majority they may have – it is entirely divided and all moderate & intelligent people have no confidence in them or in Mr Chamberlain who frightens every one & who with Sir C. Dilke, who is disgraced personally are impossible. We want a strong coalition . . .' The Queen to Salisbury (copy), 3 Dec. 1885, RA VIC/A63/88.

[30] Salisbury to the Queen, 11 Jul. 1887, RA VIC/A66/12.

marrying his sister-in-law once he had become widowed was a real and painful one in late-Victorian society, granted the strength of familial contact and attachments. Legislation to permit such marriage, and avoid the unedifying sight of couples going to Sweden or elsewhere to marry, had to wait until the Campbell-Bannerman government after 1906. But previous failed attempts raised high passion, and the interest of the 1883 episode in the current context hinges on the Court's determination to drive the Bill through. Some of the pressure came from the Queen herself, always a martyr to married love. Yet more came from the Prince of Wales – intriguing in view of his own flexibilities – and the two for once became allies in a holy war against social reaction and the stickiness of the Church. Again we have to look to private comment rather than published debates and division lists; among possible witnesses the most helpful, complete and embarrassing is the Archbishop of Canterbury, Edward White Benson – not least because no other source approaches his unpublished diary in showing how far the Court was willing to go.

The Bill had been introduced in the Commons during the spring by Lord Dalhousie and had proceeded through its initial stages. What exercised the Court was a suspicion that the bishops in the House of Lords would adopt their conventional position in regard to the biblical anathema. Rumours began to travel in Westminster that the Queen had asked Benson himself not to speak when the Bill came to the Lords, in order to encourage the peers towards acceptance. What emerges from Benson's diary is that the rumour was perfectly well-founded. Even more surprising, he alleged that pressure had simultaneously been put on the Archbishop of York by the Prince of Wales. Benson's diary, 31 May 1883:

The P of W endeavoured to persuade Abp of York to 'have an important engagement in the country at 5 [pm]' on 11 June [the date of second reading in the House of Lords]. 'Don't trouble yourself about a pair. I'll find you a pair'! This action on the part of the Royal Family is not only unprecedented in these days, but is rapidly doing a work which may grow important one day. It is fast alienating the church subjects, i.e. the most loyal subjects they have.[31]

Benson surely did not exaggerate in finding royal interference of this kind startling. On 2 June the Queen herself wrote to Davidson, plainly intending her message to be relayed to Benson, dwelling again on her displeasure that the Archbishop might speak. 'Is not Her Majesty's watch wrong?,' asked the primate with a certain bitterness. Come the day of the second reading, moreover, the Prince of Wales sent into battle a clutch of his own hearties to press the issue further. 'Just before the end of Lord

---

[31] Benson diary, 31 May 1883, Trinity College Library, Cambridge.

Coleridge's speech,' Benson wrote in his diary that evening,[32] 'a long continuous train streamed into the House of boys, dissatisfied looking boys, young Lords whom the P[rince of] W[ales] has beaten up from the Race Course and ?the Regimental Dinner. . . . The result was received with joyful howls.'[33]

A preoccupation with the exercise of power over bishops should surprise no one familiar with the Queen's understanding of her role within the Church of England. She defended, quite self-consciously, the Protestant establishment of the National Church and took seriously her responsibility to save it from fanatics, dissenters and crypto-papists. In order to achieve that protection she often operated politically, playing off Lambeth Palace against Downing Street and using her closer contacts within the Church to express her wishes and round up support for her candidates or causes. For a time her Dean of Windsor, Randall Davidson, became something of a *confidant* and that relationship helped underpin her understanding with Canterbury, for Davidson was Tait's son-in-law, Benson's former chaplain, and became the Queen's personal chaplain. It was on a visit to Davidson in 1883, that Benson found the Queen there in the Deanery shortly after John Brown's death and her conversation, which he wrote down, echoed her sense of a lost age.

'As I get older I cannot understand the world. I cannot comprehend its littleness. When I look at the frivolities and littleness, it seems to me as if they were all going a little mad . . . .'
    She said all places begin to grow sad to her: Balmoral will be sad now; sorrowful recollections of kindness & attractiveness gone from her. 'All the little corners of my life seem to be broken off.' She said a great comfort to her was the outspoken horror of Bradlaugh among the masses of the people.[34]

The last sentence catches, perhaps, her more typical mood of aggression in dealing with the Church's issues and its offices. It had been she, after all, and not Disraeli, who had appointed Archibald Campbell Tait to Canterbury after dismissing the prime minister's own nominees as ineffectual or wobbly over ritualism.[35] And had 'my faithful Commons not supported

---

[32] Coleridge in *Hansard (Lords)*, CCLXXX, cols. 178–84, 11 Jun. 1883. The Prince of Wales, the Duke of Connaught and the Duke of Albany voted in the majority (165–158). Benson did speak against: cols. 171–8.

[33] Benson diary, 2 June and 11 June 1883. A decade before, the Prince of Wales had upset Richmond when both he and the Duke of Cambridge had paired in support of a Deceased Wife's Sister's Bill, 'which', Richmond confessed in private, 'I think a great mistake': Richmond to Cairns, 14 Mar. 1873, Cairns MSS 30/51/2/f. 121.

[34] Benson diary, 11 May 1883, A5. John Brown had died on 29 March.

[35] See J. Bentley, *Ritualism and Politics in Victorian Britain: the attempt to legislate for belief* (Oxford, 1978), 7–8 and P. Marsh, *The Victorian Church in Decline: Archbishop Tait and the Church of England 1868–82* (London, 1969). Liddon took the news, as one might have

me', she told her appointee after the passage of the Public Worship Regulation Bill, 'I should have been fain to give up my heavy crown' and hand over to one of her Italian cousins, 'the representatives of the Stuarts'.[36] It was she who connived with his successor, Benson, behind Salisbury's back, neutralizing quickly his, Benson's, nominal Gladstonianism (every man is allowed one mistake) and feeding his dislike and distrust of Salisbury when it suited her, to overcome the prime minister's opinions. It was she, egged on by Benson, who insisted on Westcott's going to Durham after the death of Lightfoot. True, she had conceded that she would have to give way if pressed, but she saw Salisbury and made him feel that he could not press.[37] It was her cry of outrage that made Salisbury rethink his project of making Henry Parry Liddon bishop of Oxford: the Queen thought Liddon no better than Pusey and the rest of the ritualist subversives. And it is not as though Salisbury minced words about the injustice done:

Lord Salisbury would be wanting in his duty if he did not state frankly his opinion that the exclusion of Canon Liddon from the episcopate – or at least from the offer of it – is a severe measure, which is likely to do harm to the Church of England. He is so much the most brilliant member of the Clergy of the Established Church, that his being passed over is a conspicuous act of censure and punishment for which the members of the Church do not readily see the reason.[38]

But the Queen did; and she had her way. These were not moments of consultation, encouragement or warning: they supplied instances of naked insistence in an area where the Queen brooked no opposition to her very considerable will. Placing her success within the context of late Victorian ecclesiology and the central place of church opinion from the 1870s to the 1890s, this arena become particularly significant, and it seems a matter

expected, badly. 'It really seems as if everything were going against the Catholic party in the Church of England. Between these miserable appointments [Tait to Canterbury and Jackson to London], and these miserable decisions of a Court whose very existence is, religiously speaking, a crying outrage, we are very hard pressed': J. O. Johnstone, *Henry Parry Liddon* (London, 1904), pp. 115–6. Much of what follows here reflects from a Salisburian point of view what Professor Bahlman discovered from a Gladstonian. See D. W. R. Bahlman, 'Politics and Church patronage in the Victorian Age', *Victorian Studies* 22 (1979), 253–96, esp. 289: 'The Queen's influence had been decisive – and continued to be so . . .'

[36] Tait's diary, ?18 Jul. 1874, quoted in Peter Marsh, *Decline*, 187.

[37] See Ponsonby to Salisbury (copy), 3 Feb. 1890, and Davidson to the Queen, 5 Mar. 1890, RA VIC/D10/136, 145. Salisbury retaliated by preventing Davidson's having Winchester on which the Queen had set her heart, as had he. He got Rochester.

[38] Salisbury to the Queen, 6 Jul. 1888, RA VIC/D10/9. This letter is not even noted in the Journal. Some of the issues raised in this paragraph are taken further in M. Bentley, *Lord Salisbury's World: Conservative Environments in Late-Victorian Britain* (Cambridge, 2001), pp. 160–4.

for surprise that more has not been made of it by those attempting to estimate the boundaries of royal power in these decades.

As in matters ecclesiastical, so in domains imperial do the allegations of royal impotence often appear exaggerated or downright misleading. They seem so particularly when aimed at Indian policy, for the Queen-Empress took a special interest in it, harried ministers who did not, and had no scruple over operating unilaterally if she saw a good to be done there. Of course the Court itself saw one end of this preoccupation in the status given to the Munshi – her favourite Indian servant – in the post-Brown years. This reveals no more than a genuine concern for, and some admiration of, the Indian character coupled with a sharp dislike of those who patronized native Indian society on the ground of an assumed racial superiority. For all the froth associated with Disraeli's famous *démarche* in making her Empress of India, the Queen took her status in deadly earnest and comported herself as an Empress should, taking an obtrusive personal interest, for instance, in the visit of the Prince of Wales in 1875–6. In the case of a pliant Indian minister such as Salisbury (1866–7 and 1874–8), her influence could be brought to bear without outcry or embarrassment and may, incidentally, go some way toward explaining Salisbury's later subservience elsewhere. Randolph Churchill was a different proposition. He had hardly warmed his seat at the India Office in 1885 when he felt obliged to present Salisbury with the first of his resignations. He had objected with some violence to the appointment of HRH the Duke of Connaught to the Bombay Command only to find his views overridden, as he thought by Salisbury himself. The prime minister soon assured him that all he, Salisbury had done was to encipher the offending telegram: it was the Queen herself who had composed it and she who had sent it.[39] Churchill, not for the last time, threw a tantrum. How could he stay? 'I shall never know,' he objected to Salisbury, 'what communication may not be passing between the Queen, the Prime Minister & the Viceroy on matters of great and small importance. . . . [At] any moment this action may recur.'[40] Salisbury poured copious oil, as usual, and probably was the one who persuaded the Duke of Cambridge to write to Churchill to thank him for assenting to the arrangement. The prime

[39] Churchill to Salisbury (copy) 14 Aug. 1885; Salisbury to Churchill, 15 Aug. 1885, Churchill MSS 9248/7. On the 16th the Queen's journal recorded '[a] great bother and annoyance about Arthur's leave', which then led to an unusual outburst of passion in this guarded text on the following day. 'Startled by Ld. Salisbury telegraphing absurd behaviour of Ld. Randolph, who wished to resign, because I had asked privately of Ld. Dufferin through Ld. Salisbury, as to Arthur's fitness for Bombay, which had been answered in a most satisfactory manner . . . However he has since returned to reason . . .': RA Queen Victoria's Journal, 16/17 Aug. 1885.

[40] Churchill to Salisbury (copy), 15 Aug. 1885, Churchill MSS 9248/7.

minister insisted that the Queen's name must not be dragged into political controversy (a prohibition which she understood and used as licence) and that, as ever, it would break up the party. Churchill rescinded his resignation, and contented himself with rejecting the Queen's application for a government subvention for Maharajah Duleep Singh who had taken a shine to England and wished to remain there. A deeper significance nevertheless remained, and the cameo repays inspection. When the Empress chose to behave imperially, she would do so with or without the support of cabinet and prime minister in order to govern territories which she took in some untrivial sense to be hers.

She felt the same, of course, about much of Europe, trying to bully her various relatives into submission or insert them into positions of power. By 1895 Salisbury felt almost sorry for the Kaiser on account of the royal drubbing with which he was continually met. 'He is very susceptible & imperious', Salisbury told Devonshire, '& he would resent bitterly anything like personal remonstrance. He is more than usually resentful on that head, because our Royal Family . . . have given him more lectures and hints than he thinks a German Emperor . . . ought to receive.'[41] Wilhelm plainly took no notice of 'the old hag' and nor did anyone else except for those supplicants who hoped that Victoria's personal influence might help them up the ladder. Nor, in this segment of policy, did Salisbury – a point of some importance when one considers the length of his control over British foreign policy after 1878. She did not expect to restrain Gladstone, whose manifest wickedness in abandoning Gordon to his fate compounded a series of repellent Little Englandisms broadcast in Midlothian. But Disraeli and Salisbury ran administrations that she did expect to influence; and the undoubted role that she played in the couching of their domestic or imperial policies, led her mistakenly to assume that she could run foreign policy in the same way.

Disraeli proved the more pliable. He tried to keep the Queen broadly satisfied with the conduct of affairs by communicating with her himself and urging relevant colleagues to remember their duty to her, as we have seen. In the crisis of his majority government – the war between Russia and Turkey in 1877 – he nevertheless could not follow royal prescriptions when his cabinet fractured so sourly between Derby and Carnarvon's doves and Salisbury's hawks. As she became more excited through the summer of 1877 and brayed for blood, her minister-in-attendance, Richard Cross, faithfully copied out her memoranda for the government from Balmoral and made sure that ministers received missives such as the following in September of that year:

[41] Salisbury to Devonshire, 31 Dec. 1895, Devonshire MSS 340.2674.

The question now arises whether, in the interests of humanity, justice and of the British Empire, this [war] is to be allowed to go on to the bitter end, merely to remain neutral, and avoid all interference? The Queen is most decidedly of opinion that this should not be . . . We should, then, propose certain terms [to Russia]. . . . and should, at the same time, say – that if these are rejected, we shall support Turkey in the defence of her Capital – and in preventing her extermination. We should state this to the other Powers, asking them to join us, in preventing further bloodshed, either by enforcing our terms by negociation [sic], or else by force of arms.[42]

Thirty of those words are underlined lest the meaning remain elusive. It made no difference. Disraeli bundled her along with his usual skill, and he continued to decide policy along lines of force on which Balmoral and Osborne did not lie. Salisbury may have thought, in jealous moments, that the Queen had played her part in preventing a coercive policy toward the Turks from emerging and bringing about that 'emasculate, purposeless vacillation' that he lamented,[43] but he erred if he did. The Queen did not fight the war and did not end it. The Congress of Berlin was not a royal creation. The deepening mire into which Beaconsfield's government walked in Afghanistan and Zululand they discovered all by themselves and no tugging from Windsor would pull them out.

In Salisbury the Queen found a foreign secretary of some majesty, but the discovery had the drawbacks of its advantages. If he could be left to make policy in a way that the royal family would welcome, he refused to follow in this domain any instinct but his own, and dealt gently but very firmly with attempts to preference the royal wishes. Nowhere did this recalcitrance become clearer than over the Queen's rabid insistence that Prince Alexander of Battenberg be kept on his trembling Bulgarian throne in 1886.[44] The point of Alexander, in British eyes, lay in preventing Russian hegemony, and Salisbury had always been as keen as

---

[42] Memo. by Queen (copy by Cross), 7 Sep. 1877, Cross MSS 51265 ff. 65–6. Maybe she remembered how powerful she had been made to feel in 1863–4 in the opposite direction: that of preventing a war with Prussia over the latter's aggression towards Schleswig-Holstein. But the historian of that episode sees the Queen's minister's helping her toward power when it suited their own pacific ambitions. See K. A. P. Sandiford, 'The British Cabinet and the Schleswig-Holstein crisis, 1863–4', *History* 58 (1973), 360–83.

[43] '[A]s you know, neither the Queen nor the Prime Minister will have anything to do with' the policy of coercing the Turks: Salisbury to Northcote, 15 Dec. 1877, Iddesleigh MSS 50019 ff. 53–4, British Library. For the famous remark about vacillation, quoted by Gwendolen Cecil, see Salisbury to Carnarvon, 27 May 1877, Carnarvon MSS 60758 f. 38, British Library.

[44] Apart from his family connexion with Britain through the Battenbergs, Alexander was the son of an Austrian general, and his aunt married the Tsar. He fell to a coup in August 1886 see R. J. Crampton, *Bulgaria 1878–1918: a History* (New York, 1983), pp. 35–7.

the Queen in keeping Alexander in power.[45] But he acknowledged, as Victoria never did, the passivity of the project and tried to teach her about British difficulties when framing foreign policy. '[T]he efforts and frequent failures of Your Majesty's servants in foreign affairs', he contended, 'must be viewed with indulgence. It is their destiny always to be making bricks without straw. Without money, without any strong land force, with an insecure tenure of power, and with an ineffective agency, they have to counterwork the efforts of three Empires, who labour under none of these disadvantages.'[46] He suppressed his greatest problem – the cabinet – which, like Beaconsfield's, struggled to find any coherent view of what to do with Russia when at least three of its number seemed happy to let the Balkan peninsula go, even if Constantinople went, too.[47] The Queen had to be appeased, certainly, but she did not guide policy and certainly could not impose one. Where Salisbury did not do so, Bismarck and not she supplied the deficiency, and she died having quite failed to resolve or crush Britain's difficulties with the German Court.

II

Edward VII fared no better in that respect and he prospered less than his mother in several others.[48] He and his Court demand closer study, however, than they often receive among historians persuaded in advance by their sense of what happened after 1901 and the feeling that the reign will soon degenerate into a narrative of royal ineptitude and frivolity.[49] If he was his mother's son he was emphatically a *senior* son: almost sixty when he succeeded, a touch older than George IV had been, a little younger than William IV, at their respective accessions, and with thirty years of executive dabbling behind him. Commentators dwell on his sufferings at the Queen's hands and her view that he could not be trusted with affairs of state: all true enough. But he also learned from her, despite

---

[45] Salisbury to Smith, 29 Sep. 1885, Hambledon MSS P59/71, archive of W. H. Smith and Son Ltd. He congratulated Smith on his handling of the Queen.

[46] Salisbury to the Queen, 29 Aug. 1886, quoted in Lady G. Cecil, *Life of Robert, Marquis of Salisbury* (4 vols., London, 1921–32), vol. 4, p. 3.

[47] Salisbury to Cranbrook, 8 Sep. 1886, Cranbrook MSS T501/263. He thought Churchill, Hamilton and Smith certain, with Hicks Beach a possible fourth.

[48] His own attempt to bully the cabinet over Russia in the wake of the Anglo-Russian Convention in 1907 is a case in point. His ministers probably shared his view that Russian aspirations should to some extent be met, but not because he had lectured them on looking at the issue 'from a European & International point of view': The King to Asquith, 13 Oct.1908, Asquith MSS I, 1 f.53, Bodleian Library, Oxford.

[49] This image may have owed something initially to Sir Sidney Lee's entry on King Edward in the *Dictionary of National Biography* which occasioned distress at the Palace.

his resentments, and ingested notions about his place in the world that made him try to do what she had done. It was not merely that he wanted to play the parliamentarian with his noisy friends from the Marlborough Club. He wanted politicians to understand from the start that they should expect no lowering of demands if his turn should ever come as King. A note saying, 'I shall look forward by 4 o'clock to a list of the new Govt as at present formed', might have seemed sufficiently saucy if directed at his own prime minister; it had still more piquancy for having been aimed at his mother's some fifteen years before he had any constitutional power.[50] Once enthroned, he bullied his governments less than she had thought desirable, but he expected no less information and no less respect; he wanted to see, for instance, 'the principal points of the Old Age Pensions Bill' in 1908 quite as peremptorily as she would have done.[51] He brought no less prejudice to the exercise of authority and no less temper when he thought it flouted. He *cared* about what government was doing far more than the familiar vignettes sometimes imply, and his concern took him in directions learned from his upbringing. Nor is it accidental that his points of friction with centres of political power tended to be the same as his mother's: the Empire, the peerage, the Church, defence of the realm, dangers of insurrection. Failing as a son, he made his propitiation by extending her project.

But the balance of his interests worked differently. The Empire mattered in his mind but Edward's concerns turned as usual on personnel. Curzon he thought a good man, but he did not listen to the bleating from India suggesting that the Coronation Durbar ought to be marked by 'a special mark of Royal Favour' through a reduction in the salt tax.[52] And when Curzon finally exhausted the patience of the home government, the King had little compunction in saying that he should go and none at all in proposing that Lord Ampthill should succeed him.[53] It was all a very long away in any case for so present-minded a personality, and the refrain of Empire began to weary him: perhaps 'there [was] a little too much talk in these days of "Imperial" and "Empire"'.[54] The Church was nearer; but the King again seized on his responsibilities to it only when persons became the matter at hand. So it became pressing for him to know from

---

[50] Prince of Wales to Edward Hamilton, 3 Feb.1886, Hamilton MSS 48599 f.1, British Library.
[51] Knollys to Nash, 4 May 1908, Asquith MSS I, 1.
[52] Curzon to Knollys (copy), 12 Nov.1902, Balfour MSS 49683 f.113.
[53] Knollys to Balfour, 10 Aug.1905, Balfour MSS 49685 ff.21–2.
[54] Knollys to Haldane (reporting the King's view), 10 Oct.1909, Haldane MSS 5908 f.190, National Library of Scotland.

the prime minister which name would be submitted to him in 1903 as the next Archbishop of Canterbury, if only to prevent the Bishop of Rochester getting anything in the unseemly reshuffle that would follow.[55] All turned on the character of those who were to wield authority in the state – those with whom the King might need to deal – and not on principles or ideas involved in the discussion. The tendency followed Edward's own lines of force which were at once his limitation and strength, for what he lost in grasp he gained in focus.

He knew about the army and wanted, like his mother, to see it run by people he trusted. Having Arnold-Forster imposed on the War Office by Balfour had proved painful, and he did all he could to reduce the minister's influence and issue reprimands whenever he came across the slightest trace of rudeness or perfunctory consultation. By contrast (and paradoxically, given the Liberal record in matters military) Campbell-Bannerman's war minister, R. B. Haldane, struck the King as first-rate and he listened harder to Haldane than to anybody else in that Liberal Government formed in December 1905 that was, some alleged, to kill him by 1910. True, Haldane was impetuous. He caused endless trouble in 1907 by proposing that the Colonial Conference might best be celebrated by making Botha a British General; and the King's self-appointed guardian – the velvet but ruthless Lord Esher who controlled the Committee of Imperial Defence – entered one of his periodic crises as he strove successfully to prevent it. On the other hand, Haldane liked going to Germany and could converse comfortably in the language: a great plus from the royal point of view. He was effective as an executive minister. He had the sense not to talk to the King about Hegel and did not arouse antagonism for past radicalisms, unlike Campbell-Bannerman, or for an unfortunate manner that left Edward feeling that he was being tutored, as he tended to do when Asquith visited him.[56] Indeed, it had been Haldane who had acted as the Balmoral end of the well-known 'Relugas' conspiracy: a story that has been told many times before but stands revival here when observed from the King's point of view.

In opposition over the summer of 1905, when Balfour's government had encountered major internal difficulties, three senior shadow-ministers, Edward Grey, Haldane and H. H. Asquith, met secretly at Grey's fishing lodge, called 'Relugas', to decide what their line should be in the event of the party leader, Campbell-Bannerman, receiving a call

[55] Knollys to Sandars, 6 Jan.1903, Balfour MSS 49683 f.124.

[56] 'Asquith's visit was anything but a success . . . I fear that Asquith will never get rid of his rough, abrupt manner with him': Knollys to Haldane, 16 Oct.1909, Haldane MSS 5908 f.192.

to the Palace. They committed themselves to staying out of a Campbell-Bannerman government and to proposing rather that 'C-B' should go to the House of Lords and make way for Asquith. It was the latter who then prodded Haldane into writing to Lord Knollys, the King's secretary, to suggest a private meeting with the King in order to discuss the matter (not much 'attenuation' there), and in October 1905 Haldane made his visit to Balmoral for that purpose. They had 'a pretty full talk'. 'The plan [was] thoroughly approved in all its details.' The King would ask Campbell-Bannerman to Sandringham in November and voice doubts about his age and resilience. Asquith should talk in general terms to the leader but 'not to go so far as to let him surmise any connection between your conversation and what may be done here. They [the King and Knollys] are fully alive to the importance of secrecy and reticence.'[57] That all of this came to nothing misses the point from the royal end of the incident. What it demonstrates is that Edward was quite as ready as Queen Victoria to intervene directly in political action when politicians gave him the chance of playing a role. What she had thought acceptable in 1886 he thought no less so twenty years later. The incident also had its unspoken sequel when the King asked Asquith to kiss hands following Campbell-Bannerman's retirement in 1908. He did not bother to ask for the prime minister's advice and had made sure of his ground constitutionally by consulting Balfour before Campbell-Bannerman finally went.[58]

A less secret form of intervention concerned the issue for which the reign of Edward VII is perhaps best remembered, that of conflict between the two Houses of Parliament and the constitutional crisis that followed, with its threat of requiring the monarch to create Liberal peers to end the impasse over the Upper Houses's refusal to pass Lloyd George's 'people's budget' of 1909. Undoubtedly this matter cut to the heart of Edward's personal conception of kingship. He had worried regularly since 1906 about the Liberal government's unconciliatory approach to the Second Chamber, originally over the abortive Education Bills[59] and then over ministers' progressive heightening of tension about the Lords' lack of

---

[57] Haldane to Asquith ('secret'), 6 Oct.1906 [recte 1905] and Haldane to Knollys (copy), 17 Oct.1905, Haldane MSS 5906 ff.218–20 and 5918 ff.38–40.

[58] Balfour advised in February that the King could see Asquith at once and treat him as de facto prime minister after ascertaining what changes Asquith wished to make. The King could then go to Biarritz, which he was waiting to do, and Asquith could be called there to kiss hands, which he was: Balfour to Knollys, 24 Feb.1908, Balfour MSS 49685 ff.109–14. Lord Crewe later confirmed that Campbell-Bannerman's advice had not been sought: see R. Blake, The Unknown Prime Minister: the Life and Times of Andrew Bonar Law 1858–1923 (London, 1955), p. 514.

[59] E.g. Knollys to Nash, 21 May 1908 over a later bill (withdrawn). Asquith MSS, I, 1. For the original crisis of 1906 see J. D. Fair, British Interparty Conferences: a study of the procedure of conciliation in British politics, 1867–1921 (Oxford, 1980), pp. 59–76.

co-operation. His deprecation of Liberal language over the obduracy of the Lords reflected no mild constitutional reservation: the genuineness of his distress expresses itself in the unusual recourse he had to writing personally to his ministers about it rather than dealing through his private secretary. It is wide of the mark to suggest that his understanding could not move beyond making sure that the present situation did not change; he saw that a problem existed and he recognized that reform of the Lords had to come; he could see, too, that the Second Chamber must be encouraged to pull back from precipitate action if a wider movement towards abolishing the Lords were not to gather momentum.[60] But he held fast to two forms of resistance, and both proved inadequate to his situation. First, he expected '*his Ministers*' not to 'place him in a false position' by recommending dangerous courses of action over the Lords in vocabulary which would amount to 'if not actually unconstitutional, improper language to use when spoken by the responsible Advisers of the Crown'.[61] This made him rage against John Burns and, more especially, Lloyd George for their unbridled public attacks on the Second Chamber. Second, he believed that he could successfully mediate in an irremediable situation largely, perhaps, because he ran tapes in his head that had more relevance to the 1860s and 1870s than the world around him. When Balfour decided to resign in 1905, the King's first image (not an inaccurate one) was Gladstone's refusal of Disraeli's poisoned chalice in 1873. When the Education Bill became an early cause of friction with the Lords in 1906, his first idea was to call in the Archibishop of Canterbury as Tait had been pulled into the crisis over disestablishment of the Irish Church in 1869. As always, priority went to his memory of events from his mother's reign and to consulting those around him whom he could trust. His confidence that one could bring people round through personal contact was part of a blindness about what the Crown could achieve in an environment dominated by structures and ideologies more than the reach of personality.

III

'This is all your work', Queen Alexandra is supposed to have whispered to Winston Churchill in a bitter moment during King Edward's funeral.[62]

---

[60] E.g. his concern over the popular feeling aroused by the Lords' treatment of the Licensing Bill in 1908: Haldane to Asquith (copy), 3 Oct.1908, Haldane MSS 5908 f.60.
[61] Knollys to Campbell-Bannerman, 5 Dec.1906, Campbell-Bannerman MSS 41207 f.157, British Library.
[62] Bayford diary, 6 May 1910, in *Real Old Tory Politics: the political diaries of Robert Sandars, Lord Bayford 1910–35*, ed. J. Ramsden (London, 1984), 20.

The death of a man of seventy who lived life on an epic scale hardly demands so spectacular an explanation. It brooks no denial that the King took his constitutional impotence badly. To jump from that observation, however, to one that proclaims royal attenuation does not follow because Edward VII had given himself a personal agenda that could not be satisfied. The experience of his son, George V, shows how much the British monarchy could still achieve when it worked with the grain of social development and discovered ways in which social authority could still well up inside constitutional forms. When the constitutional crisis finally came to an end in 1911, the King did not, as his father would have done, retire to his tent to sulk. 'He has gone off happy.'[63] He intended still to play a role in his own, very different way and to make that contribution marginal makes the history of the next half century hard to follow. The central role played by George V in his secret meeting with leading politicians in 1923 to decide the succession to Bonar Law[64] – something only appreciated since the 1970s – seems less arresting once we understand the centralities of his grandmother and the heroics of his dead father. The role so unrealistically sought by Edward VIII as he tried to override ministers in order to help appease Hitler ('Who is King here, Baldwin or myself?'[65]) speaks more of a continuing attachment to authority than a claim to constitutional power. No one denies how circumscribed monarchy finds itself in the twenty-first century. Lord Blake was right when he argued, in the context of the Rev. Jeffrey John's abortive appointment to a bishopric in 2003, that 'the Queen has really no choice but to confirm the appointment of a bishop. It would be inconceivable in this day and age that she should try to block it.'[66] The late nineteenth and early twentieth centuries return a different impression. In answering differently old questions about those years, we can draw a pattern of royal power from George IV to George VI which looks more persistent than those who first framed those questions believed plausible. But we naturally need to go beyond old questions to those of our own making in order to make history resonate for a later generation, and the process takes us beyond power to authority, beyond imposition to persuasion, beyond action to language,

---

[63] Stamfordham to Nash, 11 Aug.1911, Asquith MSS I, 2 ff.240–1.

[64] M. Cowling, *The Impact of Labour, 1920–24* (Cambridge, 1971), pp. 258–66.

[65] Memo. of the Duke of Coburg, n.d. (January 1936), 'Only for the Führer and Party Member von Ribbentrop', in *Documents on German Foreign Policy*, Series C, vol. 4 (1962), p. 1063.

[66] *Sunday Telegraph*, 29 Jun. 2003. But recall Lord Charteris counselling caution to those determined to get a dissolution of Parliament three decades earlier in 1974: 'It isn't automatic for the Queen to say "Yes" or "No". You know, just watch it . . . that prerogative does still exist', quoted in P. Hennessy, *The Prime Minister: the office and its holders since 1945* (London, 2004), p. 25.

beyond constitution to practice, beyond law to *habitus*. Seen under that illumination, royal influence takes on a colour unfamiliar from the perceptions of Bagehot or Dicey, and its images suggest that the reigns of Queen Victoria and King Edward VII, once the province of constitutional fatalists, now stand ready to become postmodern.[67]

---

[67] A thought excluded none the less from the otherwise postmodern collection of essays edited by James Vernon, *Re-reading the Constitution* (Cambridge, 1996).

7 An aristocratic monarchy and popular republicanism 1830–1940*

Antony Taylor

In 1930 G. K. Chesterton wrote of the British monarchy that 'it had been profoundly modified by aristocratic traditions, both of liberty, and of license'.[1] In the nineteenth and early twentieth centuries, aristocracy, he wrote, stood at the pinnacle of the social hierarchy. Prominent at court, central to the position of society's leaders, and taking a leading role in the military, in bureaucracy, and in the nation's diplomatic circles, the aristocracy set its stamp on the culture of the court. Until the inter-war years, the links between monarchy, courtly circles and the great territorial families of the land proved indissoluble. The royal family moved in the great dynastic salons of the realm, and aristocrats in turn benefited from favours, honorific titles, and places at court. Victoria stood accused of favouring the nobility and of privileging noble retainers and imported princely German advisers over the statesmen of the nation. For republican critics of the throne like Charles Bradlaugh, the monarchy suffered from its close ties to the landed elite, which still performed the function of the 'sword-force' of the Crown, while augmenting the dignified part of the constitution by burnishing it with the archaic trappings of feudal ritual and ceremonial.[2] At the highpoint of the Victorian and Edwardian ceremonial monarchy, according to its critics, royalty stood or fell in tandem with aristocracy. On occasion, by illuminating the nature of the social elite that surrounded the Crown, the presence of aristocracy at the court exposed the pretensions of the monarchy to act as the disinterested figure-head of the nation.

The recent historiography of monarchy has noted the significant changes in the nature of royal ceremonial from the late nineteenth century and into the inter-war years. Contemporaries appreciated that

---

* My thanks to Andrzej Olechnowicz and Philip Williamson for comments on this article, and to Michael Bush for the loan of material in his collection. This chapter is in memory of Min Moss, who died in September 2005.
[1] G. K. Chesterton, *Come to Think of It* (London, 1930), p. 236.
[2] *National Reformer*, 8 Jan. 1871, p. 26 and Antony Taylor, *'Lords of Misrule': Hostility to Aristocracy in Late Nineteenth and Early Twentieth Century Britain* (London, 2004), ch. 1.

the position of royalty was changing. During this period the monarchy evolved from a narrow, insular clique of German extraction into a fully-fledged ceremonial institution.[3] The more visible public ritual surrounding the Crown symbolized the increasing democratization of the British monarchy after the 1867 and 1884 Reform Acts. Building on the patriotic re-invention of the throne under the Hanoverians, in the early twentieth century monarchy came to assume the status of a national symbol that united the nation. Under Victoria, Edward VII (the 'National Dad') and George V, it represented a fusion of familial, ceremonial, and national symbols.[4] Viewed primarily as a ritual institution, monarchy may be counted a success. The new public ritual of the throne provided a social solvent, and a focus for the pageants of domestic and imperial rejoicing. The ceremonial monarchy is, however, usually examined as an expression of the national interest, whereas the role of the narrow territorial aristocracy that clustered around the throne and took a leading part in these events is overlooked. For its critics, the ceremonial of the royal state was instrumental in consolidating the role of the aristocracy, who occupied a significant position within the demonology of radical and reform movements. On occasion, an injection of royal opulence and glamour remedied the deficiencies in outdated and rather fussy noble ceremonial. At Elizabeth II's coronation, the Scottish Labour journal *Forward* commented on 'the faultless bearing of the girl who was at its centre', but criticized the conduct of the aristocracy: 'During the communion service they fidgeted with their coronets and robes, looked through the pages of their coronation books, and whispered to one another. I suspect it was just the bad manners of rather spoilt people'.[5]

For many radicals the links between the monarch and the great families of the nation were sufficiently intimate to provide the basis for a critique that depicted monarchy and aristocracy as an alliance that suppressed the liberties of the people. The discourses of hostility to the throne that fused hatred of aristocracy with hatred of monarchy between the 1830s and the 1930s deserve recapitulation. Moreover, analysis of the monarchy's role as a paragon of aristocracy demonstrates the perils, as well as the positive benefits, for the throne of too close an identification with aristocratic patrician values.

---

[3] For differing perspectives on royal ritual, see D. Cannadine, 'The Context, Performance and Meaning of Ritual: The British Monarchy and the "Invention of Tradition", c.1820–1977', in E. Hobsbawm and T. Ranger (eds.), *The Invention of Tradition* (Cambridge, 1983), pp. 101–64, and W. Kuhn, *Democratic Royalism* (London, 1996), esp. chs. 3–4.

[4] On this theme, see M. Homans, *Royal Representations* (Chicago, 1998), chs. 2 and 3.

[5] *Forward*, 13 Jun. 1953, p. 8.

I

In 1872 the London agent for the *New York World*, Pierre Girard, wrote to the freethinker Charles Cockbill Cattell inquiring how far 'there exists in England a class of men with an appreciable political influence who really desire the substitution of a republic for a monarchy? If so, in what way are they proposing to act; and do they propose, in any practical way, immediate action? If they do, what is this action to be?'[6] Cattell's reply has not survived, but the clear omission from Girard's inquiry was an explicit question about the aristocracy and its relationship to republican agendas. Traditionally, the study of British republicanism has languished. After considerable neglect, the discourses of republicanism have recently received some scrutiny.[7] Whilst never amounting to a majoritarian movement within the mainstream of British radicalism, republicanism provided a corrective to the opulence of the royal state. Deriving from radical ideas of 'Old Corruption', republicanism had a significant incarnation in the 1870s at the time of Victoria's withdrawal from public life. Thereafter, a strain of journalistic republicanism, embodied particularly in the writings of G. W. M. Reynolds, promoted a levelling agenda against traditional social hierarchies and accentuated the deficiencies of the British throne.[8] Expressed pointedly at the time of royal jubilees, royal weddings, and the birth of royal heirs, republicanism maintained a presence both on the platform and in the Labour press into the inter-war years.

In a long-standing critique, with eighteenth-century antecedence, radicals and reformers frequently debated the degree to which monarchy or aristocracy might shoulder the blame for the travails of the nation. As John Belchem and James Vernon have demonstrated, most of the discourses of radicalism revolved around this issue.[9] Republicans were immune to the presentational and institutional changes within the British monarchy. As Brian Harrison has noted, the role of the aristocracy and its relationship to the throne changed significantly in the early part of the twentieth century. There was a marked tendency for the aristocratic carapace of the throne to fall away as landed society contracted at the end

---

[6] Girard to Cattell, 4 Dec. 1872, Special Collections, no. 635, British Library of Political and Economic Sciences.

[7] See esp. D. Thompson, *Queen Victoria* (London, 1990), chs. 5 and 6. Much of the recent discussion of British republicanism is rooted in N. J. Gossman, 'Republicanism in nineteenth-century England', *International Review of Social History* 7 (1962), 51–60.

[8] A. Taylor, '*Reynolds's Newspaper*, opposition to monarchy and the radical anti-jubilee: Britain's anti-monarchist tradition reconsidered', *Historical Research*, 58 (1995), 318–37.

[9] See J. Belchem, 'Republicanism, popular constitutionalism and the radical platform in early nineteenth-century England', *Social History*, 6 (1981), 1–32 and James Vernon, 'Notes Towards an Introduction' in Vernon (ed.) *Re-reading the Constitution: New Narratives in the Political History of England's Long Nineteenth Century* (Cambridge, 1996), pp. 1–21.

of the Great War.[10] Republican agendas, however, continued to portray an essentially nineteenth-century perspective of the throne, and the corrupt lordly courtiers who surrounded the person of the monarch. In the late nineteenth and early twentieth century this effectively hamstrung the British republican movement, which expressed an antediluvian vision of monarchy more easily challenged by supporters of the Crown. Despite the diminished role of aristocracy between the wars, hostility to landed society remained very marked in the discourses of republicanism. The republican critique was, above all, a purgative of privilege within politics. By concentrating on the manifestations of privilege within the political system, republicans hoped to undermine the stage sets of monarchy and to stifle the most vocal of its supporters. Seen as dissipated, indolent, and wealthy, the aristocracy was portrayed as incapable of reforming itself and of adapting to the straightened economic circumstances on the land, following the agricultural depression of the 1870s and during the accelerated decline of the great estate system in the twentieth century. For republicans, the touch of aristocracy compromised royalty. The presence of aristocratic figures around the throne highlighted the failings of monarchy in its unreformed state. This has led some historians to infer that aristocracy, not royalty, was the chief target of radical movements for political reform. Recent scholarship has suggested that radicals valued the stability and national symbolism provided by monarchy, but wished to see the throne shorn of the aristocratic associations that undermined the position of the Crown.[11] Without a diminution of landlord influences, some reformers argued, the Crown would succumb to the pressures exerted by aristocratic advisers and supporters. In 1869, the *Bee-Hive* newspaper commented of aristocratic influences at court that 'they retain a still more dangerous power by which they may overawe both Queen and people should any circumstances hereafter arise which they may deem inimical to the power, as opposed to the perpetuation, of their order'.[12]

This chapter challenges the view that radicals saw the social and political interests of aristocracy and monarchy as entirely separate. Rather, radicalism depicted the two strands of hereditary privilege as integral to the success of the system created by the excesses of neo-Normanism. The

---

[10] B. Harrison, *Transformation of British Politics 1886–1995* (Oxford, 1996). Social historians have argued that against the egalitarian background of the 1960s, there was an accelerated retreat by the monarchy from its aristocratic moorings: see R. Perrott, *The Aristocrats* (London, 1968), ch. 5.

[11] D. Craig, 'The crowned republic? Monarchy and anti-monarchy in Britain 1760–1901', *Historical Journal* 46 (2003), 167–85; P. Pickering, '"The hearts of the millions": Chartism and popular monarchism in the 1840s', *History* 88 (2003), 227–48; and S. Poole, *The Politics of Regicide in England 1760–1850* (Manchester, 2000), ch. 1.

[12] *Bee-Hive*, 1 Sept.1869, p. 1.

'Norman yoke' tropes of nineteenth- and early twentieth-century radical rhetoric fused the images of a dissolute aristocracy, and an equally dissolute monarchy.[13] At a time when open affirmation of regicidal and republican views could carry serious legal consequences, republicans were circumspect and indirect in their statements about monarchy, seeing the abolition of the throne as the culmination of a much longer process to reform the royal state incrementally. For most radicals, reform of the aristocracy was a necessary first step towards the abolition of the Crown itself. *The Radical* commented in 1888:

> The people are not yet ready for a republic in this country. The times, however, are ripe for many important reforms, the ultimate end of which will lead us to our desired goal. We are ripe for reform of the House of Lords, I think – for the abolition of its hereditary character. We are ripe for radical reform in land laws; for the disestablishment and disendowment of the state church, for municipal reform, and for many minor points on which I will not dwell here.[14]

Moreover, failing to distinguish between the different categories of the court, the aristocracy, the squirearchy and the poorer gentry, radical rhetoric depicted the forces of titled landlordism and of hereditary privilege as a monolithic and undifferentiated whole. In the eyes of radicals, monarchy and aristocracy were the two sides of the same social phenomenon. For many platform reformers, a strategy of undermining the aristocracy set in motion the process of change that would lead inevitably to an abolition of the throne itself.

The royal household valued the monarchy's close ties with aristocracy. In the 1870s, Prince Albert Edward, the heir to the throne, described Britain in his correspondence with his mother as an 'Aristocratic Country' and feared that reformers like John Bright hoped for an Americanized meritocracy in which 'there was the Sovereign and the people, and no class between'.[15] The significance of the close relationship between aristocracy and the monarchy was noted by reformers as central to the governing structures of Britain and of the empire. Radicals were sensitive to this relationship and saw it as mutually reinforcing and supportive. The republican *National Reformer* wrote that the political parties united in defence of the titled elite, and noted 'that they are also at one whenever a rash hand is stretched out to touch the sacred ark of royal or aristocratic avarice'.[16] Indeed, in the eyes of many reformers the integrity of monarchy suffered

---

[13] W. J. Linton, *The English Republic*, ed. K. Parkes (London, 1891), pp. 44–8.
[14] *The Radical*, 1 Sep. 1888, p. 6.
[15] Quoted in F. Hardie, *The Political Influence of Queen Victoria 1861–1901* (London, 1935), p. 188.
[16] *National Reformer*, 2 Aug.1874, pp. 68–9.

through its close relationship with the great aristocratic circles. For radicals the feeling lingered that Victoria excessively indulged both her aristocratic favourites and her German relatives at the expense of her duty to the nation, and to the detriment of the national interest. *Reynolds's Newspaper* argued that the benefits of monarchy in Britain were absorbed by 'the cold shade of aristocracy . . .its smiles and blessings are the exclusive property of the great ones of the land'.[17] While even the strongest critics of monarchy acknowledged that the throne itself had some merits, individual monarchs compromised their position by subsuming themselves in aristocratic county life and embracing the worst of its excesses.[18]

This tendency became even more pronounced after the death of Victoria. Subsequent monarchs sought to create a more homely, domestic style that countered the allegations of 'imperial' ambition that had surrounded Victoria's assumption of the title of Empress of India in 1876. The image of custodian of the land was interwoven with this public face of monarchy. As landed society contracted, perversely monarchy itself became more 'aristocratic' in its personal style to fill the gap left by the decline of the landed elite. In the case of Edward VII and George V, they lived as *de facto* country squires. The assumption of 'gentry' values by the throne is very apparent here. At Edward's court, comparisons between the monarch and the great territorial aristocracy were frequently noted. Frank Harris, who claimed a close relationship with the Prince, summed up the spirit of Edward's circle: 'Edward had all the aristocrat's tastes. He loved horse-racing, was gregarious, hated to be alone, preferred a game of cards to any conversation; in fact, he only talked freely when he went to the opera, where perhaps he ought to have been silent. He was a gambler too, as English aristocrats are gamblers, and his love of cards often got him into difficulties'.[19] The great royal estates at Sandringham became central to the mythology of monarch as country gentleman and sportsman. Edward VII also frequently played the bucolic squire. Christmas hunting meets at Sandringham became festivals of 'Merrie England' revelry with carnivalesque balls for the servants and amateur theatricals after

---

[17] *Reynolds's Newspaper*, 19 Oct. 1856, p. 7

[18] For grudging praise of the benefits of monarchy as opposed to the corruptions of American and French republicanism, which created an 'intensified empire', see *Justice*, 16 Feb. 1884, p. 3; M. D. Conway, *Republican Superstitions as Illustrated in the Political History of America* (London, 1872), p. 1; and a review of the same by Annie Besant in the *National Reformer*, 14 Jul. 1878, p. 23.

[19] F. Harris, *His Life and Adventures* (London, 1947), p. 454. Harris was a notorious liar and fantasist. Nevertheless, the unexpurgated edition of his memoirs displays an intimate knowledge of Albert Edward's intrigues and sexual affairs suggesting a close relationship with the Prince, who Harris asserted was first drawn to him by a mutual love of dirty stories: see *Frank Harris: His life and Adventures, An Autobiography*, ed. J. E. Gallagher (New York, 1963), pp. 466–9 and 655–79.

strenuous days in the saddle.[20] During the reign of George V, courtiers represented him as 'the Squire of Sandringham'. 'I like to think of Sandringham not so much as a royal residence, but as the home of an English country gentleman' wrote one admirer.[21] Both during the 1935 Jubilee and at the time of his death, George was described as a keen farmer, living 'the life of a country gentleman, among his own people, who saw in him the squire first, and the king second'.[22] Appropriately he ended his days on the estate. Even George VI was portrayed as a quintessential farmer at the time of his death, happiest on the land.[23] As recent historiography has pointed out, individual royal figures have often felt most at ease with a rural village vision of England that exalted the pre-industrial craft skills of 'our flint-knappers, our thatchers, our blacksmiths' and at the same time distanced royalty from the opulent lifestyle of aristocratic playboys on the Monte Carlo circuit.[24]

Other traits also seemed common to both aristocracy and royalty. Critics of hereditary institutions have noted the strain of 'philistinism' apparent in both aristocratic and royal upbringings. John Grigg wrote of the 'debutante stamp' on female royals, and highlighted the limitations of a conventional upper-class upbringing that reduced high-ranking senior female members of the royal family to the level of society *belles-dames*. Royal education he summarized as 'Crawfie, Sir Henry Marten, the London season, the racecourse, the grouse moor, Canasta, and the occasional royal tour.'[25] For George Bernard Shaw, Edward VII's lack of culture and rough, bucolic character made him more suited to the life of a 'sporting publican' or a 'respectable signalman'.[26] For the critics of landed society, the same boorish and oafish quality has characterized both aristocrats and royalty. In the inter-war years, allegations that the royal family routinely mistreated their household staff often surfaced, and individual cases of distress and even destitution for former servants were highlighted by the radical press.[27] Unsurprisingly, the Labour MP John Burns, himself a

---

[20] J. P. C. Sewell (ed.), *Personal Letters of King Edward VII* (London, 1931), pp. 30–2 and 'The Shooting Season at Sandringham', *English Illustrated Magazine* 2 (1893), 128–34.

[21] J. Wentworth Day, *King George V as a Sportsman* (London, 1935), p. 27.

[22] *Hail and Farewell: The Passing of King George V* (*The Times*, London, 1936), p. 71 and Sir W. Beach Thomas, 'As King and farmer: successes on the royal farm', *Portsmouth Evening News, Jubilee Supplement*, 1 May 1935, p. 21.

[23] See his obituary, *Manchester Guardian*, 7 Feb.1952, p. 7.

[24] D. Hebdige, 'Designs for living', *Marxism Today*, 1 Oct. 1989, 24–7.

[25] J. Grigg, 'A Summer Storm', in J. Murray-Brown (ed.), *The Monarchy and Its Future* (London, 1969), pp. 43–56. Recently it has been suggested that royal heirs should receive a thorough grounding in constitutional history to prepare them for their future role and to counteract the distractions of courtly life: see P. Gordon and D. Lawton, *Royal Education, Past, Present and Future* (London, 2000).

[26] See George Bernard Shaw's obituary of Edward VII, *New Age*, 2 June 1910.

[27] *Lansbury's Labour Weekly*, 27 Feb. 1926, p. 6.

former footman to a society family in Hampstead, took a radical and republican road in rebellion against his years in service.[28] Moreover, monarchy and aristocracy were closely intertwined in the annual theatre accompanying the state opening of Parliament. State ceremonial reinforced the mutual interdependence of the peerage and of the throne. From the 'monarchless' 'robe on an empty throne' ceremonial surrounding Victoria's refusal to open Parliament, through the days of Ellen Wilkinson's 'puppet show' in which 'peeresses just dripped pearls and diamonds', to Richard Crossman's comparison of the ceremony to '*The Prisoner of Zenda* but not nearly as smart or well done as it would be in Hollywood', critics stigmatized the state opening as expensive, time-consuming and irreverent flummery, that pandered to the landed hierarchy's obsession with timeless ritual and opulent public display.[29]

Ultimately, for their critics, the real connection uniting monarchy and aristocracy was their inevitable decline. Both the monarchy and aristocratic institutions were apparently in an advanced state of decay, bowed down by the burdens of their pasts, over-inflated pedigrees, and the accretions of neo-feudal symbolism. In the radical press both institutions were shown as mutually outdated. This allowed radicals to call time on hereditary institutions in general. At a debate at the Artisans' Institute in London in 1876, doubts were expressed about whether the title of Empress of India could be borne effectively by Victoria, and whether 'the throne could sustain itself . . .in its now worm-eaten condition'.[30] In his critique of aristocracy in *Our Old Nobility*, Howard Evans made the same point about the great aristocratic dynasties. Quoting Carlyle, he depicted them as a caste in terminal decline after squandering the wealth, position and good will that went with titled status:

> These old pheasant lords,
> These partridge-breeders of a thousand years,
> Who have mildewed in their thousands, doing nothing,
> . . . . . .Why, the greater their disgrace!
> Fall back upon a name! Rest, rot in that!
> Not keep it noble, make it noble! Fools,
> With such a vantage-ground for nobleness![31]

---

[28] See W. Kent, *John Burns* (London, 1950), p. 7.

[29] See, respectively, the *National Reformer*, 21 Feb.1875, p. 127; *Lansbury's Labour Weekly*, 12 Feb.1927, p. 13; and *The Crossman Diaries: Selections from the Diaries of a Cabinet Minister 1964–1970*, ed. A. Howard (London, 1975), p. 350. For a more positive view of the historical role of the state opening of Parliament from a monarchist point of view, see W. Glenvil Hall, 'The Pageant', in N. Branch (ed.), *This Britain* (London, 1951), pp. 136–51.

[30] See *National Reformer*, 16 Apr. 1876, p. 254.

[31] H. Evans, *Our Old Nobility* (London, 1907 edn.), p. 112.

Radicals were belligerent about the decrepitude of hereditary power. The decayed nature of aristocratic and monarchical institutions seemed to indicate that the age of inherited privilege was fast drawing to a close. In Mrs Humphry Ward's 1894 novel, *Marcella*, the fictionalized radical Wharton predicts that the days of the great landed families are ending: 'Since '84 the ground is mined for them – good and bad – and they know it'.[32]

Nevertheless, in the short term aristocracy added weight to the social, military, and imperial function of monarchy. Aristocrats themselves were 'little kings' in their own right. Like monarchs, they demanded unconditional loyalty and service in return for paternalistic favours. Some could boast royal descent from the Plantagenets or the House of Tudor. Others amassed immense historical power as custodians of the royal interest and as the militant arms of individual dynasties. The distribution, break-up and sequestration of land by monarchs cemented their position, and in the eyes of land reformers initiated the burdens and injustices that began the cycle of dispossession for the English yeomanry.[33] Recalling royal appropriation of public land, the radical John Wheelwright described the historical process of land redistribution to royal favourites as a kind of fraud, and concluded that 'modern landlordism conceived in sin and shapen [sic] in iniquity remains criminal to the core'.[34] Republicans who highlighted the inequities of aristocratic land usurpation and the over-concentration of wealth in the hands of a kingly and knightly caste, established a narrative of injustice that dominated the radical land reform platform from the 1850s up until the eve of the Great War. On the huge estates of Scotland and the Borders, the writ of the great aristocratic dynasties still served as law even as late as the beginning of the twentieth century. The remembered history of aristocracy in these places was one of unjust brutality and barbarism. Society and monarchy-watchers like G. W. M. Reynolds, William Howitt and Howard Evans recorded the mistreatment of their tenants in voyeuristic detail, and propounded a gospel of restitution.[35] Most radicals were impatient for change. At a meeting at Cambridge Hall in London in 1874, the chairman, Mr Wilson, pleaded to know 'How long the people intended to remain as lodgers in their own country'?[36] Given their immense power, status and position, for many

[32] Mrs H. Ward, *Marcella* (London, 1894; 1984), p. 244.
[33] See on radical criticisms of the aristocratic monopoly of land, Taylor, *'Lords of Misrule'*, ch. 2.
[34] J. Wheelwright, *Landlordism* (London, 1896), p. 6.
[35] These anti-aristocratic authors were staples of the radical canon. One reviewer described them as serving 'the radical cause in the coming struggle on the land question, and we have no doubt will furnish many weapons to radical speakers': see the *National Reformer*, 16 Nov. 1879, p. 749.
[36] Ibid., 22 Mar. 1874, p. 189.

observers of royalty it was the aristocracy, not the monarchy, who really ruled. 'The Divine Right of landlords theory has in England survived the Divine Right of Kings theory by nearly two centuries' wrote one critic of the House of Lords in the 1880s.[37] Even in the mid-twentieth century, when aristocratic power was waning, the diarist and Conservative politician Chips Channon could still comment at the time of the accession of George V:

The present king and queen are popular, very, and increasingly so, but they have no message for the Labour Party who believe them, and rightly I fear, to be the puppets of a palace clique. Certainly, they are too hemmed in by the territorial aristocracy, and have all the faults and virtues which Edward VIII lacked in this particular field. Still, it is the aristocracy which still rules England although nobody seems to believe it.[38]

Radicals concurred with this judgment. William Howitt wrote of the aristocracy in 1856 'they possess the crown, for it is the great bauble and talisman of all their wealth and honours'. For him monarchy, aristocracy and the priestcraft of the 'squarson' were indistinguishable:

Aristocracy looks to royalty as one source of honour and wealth, and to priestcraft as another. The host of priests spring from the loins of aristocracy, and become a section of it, and one of the most zealous armies of defence. Cut away aristocracy, and you unbind the whole iniquity of oppression. Kings without an aristocracy as a body-guard must rule with mildness, or soon cease to rule at all.[39]

For radicals, the monarchical system was shot through with aristocratic influences that reduced the throne to the level of a figurehead for plunderers and barbarians. Drawing heavily on popular histories of the seventeenth and eighteenth centuries, such accounts saw the national narrative as a process that had led inexorably to the subservience of the Crown to untamed aristocratic pressures. For some, the demands of aristocracy relegated the status of monarchy to that of a mere prisoner, beholden to the will of aristocratic retainers, and diminished by their incessant demands. In the 1830s James Mill wrote disparagingly of the position of the monarch:

He has put his neck into the collar of the aristocracy, and to this hour tugs like a pack-horse at their wagon. He might have done better for himself and better for the state; – he might have joined with the people in rescuing parliament from the grip of the aristocracy; and then he would have been really subservient to nothing but the public interest, which he would have felt to be his.[40]

[37] H. R. Fox Bourne, *The House of Lords* (London, 1881), p. 68.
[38] *Chips: The Diaries of Sir Henry Channon*, ed. R. Rhodes James (London, 1967), p. 130.
[39] 'John Hampden Jr' (W. Howitt), *The Aristocracy of England: A History for the People* (London, 1856), pp. 5–7.
[40] J. Mill, 'Aristocracy', *London Review* 2 (1836), p. 304.

For others, the monarchy was simply the fountainhead of snobbery, flummery and social pretension. The Labour leader George Lansbury, who preserved many of the values of nineteenth-century republicanism into the twentieth century, wrote of monarchy that it constituted an adornment for the socially ambitious and for those with *arriviste* expectations. In this sense, it served as an emblem of status and position. He wrote: 'Our protest is against the whole social order of which the monarchy is the titular head. This social order centres around the court, and garden parties, the civics and receptions at which inordinate wealth, luxury and extravagance of every sort and kind plants itself.'[41]

In the nineteenth century, marriage arrangements between scions of the royal house and the great dynastic families, reinforced this sense of a monolithic ruling elite founded on familial relationships and united by close ties of blood that transformed its network of informal 'cousinhood' into a caste. Notions of a 'vast cousinhood' remained a marked feature of radical rhetoric until the 1930s, when they informed criticisms of the elite social world of Toryism, landownership, and minor royalty.[42] Radicals believed that monarchy was an instrument of Conservatism, bound to the titled leaders of the party by bonds of blood and loyalty. Victoria was often represented as an overt Conservative, plunged into despair by Liberal victories in 1880 and 1892; George V was depicted using his royal powers to privilege Tory and Tory-dominated ministries over their opponents in 1923 and 1931.[43] In this sense, radicals suggested that royalty and the instinctively Conservative aristocracy were linked in an immense social system that buttressed reaction. Although republicans conceded some benefits in the process of royal heirs moving outside the closed circle of European royal families for their mates, they warned against closer ties with the traditional aristocracy.[44] As Jonathan Parry demonstrates in this volume, royal marriages into domestic aristocratic families, particularly in the case of the wedding between the Scottish Marquis of Lorne and Queen Victoria's daughter, the Princess Louise in 1871, carried a popular patriotic inflection that celebrated the commingling of the titled bloodlines of Scotland and England around an exalted 'Britishness'. Privileging particular domestic families over others, however, raised problems for the protocol, precedence and position of the

---

[41] *Lansbury's Labour Weekly*, 30 May 1925, pp. 10–11. Lansbury openly declared his republicanism in the 1923 Labour Party debate on abolition of the throne in which the republican motion was proposed by his son-in-law, Ernest Thurtle: see *Labour Party Annual Report, 1923* (London, 1924), pp. 250–1.

[42] For 'the cousinhood', see S. Haxey, *Tory MP* (London, 1939) ch. 6; and R. Douglas, *Land, People and Politics* (London, 1976), p. 154.

[43] See Hardie, *The Political Influence of Queen Victoria*, ch. 3.

[44] *National Reformer*, 9 March 1861.

peerage. Where marriages were seen to cement the advancement of particular families, they were vigorously opposed by radicals. Despite the successful public ceremonial surrounding the event, there was marked radical opposition to the marriage between Princess Louise and the Marquis of Lorne. For its critics, this brought the royal family together with the significant Highland landowners, the Dukes of Argyll. Whilst public opinion favoured an alliance with a major domestic dynasty in preference to a union with a foreign royal house, radicals saw the event as consolidating the monarchy's links with the semi-feudal landed baronage of Scotland. Far from representing Bagehot's 'brilliant edition of an everyday fact', for radicals this wedding demonstrated the increased power and prestige dynastic union could bring for the major landowners.[45] Moreover, they alleged that a royal dowry for Princess Louise's husband was forced through Parliament only after combined pressure applied by these powerful and privileged families. Both Argyll with a seat in the Lords, and the Marquis of Lorne with a seat in the Commons, were seen as complicit in defrauding the nation of money siphoned into the private coffers of landowners – 'and this is done by a Duke and a Marquis – by two English noblemen – by two English gentlemen'.[46] The republican *National Reformer* concluded:

If it is found that the House of Commons is so enslaved by the upper classes that it consents to the grant, and that the Marquis of Lorne lacks the dignity to induce him to refuse becoming a pensioner on the public funds, then the money given to him and his bride should be at once reimbursed to the country by the withdrawal of pensions from aristocratic imbeciles and royal hangers-on, who are only known to the nation by the questionable lives they lead, and the enormous taxation they help to keep up.[47]

Hostility to expensive grants and 'hand-outs' to relatives of the 'Grab Family' royals and a privileged network of related aristocrats helped initiate the republican moment of 1871–2.[48] Thereafter the radical press ridiculed the late Victorian emphasis on a regal court and opulent public displays. For *Reynolds's Newspaper* and other radical papers, these public manifestations of monarchism were little more than costly excess, increasing the tax burden on the people at a time when there was still a delicate balance to be maintained between revenue gained from direct and indirect sources. For this reason, the paper's emphasis on the lengthy string of royal relatives, retainers and royal refugees fleeing from revolution in

---

[45] W. Bagehot, *The English Constitution*, ed. M. Taylor (Oxford, 2001), p. 41
[46] *National Reformer*, 20 Feb. 1871, p. 136.   [47] Ibid., 29 Jan. 1871, p. 75.
[48] For the description of the royal family as the 'Grab Family', see *Reynolds's Newspaper*, 25 Jul. 1875, p. 5.

Europe, feasting and dining at the expense of the people, struck a chord with the mid-Victorian public and fed a mounting mood of cynicism about the doings of the royal family. The radical MP for Sheffield, H. J. Wilson, commented at a meeting in Barnsley:

> He did not know whether it had ever occurred to them how curiously they talked about the Queen's Government, the Queen's Army, the Queen's Navy and all manner of things. Everything they talked about was the Queen's, until they came to the debt, and then they called it the National Debt. Well, he did not want to do the Queen any wrong, but it seemed to him that if she claimed all other things, she ought to take the debt too.[49]

Such ideas were reflected back at *Reynolds's Newspaper* in the letter columns of the paper, and demonstrate the unerring populist instincts of G. W. M. Reynolds's commentaries about the throne, over the sale of titles and the role of royal, party and aristocratic placemen. This too was an issue that had a long-standing pedigree within radical circles. In the eyes of the radical press, the main beneficiaries of this process were the traditional aristocracy. The great dynastic families had a tradition of service to the throne and were familiar with the protocol and etiquette of court life. In the middle years of the nineteenth century, individual families continued to make substantial claims on the proceeds of the Civil List. Edmund Burke's comment on the Bedford family, that they were 'the leviathan of all the creatures of the Crown' was much quoted.[50] Others recalled Jeremy Bentham's description of English kingship as a 'corrupter-general'.[51] For radicals, the court in particular was stigmatized as a place where favouritism, privilege, and ostentatious waste remained rife. Pointless placemen proliferated at public expense. The *Northern Star* commented in 1840: 'The Queen requires a stirrup holder *with a salary*, and the space of placing the Queen in the saddle as a Queen should sit her horse is speedily filled'.[52] *Reynolds's Newspaper* was in no doubt that dubious court posts and positions drained the pockets of the people, and cemented the relationship between monarchy and aristocracy. It remarked: 'Now let it be borne in mind that this infamous pension list, which annually absorbs 3 millions and more of our money, is a branch of the monarchical tree, it was born and bred of monarchy; and so long as monarchy endures, it will probably exist, and the people be annually swindled out of the amount named'.[53] Its final verdict on the court with its lengthy retinue of royal retainers was a swingeing one:

---

[49] *Barnsley Chronicle*, 21 Nov. 1885.   [50] Evans, *Our Old Nobility*, p. 27.
[51] Quoted in J. S. Mill, *Autobiography* (London, 1873), p. 75.
[52] *Northern Star*, 18 Apr. 1840, p. 4.   [53] *Reynolds's Newspaper*, 7 Jan. 1873, p. 3.

A throne resembles a dung-heap in more than one point of view. Around both buzz and flutter flies and vermin that feed and fatten until they become bloated by gluttony. Both give birth to obnoxious things; a dung-heap to unsavoury odours, and the throne to a lot of lazy loafers, who thrive and prosper upon the goods of others. Round the throne of England has grown up such an immense crop of rank weeds that unless another Cromwell comes amongst us to root them out, they will remain and increase. They not only eat the bread of the people, but are almost insuperable obstacles to every enlightened or progressive movement. Amongst the rankest of these weeds is one termed 'vested interests'; or in other words, under the cloak of hereditary might, a certain number of privileged persons, a large portion being members of the aristocracy, claim the enjoyment of large incomes and do little or nothing in return for them.[54]

These criticisms of place-hunting and favouritism struck a chord with the public. They persisted as part of a radical programme into the inter-war years, and were voiced even at the time of the parliamentary debates about the continuation of Civil List payments to the former Edward VIII after his abdication in 1936. Highlighting claims that the Prince had salted away the profits of the Duchy of Cornwall to fund an ostentatious household and a life of excess in exile, critics were eager to scrutinize his income. The *Daily Worker* issued stern warnings on the subject of 'the £25,000 (or maybe £50,000) which Comrade Edward is going to loot from our till unless we object at the top of our voices'.[55]

The House of Lords came to embody many of these notions of royal favouritism and narrow aristocratic rule. There was considerable overlap in the rhetoric used against the throne, and the entrenched privilege of the House of Lords, depicted by its critics as a hereditary feudal chamber embedded at the heart of the constitution. Periodic frustration with the legislative role of the House of Lords allowed anti-heredity notions to permeate the radical mainstream. From the 1880s onwards, radicals saw Lords reform as a measure that complemented the expanding parliamentary franchise. Campaigns in the Upper House to retard progressive social legislation, and in 1884 and 1893 to delay parliamentary reform and Irish Home Rule, inspired a strong anti-Lords platform. Henry Labouchere depicted the Lords as a diseased tree, contaminating the constitutional ground around it, and requiring radical surgery to excise its influence from parliament and the constitution: 'We have met here to declare that we would so deal with it that it cumbers the earth no more'.[56] For radicals, the Lords, like the monarchy, held power by virtue of the hereditary usurpation of traditional Anglo-Saxon institutions at the time of the Norman Conquest. As descendants of Norman brigands and plunderers, the

---

[54] Ibid., 18 Jul. 1875, p. 5.   [55] *Daily Worker*, 20 Jan. 1937, p. 7.
[56] *National Reformer*, 17 Aug. 1884, pp. 116–7.

THE TALE OF A TUB

Disconsolate Duke : Now for the deuce of a ducking.

Figure 7.1. Aristocratic landowners preparing to be overwhelmed by the electorate in the first general election of 1910. From *Story of the Budget told Pictorally in the Manchester Evening New* (Manchester, 1910), p. 25. (Author's Collection).

Lords were frequently depicted as a delinquent power. *Reynolds's Newspaper* represented them as the spawn of 'land thieves' who had consolidated their position through acts of 'treason, conspiracies and rebellions against crown and people'.[57] For republicans, they were undeserving of their titles, which, held historically by force, represented a lawless and unlawful exercise of power, bearing comparison with unchecked monarchy.

[57] *Reynolds's Newspaper*, 16 Apr. 1876, p. 2 and 14 Jan. 1866, p. 3

Figure 7.2. In Mourning for the Loss of the Aristocracy. From
F. Carruthers Gould, *Cartoons of the Campaign: A Collection of Cartoons Made During the Election of 1895* (London, 1895) p. 41. (Author's Collection).

Henry Labouchere commented in 1884 that when they acted to retard parliamentary bills, they remained true to their ancestry as brigands: 'Far be it from me to compare the Lords to thieves, but it is an established fact that in the last fifty years the House of Lords has done more harm than all the thieves' dens and thieves' kitchens in the kingdom'.[58] For many republicans, curbing or reforming the Lords had implications for the monarchy. The *National Reformer* commented:

The gilded figure-head injures the state vessel less than the presence of hands on her tiller-ropes which know naught of navigation. And with the fall of the House

[58] *National Reformer*, 17 Aug. 1884, p. 117.

of Lords must crash down the throne which is but the ornament upon its roof, the completion of its elevation, so that when the toy house has fallen at the breath of the people's lips, and we can see over the near prospect which it now hides from our gaze, we shall surely see with the light of the morning on her face, with her golden head shining in the sun rays . . . that fair and glorious republic for which we have yearned and toiled for so long.[59]

The campaign against the House of Lords replicated the subversive tone of the republican agitation against the Crown. Republicans themselves noted that the Lords had been abolished in 1649 under Cromwell's Commonwealth. Like republicans in the 1870s, campaigners against the Lords traded in anonymous and subversive pamphlet literature that continued the long-standing radical traditions of anonymous radical pamphleteering.[60] For critics of hereditary power, Lloyd George's ringing cry of denunciation at Limehouse in 1907 that 'with your help we can brush the Lords aside like chaff before the wind' could apply as much to the institution of hereditary monarchy, as to hereditary landownership[61] (see Figs. 7.1 and 7.2).

II

For many contemporaries, the greatest transferences between aristocracy and monarchy occurred in the matter of personal morality. The excesses of George IV's reign provided an example of poor kingship. For delinquent royalty, he became a role-model, and a point of topical allusion. Edward Albert, the future Edward VIII, identified with him strongly in his playboy years.[62] The image of George IV as a spendthrift, a debtor and a debaucher haunted the subsequent generations of royalty. An excess of wealth, leisure and influence had created the circumstances in which George lived the life of a wayward and aged roué. Here monarchy assumed many of the characteristics of aristocracy. Like his aristocratic friends, the young Albert Edward struggled to pay his debts, and to fund his alternative and profligate court. *Reynolds's Newspaper* echoed the advice given to many profligate nobles when it suggested he pawn or sell the family silver and the presents he received on overseas visits to cover the cost of his excesses.[63] In popular mythology, debt and debauchery were the features of wayward sons. Land-reforming Cobdenite radicals in particular pointed out that primogeniture created idle and lazy heirs with time on

---

[59] Ibid., 22 Aug.1875, p. 116.   [60] See Taylor, '*Lords of Misrule*', chap. 4.
[61] E. Hughes, *The Prince, the Cash and the Crown* (London, 1969), p. 11.
[62] P. Ziegler, *King Edward VIII* (London, 1990), p. 108.
[63] *Reynolds's Newspaper*, 30 Jan. 1876, p. 5.

their hands, and fostered an effective dispossession of younger sons who lived lives of dissipation and debauchery on family pensions.[64] For eldest sons who came into the family inheritance, radicals asserted, there were strong traditions of absenteeism and indifference to their landed estates. Such complaints bore a strong resemblance to Bagehot's description of Albert Edward as 'an unemployed youth'.[65] Indeed there were echoes of absentee landlordism in Victoria's abnegation of her royal power (usually depicted as 'an empty chair with a robe thrown over it'[66]) and refusal to attend Parliament, leading to the ruination of the national estate. The indolent and supine life-styles of aristocrats that drew them into a life of pleasure and excess continued to trouble radicals into the latter half of the nineteenth century. Keir Hardie, for example, built his objections to emigration around the view that it deprived the nation of its wealth producers, leaving behind the social groups that failed to contribute: 'If we could transport the idlers, the dissolute and the worthless, then no one would object, but these are the very classes who are left behind to clog the wheels of progress'.[67] Public apprehension about Civil List payments and concerns about the expense of royalty fed radical fears that wealthy royals with a surfeit of time, and large sums of public money in their pockets, might repeat the worst features of George IV's reign, and emulate the example set by aristocratic society. This argument was raised in the debate about Civil List payments to Prince Albert in the 1840s, when the reformer Joseph Hume warned of the danger of 'setting a young man down in London with so much money in his pockets'.[68] Moreover, the issue was kept before the public eye by a succession of pretenders and claimants, asserting their claims to the paternity of prominent royals and Hanoverian princes. Whether legitimate, or in the case of Mrs Ryve, who claimed descent from the Duke of Cumberland, apparently delusional, these cases reinforced the image that 'bigamy appears to have been a fashion of the Guelph family'.[69] Here ancestral wrongdoing and a negative view of aristocracy strongly influenced the popular image of the younger, more stylish members of the royal family.

[64] See *Letters to J. E. Thorold Rogers and Mr Henry Tupper on the History and Working of the Laws of Primogeniture and Entail* (Manchester, 1864), pp. 25–8.
[65] Quoted in S. Weintraub, *The Importance of Being Edward: King in Waiting, 1841–1901* (London, 2000), p. 195.
[66] *Reynolds's Newspaper*, 30 Jan. 1876, p. 5.
[67] *Keir Hardie: His Writings and Speeches*, ed. E. Hughes (Glasgow, 1924), p. 6.
[68] Quoted in R. Nash, *Buckingham Palace* (London, 1980), p. 43.
[69] Mrs Ryve, whose claims were supported by forged papers, was described as 'insane' by the Attorney-General; see the *National Reformer*, 10 June 1866, p. 362.

Figure 7.3. Albert Edward, Prince of Wales, as an unruly child. 'L'Enfant Terrible', from *Puck*, 1 June 1891. (Author's Collection.)

Such fears about dissolute heirs came to centre around the heir to the throne, Albert Edward, the Prince of Wales.[70] The Prince cultivated many of the great aristocratic families at his home at Marlborough House. Here the fashionable circles of the land congregated. From an early stage there were persistent rumours about philandering and gambling amongst the members of the Marlborough House set.[71] Scandal compromised the public image of the Prince and added weight to radical criticisms of the royals (Fig. 7.3). As radicals gleefully pointed out, Edward rubbed

[70] For a time in the 1880s the mantle of debauchery descended on the shoulders of the Duke of Clarence, Albert Edward's oldest son, noted at the time for his alleged sexual involvement with both men and women: see T. Aronson, *Prince Eddy and the Homosexual Underworld* (London, 1994), ch. 1.

[71] See *Reynolds's Newspaper*, 2 Apr. 1865, p. 4.

shoulders with some dubious company. The *Newcastle Weekly Chronicle* highlighted the prominent presence of notorious rakes in his entourage and expressed concern about the poor public example he set. It commented that a delinquent prince 'encourages a debauched aristocracy: a debauched aristocracy makes a dissolute people. What quality of crops will the Prince of Wales's "wild oats" bear?'[72] *Reynolds's Newspaper*, condemning the 'vice, venality and vulgarity' of royal life, blamed a lack of parental restraint, and the bad example set by the worst elements amongst the aristocracy for this problem. In a fierce polemic against the Prince of Wales, it wondered how 'a nominally virtuous court, and an avowedly virtuous Princess could allow into their presence such men as the Marquis of Waterford who, it will be remembered, ran away with the wife not exactly of a commoner – for that might be set down simply as an indiscretion – but of a man of title, the Honourable Captain Vivian'.[73] Thereafter, the stories about the Prince of Wales's personal conduct became an established part of his popular image. Samuel Beeton's satirical 1872 Christmas annual, *The Coming K . . .* wrote of his predisposition for philandering in a fictionalized lament from his broken-hearted mother:

> The age that you cease to be infant in law;
> You were up to your larks,
> And the butt of remarks
> In common with other young rascally sparks;
> You kicked o'er the traces
> In manifold places
> And appeared far too fond of the prettiest faces;
> Not that I intend
> On this point to extend;
> It's one a royal Mother can do nought but end![74]

Suggestions of madness, in the eyes of republicans the hereditary Hanoverian disease that had afflicted George III, were sometimes raised to account for the Prince's aberrant behaviour. Learning that he had become the patron of Redhill Asylum, Surrey, republicans declared themselves pleased to see 'His Royal Highness in a station for which the habits of his life, and the traditions of his family so thoroughly qualify him'.[75] Memories of the insane peer, brought raving into the Upper Chamber to swing a crucial vote of censure against Peel's government in 1841, had become a folk tale that added apparent validity to these whispers about the

---

[72] *Newcastle Weekly Chronicle*, 25 Sep. 1875, p. 4. For Edward's debauched entourage of dissolute aristocrats, see also *Reynolds's Newspaper*, 6 Feb. 1876, p. 5.
[73] Ibid., 17 Mar. 1872, p. 4.
[74] S. Beeton, *Beeton's Christmas Annual: The Coming K . . .* (London, 1872), p. 9.
[75] *National Reformer*, 23 Apr. 1871, p. 265.

frail sanity of the enfeebled and incestuous hereditary classes.[76] *Reynolds's Newspaper* spoke of 'the abnormal depravity of our aristocracy:- a depravity which deepens as the years roll on'.[77] In the company of his dissolute aristocratic friends, the Prince of Wales was believed to roam the streets of London, visiting brothels, gambling dens and taverns. Accounts of his dubious conduct carried undertones of the narratives of low life and dissipation that traditionally featured in characterizations of aristocratic society in London. A visiting American writer, Daniel Kirwan, saw him at a casino in London in 1870, and noted that 'long nights of dissipation and debauchery had seamed the once youthful and unwrinkled features, and the under part of the face hung in heavy, adipose folds, like the dewlaps of a bullock'. Remarking his friendships with actresses and young ballet dancers he concluded 'for the past seven years the Prince of Wales has been a prominent actor in almost every scene of aristocratic dissipation and debauchery which has been enacted in the English metropolis'.[78] Despite his later public rehabilitation, Edward was never quite able to shake off his popular image as a rake. In later life, visits to Paris on governmental and diplomatic business revived speculation about his activities in brothels, and the specialist nature of the services that were provided for him there.[79] During her lifetime, even Victoria acknowledged the potentially destabilizing impact of such revelations on the public reputation of the monarchy, and the degree to which the Prince's involvement in celebrated affairs like the Mordaunt Divorce Case fostered public disquiet with the throne. In her correspondence, she lamented the behaviour of the 'higher classes' who 'in their frivolous, selfish and pleasure-seeking lives, do more to increase the spirit of democracy than anything else'.[80]

Monarchy was also embedded within the country-house culture of the shires. The conspicuous ostentation of the great landed families meant that royalty often competed with families like the Devonshires to create grand premises and suitable accommodation befitting their royal status. For some of the established landed families of the realm, the foreign and miserly nature of the House of Saxe-Coburg and Gotha was confirmed by their cold, draughty and cramped palaces.[81] Under Victoria, the court was branded as both dowdy and parsimonious by the nobility. The landed dynasts poured scorn on the meagre accommodation

---

[76] S. Braham, *Tales from the House of Lords* (London, 1987), p. 24. The radical press enjoyed stories about members of hereditary families who had lost their reason: for an account of the insanity of Lord Durham's wife, see *Justice*, 14 Mar. 1885, p. 5.

[77] *Reynolds's Newspaper*, 1 Oct. 1876, p. 2.

[78] D. J. Kirwan, *Palace and Hovel or Phases of London Life* (London, 1870; 1970), pp. 73, 76.

[79] See C. Rearick, *Pleasures of the Belle Epoque* (New Haven, 1985); and Weintraub, *The Importance of Being Edward*, pp. 310–1.

[80] Quoted in ibid., p. 169.   [81] See Nash, *Buckingham Palace*, chs. 1–2.

available at Sandringham and the apparent preference of the royal family
for the small hunting lodge in the grounds that served as their permanent quarters. With its echoes of 'villadom', George V's residence in York
House at Sandringham led some to see him as downright 'suburban' in
his tastes.[82] Housing and architecture, then, defined the nature of hereditary power and position. For opponents of the throne, these fine distinctions were overlooked. Royal palaces were simply the mansions of the
bandit aristocracy writ large. Radicals portrayed the opulent premises of
the county families as the unacceptable face of landed wealth and naked
class interest. Viewed in these terms, the mansions of wealthy aristocrats were a bulwark against liberty that shielded the reactionary element
within the constitution. For their critics, the self-serving and opportunis-
tic nature of the territorial landed families was amply demonstrated by
the opulence of their county seats, built on land looted from the people,
and funded with exactions drawn from their tenants. Where aristocratic
power waned, it was compared to the tottering infrastructure of the great
country house circuit. During the House of Lords crisis, H. H. Asquith
depicted the Upper Chamber as an 'ancient and picturesque structure
condemned by its own inmates as unsafe' and spoke of 'constitutional
jerry-builders . . . hurrying from every corner' to shore up its executive privilege.[83] When monarchy sought to emulate the house-building
enthusiasm of the gentry, it found itself criticized for excessive and very
public displays of wealth raised from the public purse. The *Poor Man's
Guardian* wrote of the money channelled into the renovation of Windsor
Castle and the construction of Buckingham Palace in the 1830s:

Now is this not monstrous? That we should pay not only millions for the support
of the 'King's dignity' and for his useless offices, but must be plundered thus,
every day of the year, to pay for his house repairs and his house furniture? Is
he not, in all conscience, paid enough for this? Or if not, has he not already a
sufficiency of houses, and sufficiently furnished too? Why was Buckingham house
necessary? Why, to pull down the old one, which was – 'out of fashion' and to
give to some court architects a 'job'! Why did Windsor Palace need repairs? Why,
to please the brick and mortar whims of the voluptuous 'gentlemanly' dissipated
fool, by whose 'dignity' we were last cursed![84]

The great royal palaces and opulent physical surroundings of royalty
became so central to the myth of the monarchy, that the political health of
the office of kingship was measured in terms of the structural integrity of

---

[82] Sir Harold Nicolson described York Cottage as a 'glum little villa': see J. Gore, *King
George V* (London, 1941), p. 126 and for the bourgeois traits of many of Europe's ruling
houses in their choice of accommodation, *Daily Herald*, 2 Jan. 1924, p. 7.

[83] *The Premier's Battle Cry: Mr Asquith's Speech at the National Liberal Club, November 19th
1910* (Leeds, 1910), p. 6.

[84] *Poor Man's Guardian*, 8 Oct. 1831, p. 113.

its accommodation. During Victoria's seclusion, Buckingham Palace was shown as dilapidated, abandoned and overrun by rats.[85] For some critics Buckingham Palace was simply an opulent town house, its position at the heart of ceremonial London demonstrating that the royal family, like the great aristocratic families who built the West End, were primarily urban landowners, monopolizing metropolitan rent and dominating the public spaces of the capital. Like the gated houses and enclosed private spaces of the West End squares, Buckingham Palace excluded the populace from the open ground in an overcrowded and built urban environment in which places of popular recreation were at a premium. The gates in front of Buckingham Palace were interpreted as an artistic encumbrance that formed part of this exclusionary process. James Mill described them as 'like a pillar of salt' that made the façade of the palace look 'dirty and mean'.[86] Moreover, during Victoria's retreat from the public eye, the 'To Let' notices that appeared on the gates of Buckingham Palace symbolized the excesses of urban landlordism, where unused prime accommodation was left empty and untenanted for many months of the year outside the period of the season.[87] In these terms, most of the prevailing criticisms of urban landlordism were as applicable to the royal family as to the great families of London. The *Christian Socialist* wrote of the representative urban landlord:

> You pouch the gold while we do keep the stall,
> Breathe the rank smell, and toil from morn to eve,
> To pay the all-absorbing rent which you receive.
> You roam your park, free from disease and death,
> While we pale victims draw our heavy breath,
> Living in garrets vile above thy festering slums.
> O, noble duke, king of the roaring Strand,
> Peer of the many peers, a much consuming band –
> O thou who closest iron gates against the people rude
> Lest they on thy grand squares should dare intrude.[88]

III

The transgressive aspect of monarchy was compounded by the lust for sport that was a marked feature of the aristocratic circles in which monarchy traditionally moved. Patronage of the great nineteenth-century hunts

[85] See A. Taylor, *'Down with the Crown': British Anti-monarchism and Debates about Royalty since 1790* (London, 1999), p. 82.
[86] Mill, 'Aristocracy', pp. 287–9.
[87] See J. Bellows, *Remarks on Certain Anonymous Articles Designed to Render Queen Victoria Unpopular* (Gloucester, 1864), pp. 18–27.
[88] *Christian Socialist*, 1 Aug. 1884, p. 43.

consolidated royalty's links with landed society in the shires. For supporters of the monarchy, royal involvement in fox-hunting and field sports
recalled the throne's traditional connections with estate life that dated
back at least to the reign of George III.[89] Grouse shooting was such an
established part of life at Balmoral under George V that one disgruntled
visitor complained, 'It was grouse, grouse and grouse all the day long'.[90]
There was often a sense of artful anachronism about royalty's obsession
with hunting. Writing of George V, J. Wentworth Day saw the connection as a valuable one, commenting that he was 'a sportsman of the old
school, bridging the gulf between the old and new Englands.'[91] For some
royalists, hunting and game preservation evoked the role of custodian-
ship of the landscape and of the natural rural order that the aristocracy
traditionally abrogated to itself. A. E. T. Watson wrote of Edward VII:
'Delighting as he did in the beauties of Nature, the sport that he liked most
of all was grouse-shooting in various parts of Scotland, and deer-driving
at Balmoral, where Nature has arranged such a magnificent setting for
the sportsman'.[92] This close involvement with the land was particularly
apparent at Sandringham. The link with rural Norfolk was a visceral one.
Admirers of the monarchy saw it as cementing ancestral bloodlines with
national leaders and heroes of the stature of Nelson. J. Wentworth Day
wrote of Norfolk as a repository for virtues of patriotism and of English
resolve: 'It was in such wild places, in such old untainted corners of
England, that the best of our leaders have been born and bred.'[93] Sandringham could boast one of the largest game larders in Europe. During
the reign of George V, clocks at the estate were set on so-called 'Sandringham time', an hour behind Greenwich mean time, to allow an extra
hour's daylight for shooting in the winter. Sandringham, then, became
the acme of the sporting fraternity. Following Albert Edward's lead, it
was the acknowledged meeting place for an indolent sporting set who
flouted the society dress conventions of the day by dressing entirely in
sporting tweeds, even at dinner (Figs. 7.4 and 7.5).

For radicals, opposition to 'blood-sports' provided an emotive case
against the depredations of the nation's social betters. Hunting evoked
the baser side of aristocracy, revealing the carnal urges behind the pretensions to genteel and mannered living. Rather than a haven for Englishness,

---

[89] See 'The Prince of Wales as a sportsman', *The New Penny Magazine* 7 (1900), 1–6.
[90] A. A. Michie, *God Save the Queen* (London, 1953), p. 185.
[91] Day, *King George V as a Sportsman*, p. 293.
[92] A. E. T. Watson, *King Edward VII as a Sportsman* (London, 1911), p. xxiv. In addition, Homans sees hunting in Ireland and Scotland as symbolic of a continuing royal
   subordination of the Celtic fringe: see Homans, *Royal Representations*, p. 139.
[93] Day, *King George V as a Sportsman*, pp. 126–7.

THE KING OF ENGLAND AND THE EMPEROR WILHELM OF ALMAINE
SHOOT TOGETHER AT SANDRINGHAM.

Figure 7.4. Crypto-medieval caricature of Edward VII shooting with Kaiser Wilhelm II at Sandringham. From F. Carruthers Gould, *F.C.G.'s Froissart's Modern Chronicles, 1902* (London, 1903), p. 75. (Author's Collection.)

they saw Norfolk as an artificial place, cleared of the traditional yeomanry by game preservers, aristocrats, and the visiting dignitaries, princes, and continental royals who shot with the Prince of Wales. Here the territorial aristocracy slaked their blood lust. Edward VII's neighbour, Louise Cresswell, who was financially ruined by the consequences of his obsessive game preservation, depicted the aftermath of a pheasant shoot at Sandringham as similar to a field of battle, strewn with the dead: 'When riding round after the invaders had retired, seeing the general air of devastation left in their wake, the empty cartridges strewed about, and listening to the mournful chirrupings of the poor little birds for their lost relatives, I felt it to be a dree accompaniment to my solitude'.[94] A correspondent in *Reynolds's Newspaper* spoke of the 'vicious example' set by Sandringham, and described Norfolk as 'specially cursed on account of the "felonious"

[94] L. Cresswell, *Eighteen Years on Sandringham Estate* (London, 1897), pp. 71–2. For examples of the sheer scale of shooting at Sandringham see H. S. Gladstone, *Record Bags and Shooting Records* (London, 1922). Some authors have argued that powerful royal patronage was significant in enabling fox-hunting to persist into the twentieth century. See E. W. Martin, *The Case Against Hunting* (London, 1959), pp. 105–10.

THE KING DOM CARLOS OF PORTUGAL AND THE PRINCE OF WALES
GO A-SHOOTING.

Figure 7.5. Crypto-medieval caricature of Edward VII shooting with
Dom Carlos, King of Portugal, at Sandringham. From F. Carruthers
Gould, *F.C.G.'s Froissart's Modern Chronicles* (London, 1903), p. 78.
(Author's Collection.)

class in it rearing animals at their tenants' expense in order to ape the
doings of royal princes'.[95] Other radical newspapers set out to undermine Edward's reputation as a model landowner, casting doubt on the
many plaudits he received for his good stewardship of the land. *Justice*
wrote that new cottages built at Sandringham were not designed to house
estate retainers, but were a barracks for his personal police bodyguard; in
so doing it created the impression of an army of occupation on the land.[96]
Pretensions to aristocratic status, then, could wound, as well as reinforce,
the position of monarchy. Hunting highlighted the essential conservatism
of royalty and of its landed retainers.[97] There were strong links between
the land debate, criticisms of aristocracy, House of Lords reform, and

[95] *Reynolds's Newspaper*, 11 Feb. 1872, p. 2. For the failure of petitions by Albert Edward's
tenants at Sandringham to encourage him to take a stand against the game laws and
encourage local Norfolk landowners to do likewise, see ibid, 14 Jan. 1866, p. 3.
[96] *Justice*, 2 Aug. 1884, p. 2.
[97] Alfred Watson wrote sadly of Dom Carlos, King of Portugal, a regular hunting visitor to
Sandringham and Windsor, 'barbarously murdered by the socialists', that he displayed
'exceptional skill with gun, rifle and pistol': see Watson, *King Edward VII as a Sportsman*,
p. 70.

animal welfare politics in the late nineteenth and early twentieth centuries. The monarchy's interest in game preservation enmeshed the royal estates with contemporary debates about the Game Laws and aristocratic usurpation of the people's land at the time of the Norman Conquest.[98] Radical verses frequently dwelt on the injustices this produced and its implications for the future of the monarchy:

> The earth is the lord's and the fullness thereof,
> The country and also the towns;
> Our old dear Queen is our only sov,
> And she's hardly worth three crowns;
> And we very much fear, while her loss we deplore,
> That sovereign or crown we shall never see more.[99]

These were constants of radical rhetoric that associated royal princes with the great landed proprietors, described as 'descendants of these Norman robbers, breeding game and vermin to satisfy their own selfish propensity and pleasure while thousands of our industrious poor are dying for want unable to procure the common necessaries for their miserable existence'.[100] In radical rhetoric, historical memories of feudal obligations imposed by 'William the Bastard' to preserve royal hunting rights appeared as another aspect of the traditional dispossession of the rural poor. Increasingly the restoration of peasant smallholdings and a curbing of the excesses of the great landowners were viewed as the salvation of traditional English rural society. Hunting therefore demonstrated the pampered and leisured nature of aristocratic life. *Justice* concluded that Edward's passion for pheasant shooting was valuable only insofar as it might provide him with future employment in a projected British republic as a butcher and purveyor of fine meats.[101] For its part, the *National Reformer* looked forward to a day when the intending head of state would be required 'to show that they were fit for something besides shooting pheasants' as a qualification for the position.[102]

IV

For radicals, the failings of monarchy were exacerbated on those occasions when they aspired to the virtues of the gentry and of the aristocracy.

---

[98] See A. Taylor, '"Pig-sticking princes": royal hunting, moral outrage, and the republican opposition to animal abuse in nineteenth- and early twentieth-century Britain', *History* 89 (2004), 30–48.

[99] *National Reformer*, 9 Apr. 1871, p. 239.

[100] A speech by Comrade Hardinge, entitled 'The land and the rights of the people', at the Bristol Republican club, *National Reformer*, 22 Dec, 1872, p. 398.

[101] See *Justice*, 24 Jan. 1885, p. 1.   [102] *National Reformer*, 20 Jun. 1875, pp. 389–90.

In particular, the deficiencies of the royal clan were compounded by their failings as warriors. Royal prowess in battle proved conspicuously lacking on those occasions when they sought to replicate the martial spirit of their Norman ancestors. Radicals highlighted their evident lack of chivalry, and their unwillingness to comply with the rigours of army life. Criticism of titled and well connected officers abounded following the blunders of the Crimean War and during the debates surrounding the Cardwell reforms of 1870, which overturned the aristocracy's monopoly of senior positions in the officer corps. These were the 'royal and right honourable wooden-heads' who, using connections and influence at court, had dominated the officer class for some time.[103] For critics of aristocratic influence in the military, the victory of the Federal Northern Republic in the American Civil War highlighted the effectiveness of 'citizen armies' where rank was open to talent and where 'neither fortune, position, or political influence could maintain an incompetent general in command of an army'.[104] After 1870 such aristocratic influences counted for less. For its critics, however, royalty continued to usurp military and naval titles as an addition to their lengthy list of paid public offices, honorific titles, and bogus commendations. The criticisms usually levelled against the aristocracy on these grounds remained pertinent in the case of military royals. When Albert Edward was promoted to Field Marshal in 1875, reformers criticized the extra salary that went with the position, and highlighted the Prince's unreadiness for war. Royal relatives like the notoriously inept Duke of Cambridge, who bungled the high command of the British army for much of the fifty-year period between the Crimean War and the Boer War, provided a poor model for military royals. In common with the Duke of Cambridge, Albert Edward was widely perceived as a 'carpet-soldier useless in times of war, and a burden in times of peace'.[105] The *National Reformer* wrote: 'We are not likely to be informed why the honour which was denied to some of our greatest heroes on the battlefield has been awarded to a prince who has never even seen a battle'.[106] The radical press also questioned the prince's bravery and courage. Coming as close as it dared to alleging cowardice on the part of the prince, *Reynolds's Newspaper* sardonically noted that Albert Edward's prowess on the hunting field and against the elderly rare bulls of the Chillingham herd in Northumberland were an inadequate preparation for war: 'Fortunately for the country, fortunately for himself, this mighty warrior to whom we

---

[103] *Reynolds's Newspaper*, 9 Jan. 1876, p. 5.   [104] Ibid., 30 Apr. 1865, p. 3.
[105] *National Reformer*, 18 Jul. 1875, p. 43. For a hostile caricature of the Duke of Cambridge, see *The Tomahawk*, 25 Jan. 1868, p. 39, and for attacks on his military prowess, *Reynolds's Newspaper*, 19 Oct. 1856, p. 1 and 26 Oct. 1856, p. 9.
[106] *National Reformer*, 13 Jun. 1875, p. 376.

allude passed unscathed through the terrible conflict of Chillingham, or, as it has been termed, the battle with the old cow, and likewise came unharmed from the equally daring encounters he had in India with the wild pigs of that country'.[107] The *Radical* newspaper echoed this view: 'We have royal field marshals and royal generals; but we have no royal warriors'.[108] Military royals always faced allegations of accelerated and unjustified promotions, and indifference to the exercise of the function of their office, even in time of war. When the Duke of Gloucester was promoted to Major-General in 1937, there was considerable hostility from the labourist and radical press. The *Daily Worker* commented in sardonic vein: 'If this was achieved by merit alone (and we assume that military merit is intended) then not only has this young man created something like a record, but our prospects in a future war must obviously be far better than any of us ever dared to hope. In fact we would suggest that he be appointed Commander-in-Chief immediately'.[109]

V

Edward's VII's glittering and vivacious lifestyle brought him increasingly into the orbit of the new social forces that were reshaping the aristocracy. From the 1890s onwards, new men of wealth gained prominence in his entourage.[110] Acceptance of the new plutocracy demonstrated the pliable and compliant nature of monarchy. Critics of the throne believed that the monarchy privileged 'new money' in an attempt to buttress the fading alliance of land and property that upheld the royal state. Radicals saw this new plutocracy as a social phenomenon defined by ostentatious wealth and royal favour that cohered around the rotting carcass of the old landed elite and helped 'regild decayed and ancient coronets'.[111] The new plutocrats purchased status, title and position as adornments, in the process buying up the estates of the declining landed gentry to establish holdings commensurate with their new-found status. They were notorious for raking through the detritus of extinct, dormant or unclaimed titles looking for antique peerages that might be purchased or assumed. 'A title is the fancy trimming of a plutocrat', wrote W. T. Stead, 'a big brewer has not achieved his ambition until he has scrambled over his beer barrels into the Painted Chamber'.[112] The impoverished county gentry

---

[107] *Reynolds's Newspaper*, 9 Jul. 1876, p. 5.

[108] *The Radical*, 1 Feb. 1887, pp. 41–2.   [109] *Daily Worker*, 4 Jan. 1937, p. 4.

[110] See J. Camplin, *The Rise of the Plutocrats* (London, 1978), chs. 1–2.

[111] Silas K. Hocking, *The Broken Fence* (London, 1928), p. 89.

[112] W. T. Stead, *Peers or People? The House of Lords Weighed in the Balance and Found Wanting* (London, 1907 edn.), pp. 36–7.

saw the plutocracy as buying their way into court circles and an ancestral inheritance. Drawing on mythologized and antiquarian pedigrees, they were commonly depicted as a rougher and more debased version of the county set that aped the vices and excesses of the traditional aristocracy. *Justice* called them 'new huckster cormorants (who) have all the old vices without any manners or the slightest historical claim'.[113] They featured frequently in the novels of the period as a 'hard-faced' class; the writer Richard Whiteing recoiled from them: 'One felt from the terrible look of their terrible faces, that there was no keeping them back. Nothing can stand against such men.'[114] Some social democrats like Harold Laski saw them very much in the manner of the old aristocracy as impeding progress and preventing political reform. 'The whole of those who advise the king' he wrote 'are in or about the plutocracy'[115] (Fig. 7.6). The historian Edward Freeman, who was widely read by radicals for his exposures of aristocratic land ownership, described their excesses as worse than those of the aristocracy, depicting them as even more tyrannical than the old hereditary territorial families.[116] For critics of the throne, these *arriviste* parvenus highlighted the contrived and 'invented' nature of the rituals and pedigree of the royal state. For radicals, the bogus nature of the titles handed out by royalty and the corruptability of those they adorned not only undermined the nature of inherited privilege, it also revealed the brittle foundations of monarchy itself, casting light on the dubious claims to the throne of the royal family and the legitimacy of pensions granted to key retainers.[117] Rather than fading, such concerns persisted during the nineteenth century, incensing those radicals who continued to campaign against dubious honours and excessive royal privileges up until the eve of the Great War.

VI

Leaving Britain in 1869 for exile in the United States, the militant radical James Finlen declared in a farewell oration:

He declared himself a republican in the fullest sense of the word, and felt convinced that there was no hope for the working men of England until monarchy and aristocracy were swept away as obstructions in the road to progress. He left

---

[113] *Justice*, 29 Mar. 1884, p. 1.
[114] Richard Whiteing, *No. 5 John Street* (new edn., London,1902), p. 141.
[115] Communist Party of Great Britain, *Coronation* (London, 1953), p. 8.
[116] E. A. Freeman (ed.), *The House of Lords and Other Upper Houses* (London, 1891), pp. 99–100.
[117] After Albert Edward, the court tried to distance itself from 'new money': see R. Hudson, *George V* (London, 1910), p. 18.

CORONATION

THREEPENCE

Figure 7.6. Plutocrats and monopoly capitalists clustered around the throne at the time of the coronation in 1953. Cover of *Coronation* (The Communist Party of Great Britain, 1953). (Author's Collection.)

this country without regret, cursed as it was by one of the proudest and vilest aristocracies in the world, and going, as he was, to become a citizen in the most free and famous nation on the face of the earth, where he hoped to live many years to battle on the wave of democratic republicanism.[118]

---

[118] *Bee-Hive*, 25 Sep. 1869, p. 1. For the blending and merging of British and US republican ideas in the nineteenth century see P. Krause, 'Beeswax Taylor: The Forgotten Legacy of Labor Insurgency in Gilded Age America', in E. Arnesen (ed.) *The Human Tradition in American Labor History* (Wilmington, Delaware, 2004), pp. 47–68.

Reformers who yearned for a monarchy that acted as a fountainhead of justice and liberty overlooked a fundamental reality about the throne. As Finlen suggested, in Britain royalty and aristocracy are inextricably linked. The close relationship between monarchy and aristocracy, and the power and wealth that accompanied a royal establishment tethered closely to the great landed dynasties, magnified the excesses of individual monarchs. In the nineteenth century the royal family required a close relationship with the territorial aristocracy to maintain the public face of the throne on official occasions, to represent its interests in the upper echelons of the military, to act as marriage partners and court officials, and to provide a glamorous backdrop on the hunting field or at Royal Ascot. Monarchy therefore, in part, engineered a persistence of aristocracy. In contrast to the Scandanavian countries, characterized by the absence of a large landed proprietor class, Britain's monarchy was unable to divorce its interests from those of the territorial aristocracy as a whole or to divest itself of their influences. Like the House of Lords, the monarchy was depicted by radicals as a dying institution that consolidated the remaining power of the feudal overlords and used it to block legislation inimical to the landed interest. Not confronting the decline of aristocracy, and still preoccupied with regal ritual and its aristocratic impresarios, the critique provided by British republicanism has struggled to move beyond a vision that sees monarchy and aristocracy as the same social phenomenon.[119] For its critics, the throne was a screen behind which the aristocracy still marshalled its considerable hidden powers over the land, in urban investments, and in relation to political and social position. The misdeeds of the aristocracy remained a potent element in the platform rhetoric of radicalism that provided evidence against titled rakes, and a condemnation of the social lottery that defined access to wealth and privilege. Individual monarchs found themselves measured against the failings of their aristocratic courtiers. The failings of aristocracy therefore, were also the failings of monarchy. For better or for worse, the monarchy was (and still often is) judged in terms of the behavior of its closest allies.

[119] S. Haseler, *The End of the House of Windsor: The Birth of a British Republic* (London, 1993), ch. 5.

Part III

8   The monarchy and public values 1910–1953*

Philip Williamson

As a former imperial proconsul and cabinet veteran of the Abyssinian and Rhineland crises, the Marquess of Zetland was not easily alarmed; yet in November 1936 he described the government as 'faced with a problem compared with which even the international issues, grave as they assuredly are, pale into comparative insignificance'. This and similar comments by other public figures during that year[1] might be dismissed as over-reactions, characteristic of the loss of proportion which afflicts many statements about the British monarchy. King Edward VIII's wish to marry Mrs Simpson hardly seems so menacing as the activities of Franco, Mussolini, Hitler and Stalin. There was no constitutional conflict and no civil disorder, only an exercise in political management; fears of national and imperial calamity were swiftly dispelled by a straightforward dynastic adjustment, substituting one brother for another on the throne.

Yet a retrospective view that the severity of the 'abdication crisis'[2] was exaggerated begs the question of why contemporaries regarded the King's proposed marriage as such a fundamental problem. It also raises larger questions about the monarchy's position in early twentieth-century public life. A leading theme of statements about the monarchy was that although its political power had declined, its public significance had increased. Baldwin, for example, declared in 1935 that 'the influence of the Crown, . . . the necessity of the Crown, has become a thing of paramount importance'.[3] The monarchy also appeared to have become

* I am most grateful to Peter Ghosh, Ged Martin, Andrzej Olechnowicz, Jonathan Parry and David Craig for constructive criticisms of an earlier draft; to the British Academy for a research readership; and to Pamela Clark at the Royal Archives for valuable advice. After the first citation, titles of royal biographies are abbreviated as *KGV*, etc.

[1] Zetland to Linlithgow, 27 Nov. 1936, Zetland papers, Mss Eur D 609/7/136, Oriental and India Office Collections, British Library; and see e.g. *The Reith Diaries*, ed. C. Stuart (London, 1975), p. 188 (28 May, 10 July 1936); T. Jones, *A Diary With Letters 1931–1950* (London, 1954), p. 290 (3 Dec. 1936); *The Diary of Virginia Woolf*, ed. A. O. Bell, vol. 5 (London, 1984), p. 39 (7 Dec. 1936).

[2] In strict terms this traditional designation is misleading. The problem was the King's proposed marriage; his abdication was not the cause of the crisis, but its solution.

[3] *The Times*, 4 May 1935.

more popular, as shown spectacularly in 1935–7 by the Silver Jubilee, George V's death, and George VI's coronation, and again in 1952–3 by George VI's death and Elizabeth II's coronation. So remarkable was the public interest on each occasion that for the first time since Bagehot, commentators and academics began to regard the monarchy's popularity as an intellectual problem.[4] By 1953 there seemed to have been an 'extraordinary upsurge and renaissance of monarchical feeling . . . in the last thirty or forty years'.[5]

During those years the conditions for monarchy had been transformed, and not obviously in ways which assisted it: still greater concentration of power in the hands of politicians and officials; the establishment of a fully democratic electorate and emergence of a powerful labour movement; prolonged periods of economic difficulties, social distress and industrial unrest; millions conscripted and hundreds of thousands killed and wounded in 'the King's service', and the civilian population exposed to the bombings, privations and dislocations of total war; republican secession from the United Kingdom, and an Empire becoming a Commonwealth of autonomous nations. Across Europe other monarchies collapsed, and were often succeeded by fascist or communist dictatorships. Although Britain did not suffer the military defeats or revolutions which destroyed continental monarchies, these new conditions were challenging for its own monarchy and some could be regarded as dangerous. During the first decade of George V's reign, he and his advisers were fearful of the monarchy's chances of survival, particularly because they suspected the Labour party of republican aims. Anxiety about public feeling had very personal repercussions: during the First World War the King replaced his family's German name and titles with English neologisms, renounced his German relatives, and refused refuge for his Russian cousins.[6] Edward VIII's marriage proposal and abdication were certainly crises for the royal family itself, and George VI thought he had been

---

[4] E.g. E. Jones, 'The psychology of constitutional monarchy', *New Statesman*, 1 Feb. 1936; K. Martin articles in *Political Quarterly* and *New Statesman* 1936–7, summarized in his *The Magic of Monarchy* (London, 1937); H. Laski, *Parliamentary Government in England* (London, 1938), pp. 388–96. The 1936–7 royal occasions also prompted the creation of the social research organisation, Mass-Observation: see P. Ziegler, *Crown and People* (London, 1978), pp. 9–10, and H. Jennings and C. Madge (eds.), *May The Twelfth* (London, 1937; 1987).

[5] S. Haffner, 'The renascense of monarchy', *Twentieth Century* 154 (1953), 418. See also E. Shils and M. Young, 'The meaning of the coronation', *Sociological Review* 1 (1953), 63–81, and for a historical verdict R. McKibbin, *Classes and Cultures. England 1918–1951* (Oxford, 1998), pp. 3, 7.

[6] F. Prochaska, 'George V and republicanism 1917–1919', *Twentieth Century British History* 10 (1999), 27–51, and F. Prochaska, *The Republic of Britain* (London, 2000), pp. 154–78.

encumbered with a tarnished and unsteady throne. Yet the monarchy emerged unscathed, and by the time of Elizabeth II's accession none at the Palace could have been disturbed by republican nightmares.

How did the monarchy remain secure and popular? Why, in the new political democracy from 1918 and social democracy from the mid 1940s, was it presented as more, not less, important? Why did it preserve its considerable prominence rather than subsiding, as some in the 1930s suggested it should,[7] into the more discreet role of the Scandinavian monarchies? Answers to these questions also provide the best context for understanding Edward VIII's abdication. Despite excellent and well documented accounts of the episode,[8] speculation continues about suppressed political or policy causes – that his marriage proposal was a ministerial or 'establishment' pretext for removing a King with inconvenient sympathies towards the unemployed or Nazi Germany, and still more inconvenient populist political ambitions. Such claims persist largely because since 1936 the contemporary public considerations have lost most of their force and so seem, wrongly, to provide insufficient explanation for the King's departure.[9] Understanding the reasons for the monarchy's continued significance shows why as late as the 1930s a royal marriage could still be a major problem of state.

I

With an institution so long established and so central to public life as the monarchy, in any relatively short period little is wholly new: the main patterns are continuity, adaptation and renovation. The constitutional position and political role; the alluring combination of ceremonial display, domesticity and 'ordinariness'; the Christian example and philanthropic endeavours, and the provincial and imperial visits of the royal family – all have antecedents in the reign of Victoria or even George III. Even projection in the new mass media of radio, film and television added only greater immediacy to the already enormous coverage of the monarchy in the existing mass media of print and photographic

---

[7] *New Statesman*, 12 Dec. 1936, and see below, p. 241.
[8] The 'abdication' files released by the National Archives in 2003 add little to the essentials cumulatively established from other sources by K. Middlemas and J. Barnes, *Baldwin* (London, 1969), ch. 34; F. Donaldson, *Edward VIII* (London, 1974), chs. 14–23; M. Bloch, *The Reign and Abdication of Edward VIII* (London, 1990); and also, with early access to the government files as well as Edward VIII's papers, by P. Ziegler, *King Edward VIII* (London, 1990), chs. 14–18.
[9] A recent example, notwithstanding valuable documentary research, is Susan Williams, *The People's King* (London, 2003).

reproduction.[10] Nevertheless, reflection on the monarchy's adjustment to early twentieth-century conditions reveals much about its character and, more significantly, about the support it received from other institutions and voluntary organizations. The instances of renewed royal effort are mostly familiar: more public ceremonies, more frequent royal visits, increased patronage of voluntary social and medical services, and the innovation of a *silver* jubilee, where the precedents were only for golden and diamond jubilees.[11] There was, however, a further development deserving closer examination: the monarchy became more vocal.[12] As the royal family's activities and visits increased, so its members made more speeches and issued more messages, heard or received more public addresses, and attracted greater media commentary. Collectively these statements provided sustained expositions of what the monarchy represented and commended, and explanations of the social meanings of its ceremonies, visits and philanthropy. The effect was to enhance what had become its chief function – to express and symbolize public values.

The pressure upon members of the royal family to speak could be inexorable, overcoming their own reluctance. This was especially so for what became the monarchy's most important speaking occasion. It was nine years before George V could be persuaded to broadcast a Christmas Day message, but in 1932 it made such an impact that he found he could not escape its annual recurrence.[13] So necessary a royal attribute did public speaking become that serious difficulties arose with George VI. Before 1914 a royal stammer would have been a minor matter, but in the 1920s it raised doubts about the then Duke of York's suitability for public duties. Even with assistance from a speech therapist and a BBC sound engineer, the preparation, rehearsal and delivery of his speeches were an ordeal for himself, his staff, and event organizers. His first Christmas broadcast, in 1937, was explicitly intended to end the new 'tradition';

---

[10] See, notably, L. Colley, *Britons. Forging the Nation 1707–1837* (New Haven, 1992), ch. 5; F. Prochaska, *Royal Bounty* (New Haven, 1995); W. H. Kuhn, *Democratic Royalism* (Basingstoke, 1996); J. Plunkett, *Queen Victoria: First Media Monarch* (Oxford, 2003); and Jonathan Parry's chapter in the current volume. These qualify the chronology and main thesis of D. Cannadine, 'The context, performance and meaning of ritual: the British monarchy and the "invention of tradition" c.1820–1977', in E. Hobsbawm and T. Ranger (eds.), *The Invention of Tradition* (Cambridge, 1983), pp. 101–64.

[11] In early discussions it was called a 'semi-jubilee': Bishops meeting, 24–25 Oct. 1934, Lambeth Palace Library. Little evidence appears to have survived on the jubilee's origins. It would not have occurred without ministerial approval, but it does not follow that the motives were party-political: see below note 48.

[12] Though again this was not entirely new: see *The Principal Speeches and Addresses of His Royal Highness the Prince Consort* (London, 1862).

[13] T. Fleming (intro.), *Voices out of the Air. The Royal Christmas Broadcasts 1932–1981* (London, 1981), pp. 5–9; *Reith Diaries*, pp. 181–3; K. Rose, *King George V* (London, 1983), pp. 393–4.

Figure 8.1. King Geoge VI delivering the 1944 Christmas Day broadcast (The Royal Collection).

only with great difficulty was he persuaded after the outbreak of war to revive it.[14]

Monarchs and their family members rarely spoke extempore or wrote their own speeches and statements. Royal pronouncements received immense publicity and required elegance and tact, but royal individuals themselves lacked the literary ability, application and confidence to produce suitable prose.[15] A few speeches (not just the parliamentary King's Speeches) were written by government ministers, who certainly vetted any significant statements bearing on constitutional or policy issues. More were drafted by civil servants, and for overseas tours an official was either

[14] J. Wheeler-Bennett, *King George VI* (London, 1958), pp. 133–5, 207–8, 212–5, 361, 428, 449; S. Bradford, *George VI* (London, 1989), pp. 159–63, 272–3, 276–9, 419; R. Rhodes James, *Spirit Undaunted. The Political Role of George VI* (London, 1998), pp. 176–8; and for 1937, *Voices out of the Air*, pp. 21, 26. In a later controversy about the monarchy's standing, Elizabeth II's speeches were a leading point of criticism: see Lord Altrincham, 'The monarchy today', *National and English Review* 149 (1957), pp. 63, 65.

[15] On the shortcomings of their unaided written and spoken statements, see e.g. Rose, *KGV*, pp. 15, 56, 182–3; *Letters from a Prince 1918–1921*, ed. R. Godfrey (London, 1998), p. ix and *passim*.

seconded to the royal staff for the purpose or supplied by the local governor or ambassador.[16] Recognized masters of public prose were also recruited. Kipling composed several speeches for George V and his sons, and the first two Christmas broadcasts.[17] Archbishop Lang wrote the next two. During the Silver Jubilee, Lang drafted both the King's broadcast and the House of Lords' address to the King, John Buchan wrote the House of Commons' address, and G. M. Trevelyan the King's reply to these two addresses.[18] Authors of George VI's Christmas broadcasts included Baldwin, Churchill, R.A. Butler, and Arthur Bryant.[19] Material for speeches to corporations and societies was usually provided by one of the organization's officers, or another expert in the field. Most of the work was done by the private secretaries to each member of the royal family: they selected draftsmen, revised their texts, and wrote many speeches and statements themselves, just as they drafted most official letters from the King and his family members as well as explicitly writing letters on their behalf. Stamfordham, George V's secretary until 1931 and a 'masterly draftsman', set the standard;[20] his successors Wigram and Hardinge presumably contributed too, but the most prolific speech-writer was Sir Alan Lascelles, beginning with Edward as Prince of Wales and continuing with George VI and Princess Elizabeth.[21]

Royal public language was, therefore, the work of numerous minds, which itself indicates that the monarchy was associated with a well recognized vocabulary and set of messages. Notwithstanding the contemporary legend and historical shorthand which speak of monarchs alone deciding the institution's course, such collective effort was also true of

---

[16] E.g. Ziegler, *KEVIII*, pp. 139, 157; Wheeler-Bennett, *KGVI*, p. 216; James, *Spirit Undaunted*, pp. 69, 161, 249, 282; Bradford, *KGVI*, p. 500. Identifying the original authors of the speeches is not easy, as they observed a protocol of confidentiality and the Royal Archives preserve the convention that the words of royal persons are their own.

[17] Not, as usually stated, just the first one: see Kipling papers 21/7–9, 17, University of Sussex Library, and for drafts of other speeches, D. Gilmour, *The Long Recessional* (2002), p. 308.

[18] A. Don diary, 6, 9 May 1935, Lambeth Palace Library; D. Cannadine, *G. M. Trevelyan* (London, 1992), pp. 122–4 (Trevelyan also wrote the Jubilee leader in *The Times*); MacDonald to Wigram, 21 Feb. 1935, PREM 1/173, National Archives: this file contains further documents showing that the prime minister's office staff co-ordinated and refined all these addresses.

[19] Hardinge to Baldwin, 29 Nov., 16 Dec. 1939, Baldwin papers 178/313–4, Cambridge University Library; M. Gilbert, *Winston S. Churchill. iv 1939–1941* (London, 1983), p. 961; A. Howard, *R. A. Butler* (London, 1987), p. 131; Lascelles to Bryant, 21 Dec. 1946, Bryant papers D4, King's College, London; Cf. Bradford, *GVI*, p. 605.

[20] Oddly, on this point the earliest official biography is the most frank: J. Gore, *King George V* (London, 1941), pp. 147–8, 209, 220.

[21] Donaldson, *EVIII*, pp. 102, 398; Ziegler, *KEVIII*, pp. 178, 183, 250; *In Royal Service. Letters and Journals of Sir Alan Lascelles 1920–1936*, ed. D. Hart-Davis (London, 1989), pp. x, 10, 117; James, *Spirit Undaunted*, pp. 176, 249.

its general position in public life. It was not just that for state business, ceremonies and other public duties, they were advised and organized by their private secretaries and senior court officials. Nor was it only that this royal bureaucracy was assisted by a network of government and unofficial advisers – civil servants, ministers, elder statesmen, churchmen, the editor of *The Times*, officers of voluntary societies and charities.[22] The modern monarchy's public character had never been determined only by those close to the Palace.[23] In a society becoming less hierarchical and more plural, it could not have preserved its position and popularity without much broader institutional support. Members of the public did not just admire or accept the monarchy for itself and because of its own efforts; they did so also, and crucially, because it was approved by most of the public bodies and voluntary organizations to which they belonged or which they supported or respected, and by most of the media which further influenced their opinions.

Why did this wide organizational support remain available? One answer is that the monarchy had become uncontroversial. Since the 1830s it had been publicly distanced from electoral and party politics. From 1910 limitation of the House of Lords' powers and George V's relative disengagement (in contrast to his father) from London 'society' made it seem less tied to the aristocracy and plutocracy. The Great War ended its links with the autocratic continental monarchies, and renewed its position as the focus for patriotic sentiment.

Yet if ostensible non-partisanship was a necessary condition of its public status, it is not a sufficient explanation. The monarchy was for many not just a matter of indifference, or simply tolerated: it was positively, enthusiastically, admired. Nor was it – nor could it be – entirely neutral, however much it was removed from public controversies: the royal family's instincts were conservative,[24] the sovereign remained supreme governor of the Church of England, and monarchy was the epitome of social inequality and privilege. It was able to be uncontroversial only because organizations which might have been critical or cool chose to treat it as such, overlooking its remaining partisan features.

---

[22] See Nicolson, *KGV*, p. 452, for George V saying that Stamfordham 'taught me how to be a King', and for other examples Prochaska, *Republic of Britain*, pp. 157–60, 162–3, 165–76, 178–9. For the general point see also D. Cannadine, 'From biography to history: writing the modern British monarchy', *Historical Research* 77 (2004), 300–1.

[23] See e.g. Colley, *Britons*, pp. 217–29, and Plunkett, *Queen Victoria*, ch. 1.

[24] Remarkably, James, *Spirit Undaunted*, pp. 286, 278, describes George VI as a 'progressive liberal', even a 'radical', presumably because of his earlier association with voluntary social welfare. But that was entirely compatible with Conservatism, and hardly justifies aligning him with Attlee's socialism: see also Prochaska, *Royal Bounty*, pp. 229–47; R. McKibbin, *Classes and Cultures. England 1918–1951* (Oxford, 1998), p. 6.

Why was this so? The bodies which approved of the monarchy were not, or not wholly, passive recipients of its messages and symbolism. As Prochaska has argued for voluntary service societies seeking royal patronage, it is misleading to regard such bodies as simply deferential or dazzled. They identified with royalty because they expected benefits for themselves. Most directly, these could be status, publicity, increased donations, or honours for their leaders; but more generally, the benefits were assistance in preserving or promoting conditions and attitudes which upheld or advanced their own purposes. These organizations contributed to the monarchy's public character by projecting on to it what they themselves admired; and the Palace was usually responsive, indeed it commonly arranged for royal individuals to say what particular organizations wanted, provided it was expressed as uncontroversially as possible. Besides hospitals and welfare charities, these bodies included numerous religious, educational, youth and sporting associations, and the patriotic and ex-servicemen's organizations that emerged from the Great War, notably the British Legion. Commercial groups used royal patronage or images to help sell their products, and the Prince of Wales became the first member of the royal family to promote British goods in overseas markets, visiting and speaking at South American trade fairs in 1925 and 1931. The various media gave huge coverage to royalty not just in order to boost their circulations or audiences, but also to underpin their own political and social stances or, for the BBC, public service aims – concerns which, as the newspapers' self-censorship over Edward VIII's affair demonstrated, induced a sense of public responsibility which overrode their journalistic instincts and commercial interests. Most important, to the traditional support from the armed forces, civil and diplomatic services, political government, and Conservative and Liberal parties was now added, contrary to royal suspicions, that of the Labour movement.

Plainly these different organizations did not always approve of the monarchy for the same reasons, but the cumulative effect was to create considerable public expectations about the reputation and behaviour of the royal family. Most of its members understood that royalty had become much less about power and privilege, and much more about public example and service. It was now a vocation, or more prosaically a job in what George VI privately called 'the family firm'.[25] The strength of these expectations was shown in November and December 1936.

The public language of monarchy had some notable characteristics. Ceremonial addresses and official documents retained their studied archaisms but after 1918, in accordance with the new demotic conditions,

[25] Bradford, *GVI*, p. 5.

most royal speeches and organizational addresses became rather less elevated.[26] Even so, royal language remained inflated and generalized, and
might be considered so artificial, stylized and obsequious as to be vacu-
ous. Certainly its literal accuracy was slight: it had only loose and selective
connections with political and social realities and with the private characters of royal persons. George V, George VI, and even Edward VIII
were hardly impressive or accomplished in their own right, yet like their
predecessors they were publicly invested with exceptional qualities of
knowledge, insight, sympathy, piety and power. Incongruously, again in
response to the new democracy, there was also renewed emphasis on the
Victorian trope of members of the royal family as also being 'ordinary'
people. Yet even in their ordinariness they were, it seemed, extraordinary:
the perfect family with blissful home lives, outstanding in their hobbies
of shooting, stamp-collecting, yachting, riding or gardening.

However, to expect literal meaning from royal language is to misunder-
stand its purpose, which was not descriptive but exemplary – to express
and endorse public values. The more the monarchy had become elevated
above sectional controversies, the more convincing and useful it became
in symbolizing and universalizing values which most public and voluntary bodies considered essential for the general interest. Consequently,
preserving respect or reverence for the monarchy and maintaining idealized images of members of the royal family seemed matters of great
public importance, an attitude shared by very nearly all the media: in this
period, public criticism of royalty became something close to taboo.[27]
In commissioning George V's official biography, Lascelles told Harold
Nicolson that the King had been 'the subject of a myth' and that his book
would 'have to be mythological'.[28] But such attitudes were not, could not
be, just manufactured by the Palace or sustained by the government; their
sources were wider and more spontaneous. As Tom Jones, the adviser of
many public figures, observed just before Edward VIII's abdication, 'we
invest our rulers with qualities which they do not possess and we connive
at the illusion – those of us who know better – because monarchy is an
illusion that works'.[29]

---

[26] As is evident from comparison of the pre-1914 and post-1918 speeches in *The King to His People 1911–35* (London, 1935).

[27] See Martin, *Magic of Monarchy*, pp. 9–10. Altrincham's mild comments in 1957 (like those of Muggeridge in the *New Statesman* a little earlier) attracted remarkable degrees of outrage: P. Brendon and P. Whitehead, *The Windsors* (1994; 2000), pp. 152–4.

[28] *Harold Nicolson. Diaries and Letters 1930–1964*, ed. S. Olsen (London, 1980), p. 334. Lascelles added, however, that this meant omission of any discreditable matters, not writing untruths or exaggerations; and despite occasional hyperbole, Nicolson's biogra-phy remains one of the most intelligent books about the modern monarchy.

[29] Jones, *Diary with Letters*, p. 291 (8 Dec. 1936).

This is not to argue that the monarchy reflected some 'natural' moral consensus in British society, nor that it could genuinely symbolize the whole nation or empire. The values projected upon and expressed by the monarchy were 'ideological' responses by various groups to particular early twentieth-century conditions.[30] Economic and social strains, war mobilization, civilian exposure to bombing, and totalitarian and atheistic threats meant that despite many continuing and new internal disagreements, there was a shared and pressing concern for basic political, social and moral stabilization – obviously so from conservative perspectives, but also within the Labour and other progressive movements which dreaded communism nearly as much as fascism, and which wanted to preserve arrangements and attitudes conducive to reform. Consequently a long-established and conventional monarchical language and symbolism were now renewed or acquired new references. A private comment in 1935 by Beatrice Webb gives one view of the outcome:

The universal popularity of the royal family is the biggest asset of the *status quo* within Great Britain and its Empire. What a political paradox! Powerless puppets saving the face of the British constitution. The King and Queen, the royal dukes and their Duchesses, above all the Prince of Wales, are good souls and do their duty with exemplary piety. How long will they save the situation for western civilization – i.e. capitalist dictatorship plus political democracy, plus a veneer of the Christian faith?[31]

Webb was an admirer of Soviet Russia, but if her more pejorative terms had been toned down only a little and if the *status quo* were taken to mean the institutional and moral framework rather than the distribution of wealth, most public figures of all political persuasions would have accepted the truth of her statement, including the verdict that civilization was at stake. The paradox of a powerless monarchy having great public importance is resolved by understanding its function in expressing and symbolizing public values. Five aspects had particular significance: constitutionalism, social cohesion, the empire, Christian witness, and public morality.

II

Royal and constitutional historians commonly claim that early twentieth-century monarchs retained significant *direct* political influence,

---

[30] So in terms of a celebrated debate, the following argument is closer to N. Birnbaum, 'Monarchs and sociologists', *Sociological Review* 3 (1955), 5–23, than to Shils and Young, 'The meaning of the coronation'.
[31] Beatrice Webb diary, 9 Feb. 1935 (microfiche edn.).

underpinned by the continued importance of their residual constitutional prerogatives. Yet for contemporaries the key feature of their public position was, as Webb wrote, their lack of power. Historians of government and political leadership, who rarely find it necessary to bring the sovereigns into their explanations, have agreed, with much more justification than commentators on the Victorian period.[32] George V and George VI were certainly active, because for them and their secretaries what Bagehot had described as the monarch's rights – consultation, encouragement and warning – were positive duties. They and their secretaries diligently read government papers and collected further advice and information, and sent a stream of enquiry, exhortation, suggestion and sometimes protest to ministers and officials on innumerable large and small subjects. Constitutional niceties and civil service procedures ensured that they were normally kept informed, and that their comments and questions received respectful and considered responses. Nevertheless the quantity of this activity far exceeded its importance and effect. For ministers, parliamentary, party and electoral considerations and their own assessments had long been decisive, and Palace views had influence only where these coincided with these pressures or calculations. Even prime ministerial attentiveness towards the monarch had ceased to be an official or political necessity, and become a matter of personal inclination. Exchanges with the Palace were now routinely handled by private secretaries rather than by ministers themselves.[33] Lloyd George hardly bothered communicating with the Palace at all, and Baldwin never corresponded with the King on business and spoke with him only about every six weeks. Only during the Second World War did Chamberlain and Churchill establish what came to be regarded as a 'tradition' of weekly meetings with the monarch during parliamentary sessions, and then only as a pleasant courtesy and to help keep him informed.[34] George V could be awkward and persistent,

---

[32] See Michael Bentley's chapter in the current volume. From publication between 1907 and 1932 of selections from the Queen's correspondence, contemporaries knew that political practice had only recently caught up with constitutional theory (and with Bagehot): see F. Hardie, *The Political Influence of Queen Victoria* (Oxford, 1935); Martin, *Magic of Monarchy*, pp. 46–53; Laski, *Parliamentary Government*, pp. 397–401.

[33] As is evident from prime ministerial files; and for the particular case of the 'King's letters', the traditional daily report from the Commons leader or home secretary on House of Commons proceedings, see *Baldwin Papers. A Conservative Statesman 1908–47*, ed. P. Williamson and E. Baldwin (Cambridge, 2004), pp. 3, 503.

[34] Brendon and Whitehead, *The Windsors*, pp. 44–5; Baldwin in Mackenzie King diary, 7 Oct. 1928, online at http://king.collectionscanada.ca; James, *Spirit Undaunted*, p. 206. More frequent meetings (usually luncheons) are not in themselves evidence of political significance; and the claims that George VI had 'considerable' influence with Churchill and became 'a major element in government' (ibid., pp. 207–8, 221, 230, 284) are simply incredible: cf. the verdicts in D. Cannadine, 'Churchill and the British monarchy', *Transactions of the Royal Historical Society* 6s. 11 (2001), 264, 271.

but he well knew that he had to act according to ministerial advice, and he did not obstruct and wear down ministers as Queen Victoria had done. By 1918 the dangers of public criticism for the monarchy's reputation, privileges and even – as he would have thought – survival seemed all too great; fear of socialism was a powerful constitutional check. The instinct for safety also emasculated the prerogative powers. When during the 1910–14 constitutional deadlocks Liberal and Unionist leaders each pressed him to exercise these powers in their own interest, the King was haunted by the fear that if he took the advice of either he would embitter half the nation; and it was only in the desperate hope of escaping this choice and forcing the politicians to compromise that, paradoxically, he resorted to (empty) threats of ignoring ministerial advice and exercising his ostensible powers. Thereafter, while the Palace guarded the principle and spirit of the prerogative as a guarantee for the monarchy's status, in practice its aim was to avoid the exercise of its powers, or failing that, to minimize the effect. When a possible decision loomed, advice on constitutional principle was sought; but the real purpose of this consultation was political calculation – to ascertain what would cause least controversy and the least harm to the monarchy, and what the leading politicians themselves wanted or would accept responsibility for.[35] This is evident in the monarchy's major political acts during this period. In 1923 Baldwin as a member of the House of Commons was manifestly the safer choice as prime minister than Lord Curzon, given that the Labour opposition then lacked any representative in, and was still committed to abolishing, the House of Lords. In August–October 1931, the King certainly helped to establish and perpetuate a 'National' coalition government, but he did so on the well informed and accurate understanding that, given the unusually awkward political circumstances, this was already being considered by the Labour prime minister and leaders of the other parties.[36] By the 1940s, George VI and his secretaries welcomed party arrangements and civil service procedures which relieved them of the embarrassment of political choices.[37]

As was routinely observed at the time, the end of the monarchy's direct political power had been vital for the elevation of its *indirect* political significance: it became a purer symbol of constitutional government.

[35] Nicolson, *KGV*, p. 115, sensibly emphasizes the distinction between the historical survival of powers and the political expediency of their exercise.
[36] P. Williamson, *National Crisis and National Government 1926–1932* (Cambridge, 1992), pp. 152–3, 232, 274, chs. 9, 12, and see the Bogdanor-Williamson exchange in *Twentieth Century British History* 2 (1991), 1–25, 328–43, ignored in V. Bogdanor, *The Monarchy and the Constitution* (Oxford, 1995), pp. 104–12.
[37] E.g. James, *Spirit Undaunted*, pp. 305–6, 319–22.

For two centuries the essence of the monarchy's strength had been its personification of a parliamentary constitution in which the 'Crown-in-Parliament' was the sovereign body. This constitution and its associated 'Whig' history of unfolding freedoms had long been at the core of British national identity, and this gave the monarchy broad and deep ideological foundations.[38] But two new elements preserved its prestige: its publicly smooth transition into a symbol of parliamentary *democracy*, and a succession of pressures which made constitutional government seem still more precious. During the First World War the King's speeches identified him with the 'cause of freedom, liberty and justice' against tyranny and militarism.[39] After 1918 the monarchy symbolized a constitutional system of government which had not only secured military victory, but which in comparison with other European regimes seemed to guarantee stability and liberalism against the threats of both revolution and reaction. During the Labour party advances of the 1920s and 1940s a public absence of royal opposition seemed to confirm that this system was impartial not just between parties, but also between classes and socio-economic doctrines. More fundamentally still, just as in earlier centuries the British constitutional monarchy had represented resistance to foreign despotisms, so during the 1930s and 1940s it became a leading symbol in the defence of democracy against the continental dictatorships.

In these senses, the monarchy remained or became valuable for each of the main political parties. Reduced public discussion about its political role and about the monarch's opinions is indicative. This was due as much to the restraint of the politicians as to that of the monarchs: in contrast to 1910–14, after 1918 the monarchy was too important to be dragged into party politics.[40] For Conservatives, calls for royal obstruction to a Labour government were not worth the risks of provoking a Labour backlash which might weaken the monarchy's place in the implicit ideological and institutional checks against socialism. Conversely, Labour leaders feared that criticism of the monarchy might stiffen conservative resistance and reduce the opportunities for advancing socialism. Labour attitudes were obviously crucial. The party had never been republican, but before 1914 it contained some outspoken republicans and a larger number of other socialists who disliked the monarchy as the apex of the system of inherited

---

[38] See J. Parry, chapter 2 above; also, from a quite different perspective, T. Nairn, *The Enchanted Glass. Britain and its Monarchy* (London, 1988).

[39] *The King to His People*, pp. 66–7, 71–2, 75, 88, 94–6, 110, 117–8.

[40] The main, but only momentary, exceptions were Asquith in late 1923 and Lloyd George in early 1929, because royal intervention after indecisive general elections had become one of the last hopes for the Liberal party's return to government: M. Cowling, *The Impact of Labour 1920–1924* (Cambridge, 1971), p. 351; Lloyd George speech discussed in Stamfordham to Vansittart, 29 April 1929, Royal Archives PS/GV/K.2223/11.

privilege. In 1910 its parliamentary leaders pointedly treated the King's civil list as if it represented the income of 'a President of a Republic'. In 1936 and 1937 their successors again wanted reduction of the monarchy's costs.[41] But only a handful of (mainly Scottish) left-wing MPs called for its abolition, and the reallocation of its palaces, wealth and income to the poor.[42] Most Labour politicians took it for granted that the monarchy was popular among the working population, and regarded changes to its status as a lower priority than economic and social reform. The more republican members assumed that it would wither away as socialism advanced, and for the meantime considered a hereditary non-partisan monarch less inconvenient than an elected, politicized, president.[43] But the chief reason for the Labour party's acceptance of the monarchy, and for some of its members being monarchists, was its absorption of a long tradition of popular constitutionalism and its understanding that monarchs no longer governed and were not an obstacle to further political and social progress. Faith in and commitment to established political procedures outweighed objections to the monarchy as the embodiment of social inequalities.[44] It was assumed that just as monarchs in the past had acted on Liberal and Conservative ministerial advice, so they would accept the advice of Labour ministers; only if any obstruction were attempted might the monarchy's position be reassessed.[45] As is well-attested, the Palace's attitude towards the first Labour government was vital. In 1923–4, George V and Stamfordham did not want socialists as the King's ministers, and only after unco-operative Conservative and Liberal decisions made this inescapable did they decide that it would be wise to treat Labour leaders with an elaborate display of accommodation, trust and friendliness. The tactic was highly successful. For working-class ministers and their families it sealed their sense of arrival and achievement, and for the Labour

---

[41] *House of Commons Debates, 5th. series* [HCDeb] 19, c. 1627–40 (Barnes, 22 July 1910); 311, cc. 1590–5, 1615–21, 1634 (Pethick-Lawrence and Cripps, 5 May 1936); 324, cc. 40–5, 72–7, 455–60 (Attlee and Pethick-Lawrence, 24 May, and Greenwood, 27 May 1937).

[42] E.g. *HCDeb*, 311, cc. 1603–15, 1637–52 (5 May 1936); 318, cc. 2191–6, 2206–12, 2218–9 (10–11 Dec. 1936); 324, cc. 49–56 (24 May 1937).

[43] E.g. S. and B. Webb, *A Constitution for the Socialist Commonwealth of Great Britain* (London, 1920), pp. 108–10; Lansbury in *Labour Party Annual Conference Report 1923*, p. 251, and see Prochaska, *Republic of Britain*, pp. 188–9.

[44] R. McKibbin, *The Ideologies of Class. Social Relations in Britain 1880–1950* (Oxford, 1990), pp. 17–27; N. Kirk, 'The conditions of royal rule: Australian and British socialist and labour attitudes to the monarchy 1901–11', *Social History* 30 (2005), 64–88; and see N. Owen, 'MacDonald's parties: the Labour party and the "aristocratic embrace" 1922–31', *Twentieth Century British History* 18 (2007), 1–53, at 9–16.

[45] This was the purport of the only significant interwar public admonitions to monarchs from leading Labour politicians, in 1924 and 1934: R. Postgate, *George Lansbury* (London, 1951), pp. 224–5, and C. Cook, *Stafford Cripps* (London, 1957), pp. 159–60.

party it seemed the ultimate endorsement of its own legitimacy, fitness to govern and right to seek reform.[46] It now seemed fully in the party's interest to subscribe to the principle – more accurately, a convenient fiction – that monarchs were entirely neutral in their personal political opinions, and to observe the convention that ministers should not divulge their sometimes strongly expressed views. Labour leaders made little of some socialist intellectuals' charges that the 1931 National government was 'born of a Palace Revolution'. Nor did they (any more than did the Liberal and Conservative anti-appeasers) criticize George VI's very public support for Chamberlain after the Munich agreement.[47]

The apotheosis of the monarchy as the symbol of democratic constitutionalism came in the mid 1930s. An official theme for George V's Jubilee in May 1935 was celebration of the 'constitutional progress' during his reign,[48] but implicitly and often explicitly a further message was comparison with the regimes of Hitler, Mussolini and Stalin. The King's address to Parliament declared that 'the perfect harmony of our Parliamentary system with our Constitutional Monarchy' had been found to be the 'best way to secure government by the people, freedom for the individual, the ordered strength of the state and the rule of law over governors and governed alike'.[49] Ministers and opposition leaders presented constitutional monarchy as a barrier to dictatorship,[50] and the remarkable popular enthusiasm for Jubilee events was attributed partly to 'the people realizing the contrast between the homely ways of the King and the bullying of the continental despots'.[51] On George V's death it was not

---

[46] It should, however, be recorded that while the often-quoted account of the King's reception of his new Cabinet in J. R. Clynes, *Memoirs* (London, 1937), i. 343–4, no doubt accurately reflected Clynes's sentiments, these 'memoirs' were actually written by Frank Stuart, a professional ghost-writer: Stuart to Gilmour, 26 Aug. 1937, Gilmour papers GD383/69/16, National Archives of Scotland.

[47] The King was plainly imprudent in early October 1938, and was nearly even more so: James, *Spirit Undaunted*, p. 144. But the claim that his actions were 'unconstitutional' originated much later, with John Grigg in 1989: A. Roberts, *Eminent Churchillians* (London, 1994), p. 21.

[48] MacDonald to Wigram, 21 Feb. 1935, PREM 1/173. There is no evidence for a common assumption that the National government planned the jubilee specifically in order to boost its re-election prospects (e.g. Rose, *KGV*, p. 394). Ministerial files show that care was taken to avoid party-political implications and to involve all major parties in jubilee events. Moreover, at the time of the jubilee a general election was not due for another seventeen months; only in October did Baldwin decide on an earlier election, in the unexpected conditions created by the Abyssinian war. But as Jonathan Parry suggests (above p. 70), the decision was probably connected more generally with the government's claim to be a 'National', non-party, arrangement.

[49] *His Majesty's Speeches. The Record of the Silver Jubilee* (London, 1935), pp. 50–1, and see the Lords and Commons addresses, pp. 42, 43.

[50] Baldwin in *Times*, 4 May 1935; other party leaders in *HCDeb* 301, cc. 977–87 (8 May 1935), 308, c. 17 (23 Jan. 1936); and Martin, *Magic of Monarchy*, p. 15.

[51] Jones, *Diary with Letters*, p. 148 (20 May 1935).

Conservative or Liberal politicians but the Labour leader, Attlee, who praised him as a 'democrat'.[52] At the 1937 coronation, which received the same blanket coverage in the Labour movement's newspaper, the *Daily Herald*, as in the conservative popular press, Labour spokesmen described the institution itself as democratic: 'the monarchy exists by the will of the British people'.[53] During the Second World War the anti-fascist crusade, an all-party coalition government, and Churchill's constitutionalist rhetoric cemented this identification of monarchy with democracy and freedom. Major Crown honours, first accepted by trade-union leaders in 1935, now began to cascade through the party.[54] There was simply no reason to withhold support from an institution that proclaimed many political values admired by the Labour party, and which represented a parliamentary system which from 1945 ensured consent to socialist legislation. As the *Daily Herald* had declared in 1937, the monarchy symbolized the 'underlying unity of a community in agreement, not about everything, but about the political method by which everything will be decided'.[55]

It was in these terms that the 'abdication crisis' seemed alarming, yet passed so easily. The issue was not any attempt by Edward VIII to revive royal power, nor political differences with his ministers. His views on peace, Anglo-German friendship and social issues were virtually identical with those of his father, and indeed his successor – and, more to the point, with those of most Cabinet members. He was less discreet than his father, but his notorious phrases that 'something should [must, will] be done' about South Wales unemployment were uncalculated and became significant only when they were exploited by anti-government newspapers, for which he expressed regret.[56] If ministers heard of his occasional

---

[52] *HCDeb* 308, c. 16 (23 Jan. 1936).   [53] Ibid., 324, c. 457 (27 May 1937).

[54] Some trade union leaders had accepted the lesser OBE awards instituted in 1917, but Citrine's and Pugh's 1935 knighthoods had been controversial. The 1924 and 1929–31 Labour governments had recommended the creation of several peers, but for the practical purpose of conducting House of Lords business; only after 1940 were peerages accepted as 'honours': see P. Williamson, 'The Labour party and the House of Lords 1918–31', *Parliamentary History* 10 (1991), 317–41.

[55] *Daily Herald*, 13 May 1937. It is commonly stated that during the debate on the Abdication Bill in December 1936, some 100 MPs would have voted for a republic if the Labour party had allowed a free Commons vote; but this is one of those persistent misunderstandings which beset accounts of the modern monarchy. The story can be traced back through Wheeler-Bennett, *KGVI*, p. 299, to C. Petrie, *Monarchy in the Twentieth Century* (1952), p. 111. But Petrie had misread his source, which not only has the lower figure of 40 to 50 MPs but offered these numbers as a 'fancy', a speculation – and this from a hostile, right-wing, Conservative MP: see C. Petrie, *The Modern British Monarchy* (1961), pp. 24, 177, this time correctly citing A. Wilson, *Thoughts and Talks* (1938), p. 246. No other source indicates division among or pressure on Labour MPs over the relevant vote, on an ILP republican amendment supported by just seven MPs.

[56] Cabinet minutes, 27 Nov. 1936, in *Baldwin Papers*, p. 396. The King used different versions of the phrase (should, must, will) in statements at different stopping places

offhand boasts about imposing his will in government, they knew from his lack of application to state business how empty such statements were: compared to George V, he was in these terms very much a lightweight. Pressed by Mrs Simpson, he did make suggestions for keeping himself on the throne, but he himself never seriously resisted Baldwin's opinion that marriage required his abdication. Nor did he countenance a political campaign on his own behalf. Rather, the real danger lay elsewhere: that anti-government mavericks like Churchill and the Beaverbrook and Rothermere newspapers, or the anti-parliamentary fascists and communists, might make the King's wishes an issue for political division, in effect if not intention reviving royal independence in public affairs and, at a time of international difficulties, distracting government and the nation with constitutional disputes. It was towards forestalling this type of political division that Baldwin directed his efforts, particularly by ensuring it was made plain that the King himself chose abdication rather than renunciation of Mrs Simpson. Like almost every other public body, the Labour party took the strictest constitutional view: that irrespective of opinions about the King's proposed marriage and despite its own hostility towards the National government, it was vital to uphold the principles of ministerial authority and parliamentary supremacy. The *Daily Herald* even argued that any other course 'might easily lead to fascism', and stigmatized public demonstrations in the King's favour as 'anti-democratic'.[57] The most significant political feature of the episode is that there was, after all, no real crisis; the speed and completeness of Baldwin's success testifies to the enormous importance attached to constitutionalism, the more so in an ideologically tense period.

III

Total war and chronic economic difficulties gave renewed momentum to the traditional conception of the monarchy as a focus and force for social cohesion. With the mass mobilization of the First World War, through appeals for volunteers, exhortations to conscripts and civilian workers,

during his tour (*Daily Herald* and *Daily Mail*, 19, 20 Nov. 1936), but except for a critical comment in MacDonald diary, 21 Nov. 1936, these passed unremarked by ministers until the *Daily Mail* used them several days later for its own purposes: Baldwin in Jones, *Diary with Letters*, p. 288 (25 Nov. 1936). The King had already said he would abdicate, and privately he blamed the Welsh unemployment problems not on the government but on local 'socialists' and 'bolshevism': R. Rhodes James, *Victor Cazalet* (London, 1976), p. 186 (diary, 19 Nov. 1936). For the King's distinctly callow political views, see Donaldson, *EVIII*, pp. 191–206, 253–6, and Ziegler, *KEVIII*, pp. 182–6, 204–11, 266–75.

[57] *Daily Herald*, 5, 7, 10 Dec. 1936: it attributed the demonstrations to incitement by the British Union of Fascists and the Communist party.

investitures, hospital and factory visits, and messages to bereaved families, the royal family touched the lives of more people than ever before. From evoking patriotism and endurance for a united war effort and then leading national acts of remembrance for the war dead, there were easy transitions to appealing for united efforts in post-war reconstruction and later in mitigating the effects of unemployment. In the face of industrial unrest and social distress, governments and voluntary organizations were as eager to exploit the monarchy's ability to inspire loyalty and co-operation as the Palace was to demonstrate its social relevance. Precisely because class conflict and social alienation were feared, royal rhetoric presented 'the people' as united and wanting still closer 'brotherhood' or 'fellowship'.[58] Speeches and commentaries, as well as royal visits and patronage, systematically created an impression of closeness between the monarchy and the working population. Royal persons were said to share the 'hopes and joys, and fears and sorrows' of all classes of 'the people',[59] and were, it seemed, prodigious in their 'deep' or 'constant' interest in medical, child-care, educational, housing, sanitation, industrial, scientific and artistic schemes. For the royal family it was important that their eldest son, like the sons of other families, could be said to have 'shared with My Armies the dangers and hardships of the campaign'.[60] Famously, the Prince of Wales was later projected as a champion of ex-servicemen and the unemployed, particularly as patron of the British Legion and the National Council of Social Service.[61] But by the 1930s, building upon a long tradition, encouragement and appeals for those in distress – the sentiments that 'something must be done' – were expected not just from any one royal individual but from the whole royal family, supporting both voluntary organizations and the National government's private-public partnership schemes. George V's Jubilee broadcast declared that 'I grieve to think of the numbers of my people who are still without work. We owe to them . . . all the sympathy and help that we can give. I hope that . . . all who can will do their utmost to find them work and bring them hope'. The purpose of his son's Jubilee Trust, to assist youth welfare organizations, was chosen to commemorate the 'devotion to the welfare of the people which His Majesty has personified supremely throughout

---

[58] E.g. *The King to His People*, pp. 95, 156–8, 280–3, 308–9.

[59] E.g. Lord Halifax in *Times*, 4 May 1935; MacDonald in *HCDeb*, 301, cc. 979–80 (8 May 1935).

[60] *The King to His People*, p. 53. There was no indication that, to Prince Edward's own dismay, he was kept away from military action. Curiously, Prince Albert's service in the navy (which included battle experience) and later in the air force went unmentioned in the King's collected public statements, presumably to preserve the focus on his heir.

[61] Though see Prochaska, *Royal Bounty*, pp. 190, 196, 201–4, 210, for a gap between public image and personal commitment.

his reign'.[62] Edward VIII's replacement by George VI did not change this style of presentation, because the former Duke of York had as considerable a record as his brother of 'keen interest in social questions'.[63] And the new King and his Queen soon acquired a public cult of their own. The Second World War had an even greater effect than the first in identifying the monarchy with a genuinely national purpose, and the Queen proved at least Edward's equal in conveying spontaneous human interest. The story that after the bombing of Buckingham Palace in September 1940, she said that she now felt she could 'look the East End in the face' is apocryphal;[64] nevertheless this does capture the royal family's determination, amplified by official propaganda, to be seen to share the dangers and privations of the 'people's war', and to set an example of fortitude and defiance.

For a leading Conservative in 1935, the Crown was 'symbolic of all the persons and things that together compose the life of our nation . . . and speaks of the essential unity that is greater than all the accidental differences that may exist between us'.[65] Again, statements by Labour politicians reveal the widespread absorption of such attitudes. Lansbury spoke of how the royal family's social sympathies had helped break down Labour suspicions that 'the Monarchy would preserve for ever the domination of class'. After George V's death, Attlee described him not just as a 'democrat' but still more surprisingly as a 'real social reformer', who had 'recognized the claims of social justice'.[66] For the Labour leaders monarchy had, it seems, become compatible with their party's commitment to social equality. They did treat the abdication as an opportunity for a 'new start', but they meant only that the monarchy should be made more accessible and still more popular. Occasional and 'reasonable' pageantry was desirable, but continual ritual and the 'narrow and privileged' courtier class hampered the monarch's true work. In 1937 they proposed an enquiry into the royal family's 'mode of life', on the principle that 'utmost simplicity in the monarchy, . . . will . . . bind together the people and the Monarch

---

[62] *The King to his People*, p. 299; National Council of Social Services memo., Jan. 1935, PREM 1/173, and more generally Prochaska, *Royal Bounty*, chs. 6–7.

[63] *Crown and Empire. The Coronation of King George VI* (*Times*, 1937), pp. 8–9.

[64] The source is not contemporary, but a sentimental biography by an author who became a court correspondent only after the war had ended: B. S. Shew, *Queen Elizabeth, the Queen Mother* (London, 1955), p. 76. The phrase was lent authority by Wheeler-Bennett, *KGVI*, p. 470.

[65] Halifax, *Times*, 4 May 1935.

[66] *HCDeb* 301, c. 981 (8 May 1935); 308, c. 17 (23 Jan. 1936), and see Laski, *Parliamentary Government*, p. 392, for the cynical observation that 'the Monarchy . . . has been sold to the democracy as a symbol of itself'.

Figure 8.2. The royal family as 'ordinary' and domestic: 'Conversation piece at the Royal Lodge', 1950, by Sir James Gunn (National Portrait Gallery).

more closely than before'.[67] Ten years later, they presumably thought that war and austerity had effected these changes. In the depths of post-war economic crisis, Labour ministers agreed that Princess Elizabeth and the Duke of Edinburgh should have a full ceremonial wedding and, against opposition from their own backbench MPs, a generous civil list. According to Attlee, 'our British monarchy today . . . is in essence simple . . . and

[67] Attlee, Pethick-Lawrence and Greenwood in *HCDeb* 318, cc. 2204–5 (11 Dec. 1936), and 324, cc. 40–5, 72–7, 455–60 (24, 27 May 1937).

approachable', and the couple needed the money to do what the general public wanted them to do, 'visiting round the country . . . [and] coming into contact with the people'.[68]

Symbolizing and cementing unity was a still more insistent theme in relation to the Empire and Commonwealth. The zenith of the imperial monarchy is usually placed in the late Victorian and Edwardian periods, but the association of monarchy and Empire actually increased after 1914. On the one hand, the two world wars showed the extent to which British international power and even national defence now depended on imperial resources, and during the interwar years and again after 1945 both British and Dominion governments regarded an imperial trade and sterling bloc as the chief means of escape from economic depression. Yet on the other hand, the Dominions and India were obtaining greater self-government and had stronger nationalist movements. As a more challenging world made the overseas empire more valuable, so a 'non-political', supra-national and liberal monarchy was considered vital for preserving the sense of imperial unity. Within Britain itself, organizations, events and media aiming to stimulate popular imperial sentiment continued to proliferate, and to be leading vehicles for publicizing the monarchy's importance.[69]

The belief that the Empire depended on the monarchy was as central for George V's and his advisers' strategy of royal survival as the display of social benevolence.[70] At the Unionist government's urging, he himself had as Prince of Wales been sent around the Dominions in 1901 and to India in 1905–6 in order to make the Crown and empire visible to their populations, and in 1911 he insisted on attending the Indian Durbar. From 1919 to 1925 he sent his eldest son on even longer Dominion and Indian tours to capitalize on and consolidate wartime imperial patriotism. The King privately disliked the increasing concessions made towards self-government, yet because his various governments used the monarchy to endorse the Empire's re-constitution and publicize its revised ideology, the effect of these concessions was to enhance his own status. The 1926 Balfour formula and 1931 Statute of Westminster 'exalted' the monarch by making him king of each Dominion, leaving the sovereign as the sole constitutional link between Britain and the Dominions, and declared

---

[68] Ibid. 445, cc. 1745–7 (17 Dec. 1947); B. Pimlott, *The Queen. A Biography of Elizabeth II* (London, 1996), pp. 125–32, 146–8. The 160 dissident Labour MPs were hardly radical: they wanted only a lower grant, not complete rejection. Nor did the Labour government curb the royal family's tax exemptions: see P. Hall, *Royal Fortune* (London, 1992).

[69] See J. M. MacKenzie, *Propaganda and Empire* (Manchester, 1984).

[70] E.g. 1918 statements in Prochaska, *Republic of Britain*, p. 169, and Wheeler-Bennett, *KGVI*, pp. 159–60.

the new Commonwealth to be united by its 'common allegiance' to the Crown. Against the Congress party's demand for Indian independence, the King-Emperor was similarly elevated as the focus of allegiance for the various princes, provinces, races and religious groups within new all-India political structures.[71] Baldwin expressed the conventional view during Jubilee week:

> If in any cataclysm the Crown vanished, the Empire would vanish with it . . . [No] political party . . . would hold together an Empire scattered throughout the world and that great Indian Empire besides. More and more as the older [Imperial] ties became attenuated, the ties of the Crown become stronger and more personal every year.[72]

Royal speeches welcomed self-government while speaking of indissoluble imperial links, links which would become stronger because now based on co-operation and shared ideals: the Empire-Commonwealth was a 'great instrument for justice, peace and goodwill'.[73] The 1935 Jubilee was staged as much to proclaim Dominion and Indian 'devotion and affection' for the King as to celebrate national cohesion,[74] and when on his deathbed he supposedly asked 'How is the Empire?', this was treated as hugely significant: it was even, unlike most royal stories, 'very nearly true'.[75]

In 1919 Stamfordham had told the Prince of Wales that 'the throne is the pivot upon which the Empire will more than ever hinge. Its strength and stability will depend entirely on its occupant'.[76] When in late 1936 King Edward, supposedly much impressed by his imperial tours, remained unmoved by appeals to the importance of Dominion opinion, this came as a shock. The marriage proposal and then the abdication had potentially harmful consequences for imperial relations, even aside from the Irish government immediately exploiting the episode to reduce its constitutional links with Britain still further. In public, the only possible course was to pretend that nothing had happened. In his coronation broadcast George VI declared that he had 'felt . . . that the whole Empire was in very truth gathered within the walls of the Abbey'. Royal tours of

---

[71] Nicolson, *KGV*, pp. 479–82, 485; N. Mansergh, *Survey of British Commonwealth Affairs. Problems of External Policy 1931–1939* (Oxford, 1952), pp. 31, 35–6, 47; D. Cannadine, *Ornamentalism* (London, 2001), pp. 54–6.

[72] *Times*, 4 May 1935.

[73] *The King to his People*, pp. 67, 207, 248–51, 270, 274, 295.

[74] *Record of the Silver Jubilee*, pp. 14–17, 27–38.

[75] For the stages by which an incoherent word was transformed into an internationally famous phrase, see *In Royal Service*, pp. 197–8; *Reith Diaries*, p. 185, and S. Baldwin, *Service of our Lives* (London, 1937), pp. 17–18.

[76] Ziegler, *KEVIII*, p. 114.

the Dominions resumed, beginning with Canada in 1939 and only postponed by the war; the King became patron of the Empire Day movement, and he spoke of 'a new vision' of an Empire of 'free peoples' opposed to 'the spirit of domination and the lust of conquest'.[77] Even when the Empire began to vanish in the late 1940s, with India becoming a republic and the King-Emperor turned into 'Head of the Commonwealth', to all appearances this was not loss but evolution. In Churchill's broadcast on George VI's death, the crown was 'the magic link . . . which unites our loosely bound but strongly interwoven Commonwealth of nations'; indeed the character of the sovereign was 'vital to the future . . . of world freedom and peace'. In public presentation, at the 1953 coronation the monarchy was no less an expression of British leadership of a 'fellowship' of nations than it had been at the 1935 Jubilee.[78]

The monarchy's function of symbolizing unity was made more effective by two additional elements. The pressures on social cohesion, on the Empire and on the monarchy itself stimulated further development of the traditional metaphors of the king as father, the nation and Empire as families, and the royal family as emblematic of all ordinary families. Even more than during the previous century, royalty's own family occasions – weddings, births, anniversaries, funerals – were presented as public events, encouraging in ways that Bagehot would have recognized 'a curious process of identification of royal family life with the individual life of the subject'.[79] But what especially evoked this sense of closeness was the use of radio. The earliest royal broadcasts were for the imperial service, and the BBC wanted a King's message on the family occasion of Christmas because it would reach exceptionally large and susceptible audiences.[80] With monarchs able to speak to millions of people in their homes, the speech writers saturated the broadcasts with personal pronouns and family references: 'I would like to think that you . . . and all the peoples of this Realm and Empire are bound to me and to one another by the spirit of one great family'.[81] Commenting on George V's last Christmas message in his own imperial broadcast on the King's death, Baldwin made the extraordinary assertions that 'it is as members of a family that we are

---

[77] *King George VI to His Peoples* (London, 1952), pp. 2, 7–9, 22–4; MacKenzie, *Propaganda and Empire*, pp. 234–5.

[78] *The Listener*, 14 Feb. 1952, and see Elizabeth II's first two Christmas broadcasts in *Voices out of the Air*, pp. 70–4.

[79] Martin, *Magic of Monarchy*, p. 15; see W. Bagehot, *The English Constitution*, ed. M. Taylor (Oxford, 2001), p. 41.

[80] MacKenzie, *Propaganda and Empire*, pp. 91–3; P. Scannell and D. Cardiff, *A Social History of British Broadcasting 1922–1939* (Oxford, 1991), pp. 7, 29, 280–6.

[81] 1934, in *Voices out of the Air*, p. 14, but see all his and George VI's Christmas broadcasts, pp. 11–18, 28–60.

mourning him' and that 'there must be millions who feel as I do that a wise and loving friend and counsellor has been taken from us'. More remarkably still, this had some truth: as Labour commentators observed, among the general public large numbers appeared to feel something akin to personal loss.[82]

IV

Secularization has made it difficult to appreciate the continued significance of religion in public life during the early twentieth century. Until the 1960s, Britain remained a Christian nation. Total church membership reached its historic peak in the 1900s and declined only slowly, with recoveries in the late 1920s and the 1950s; and although a large majority of the population were not regular church-goers, most retained Christian beliefs, respected Christian moral rules and observed the churches' rites of passage.[83] The monarchy's Christian witness and identification with the established English and Scottish churches remained important for the nation's explicitly Christian life, and royal rituals were at the core of a more diffuse 'civil religion';[84] while for all the churches, the pressures of growing secularization and challenges from fascist paganism and communist atheism made the monarchy's example seem still more valuable. The royal family was upheld as a model of Christian fidelity, charity, probity, and domestic virtue. Prayers for the sovereign and singing of the national anthem – 'God Save the King' – were still part of common experience. Much royal philanthropic endeavour was emblematic of religious values, and the connection was made still clearer by the revival in 1932, for the first time since 1698, of the sovereign personally distributing alms at the annual Royal Maundy service.[85] Many royal ceremonies were also national religious events, and the coronations, deaths and funerals of

[82] Baldwin, Service, pp. 11–12; Attlee in HCDeb 308, c. 15 (23 Jan. 1936); New Statesman, 25 Jan. 1936.

[83] C. G. Brown, The Death of Christian Britain (London, 2001); R. Currie, A. Gilbert and L. Horsley, Churches and Churchgoers (Oxford, 1977), pp. 28–33; McKibbin, Classes and Cultures, pp. 272–6, 289–92.

[84] See I. Bradley, God Save the Queen. The Spiritual Dimension of Monarchy (London, 2002), esp. pp. x–xiii and ch. 6; R. Bocock, 'Religion in modern Britain', in R. Bocock and K. Thompson (eds.), Religion and Ideology (Manchester, 1985), pp. 210–11, 219, 266, 231; J. Wolffe, 'The religions of the silent majority', in G. Parsons (ed.), The Growth of Religious Diversity, vol. 1 (London, 1993), pp. 309–10, 318–27.

[85] See Times, 22–24, 26 March 1932 and B. Robinson, Silver Pennies and Linen Towels. The Story of the Royal Maundy (London, 1992), pp. 41–50. The ceremony had long been left to the sovereign's clerical representative, the Lord High Almoner, but the King's mother and sister attended during the Great War and after 1932 members of the royal family were normally present. Edward performed the distribution in 1936 and George VI in 1940, and since 1944 it has been an almost annual sovereign's occasion.

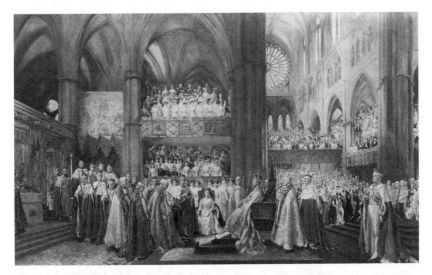

Figure 8.3. The Christian monarchy: 'The Coronation ceremony of His Most Gracious Majesty King George V in Westminster Abbey, 22 June 1911', by J.H.F. Bacon (National Portrait Gallery).

sovereigns evoked both church appeals for reaffirmed Christian commitment and, it seemed, considerable evidence of continuing popular Christian belief.[86] During the First World War there was a revival of national days of prayer – united appeals for divine intercession during extraordinary national anxieties, or thanksgiving for divine assistance after reliefs or victories – which had fallen into abeyance since the 1850s. The King 'called his people to prayer'; the royal family usually attended a state service at St Paul's Cathedral or Westminster Abbey, accompanied by the nation's other leaders; and churches throughout the nation and empire were crowded for special acts of worship. During the Second World War, national days of prayer became frequent – usually twice a year – and the last one, a call for national re-dedication in the face of economic difficulties, was approved by the Labour government in 1947.[87] All this carried greater force from the traditional British Protestant doctrine that the nation and its monarchy enjoyed exceptional divine favour. Coronations were presented as national re-consecrations, renewing the sacred

---

[86] M. Grimley, *Citizenship, Community and the Church of England* (Oxford, 2004), pp. 184–93, and see J. Wolffe, *Great Deaths* (Oxford, 2000), chs. 8–9, for these effects associated with sovereigns' funerals from Victoria to George VI.

[87] Aside from those during the wars and in 1947, a day of prayer was called during the 1931–2 economic slump and two more during and after the 1938 Czechoslovakian crisis. For 1947 see P. Howarth, *George VI* (London, 1987), p. 204.

qualities of the nation's institutions and 'the organic union of the people and their sovereign under divine providence'.[88] As the Dean of Durham wrote in 1937, it was 'no mere accident that the one royal house which has been for a century consistently true to its Master's teaching is the one which has survived a century of unrest with ever growing honour'.[89] The kings themselves customarily spoke in quasi-priestly terms, bestowing God's blessings, invoking God's help, offering thanks to God.[90] George VI was especially fervent, overcoming his hatred of broadcasting twice for national days of prayer, and again to call for special prayers on D-Day: 'we dare to believe that God has used our Nation and Empire as an instrument for fulfilling His high purpose'.[91]

Notwithstanding the sovereign being supreme governor of the Church of England, the other religious denominations had long shared the admiration for the monarchy, and successive modern sovereigns, notably Queen Victoria, had given indications of reciprocating this regard.[92] This convergence continued, reinforcing the monarchy's representative character and making it more ecumenical. George V and George VI were devout yet undoctrinaire in their faith, ready to encourage closer relations between the various churches and, as they saw it, to solidify their allegiance; and in a spiritually more threatening world, the denominations themselves sought closer association with a Christian king as reinforcement for their own efforts and as confirmation of their integration into national life. In 1910 George V successfully backed a movement to modify the statutory 'Protestant declaration' in his parliamentary accession oath, removing the imprecations against Catholic doctrines likely to offend the Roman Catholic populations of the Empire.[93] Although originally national days of prayer had strictly concerned only the established

---

[88] G. Martin, *Past Futures* (Toronto, 2004), pp. 28, 170; C. Longley, *Chosen People* (London, 2002), ch. 2; Bradley, *God Save the Queen*, ch. 2; and for evidence of substantial popular belief that God and sovereign were linked, see Ziegler, *Crown and People*, p. 36.

[89] C. A. Alington et. al., *Sermons for the Coronation of . . . King Edward VIII* (London, 1936), pp. 16–17. A Church of England collection of model sermons was published as part of the preparations for each (planned) coronation from 1902 to 1953.

[90] See most pages of *The King to His People* and *George VI to His Peoples*.

[91] *George VI to His Peoples*, pp. 24, 38–9; *Times*, 30 March 1942; Wheeler-Bennett, *KGVI*, pp. 449–50, 597–8, 607–8. Similarly, in an acclaimed broadcast (drafted by Bishop Woods of Lichfield, Lascelles, and Churchill) his Queen spoke of 'the creative and dynamic force of Christianity' as the vital basis for post-war reconstruction: *Times*, 12 April 1943; *King's Counsellor. Abdication and War. The Diaries of Sir Alan Lascelles*, ed. D. Hart-Davis (London, 2006), pp. 121–3.

[92] Her partiality for the presbyterian Church of Scotland was well known, but for her open-mindedness towards even non-Christian religions (but not atheists), see W. Arnstein, 'Queen Victoria and religion', in G. Malmgreen (ed.), *Religion in the Lives of English Women 1760–1930* (London, 1986), pp. 112–21.

[93] Nicolson, *KGV*, pp. 162–3; Longley, *Chosen People*, pp. 56–8, 61.

churches, the Free Churches and the Roman Catholic Churches, and indeed the Jewish community, came to observe them in their own ways. In 1917, during the Palace's reassessment of the monarchy's role, Archbishop Davidson persuaded the King himself to take over the public initiative in calling days of prayer on the grounds that this would 'evoke enthusiastic support' from 'religious people of all denominations', people on whom the King 'might have to rely in hours of national strain and confusion',[94] and thereafter, on the King's behalf, the archbishops made them truly national by routinely consulting the other religious leaders in advance. When after the 1918 armistice George V became the first sovereign to worship at a Free Church service, their leaders regarded this as a historic lifting of 'the social stigma' on their denominations. They successfully lobbied for participation in the 1935 royal jubilee service (the Free Church Federal Council president read a lesson), and received places in the ceremonial processions at the 1937 and 1953 coronations – though they remained disappointed that these were still Anglican rather than fully 'national' occasions.[95] Matters were easier with the Scottish churches. In 1929–30 the Duke of York became the first member of the royal family to be appointed Lord High Commissioner to the Church of Scotland in order to mark its reunion with the Free Church of Scotland, and in 1953 the Moderator of its General Assembly, as representative of the nation's second established church, became the first non-Anglican to participate in a post-Reformation English coronation service.

A considerable weight of religious expectation lay upon the sovereign. Archbishop Lang was probably right in saying that the British people felt that George V's 'life was founded, as they instinctively desire the life of themselves and of their country to be founded – on the faith and fear of God'.[96] In some sense the monarch's religion was regarded as standing for that of the whole nation, or as Baldwin expressed it in social terms to George VI:

---

[94] Davidson to Stamfordham, 21 April 1917, Archbishop Davidson papers 6/19, Lambeth Palace Library.

[95] *Christian World*, 21 Nov. 1918; J. Marchant, *Dr John Clifford* (London, 1924), p. 235; correspondence with Gilmour, Wigram, and Rev. S. Berry, 4–16 Feb. 1935, Archbishop Lang papers 36/46, 54–6, 78–9, Lambeth Palace Library; E. K. H. Jordan, *Free Church Unity* (London, 1956), pp. 152, 217–8. From the 1887 jubilee, a small number of Free Church representatives were invited to attend great royal services, but had been allocated seats only at a distance from the actual ritual. The Archbishops were more accommodating at the state funerals of monarchs (Wolffe, *Great Deaths*, pp. 89–93, 266, 269), and were keen that the Christmas broadcast should remain undenominational, rather than tied in with any Anglican service: Bishops meeting, 20–21 Oct. 1937.

[96] Lang in *Record of the Silver Jubilee*, p. 12.

the average working man likes to spend Sunday morning in bed reading the newspaper, if possible to the accompaniment of a pint of beer. But he says to himself all the time, 'Well, anyhow, I am glad that the King and Queen are going to Church even if I am not doing it myself this morning'.[97]

A king who 'knows little . . . and cares little, about the Church' was always likely to stumble into difficulties. It was Edward VIII's failure to attend church regularly that prompted the famous rebuke of Bishop Blunt, which gave the newspapers their pretext for revealing his relationship with Mrs Simpson.[98]

Christian witness was not the only way in which the monarchy remained, in Bagehot's term, 'the head of our morality'. A royal household official, the Lord Chamberlain, was still responsible for theatre censorship, and George V had more direct influence here than in most other public matters. He also commented freely to government ministers on issues of public morality. His expressions of 'disgust' at newspaper reports of 'gross' intimate details in divorce cases made some contribution towards 1926 legislation which prohibited publication of 'indecent matter' from judicial proceedings.[99] Disapproval of matrimonial irregularity itself was still more evident. 'Guilty parties' in divorces were excluded from Palace functions until at least the late 1950s, except that – perhaps after a divorcé was included in the first Labour Cabinet – divorced government ministers were invited in their official rather than personal capacities. Even 'innocent parties' were only admitted from the late 1920s, and only after they had submitted their divorce decree and even the case proceedings for inspection by the Lord Chamberlain's office, as proof that their own behaviour really had been irreproachable. Mrs Simpson certainly knew about this royal convention: before her presentation at court in 1931, she had to submit the records of her first divorce.[100]

By the standards of the time, most politicians were not especially censorious about sexual and marital conduct.[101] Many had long known of Edward's attachment to Mrs Simpson and, as Baldwin indicated to an

---

[97] *Baldwin Papers*, pp. 445–6 (1 Dec. 1937).

[98] J. G. Lockhart, *Cosmo Gordon Lang* (London, 1949), p. 395; J. S. Peart-Binns, *Blunt* (Queensberry, 1969), pp. 152–4, and see Donaldson, *EVIII*, p. 188.

[99] Bagehot, *English Constitution*, p. 50; J. Johnston, *The Lord Chamberlain's Blue Pencil* (London, 1990), esp. pp. 84–6, 103–4; Nicolson, *KGV*, p. 429; S. Cretney, *Law, Law Reform and the Family* (Oxford, 1998), ch. 4 – though Joynson-Hicks, the puritanical home secretary, hardly needed royal prompting.

[100] D. Laird, *How the Queen Reigns* (London, 1959), p. 264; Rose, *KGV*, p. 366; *Wallis and Edward Letters 1931–1937*, ed. M. Bloch (London, 1986), pp. 24–5, 29, 30. The divorcé in the 1924 Labour Cabinet was Wedgwood, who in 1936 was one of the few parliamentary 'King's friends'.

[101] Remarkably, no one seems to have commented that the prime minister's eldest daughter had obtained a divorce in 1934.

unshocked Archbishop Lang, ministers would have been content if she had remained an unpublicized mistress. He even intimated this, more cautiously, to the King himself. Edward's objection that this would be hypocritical[102] showed an entire misunderstanding of prevailing public codes. For a sovereign to want a divorcée as his wife, let alone as queen, was scandalous – not simply in the modern sense of media prurience, but in the older meaning of deep moral disturbance. That Mrs Simpson was obtaining a second divorce that might well face legal challenge, publicly exposing the King to charges of adultery, only made matters worse.[103] All the churches taught that marriage was an indissoluble union, and such royal flouting of Christian principle seemed certain to weaken the respect and loyalty of Free Churchmen and Roman Catholics, in the Dominions as much as Britain. For the Church of England the difficulty was still greater: since the 1900s its strictures against re-marriage of divorced persons had been made more explicit,[104] and in these circumstances it could hardly allow even its own supreme governor a religious marriage. Nor would its archbishops feel able to admit the King to the sacrament of coronation – given its themes of Christian virtue, adherence to church principles and sacrifice for the sake of duty – with all the damage that might imply for church–state relations, the nation's spiritual life and, as many would suppose, the British Empire's place in the divine order.[105] The recitation of Edward's titles in the abdication legislation silently but eloquently omitted the statutory epithet, 'Defender of the Faith'.[106]

Even so, although the government was sensitive to Archbishop Lang's anxieties and the anticipated wider religious criticism, it did not act on

---

[102] Ziegler, *KEVIII*, pp. 248, 293; *The Duff Cooper Diaries*, ed. J. Norwich (London, 2005), p. 230; *Baldwin Papers*, pp. 394, 421.

[103] For the legal issues see S. M. Cretney, 'The King and the King's Proctor: the abdication crisis and the divorce laws 1936–1937', *Law Quarterly Review* 116 (2000), 583–620, and 'The divorce law and the 1936 abdication crisis: a supplemental note', ibid. 120 (2004), 163–71.

[104] See e.g. *The Lambeth Conference 1930* (London, 1930), p. 42 (resolution 11). If anything, the stricture was even stronger in *The Lambeth Conference 1948* (London, 1948), p. 49 (resolutions 92, 94).

[105] G. I. T. Machin, 'Marriage and the churches in the 1930s: royal abdication and divorce reform 1936–7', *Journal of Ecclesiastical History* 42 (1991), 68–81; and see the verdict in A. Hastings, *A History of English Christianity 1920–1985* (London, 1986), pp. 248–9. A further embarrassment was that the Archbishops had prepared a 'Recall to Religion' in association with the coronation, to exploit its message of 'service and self-dedication': Bishops meeting, 1–2 July 1936; Lockhart, *Lang*, pp. 398, 400. Even when no longer king, Edward's eventual marriage caused much ecclesiastical difficulty: Donaldson, *EVIII*, pp. 320–1.

[106] When the omission was noted in Parliament, Simon as home secretary replied in *HCDeb* 318, cc. 2226–7 (11 Dec. 1936) that it had occurred because the King had not used the term in his own 'Instrument of Abdication'; but that document had been drafted by ministers and officials.

church advice but on broader and more secular concerns. Preservation of family life remained one of the highest social goods, considered by every organization involved in social and political issues to be essential for moral health, social cohesion and social improvement. For the largest women's organizations and much of the Labour movement, maintaining the security of marriage was also the foundation for raising the status of women. Conversely, many assumed that, as Princess Elizabeth's speechwriters would declare in 1949, divorce and separation were 'responsible for some of the darkest evils of our society today'.[107] Divorce remained circumscribed by social disapproval and legal restriction, permitted only as an extreme and exceptional resort: even the advocates of the divorce law reform bill which was passing through Parliament during the discussions over Edward's proposed marriage justified it as a means to strengthen the institutions of marriage and the family. Such priorities explain why private sexual irregularity could indeed seem a lesser evil than public divorce, or a divorcée becoming queen. Not only was the royal family assumed to be a model family; a leading function of the monarchy was to set an example in upholding the sanctity of marriage – as in other matters, precisely because this now seemed under pressure. 'Since the War', Baldwin told King Edward, 'there has been a lowering of . . . public morals, but people expect even more of the Monarchy'. Later he would epitomize the point in a supposed saying of a 'Yorkshire yokel': '<u>You</u> can marry a whore & <u>I</u> can marry a whore, but the King can't. Because the King is not a man but a job'.[108]

V

The most ubiquitous public values were those clustered around the concept of 'service': duty, self-sacrifice, mutual assistance. Obviously this was the ethic of government itself and the public services, but it was still more fundamental not just for the churches but also for the charities and voluntary services which before the creation of the welfare state helped sustain medical and social care. For many organizations the spirit of 'service' provided much of the answer to actual or feared social and political problems, whether poverty, industrial conflict or revolutionary or reactionary movements. It was for Liberals integral to good citizenship, for Labour the essence of socialism, and for Conservatives an antidote to

---

[107] Pimlott, *The Queen*, pp. 160–1. For the general issues see S. Cretney, *Family Law in the Twentieth Century* (Oxford, 2003), pp. 205–50. The Labour party was divided over the issue of divorce law reform.

[108] *Baldwin Papers*, pp. 393–4, 421; *Champion Redoubtable. The Diaries and Letters of Violet Bonham Carter 1914–45*, ed. M. Pottle (London, 1998), p. 280 (28 Sept. 1943).

socialism. Clearly its particular meanings and purpose varied, but everyone in public life extolled the general principle – and so were irresistibly drawn into extolling what had long been its most prominent and willing exponent, the monarchy. After the 1918 armistice George V's 'message to the people' declared that the 'sacrifices made, the sufferings endured, the memory of the heroes who have died that Britain may live, ought surely to ennoble our thoughts and attune our hearts to a higher sense of individual and national duty'.[109] The point was reinforced by the royal family's leadership of annual acts of remembrance and at the funeral of the Unknown Warrior, and their recurring tributes at his Tomb. 'Public spirit', 'unselfish service', an Empire 'united by bonds of willing service', were characteristic royal phrases; and honouring the sacrifices of troops and appealing for service to assist the unemployed were the basis of the Prince of Wales's reputation for sympathy towards the working population. Even more than with other public values, there was an implied compact: to be respected, to retain its privileges, perhaps even to survive, the royal family had to practise, or appear to practise, what it preached. The new democracy, and the belief that only special moral qualities could hold it together, gave new force to the old notion of the king as servant of his people; and because of his exemplary role, the sovereign was presented even by Labour leaders as bearing a huge, almost unbearable, burden of work and responsibility.[110] George V's Jubilee was a liturgy to mutual service, and on his death Baldwin as prime minister declared that 'the doing of his duty . . . was the guiding principle of his life'. The King had 'rigorously trained [his will] to place the public interest first and last', his 'own ease and pleasure were never considered', and through his example 'men had led better lives in the accomplishment of their daily duties . . . at home and to their country'.[111]

Given the force of royal image-making and the interests of the state, the churches, the bodies under royal patronage, and many other voluntary organisations, this was the example that his eldest son was expected to follow. As the poignantly entitled *Sermons for the Coronation of His Majesty King Edward VIII* stated, 'our king is our King by virtue of the service he renders', and 'true royalty reveals itself in self-denying sacrifice'. Edward's speech-writers ensured that he appeared to subscribe wholly to this image: just as his father 'was ever actuated by His profound sense of duty', so he was 'resolved to follow in the way he was set before

---

[109] *The King to His People*, pp. 95–6.
[110] E.g. Attlee in *HCDeb* 308, c. 16 (23 Jan. 1936), and 495, c. 964 (11 Feb. 1952).
[111] Baldwin, *Service*, p. 18 (broadcast, 21 Jan. 1936); *HCDeb* 308, c. 13 (23 Jan. 1936), and see *Record of the Silver Jubilee*, *passim*, for many similar statements from other public figures.

me'.[112] It was not just his choice of a divorcée for his wife that offended conventional opinion; more disturbing still was his determination to place personal desire before public interest, a selfishness that struck at the heart of the most obvious and essential royal and public principles. Baldwin was astounded that he showed no moral or spiritual struggle, 'no idea of sacrifice for duty'.[113] Once the affair became public, numerous newspapers drew the social parallels: 'sacrifice of personal feelings is one which men and women in all ranks of life are often called upon to make . . . in obedience to the call of duty'.[114] The contrast between the King's behaviour and that of the millions who had served in the King's armed forces was all too plain. As Queen Mary tried again to explain to her still uncomprehending son eighteen months later: 'It seemed inconceivable to those who had made such sacrifices during the war that you, as their King, refused a lesser sacrifice'.[115]

The rest of the royal family also knew what was at stake: in a reversal of the monarchy's presumed relations with ministers, they turned to the prime minister in entreaty, apology, even shame, and then gratitude. George VI well understood that his main task was 'to make amends' to the nation and empire.[116] The verbal rehabilitation of the monarchy testifies to what had become central to its public position. The King's coronation broadcast reiterated over and over the key message: 'The highest of distinctions is the service of others, and to the Ministry of Kingship I have in your hearing dedicated myself, with the Queen at my side, in words of deepest solemnity. We will, God helping us, faithfully discharge our trust'. Baldwin's coronation broadcast drummed home the wider moral: like the King and Queen, 'let us dedicate ourselves . . . to the service of our fellows, a service in widening circles, service to the home, service to our neighbourhood, to our county, our province, to our country, to the Empire, and to the world'.[117] That George VI came to the throne unexpectedly, reluctantly and, disadvantaged by his stammer, not obviously

---

[112] Alington et. al., *Sermons*, pp. 37, 40, and *passim*; the King's message in *HCDeb* 308, c. 10 (23 Jan. 1936).

[113] *Baldwin Papers*, pp. 421–2. For a courtier's observations on the King's fatal selfishness, see Hart-Davis, *King's Counsellor*, pp. 108–9, 415: 'fundamental ideas of duty, dignity and self-sacrifice had no meaning for him'.

[114] *News of the World*, 6 Dec. 1936; *Morning Post*, 7 Dec. 1936; *Birmingham Post*, *News Chronicle* and *Scotsman*, 11 Dec. 1936; and see Donaldson, *EVIII*, p. 299, describing a cartoon of a workman throwing down his tools with the comment 'How can I do my work without the woman I love beside me?'.

[115] J. Pope-Hennessy, *Queen Mary 1867–1953* (London, 1959), p. 575. Letters from the general public in Baldwin papers, volumes 143–50, contain numerous references to the war dead and other personal sacrifices.

[116] *Baldwin Papers*, p. 416, and letters from other royal persons, ibid., pp. 413n, 415n, and in Baldwin papers volumes 176–7.

[117] *King George VI to his Peoples*, pp. 2–3; Baldwin, *Service*, p. 144.

suited to the position, had the effect of emphasizing this renewed commitment to duty and service, and in time won him sympathy and respect. The message and example were made still more relevant – and more useful for the purposes of the government and most other public bodies – by the mobilization for the Second World War, the effort required for post-war reconstruction and the introduction of sweeping welfare and economic reforms. According to the King's 1941 Christmas broadcast, it was 'in serving each other and in sacrificing for our common good that we are finding our true life'.[118] The ethic became very strong in the next royal generation. In a broadcast to mark her twenty-first birthday, Princess Elizabeth proclaimed 'a solemn act of dedication' which would resonate through her 1953 coronation and in the buoyant notions of a 'new Elizabethan age':

I declare before you all that my whole life . . . shall be dedicated to your service and the service of our great Imperial family . . . But I shall not have the strength to carry out this resolution alone unless you join in with me, as I now invite you to do. God help me to make good my vow and God bless all of you who are willing to share in it.[119]

VI

The monarchy retained its considerable prominence in the more democratic conditions of the early twentieth century because it became more purely the symbol and exponent of a particular set of public values, values promoted by almost all public organizations and respected by most of the general public. The abdication occurred because Edward VIII was, ultimately, indifferent or dismissive towards those values. No supposedly hidden political motives are required to help explain his departure: the public reason, his proposed marriage, was sufficient. The sensitivity of divorce for the monarchy was shown again in 1955 when, without any question of political complications, Princess Margaret was prevailed upon to renounce marriage to a divorced man, 'mindful of the Church's teaching that Christian marriage is indissoluble, and conscious of my duty to the Commonwealth'.[120] Edward VIII's marriage proposal mattered so much because it bore upon wider aspects of public morality – and also because it raised a still more straightforward principle. For rhetorical purposes, political leaders commonly claim to speak for the whole

---

[118] *King George VI to his Peoples*, p. 29.
[119] Pimlott, *The Queen*, pp. 115–18. The broadcast was written by Lascelles, who from the 1920s had been one of the Palace officials most critical of Edward's conduct, even resigning from royal service for a period: see Hart-Davis, *King's Counsellor*, pp. 104–10.
[120] Pimlott, *The Queen*, pp. 201–2, 218–20, 232–9; Hart-Davis, *King's Counsellor*, pp. 398–400.

'people' or nation, and Baldwin did so in his discussions with the King and in his House of Commons speech after the abdication. But what he and the Cabinet and officials really anticipated was public and newspaper division over the King's marriage proposal.[121] In royal image-making the individual and the institution could not easily be separated; many might feel attached to Edward the person, rather than to the monarch as personified virtue. Yet the monarchy's greatest function was to symbolize national and imperial unity, and it was unacceptable that any individual monarch should be a cause of division on matters of public importance. In this sense the actual balance of public opinion was immaterial – though there is little doubt that Baldwin and the Cabinet did express the majority view and certainly that of most organizations, including the Labour movement.[122]

Understanding the monarchy's popularity is notoriously difficult. Different individuals admired it for different reasons, and in various degrees of intensity. These reasons were not necessarily consistent. Some felt reverence towards a sanctified institution. Some were impressed by the pageantry, some by the illusion of proximity created by royal visits and radio broadcasts. Some admired royal philanthropy, and some idolized the romance of royal persons. Many respected the institution while responding to different aspects of what it represented. In November 1936 industrial South Wales cheered the King for his sympathy towards the unemployed, but in December religious South Wales – largely the same people – was appalled by his proposed marriage.[123] What can be said with some certainty is that various pressures and anxieties gave almost every other institution and association causes to approve and promote idealized notions of the monarchy and the royal family, and that the kings, their advisers and their speech-writers developed styles of presentation and statement which preserved high levels of public respect. The public was deluged with reasons to admire the monarchy, and during the Silver Jubilee and the coronations and royal funerals, the radio, newsreels and print media made it almost physically impossible to escape these messages. Even if these were not the only cause of royal popularity, they

---

[121] As was also explicit in the discussions and the speech: *Baldwin Papers*, pp. 393–4, 396, 401–2: *HCDeb* 318, c. 2180–1 (10 Dec. 1936)..

[122] Williams, *The People's King*, reveals that the King received large numbers of letters of support, and argues that the abdication was contrary to the wishes of 'ordinary people'. But Baldwin, Queen Mary and other public figures also received very many letters of concern or support from individuals of all classes. What is certain (and what was crucial) is that 'public opinion' was divided. See also the observations in Ziegler, *Crown and People*, pp. 35–9.

[123] *New Statesman*, 12 Dec. 1936; H. Dalton, *The Fateful Years. Memoirs 1931–45* (London, 1957), p. 114. The area had exceptionally high levels of chapel affiliation.

supplied a vocabulary for individuals to help express whatever other feelings of admiration or tolerance they felt towards it. These themes are aptly indicated by the comments of a road-sweeper and old soldier recorded by the novelist Philip Gibbs during the 1935 Jubilee:

The Royal Family . . . is a very respectable lot . . . Human, if you know what I mean. They feel kindly towards us, and we feel kindly towards them . . . [The King's] all right! A nice fellow – not like that there Hitler in Germany who puts folks into concentration camps because they don't see eye to eye with him. [He] does his duty like the rest of us, like I do mine, and I don't envy him his job. That's why I'm loyal. That's why we're all loyal.[124]

[124] P. Gibbs, *England Speaks* (London, 1935), p. 1.

9   The monarchy and film 1900–2006

Jeffrey Richards

Traditionalist defenders of the monarchy are fond of quoting the dictum of the great nineteenth-century constitutional expert Walter Bagehot who warned: 'Above all things our royalty is to be reverenced, and if you begin to poke about it, you cannot reverence it. Its mystery is its life. We must not let daylight in upon the magic.'[1] They therefore denounce the intrusion of the mass media, notably television and the tabloid newspapers, into the affairs of monarchy, claiming that it has been seriously undermined by the loss of its magic.

Bagehot was writing before cinema, television and wireless transformed the world and made the letting in of light inevitable. Contrary to Bagehot, this essay argues that the letting in of daylight which had already begun in the nineteenth century has not destroyed the magic. Rather it has replaced one magic, the magic of distance, with another, the magic of familiarity, but a familiarity conditioned in the twentieth century by the conventions of Hollywood, which have reclothed the royals in the divinity of stardom and celebrity.

Where Bagehot was indubitably correct was in stating: 'So long as the human heart is strong and the human reason weak, Royalty will be strong because it appeals to diffused feeling, and Republics weak because they appeal to understanding.'[2] The republican case in this country is grimly rationalist, and while practical political, constitutional and even economic reasons (the 'it's good for tourism' argument) can be adduced to support monarchy, its justification at bottom is emotional. 'Britain wouldn't be Britain without the monarchy' said one of the 200,000 people queuing for the lying-in-state of the Queen Mother. This encapsulates the idea that the monarchy is one of the things that makes Britain distinctive. It is seen as an integral part of the national identity, representing continuity, tradition, history and pageantry. 'All ritual is fortifying', said Kipling,

---

[1] W. Bagehot, *The English Constitution*, ed. M. Taylor (Oxford, 2001), p. 54.
[2] Ibid., p. 41. On the nineteenth-century popularization of the monarchy, see J. Plunkett, *Queen Victoria: the First Media Monarch* (Oxford, 2003).

and the events surrounding the death of the Queen Mother abundantly justify that view.

Large sections of the intelligentsia and three national newspapers, the *Independent*, the *Observer* and the *Guardian*, convinced themselves during the past decade that monarchy was finished and that their longed for republic was at hand. The *Guardian* in particular has campaigned against the monarchy, culminating in the combination of venom and glee with which some of its contributors greeted the death of the Queen Mother, predicting universal indifference to her passing.[3] One million people turned out on the day of her funeral to prove them wrong. A similar number packed the Mall for the climax of the Golden Jubilee celebrations.

They only needed to consult the opinion polls to discover the true situation. Since opinion polls began to be taken in the early 1950s about whether the public wanted Britain to be a monarchy or a republic, there has almost never been less than 70 per cent for a monarchy and rarely more than 20 per cent for a republic.[4] In the week following the funeral of Princess Diana in 1997 – the culmination of the greatest period of crisis for the monarchy since the abdication of Edward VIII – all the major polling agencies published their latest findings: Gallup found 71 per cent in favour of a monarchy and 11 per cent for a republic, MORI found 73 per cent for a monarchy and 18 per cent for a republic, and ICM found 74 per cent for a monarchy and 12 per cent for a republic. On the first anniversary of Diana's death, MORI reported 75 per cent for a monarchy and 16 per cent for a republic.[5] On the day of the Queen Mother's funeral, the *Independent* published a new NOP poll which found 84 per cent for a monarchy and 12 per cent for a republic, a return to the levels recorded in Silver Jubilee Year of 1977, when there was a broadly similar result.[6] These levels have been sustained despite the letting in of daylight or, as I would argue, because of it.

In the twentieth and twenty-first centuries the faces and voices of the royal family have been instantly recognizable, thanks to the mass media and in contrast to earlier ages, which knew their monarch only from coin portraits or paintings. But the media have done more than just promote

---

[3] See, for example, Christopher Hitchens, 'Mourning will be brief', *Guardian*, 1 Apr. 2002, in which he dismisses the Queen Mother as 'a woman who symbolised and endorsed luxury and idleness in personal life, philistinism in culture, ruthlessness in eugenics and reaction in politics'. A more measured and realistic assessment from republican columnist Jonathan Freedland appeared on 12 Apr.

[4] P. Ziegler, *Crown and People* (London, 1978), p. 127.

[5] J. Richards, S. Wilson and L. Woodhead (eds.), *Diana: the Making of a Media Saint* (London, 1999), pp. 72–3.

[6] *Independent*, 9 Apr. 2002.

familiarity. They have popularized the monarchy in a democratic era when monarchy exists only by maintaining popular approval.

Television is now inextricably intertwined with monarchy and we can trace that process from the decision of the Queen, overruling the Prime Minister and the Archbishop of Canterbury, to allow television cameras into Westminster Abbey for the coronation in 1953, through the introduction of the televised Christmas Day broadcast in 1957, through the ground-breaking documentary *Royal Family* in 1969 (a programme watched by 68 per cent of the population) and through a series of royal marriages staged as television spectaculars, to the utilization of television by Charles and Diana during their marital troubles and only recently the lying-in-state and funeral of the Queen Mother, and the Golden Jubilee celebrations of Queen Elizabeth II.

I

Before television, it was the cinema which helped to sustain popular monarchy, by playing to two different but complementary sides of the institution. Newsreels and documentaries stressed the public face of monarchy and the idea of monarchy as the epitome of a life of duty and service. Feature films helped to humanize the institution by turning past royal figures into stars, and inviting the public to sympathize with them in their private tragedies and tribulations.

The cinema had arrived as a mass medium of entertainment in Britain in 1896, just as the British Empire was reaching the high noon of its power and splendour. So the cameras were there to capture in short flickering films the great ceremonial milestones of the era: Queen Victoria's Diamond Jubilee (1897) and funeral (1901), the coronation procession of King Edward VII (1902) and his funeral (1910), the coronation procession of King George V (1911) and the Delhi Durbars of 1903 and 1911, all of them staged and viewed as royal and imperial spectaculars.[7]

British cinema newsreels began in 1910–11. Relying on the visual image and captions, they were simpler than their sound counterparts, but they became an integral part of the cinema programme. It was only during the First World War that, as Luke McKernan has noted, the royal family became 'the dominant home subject' in the newsreels.[8] Before the War, regular access to the royal family had been denied to the newsreels and the cameras had to keep their distance. But by the latter part of the

---

[7] On the earliest films of royalty, see J. Barnes, *The Beginnings of the Cinema in England 1894–1900*, 5 vols. (Exeter, 1997).

[8] L. McKernan, *Topical Budget* (London, 1992), p. 56.

Great War, the propaganda and morale-boosting value of the cinema had come to be appreciated by the authorities and greater access to the royal family was granted. King George V, for instance, appeared in only five items in Topical Budget newsreels in 1916, but in thirty-six in 1918.

After the War, the newsreel cameras became an indispensable part of the royal routine. Royal weddings such as those of the Princess Royal and Viscount Lascelles in 1922, and of the Duke of York and Lady Elizabeth Bowes-Lyon in 1923 received extensive and admiring coverage. But the newsreels' favourite subject matter was the Prince of Wales, whose domestic public appearances and Empire tours were fully covered. According to McKernan, 'the extraordinary worldwide enthusiasm generated by his presence came in large part from the constant exposure on cinema screens'.[9] The newsreel cameras accompanied him on his 1920 Empire Tour of the West Indies, the Pacific Islands, Australia and New Zealand, and at the end of it, Topical Budget's individual newsreel items were put together in a feature-length documentary *50,000 Miles with the Prince of Wales*.

The attitude adopted towards the royal family is typified by the captions in Topical Budget's three items on the death of Queen Alexandra in 1925:

It is with profound regret that Topical Budget records the death of the Queen Mother at Sandringham. The passing of the beloved consort of King Edward VII and the mother of our King plunges the whole Empire into mourning. Pictures which recall the gracious personality of the adored Queen . . . Nation's tribute of tears as the beloved lady passes to her rest.[10]

There is almost no alteration of tone in the way in which Pathé News reported the death of Queen Mary in 1953: 'The whole world mourns as a very great and gracious lady, the mother and grandmother of sovereigns, passes from our lives . . . grief born of respect and love . . . a grand old lady we called her – in those words was expressed a wealth of affection . . . so great and gracious a lady, so kindly and dignified a Queen.'

The coverage of royalty by the newsreels from their inception to their demise in the mid-1960s – after television had taken over their functions – was uniformly deferential, respectful and supportive. Just as there was a continuity of tone, there were continuing themes in the newsreels' depiction of royalty: the close association of Crown and Empire, the predominance of the ideas of duty and service, the concern of the royal family for the people and the reciprocating loyalty of the people for the Crown; the idea of a family on the throne and the innate humanity and naturalness of the royals.

---

[9] McKernan, *Topical Budget*, p. 118.   [10] Ibid., pp. 120–1.

The coming of sound added a new dimension to the newsreels – background music and the voice of a commentator. That voice was the voice of the Establishment, for as newsreel chiefs put it in 1938: 'The newsreel companies were always ready to give, and in fact frequently gave, assistance to the government in portraying matters that were deemed to be in the public interest'.[11] That certainly included coverage of the royal family. By 1935, the twenty-fifth anniversary of his accession, King George V was in poor health, but his ministers thought it both fitting and politically expedient to stimulate patriotism and support for the monarchy and the Empire, and so Silver Jubilee celebrations were organized. The newsreels' coverage of the service of Thanksgiving at St Paul's Cathedral on 6 May, 1935, showed the streets were packed with cheering crowds, causing the King to record 'the greatest number of people in the streets that I have ever seen in my life.'[12] Movietone's version has the procession to and from St Paul's Cathedral, and the commentator noted:

The whole world rejoices as their majesties drive in procession to St Paul's . . . the spectacle of a nation exalted . . . a tempestuous ovation roared by 10,000 voices . . . the nation's exaltation breaks all bounds in expressing that veneration that the British people feel for the King and Queen . . . the most impassioned demonstration of loyalty within memory . . . Has the Queen ever looked so beautiful?

The service itself is represented by photographs, as cameras were not allowed inside the cathedral. Then after the drive back, the crowds surge round the palace: 'It is the example of noble lives lived in public-spirited endeavour which really influence humanity, so that the example of the Royal House of Windsor must exercise a glorious influence on generations yet to come'.

Pathé News adopted a different strategy, showing the same scenes but superimposing the King's broadcast from Buckingham Palace on the evening of Jubilee Day:

I can only say to you, my very dear people, that the Queen and I thank you from the depth of our hearts for all the loyalty – and may I say so – the love with which this day and always you have surrounded us. I dedicate myself anew to your service for the years that may yet be given to me.

Then speaking specifically to the children:

---

[11] A. Aldgate, *Cinema and History: British Newsreels and the Spanish Civil War* (London, 1979), p. 193.
[12] K. Rose, *King George V* (London, 1983), pp. 395–7.

In days to come you will be citizens of a great Empire. As you grow up, always keep this thought before you. And when the time comes, be ready and proud to give to your country the service of your work, your mind and your heart.[13]

The use of the wireless was another prime example of the utilization of the mass media to increase the accessibility of the Crown. The voice of a reigning monarch had never been heard by his peoples before the reign of George V. It was first heard opening the Empire Exhibition at Wembley in 1924, and thereafter thirteen times on the wireless making speeches on formal occasions. But he had resisted repeated requests from Sir John Reith to broadcast at Christmas. Finally in 1932 he agreed and he broadcast from Sandringham on Christmas Day a simple message of greeting, scripted for him by Rudyard Kipling. The King proved to be a natural broadcaster. As Tom Fleming has written:

Never had the voice of a British monarch been heard speaking personally, and from a room in his own home, to his people throughout the British Isles, let alone simultaneously to his other peoples, scattered across the seven seas and the five continents . . . the sound of a gruff, unaffected voice, speaking kindly and unpretentious words to an expectant audience of millions, much in the manner of a revered grandfather addressing his assembled family, and doing so at the essentially family festival of Christmas was a new experience, which few who shared it were ever likely to forget.[14]

The same tones can be heard in the Jubilee Day broadcast, an intimate and human dimension added to the public pomp. The Christmas Day broadcast became a national institution, taken up by King George VI and Queen Elizabeth II.

During Silver Jubilee Year, Pathé covered the Naval review at Spithead and the Royal Air Force review at Mildenhall, noting that the King was appearing for the first time in the uniform of a Marshal of the Royal Air Force. He inspected the aeroplanes by car, covering a total of five miles. Both reports ended with the assembled servicemen giving three cheers for the King. Pathé also covered the Silver Jubilee Garden Party at Buckingham Palace. The commentator noted that the King and Queen greeted the King's Indian Orderlies first, and that High Indian officials and their wives mingled with the cream of the English aristocracy at the event. He also stressed the 'informality of modern royalty', as we see

---

[13] All the Pathé newsreels analyzed in this essay are taken from the video compilation *King and Queen: the Reign of George VI and Elizabeth* (Castle Vision, 1993). All the Movietone newsreels analyzed are taken from the video compilation *The Silver Heritage Collection: the Best of British Movietone News*, vol. 2: Great Events (1987).

[14] Tom Fleming (intro.), *Voices out of the Air: the Royal Christmas Broadcasts 1932–1981* (London, 1981), p. 1.

footage of the King and Queen chatting and joking with guests: 'What a delightfully informal host and hostess Our King and Queen are.'

There were several newsreel compilations to celebrate the Silver Jubilee: Gaumont British's *The King's Jubilee*, Paramount's *Long Live the King* and Pathé's *25 years a King*. Associated British Pictures produced a major all-star drama-documentary, *Royal Cavalcade*, which followed the progress of one of the first coins of George V to be struck in 1911. As it proceeds from one person to another, the film interweaves fictional personal stories, filmed in the studio with actors, with newsreel and documentary footage of the great events of the reign. They are all bound together by a strident and over-assertive commentary. The use of a coin as a linking device was particularly apt, for it served to blend the personal and the national stories together and bind them all to the monarch, whose image was stamped on the coin. The film ended with the coin being contributed to the King's Jubilee Fund. It was very much the official version of the reign with the stress laid on tradition, pageantry, service and duty.[15]

But King George V barely made it through Jubilee Year, dying on 20 January 1936. In February, Pathé covered Edward VIII's first official engagement as King and it was significantly imperial. As Prince of Wales, we are told, Edward was 'the supersalesman of the Empire' and now he opens the 1936 British Industries Fair at Olympia. The King makes straight for the Dominion stands and visits all the empire displays. Then in December came his abdication. The British media had been reticent in their treatment of the looming crisis surrounding the King and Mrs Simpson. Movietone lost no time in drawing a line under Edward VIII's reign. It notes that the episode is now closed. Mr. Baldwin's role in it is 'recognized and honoured.' The new King and Queen are already acclaimed and it plays Edward VIII's abdication speech over scenes of the new King and Queen and their family, and ends with the proclamation of George VI and a photograph of the new King. Edward VIII had said in his broadcast of his brother: 'He has one matchless blessing, enjoyed by so many of you and not bestowed on me, a happy home with his wife and children', and Pathé showed charming informal pictures of the new King and Queen and the two little princesses. The imperial dimension was, however, always present. In December 1936, Pathé ran an issue called *Our King and Queen* devoted entirely to their imperial tours as Duke and Duchess of York helping 'to forge the links of Empire.' The commentator concludes: 'We know they will uphold the glorious tradition of King George V and Queen Mary.' In May 1937 came the coronation, and for

---

[15] For a detailed discussion of *Royal Cavalcade*, see J. Richards, *The Age of the Dream Palace* (London, 1984), pp. 269–71.

the first time the newsreel cameras were allowed to film the ceremony inside the Abbey. 'The most solemn and sacred pictures ever taken by a newsreel', the Pathé commentator called the scenes. The stress in Pathé's coronation issue was on tradition, pomp and empire.

There was clearly an anxiety to project the monarchy as simple and unaffected. So Pathé reported in August 1937 on the King's Camp, at which industrial workers and public schoolboys mingled. It had been founded sixteen years before when he was Duke of York, but was still continuing now. The King is seen singing with his people, 'Oh, we are a happy family' and the commentator praises the pictures of 'democratic royalty.'

There was another media milestone in 1938 when the voice of the Queen was heard for the first time as she launched the liner *Queen Elizabeth* on the Clyde. 'The soft and mellow voice of the Queen puts into ringing tones what the whole Empire thinks and feels today' says the commentator. She reads out a message from the King urging his people to be of good cheer despite the dark clouds hanging over them.

There was extensive coverage by Pathé of the North American tour of the King and Queen, which featured the first visit of a reigning British sovereign to the United States. When the royal family see off the King and Queen at Victoria Station, we are treated to 'the most charming, informal close-ups of every member of our royal family'. Their return on the liner *Empress of Britain*, headed 'Welcome Home!' is accompanied on the soundtrack by *Land of Hope and Glory*. The trip is pronounced a diplomatic triumph.

It is at least arguable that it was the war that was the making of King George VI, and that he and the monarchy benefited strongly from cinema coverage of his activities. He had come to the throne unexpectedly, painfully shy and afflicted by a speech impediment which he struggled to overcome and which sometimes makes his speeches painful to listen to, as you wonder if he will get the next word out. Indeed there is evidence that some of his speeches were deliberately suppressed by the newsreel companies for this reason. But he became something of a symbol of democratic Britain at war.

George VI's role was not that of the inspiring orator. It was Prime Minister Winston Churchill who, in President Kennedy's words, 'mobilized the English language and sent it into battle'. The King and Queen played a different role: one of quiet and selfless service, encouragement and example. This was the image that the newsreels reflected.[16]

---

[16] R. Brunt, 'The family firm restored: newsreel coverage of the British monarchy 1936–45', in C. Gledhill and G. Swanson (eds.), *Nationalising Femininity* (Manchester, 1996), pp. 140–51.

The newsreels reported on 'Her Majesty's Sewing Bee' when the Queen and the ladies of the palace staff knitted comforters for the troops ('There's a complete absence of formality – there's just a job to be done'). This emphasis on informality and service provided a running theme, as Pathé newsreels filmed the King and Queen visiting salvage centres, munitions factories, feeding and clothing centres for the homeless, preserving depots, uniform manufacturers, evacuees, hospitals, wounded servicemen, and above all, blitzed and bombed areas. 'With a complete absence of pomp he talks to the men' says the Pathé commentator of the King at a munitions factory; 'a visit from Her Majesty is as good as a tonic', he says as the Queen visits wounded servicemen.

The cameras recorded a visit by the King and Queen to a vehicle maintenance depot where Princess Elizabeth, a subaltern in the ATS, was repairing an ambulance engine. The King turns the whole of the Sandringham estate over to food production, and the royal family are filmed touring the fields on bicycles. Gaumont British News film a visit by the King and Queen to the Dambusters' base in 1943 after the famous raid. Everywhere they go, they are greeted by cheering crowds. The Queen's broadcasts to the women of Britain, sympathizing in their suffering and loss and paying tribute to their contribution to the war effort, were filmed by the newsreel cameras.

In documentaries too, the King and Queen are depicted as remaining amongst their people. In Humphrey Jennings's masterpiece, *Listen to Britain*, a sound picture of Britain at war, in a sequence of a lunchtime concert by Dame Myra Hess at the National Gallery, there in the audience alongside the office workers and off-duty service personnel is the Queen (Fig. 9.1). In *London Can Take It*, the King and Queen are seen inspecting bomb damage. Their continued presence in the capital was recorded in a popular song 'The King is still in London, in London, in London, Like Mr. Jones and Mr. Brown, the King is still in London town.'

The King's main contribution to inspirational broadcasting was his annual Christmas message to Britain and the Empire. One of these led directly to a film. He ended his 1939 Christmas message by quoting from a poem by Minnie Louise Haskins, *The Gate of the Year*:

I said to the man who stood at the Gate of the Year, 'Give me a light that I may tread safely into the unknown' and he replied, 'Go out into the darkness, and put your hand into the Hand of God. That shall be to you better than light, and safer than a known way.'

He concluded 'May that Almighty Hand guide and uphold us all'. Film tycoon J. Arthur Rank, a devout Methodist, was so moved by this that

Figure 9.1. Queen Elizabeth in the audience for a lunchtime concert at the National Gallery in Humphrey Jennings's picture of 'the People's War' – *Listen to Britain* (1942) (Crown Film Unit. The Jeffrey Richards Collection).

he commissioned an inspirational film to be built round it. He turned for it to Norman Walker, who had directed his award-winning first feature film venture, *Turn of the Tide* in 1935.

Walker took his cue from an earlier passage in the King's speech:

We look with pride and thankfulness on the never-failing courage and devotion of the Royal Navy . . . and when I speak of our navy today, I mean all the men of our Empire who go down to the sea in ships, the mercantile marine, the minesweepers, the trawlers and drifters, from the senior officers to the last boy who has joined up.

In doing so, he turned back to the world of fisherfolk featured in *Turn of the Tide*. In *The Man at the Gate* (1941), he tells the story of a fisherman's wife who has lost two sons to the sea and when her remaining son, a wireless operator on a steamer is reported lost after the ship is sunk by German bombs, she loses her faith in God. She comes to believe that 'there's no love left in the world and only fear, hatred and cruelty'. But listening to the King's Christmas broadcast and the Haskins poem, she regains her faith and repeats his words 'better than light and safer than a known way.' Immediately after the broadcast comes news on the radio that her son has been rescued and landed safely in Scotland. The King's words have restored faith and hope. Indeed, those words became so closely associated with the King that they were inscribed on the gates of his memorial chapel at Windsor.

When victory finally came, people sought to express their gratitude to the King and Queen for their wartime work. The British Movietone News Victory issue began with film of Mr Churchill broadcasting the news of victory in Europe, concluding 'Advance Britannia. Long live the cause of freedom. God save the King.' There followed scenes of crowds converging on Buckingham Palace. The King, the Queen, the Princesses and Mr Churchill appear on the balcony in answer to the insistent chants of 'We want the King'. 'This is the way we have in Great Britain,' says the commentator. 'The family and the head of the family rejoice together.'

After the War, the newsreels covered the King and Queen's victory tours of Great Britain, their tour of South Africa, the engagement and marriage of Princess Elizabeth and Prince Philip. Characteristically, the South African tour was depicted as an unalloyed triumph. In reality it was fraught with problems. The King was sensitive to criticism that he had headed for the sun during the freezing winter of 1946–47, which had caused chaos in Britain. Prime Minister Smuts, facing an election, was endeavouring to use the tour for political purposes. The Nationalist Party boycotted the visit. The King was greatly disturbed by the first stirrings of apartheid. The newsreels also covered the silver wedding of the King and Queen ('The nation rejoices with the Our King and Queen. None of the pomp and ceremony can hide the simple significance of it all. The King and Queen give their people inspiration and youth an example'). It was the sense of oneness with the people, and the linked ideas of family and service, so regularly stressed by the newsreels, that explains the genuine and widespread grief at the sudden and unexpected death of the King in 1952 at the age of fifty-six. There was general recognition that he had worn himself out in the service of his country.

The British Movietone News issue on the death of the King began with the statement: 'The British people will cherish the memory of a brave and beloved King' and spoke of a sudden and grievous shock to his peoples. The retrospective of his reign covered his coronation in 1937, the simplicity of his family life and his 'quiet happiness' with the Queen and his daughters. There is footage of his wartime visits, and it is noted that the King stayed in his capital and that his palace was bombed. Then came victory and the familiar scenes of rejoicing at the palace. After footage of the South African tour, the silver wedding and the christening of Prince Charles, there is the news of the King's illness and the operation on his lung. Finally, there is that most poignant airport farewell, when the King, gaunt and visibly already shadowed by death, saw off his daughter and her consort on the Commonwealth tour which he was unable to undertake. After expressing deepest sympathy to the Queen, the commentator concludes: 'the nation mourns a King who served it so well.'

Pathé echoes the sentiments of Movietone: 'Britain mourns the passing of a monarch whose life was an inspiration to all over whom he ruled'. Repeating the words used of George V in the 1935 newsreel coverage of his death, the commentator talks of George VI as the King to the rest of England and the Empire, but squire to his people at Sandringham. The solemn BBC announcement of the King's death was replayed. 'The heart of the nation stops; the flags lower in tribute . . . The great dominions join us in our sorrow . . . the King – Our King – is no more with us.' There is footage of the coronation ('He was crowned ruler of the greatest Empire in history.') The commentator talks of 'a life of unselfish service', adding, 'Wherever a man's life is measured in service to his fellow men, they mourn George VI.' His love of the countryside is recalled and his life as a family man, with scenes of the King and the Princesses bicycling over the Sandringham estate during the war. Over scenes of the war, we are told: 'Wherever his people suffered, he came and by his presence brought comfort and assurance in their ordeal'. At the lying-in-state, 300,000 people file past his coffin: 'Of George VI it will be written this was a king his people loved'. The King's coffin leaves Buckingham Palace and the procession passes the Cenotaph, silently linking his death with those millions who gave their lives for their country. Then from Paddington Station, he takes his last journey to Windsor. 'George VI whom history will name the Good.'

The coronation of Queen Elizabeth II on 2 June 1953 marked not just the beginning of a new reign but of a new era, coming at the end of a period of post-war austerity. It was widely promoted as the 'new Elizabethan age' and great hopes were expressed for an era of achievement, hopes which received a boost when Mount Everest was conquered by a British-led expedition, news of which reached London on Coronation Day.

Both British Movietone and Pathé, customarily filmed in black and white, went into colour for their coronation editions. Both major cinema networks, Rank and Associated British, produced feature-length colour documentaries of the coronation. Rank's was *A Queen is Crowned*, produced by Castleton Knight, scripted by the poet Christopher Fry, narrated by Sir Laurence Olivier, scored by Guy Warrack, and with extra music selected by Sir Malcolm Sargent. The Associated British film, *Elizabeth is Queen*, was scripted by the poet John Pudney, narrated by Leo Genn and featured music conducted by Sir Adrian Boult. Both were completed and released on 8 June, a mere six days after the actual event. By common consent *A Queen is Crowned* was the better of the two. It became the year's most successful film at the British box office, was popular throughout the Commonwealth and was a surprise success in the United States.[17] The film was woven together of elements which were seen as timeless and traditional: Empire, Protestant Christianity, popular approval and the coronation confirmed the monarchy as an integral, inevitable and desirable part of ongoing history. Parties of schoolchildren all over the country were marched to their local cinema to watch it, and it was undeniably a more powerful and vivid experience than the small black and white images on television.

A Queen is Crowned was followed up by a now forgotten feature film which complements it perfectly, a 95-minute documentary in Cinemascope and Eastmancolor, released in June 1954 by Twentieth Century-Fox and recording the 1953–4 Commonwealth tour of the Queen and the Duke of Edinburgh, which encompassed Fiji, Tonga, New Zealand, Australia, Ceylon, Uganda, Malta and Gibraltar. It was shot by British Movietone News, produced by Jack Ramsden and narrated by Leslie Mitchell from a script by Gerald Sanger. It was called *Flight of the White Heron* and despite its billing as a film record of the 'Commonwealth tour', it has an undoubted imperial feel to it, right from the opening titles: a Maori greeting to the Queen:

A stranger from beyond the horizon, the rare White Heron from a Single Flight, welcome to this outflung post of your Empire, Queen of a mighty throne, built on the affections of countless peoples, enter your domain.

The Kotuku, the White Heron, is a cherished bird rarely seen in New Zealand.

The film is structured around several recurrent themes. The first is constitutional monarchy and parliamentary democracy, symbolized by the scenes in which the Queen as head of state opens the parliaments in New Zealand, Australia and Ceylon. She wears her coronation gown and a tiara for each event. 'Her youthful radiance is breathtaking', rhapsodizes Leslie Mitchell. In Ceylon she is 'serene, cool and graceful'.

A second theme is Protestant Christianity. The Queen visits churches, and worships wherever she goes. The film stresses the Protestantism of Tonga brought by the missionaries ('Christianity is cherished in Tonga with a devotion that has become a tradition.'). The royal couple leave to the singing of *The Lord is My Shepherd*. They celebrate Christmas in Auckland with a chorus of children singing *Hark the Herald Angels Sing*, and they visit a church for a Christmas service. In Ceylon, they visit Holy Trinity Church, Nuwara Eliya.

---

[17] J. Chapman, 'Cinema, monarchy and the making of heritage: *A Queen is Crowned* (1953)', in C. Monk and A. Sargeant (eds.), *British Historical Cinema* (London, 2002), pp. 82–91.

The Second World War as a linking experience for the Empire is stressed. The Queen lays wreaths and unveils new war memorials. There are recurrent images of the modern armed forces, indicating the preparedness of the Commonwealth. The Empire is largely constructed as exotic, featuring as it does the Blue Mountains of Australia, the hot springs at Rotorua, the Royal Botanic Gardens in Colombo, elephants and tea plantations in Ceylon. In almost every place they visit, the royal couple are entertained by native dancers. But there are also reminders of England everywhere, cricket and tennis matches, race meetings, English-style churches, formal garden parties. Throughout the trip at every stage, loyalty is stressed. As the Queen arrives home, the commentator announces: 'she is destined to become one of the famous queens of history', praises the perfect organization of the 50,000 mile tour in which not a single engagement was missed and she became the first reigning monarch to visit Australia and New Zealand. One is struck viewing it today by the extraordinary sense of imperial timelessness, as the trip repeated many of the elements of the visit of the Duke and Duchess of York to Australia and New Zealand in 1926, itself covered by newsreel cameras: the opening of the federal parliament, the unveiling of memorials, the parade of ex-servicemen, Maori dances, visit to the Rotorua hot springs.

A further major Technicolor film of the period deserves mention too in this context. British Lion released in November 1953 a feature-length documentary *Conquest of Everest*, scripted by the poet Louis MacNeice and narrated by Meredith Edwards. It followed the British expedition led by Colonel John Hunt, culminating in New Zealander Edmund Hillary and Sherpa Tenzing Norgay reaching the summit: the identity of the conquerors of the summit giving it a real imperial flavour. But it set the achievement squarely in the context of the coronation, opening with the procession of the golden coach through the streets of London and the headlines that greeted news of the achievement: 'The crowning glory'. The cumulative impression gained from *A Queen is Crowned, The Flight of the White Heron* and *The Conquest of Everest* is of the centrality, timelessness and continuing vigour of the monarchy and the Empire. Together they mark 1953 as a high point in the history of modern monarchy, and of the role of cinema in its positive promotion.

II

The censorship rules under which the cinema operated in its heyday decreed that no reference to, or depiction of, the current royal family should be made in fictional films. Not only was the current royal family sacrosanct, but so too initially was Queen Victoria. But the ban on

Figure 9.2. Anna Neagle in *Victoria the Great* (1937) – affirming the soundness of the monarchy at a time of crisis (RKO Radio Pictures. The Jeffrey Richards Collection).

depictions of Queen Victoria was lifted by agreement between the Lord Chamberlain and the President of the British Board of Film Censors on 20 June, 1937, the hundredth anniversary of her accession. King George V, who had not wanted his grandmother portrayed on the screen, had died the previous year and King Edward VIII, perhaps because his father had taken the opposite view, was keen to see her life filmed and had given producer Herbert Wilcox permission to make such a film. Wilcox produced and directed *Victoria the Great* in 1937 (Fig. 9.2). It was such a box office success that he promptly remade it in Technicolor as *Sixty Glorious Years* in 1938. Anna Neagle played Queen Victoria and Anton Walbrook Prince Albert in both films. Taken together, the films represent the definitive hagiographical account of Queen Victoria.

Both films have the ritual formality of a pageant or a mystery play, detailing, step by pre-ordained step, the progress towards apotheosis. Many scenes allegorically represent one or other of the divine virtues (compassion, dedication, peace); and the loss of the Prince Consort, who dies worn out by his service to the nation, emphasizes the loneliness and destiny of the Great White Mother. Her centrality to the life of the nation is confirmed by the appearance of almost all the other great myth figures of the age in the two films, revolving around her like a constellation of stars around a planet – Wellington, Peel, Palmerston, Gladstone, Disraeli, Gordon and Rhodes. The major events of the reign (the repeal of the Corn Laws, the Charge of the Light Brigade, the Great Exhibition, etc.) are recreated.

The critics loved both films. But so too did audiences. Queen Mary was so moved by *Sixty Glorious Years* that she left the cinema in tears and Anna Neagle, making personal appearance tours with the film in the North of England, noticed many working-class women in clogs and shawls leaving the cinemas in tears also.[18] The film paralleled the theme of the newsreels, celebrating as it did the happy family life of the dynasty, pride in the Empire, a career of royal duty and service, and the link between Crown and people, something that was particularly important in the aftermath of the Abdication.

Films critical of Queen Victoria or the monarchy, however, were still not permitted. When both MGM and Warner Brothers submitted to the British censors Vaughan Wilkins' novel *And So – Victoria* as a possible project for filming, the senior censor, Colonel J. C. Hanna, noting that the plot centred on the intrigues among the sons of King George III to secure the succession to the throne and involved a plot by the Duke of Cumberland to murder Victoria, reported: 'If the intention is to show up the evil lives that were lived by our Royal Family in those days, then I have no hesitation in saying I think it would be most undesirable.' It was never made. Nor was a proposed film *John Brown, Servant of the Queen*, of which Colonel Hanna reported:

I suggest that to revive these ugly rumours after this lapse of time would be worse than 'bad taste'. It would be a deliberate attempt to belittle the dignity of the crown. I consider that a film with this motif would be extremely improper and quite unfit for exhibition in this country.[19]

But earlier monarchs were fair game for the cinema, and both in Britain and in Hollywood there has been a thriving cinema of monarchy. Despite the fact that such films often reveal cruelty, immorality and ill treatment within the royal family, their net effect is to strengthen and entrench it as they simultaneously mythologize and humanize the institution.[20]

They mythologize by casting famous film stars as famous monarchs, for instance Bette Davis as Elizabeth I, Charles Laughton as Henry VIII and Anna Neagle as Queen Victoria. These stars became so identified

[18] Richards, *Dream Palace*, pp. 264–6.   [19] Ibid., pp. 117–8.
[20] On the cinema of monarchy, see J. Richards, 'Imperial images: the British Empire and monarchy on film', *Cultures* 2 (UNESCO, 1975), pp. 79–114.

with the roles that after initial appearances in the 1930s, they were called on to repeat them in films of the 1950s.[21] The charisma of the stars and the charisma of the monarchs commingled to elevate both the person and the role.

Mythologization has been accompanied by humanization. But it is humanization embodied in 'the private life' syndrome. There is an apparently endless appetite amongst ordinary people to know about the personal, behind-the-scenes behaviour of the great and famous. Films like *The Private Life of Henry VIII* or *The Private Lives of Elizabeth and Essex* cater to this need but in so doing, emphasize the very greatness of their subjects. For if they were not great, there would be no interest in their private lives.

Such films avoid concentrating on real, substantive historical issues – social, political, economic, religious – which might cause controversy, invite censorship or affect profitability. Thus *The Private Life of Henry VIII* (1933) and *Anne of the Thousand Days* (1969) ignore the Reformation to concentrate on Henry's marital misadventures. King Charles II is most frequently depicted in films dealing with his relationships with his mistresses: *Nell Gwynne* (1926), *Nell Gwyn* (1934), *Forever Amber* (1947), *Restoration* (1995).

There has been a distinct fondness for famous royal scandals of history, such as *Mrs Fitzherbert* (1947), dealing with the morganatic marriage of King George IV to Mrs Fitzherbert, and *Saraband for Dead Lovers* (1948), about the unhappy love affair between Sophie Dorothea, wife of King George I, and Count Konigsmarck. The important point about these scandals is that they all end in tragedy. So too do the special friendships formed by monarchs, when ties of personal affection come up against issues of public policy as they do in such films as *Beau Brummell* (1955), *Becket* (1964), and *A Man for All Seasons* (1966).

Ever since Sarah Bernhardt recreated her stage success *Queen Elizabeth I* on the screen in 1911, the figure of Elizabeth has fascinated film-makers. At times of national danger, such as the 1930s and 1940s when the rise of fascism and the outbreak of war threatened the very survival of Britain, Elizabeth as played by Athene Seyler in *Drake of England* (1935) and by Flora Robson in *Fire Over England* (1936) (Fig. 9.3) and *The Sea Hawk* (1940), was invoked as the spirit of English resistance to foreign aggression. But she has more often been depicted in films which show

---

[21] Bette Davis played Elizabeth I in *The Private Lives of Elizabeth and Essex* in 1939 and *The Virgin Queen* in 1955; Charles Laughton played Henry VIII in *The Private Life of Henry VIII* in 1933 and *Young Bess* in 1953; Anna Neagle played Queen Victoria in *Victoria the Great* and *Sixty Glorious Years* in 1937–8, and in *Lilacs in the Spring* in 1954. Similarly Peter O'Toole played Henry II in both *Becket* (1964), and *The Lion in Winter* (1968), and George Sanders played Charles II in *Forever Amber* (1947) and *The King's Thief* (1955).

Figure 9.3. Flora Robson in *Fire Over England* (1936) – Elizabeth I as anti-fascist icon (United Artists. The Jeffrey Richards Collection).

her womanliness in conflict with her duty as queen. Time and again the cinema has returned to her unhappy love life. In *The Virgin Queen* (1923), *The Private Lives of Elizabeth and Essex* (1939), *Young Bess* (1953) and *The Virgin Queen* (1955), Elizabeth (played by Lady Diana Manners in 1923, Bette Davis in 1939, Jean Simmons in 1953, Bette Davis again in 1955) falls in love with a handsome young aristocrat (Lord Robert Dudley, the Earl of Essex, Lord Thomas Seymour, Sir Walter Raleigh) but each time sacrifices her love as a woman to her duty as Queen. Elizabeth says in *Elizabeth and Essex*: 'The necessities of a Queen transcend the necessities of a woman . . . England – that is my greatest and most enduring love'. All the Elizabeth films contain similar speeches.

The implicit assumption behind all these films is that being king or queen does not make you happy, and you should leave the job to those who have been trained to do it. The setting of the films further distances the ordinary spectator from the action. Most royal films take place almost entirely within castles, palaces and country houses. This emphasizes the fact that whatever personal traumas the royal personages are undergoing, they remain above and beyond ordinary men and women. They are a race apart, special beings impersonated by the gods and goddesses of

Figure 9.4. Ronald Colman and Madeleine Carroll in *The Prisoner of Zenda* (1937) – its production inspired by the abdication crisis (United Artists. The Jeffrey Richards Collection).

Hollywood, whose lives and loves we the lesser mortals are privileged to glimpse. So humanization and personalization take place, but within a framework which reinforces the elevated status of the monarchy.

Although the cinema in its heyday was not permitted to depict living royals, it was not above making coded comments on royal events in the public mind. It is hard not to see *Victoria the Great* and *Sixty Glorious Years* as reaffirmations of a life of royal service, after King Edward VIII abandoned the throne. Similarly David O. Selznick's production of *The Prisoner of Zenda* (1937), made in Hollywood with a largely British cast (Fig. 9.4), was inspired in part by the publicity surrounding the Abdication crisis. It gave Hollywood's traditional answer to the dilemma, the putting of duty before personal inclination.[22] Englishman Rudolf Rassendyll (Ronald Colman) impersonates the kidnapped Ruritanian King Rudolf V to ensure the success of his coronation. But he falls in

[22] David O. Selznick, the producer of *Zenda*, declared in a speech given in 1937 that the subject of the film had 'become a topical problem as a result of the Windsor case': R. Behlmer (ed.), *Memo from David O. Selznick* (London, 1972), p. 110.

love with the King's fiancée, Princess Flavia. They briefly toy with the idea of going away together. But the call of duty is too strong. Unlike Edward VIII, Rassendyll gives up the woman he loves. He rescues the King, parts sadly from the Princess and retires to England, having ensured the survival of the royal house of Elphberg.

In 1953 the charming romantic fable *Roman Holiday* was released. In it, beautiful young Princess Ann (Audrey Hepburn) from an unnamed European country is paying a state visit to Italy. Weighed down by her official duties, she goes missing and explores Rome incognito. An American reporter, Joe Bradley (Gregory Peck), spots her and scenting a story, shows her the town. But they fall in love. After a brief idyll, she decides that she must return to her duties and her country. They part sadly but she has a newfound confidence and maturity as a result of the experience. The film appeared at a time when the gossip columns had been dominated by rumours of a romance between Princess Margaret and the dashing divorcé Group Captain Peter Townsend. Two years after the film came out, Princess Margaret made the same decision as Princess Ann.

While they may not have depicted living royals, the film industry regularly stressed the link between ordinary people and the Crown. In the 1944 hit film *This Happy Breed*, the Gibbons family filed reverently past the coffin of King George V at his lying-in-state. In *Here Come the Huggetts* (1948), the archetypal working-class family set out to watch the wedding procession of Princess Elizabeth and Prince Philip, describing it as 'a family affair of the nation'. *It's a Great Day* (1955), featuring another archetypal family, television's Grove family, centred on the selection of the Groves to receive a visit from Princess Margaret, whose arrival formed the climax of the film. *John and Julie* (1955) told the story of two six-year-olds who run away to see the coronation and are helped in their endeavour by a cross-section of the population.

The Princess Diana affair, which led to much rash talk of the imminent end of the monarchy, has in cinematic terms, strengthened it. Diana's story was from the first transmitted in pure Hollywood terms.[23] In 1982, rival American television networks produced all-star rose-tinted versions of the romance of Charles and Diana culminating in the fairy-tale wedding and the balcony kiss: *The Royal Romance of Charles and Diana* and *Charles and Diana: a Royal Love Story*. The marriage break-up inspired the three-hour television film *Diana: Her True Story* (1993), based on Andrew Morton's book. This was almost a re-run of the 1948 film *Saraband for Dead Lovers* with a beautiful, innocent and romantic princess married off for reasons of state to the future King George I and thereafter ill-treated

---

[23] See J. Richards, 'The Hollywoodisation of Diana', in Richards, *Diana*, pp. 59–73.

by the cold and cruel Hanoverian royal family, the moral of *Diana* being the one enunciated by Electress Sophia in *Saraband*: 'Royalty may not look for happiness such as others may find.'

The recent travails of the royal family sparked off a new cycle of historical royal films but amazingly they all conformed to the well-established templates. *Elizabeth* (1998), a vivid and gripping political thriller charting the intrigues swirling round the young Queen Elizabeth I, also focused on her sacrifice of personal happiness with Lord Robert Dudley and her decision to remain the Virgin Queen ('I am married to England'). *Mrs Brown* (1997) was the latest 'unhappy friendship of a monarch' film sympathetically exploring the relationship of the lonely and bereaved Queen Victoria and her highland servant, John Brown, the very subject which the censors had vetoed in the 1930s. *The Madness of King George* (1995) written by Alan Bennett, recounted the humiliating medical treatment of the deranged George III and the intrigues of his son to assume the Regency. It was impossible not to sympathize with the fundamentally decent and well-meaning King (Nigel Hawthorne) and to rejoice at his final restoration to health. In every case, the themes are the loneliness of power, the conflicting demands of duty and personal inclination, the natural unhappiness of princes, exactly as they had been rehearsed in feature films since the birth of the medium.

If anything, these films had added strength as they conformed to two important cultural developments. One is the idea, imported from America, that everyone is a victim.[24] In these films, the monarchs are spectacular victims of conspiracy, betrayal, familial opposition and ill-treatment. The monarch-as-victim chimes with the culture of the talk shows, the confessional tabloid, the tell-it-all autobiography. It is reflected in the construction of Diana as a classic victim. But in the case of these three films, Elizabeth I, George III and Queen Victoria all rise above the pressures triumphantly to do their duty and serve the nation, confirming that they are remarkable individuals.

III

The other recent cultural development has been the transformation of public events into soap opera. As modern life has become steadily more privatized, and as for many people the insulated world of the private car, the owner-occupied house and the television have superseded the once dominant communal experiences of public transport, the cinema and the street, soap opera has come to replace real life as a source of gossip,

---

[24] R. Hughes, *The Culture of Complaint* (New York, 1993).

attitudes and role models. The 'soaps' which are Britain's favourite television viewing, and American-influenced talk shows in which people parade their problems and bare their souls before openly partisan audiences, have conditioned the public's reaction to the trials and tribulations of others, both real and fictional. Some people seem unable to distinguish between the two. The Louise Woodward and O. J. Simpson court cases are perfect examples of this new phenomenon of real-life events which are treated, viewed and consumed as soap operas.

The British Royal Family has become a supreme example of the participatory soap. Because through the media the public has shared the ups and downs, the joys and sorrows of this family, has taken sides and passed judgement as they would on characters in *Eastenders*, or *The Archers*, they feel that they know them personally. The sociologist Michael Billig discovered in his research into current attitudes to the royal family that people familiarly refer to its members as Charles, Di, Philip, Fergie, Andy and the Queen Mum, as if they were characters in a long-running soap, though significantly the Queen was always referred to as the Queen.[25] Princess Diana was the undoubted star of this supersoap. Her eating disorders, suicide attempts, the broken marriage, the unhappy love affairs that ensued were all followed with the same eagerness and fascination with which earlier generations of soap fans had followed the fictional careers of Meg Richardson and Elsie Tanner. Her life inspired no fewer than four television films, in which all the members of the royal family were impersonated by actors. So television has merely continued the cinematic practice of mythologizing and humanizing royalty and has already extended it to include the current royal family along with its predecessors, which it continues to celebrate in such popular all-star costume drama series as *Edward VII* (1973–4), *Edward and Mrs Simpson* (1978), *Victoria and Albert* (2001), *Bertie and Elizabeth* (2002), *The Lost Prince* (2003, the story of the epileptic youngest son of King George V and Queen Mary, Prince John), and *Wallis and Edward* (2006).

Far from undermining the monarchy, the mass media have helped to perpetuate and transform the institution by the twin-track approach which has on the one hand preserved a positive image in newsreels and documentaries of the royals assiduously performing their public duties and on the other hand mythologised and humanised them in dramatised soap-opera accounts of past and present royal families which permit identification and sympathy with them as human beings albeit as special human beings.

[25] M. Billig, *Talking About the Royal Family* (London, 1992).

10 'A jealous hatred': royal popularity and social inequality

Andrzej Olechnowicz

Why over the last 130 years have a majority of British people who were neither wealthy, nor privileged, nor leisured identified with and enthusiastically supported a monarchy which appears to be all three? In 1934, H. G. Wells recollected his youthful hostility towards the Royal Family who possessed what his own family lacked:

I conceived a jealous hatred for the abundant clothing, the magnificent housing and all the freedoms of her [Queen Victoria's] children and still more intensely of my contemporaries, her grandchildren.[1]

The monarchist Geoffrey Dennis considered that Wells's statement 'was no doubt the desirable reaction for a free-born man, and the natural reaction for an assertive one'.[2] And yet this 'natural' reaction has been the response of very few.

Socialists have argued that the monarchy has been the beneficiary of a generally unequal society, and actively promotes it. In the 1930s, Frank Hardie wrote that 'the Monarchy in its present form will last as long as inequality . . . last[s], and not very much longer',[3] and Harold Laski that 'the whole impact of the Crown and the social system it necessitates is to preserve that temper of inequality it is the purpose of a Labour Party to deny'.[4] Socialists have, however, avoided considering exactly why conditions of social inequality produce popular monarchy.

There is a powerful heterodox voice on the left: Tom Nairn. He argues that the monarchy's identification with a particular class and its expense do not matter to the mass of subjects, because 'both the genesis of the contemporary monarchy and its apparently unstoppable popularity are quite clearly phenomena of *national* rather than merely social significance'.[5]

---

[1] H.G. Wells, *Experiment in Autobiography* (Boston, 1962 edn.), p. 28.

[2] G. Dennis, *Coronation Commentary* (London, 1937), p. 131.

[3] F. Hardie, Review of K. Martin, *The Magic of Monarchy*, *Political Quarterly* 8 (1937), 460.

[4] H. J. Laski, *Democracy in Crisis* (London, 1933), p. 117.

[5] T. Nairn, 'Britain's royal romance', in R. Samuel (ed.), *Patriotism, Vol. III* (London, 1989), p. 76; Nairn, *The Enchanted Glass* (London, 1994), pp. 127, 183, 231.

The problem with this account is that the British people are troubled by the monarchy's social character and its expense, and do not see their national identity in obsessively 'regal-popular' terms.[6] Nairn's distinctive emphasis on the nation is the very thing which makes this incomprehensible.

There are other, non-leftist arguments for the view that the British people have been unconcerned about social inequality and their place in a class system. David Cannadine has argued that the hierarchical view of society as a 'seamless web' had the 'widest, most powerful and most abiding appeal' in modern Britain.[7] An alternative argument maintains that in contemporary society privatized life-styles, individualized home- and family-centred social identities and a common culture of consumption have left people with little sense of collective identities or the real extent of inequality.[8] A different approach in effect dispenses with the possibility of viable collective identities being formed by emphasizing the postmodern self as possessing fragmented, multiple identities, with a stable 'self-identity' being 'routinely created and sustained in the reflexive activities of the individual', which enable a particular biographical narrative to be kept going.[9]

The study of social class in modern Britain by Gordon Marshall and his colleagues showed that these positions lack empirical foundations. It found that in the 1980s, 'class is still the most common source of social identity and retains its salience as such'. Sixty per cent of their sample claimed that they thought of themselves as belonging to a particular social class, understood as an occupational, income or status grouping. Moreover, three-quarters stated that birth determined class membership. Seventy per cent thought the distribution of income and wealth was unfair, and over 80 per cent wanted to redistribute wealth to those at the bottom. Moreover, 'only a small minority (some 16 per cent or so) . . . could be identified as existential fatalists, at least as far as issues of redistributive justice were concerned, in that they judged these simply to be beyond human volition'. So the great majority of people were aware of inequality, considered it unfair, and thought something could be done about it if governments had the political will to do so. However, their general perspective was an 'informed fatalism', for although people were often aware of alternatives, 'they are, on the whole, resigned to the fact that they can

---

[6] See below, pp. 300–1.

[7] D. Cannadine, *Class in Britain* (New Haven, 1998), pp. 19, 22, 155–7, 186.

[8] Summarized in G. Marshall, H. Newby, D. Rose and C. Vogler, *Social Class in Modern Britain* (London, 1988), pp. 8–11.

[9] A. Giddens, *Modernity and Self-Identity* (Cambridge, 1991), pp. 52, 54; C. Barker, *Cultural Studies* (London, 2000), pp. 166–70.

do little or nothing to help achieve these'. Perhaps for this reason there was 'little ideological consistency in the British population as a whole', and little developed class consciousness which went beyond class identity and encompassed a radically different society. Finally, Marshall and his colleagues outlined how this pattern had characterized British workers since the mid-nineteenth century.[10] These empirical facts suggest that the possibility of an incongruity between resentment of social inequality and popular support for a privileged institution cannot be wished away.

Nor has the monarchy made light of this incongruity. True, royalty has sometimes resisted the courting of popularity. Victoria, for example, had personal and political reservations. She dreaded the eruption of 'hustle & bustle' during the Golden Jubilee.[11] Prince Philip had a more worldly objection: 'Safer not to be too popular. You can't fall too far'.[12] Monarchists and republicans alike have reflected on the fickleness and irrationality of royal popularity. The courtier Lord Esher noted in 1903 that 'like all popular favour, it is worth nothing and is blown away by the first breath of adverse breeze'.[13] Yet all knew what was at stake: the legitimacy of the kind of constitutional monarchy fashioned in Britain from the 1840s onwards depended on monarchs demonstrating that they commanded the approval of their subjects.[14] A major function of the court has always been to devise ways of securing that approval, and politicians of all parties have assisted in bolstering royal popularity. As Elizabeth II acknowledged at the start of her reign, the monarchy 'could easily stand as an archaic and meaningless survival' unless it 'received visible and audible proof that it is living in the hearts of the people'.[15] Her eldest son

---

[10] Marshall, *Social Class*, pp. 143–8, 157–8, 190, 202–6. The extent of social mobility before 1945, as well as after, is a matter of debate: see e.g. M. Savage and A. Miles, *The Remaking of the British Working Class, 1840–1940* (London, 1994), pp. 32–8; A. Miles and D. Vincent, 'A land of "boundless opportunity"?: mobility and stability in nineteenth-century England', in S. Dex (ed.), *Life and Work History Analyses* (London, 1991), pp. 43–72; D. Baines and P. Johnson, 'In search of the "traditional" working class: social mobility and occupational continuity in interwar London', *Economic History Review* 52 (1999), 692–713. Nonetheless, the reality of a 'workers' caste' between the wars – 'a social group whose status is permanent and hereditary' – seems clear. On its defensive culture of consolation, G. Stedman Jones, 'Working-class culture and working-class politics', *Languages of Class* (Cambridge, 1983), pp. 179–238; R. McKibbin, *The Ideologies of Class* (Oxford, 1990), pp. 111–2.

[11] E. Longford, *Victoria R. I.* (London, 1966), p. 622.

[12] G. Brandreth, *Brief Encounters* (London, 2003), p. 116.

[13] *Journals and Letters of Reginald, Viscount Esher*, ed. M. V. Brett, vol. 2 (London, 1934), p. 7.

[14] J. Plunkett, *Queen Victoria: First Media Monarch* (Oxford, 2003), esp. pp. 14–7, 67 on 'royal populism'; A. Tyrrell and Y. Ward, '"God bless Her Little Majesty": the popularising of monarchy in the 1840s', *National Identities* 2 (2000), 109–24.

[15] E. Longford, *Elizabeth R* (London, 1984), p. 208.

too has said of the monarchy that 'if people don't want it, they won't have it'.[16]

Most recent historical writing has concentrated on documenting the 'production' of a popular monarchy through the media, fiction, visual images and material culture, and the technological, commercial and artistic developments which made this possible. In the case of national royal ceremonies, the papers of the courtiers, politicians and clergymen who organized them have been relied on. Yet the same attention has not been paid to the 'reception' of these productions by the people. John Plunkett acknowledged in his study of Victoria's 'media making' that the 'assimilation of the monarchy into individual subjectivities, as revealed through diaries and letters' had not been extensively examined.[17] It may be misleading to assume that the meanings of a royal ceremony for its audience were the same as for its creators, and that the social groups targeted were those that were reached.[18]

The purpose of this concluding chapter is to sketch the cognitive and affective structures which have underpinned the popularity of the Royal Family, and to speculate whether these structures can continue to operate. In assuming that popularity is a relatively stable phenomenon and a product of underlying structures of thoughts and emotions, the chapter rejects the alternative view, that popularity is a will-o'-the-wisp. The monarchy is popular not simply because of success in staging a series of national ceremonies, patronizing worthy charities and avoiding or removing unsuitable royals such as the Duke of Clarence, or Edward VIII.

The problem for the approach taken here is one of sources. By their nature, diaries and letters, as well as autobiographies, speeches, novels or newspaper comments, may be deliberately biased, or may be suggestive but 'unrepresentative'. Consider Carolyn Steedman's recollection:

My mother had wanted to marry a king. That was the best of my father's stories, told in the pub in the 1960s, of how difficult it had been to live with her in 1937, during the Abdication months. Mrs. Simpson was no prettier than her, no more clever than her, no better than her. It wasn't fair that a king should give up his throne for her, and not for the weaver's daughter. From a traditional Labour background, my mother rejected the politics of solidarity and communality, always voted Conservative, for the left could not embody her desire for things to be *really* fair, for a full skirt that took twenty yards of cloth, for a half-timbered cottage in the country, for the prince who did not come.[19]

[16] Quoted in R. Rose, *Politics in England* (London, 1985), p. 75.
[17] Plunkett, *First Media Monarch*, p. 8.
[18] D. M. Craig, 'The crowned republic?: monarchy and anti-monarchy in Britain, 1760–1901', *Historical Journal* 46 (2003), 171–2, 184.
[19] C. Steedman, *Landscape for a Good Woman* (London, 1986), pp. 46–7.

Social evaluations, social ambition, the understanding of 'fairness' – each is striking here; but how representative or idiosyncratic is this? The problem of the 'representativeness' of opinions was evident on a larger canvas with Susan Williams's study of popular responses to the Abdication. Examining the thousands of letters and telegrams sent to Edward during the crisis by ordinary people, she found that 'overwhelmingly they offered loyal and heartfelt support to the King', and many accepted Wallis Simpson as a suitable wife since she was 'someone who had come from an ordinary family and had struggled as they had themselves'. She argued that they offered a 'unique window on to the attitudes and feelings of ordinary people', and endorsed the assessment of a former assistant private secretary to Edward that they contained a 'remarkable cross-section of public opinion'.[20] They certainly do the first; but how can we be sure they do the second? Baldwin also received hundreds of letters from people appalled that the King's elevation of personal happiness 'threatened to destroy respect for the Crown as a symbol of selfless duty'.[21]

There is no rule of thumb to decide how many diaries, autobiographies or letters must be consulted before any patterns of thoughts and emotions that occur can be plausibly presented as widely shared. Of necessity these sources must be used where there is nothing else; but this chapter will attach greater weight to three sources which set out to gauge 'public opinion' – opinion polls, Mass-Observation surveys for the coronation in 1937 and beyond, and the interviews in Michael Billig's book, *Talking of the Royal Family*.[22]

The chapter is divided into two main sections. The first considers the course of royal popularity over the last 130 years, finding increased evidence of criticism but also considerable persistence of support. The second section advances an explanation which starts from the assumption that how people have reconciled themselves to living with social inequality has been central to the riddle of royal popularity. Social inequality denies most people the opportunities that some people enjoy, and forces them to behave in ways and to endure lives they would not freely choose. Moreover, the ubiquity of the Royal Family in everyday life – a result of persistent media interest – as well as on grand ceremonial occasions, has meant that people cannot but compare their own lives with theirs. Ordinary people have found a compensation for the restrictions on their own freedom to choose as dictated by their class position in the apparent fact

---

[20] S. Williams, *The People's King* (London, 2003), pp. xviii–xix.

[21] P. Williamson, *Stanley Baldwin* (Cambridge, 1999), p. 327.

[22] H. Jennings and C. Madge (eds.), *May the Twelfth* (London, 1937); L. Harris, *Long to Reign Over Us?* (London, 1966); P. Ziegler, *Crown and People* (London, 1978); M. Billig, *Talking of the Royal Family* (London, 1992).

that the most privileged family in the land have also not been free to do as they will, because of rigid court protocol, elaborately rule-governed grand ceremonies and routine visits, and the relentless demands of royal 'duty' and 'service'. People have a compelling psychological need to think and feel that in an unequal society money does not buy freedom and happiness,[23] and that those without money can be freer and happier than those with it, and the public face of royal life allows them to do just that. In short, ordinary people have supported the Royal Family because they have been able to sympathize with it.

This chapter takes issue with the recent trend of dismissing psychological or sociological models as 'rather crude and elitist'.[24] All models are of necessity reductionist to some degree; but that does not automatically mean they can have little explanatory value. At the very least, the psychological model outlined here points to why what the monarchy has projected has resonated with ordinary people, and therefore addresses the much neglected problem of the reception of royal messages.

I

It is helpful first to distinguish between three distinct phenomena: recognition, interest and popularity. Recognition of the Royal Family has been consistently high.[25] As for interest, there have often been fears in royal circles, which always proved to be groundless, that some major celebrations would not attract enough support.[26] Interest – until very recently perhaps[27] – appears to have been consistently very great among all types of people. Evelyn Waugh, for instance, recorded in his diary for December 1936: 'The Simpson crisis has been a great delight to everyone'.[28] In the

---

[23] This is wishful thinking for two reasons. First, there is strong empirical evidence for the view that money does bring happiness. The economist Andrew Oswald's ten-year Warwick study measuring how happy 9,000 individuals became after winning or inheriting large amounts of money 'found a strong link between the influx of money and an improvement in the average person's happiness and psychological health': *Guardian*, 9, 12 Jan. 2002. Second, there is a compelling theoretical argument that 'lack of money *is* (a form of) lack of freedom, in the favoured sense of freedom, where it is taken to be absence of interference': G. A. Cohen, 'Back to socialist basics', *New Left Review* 207 (1994), 15–6.

[24] Craig, 'Crowned republic?', 184.

[25] See e.g. R. Rose and D. Kavanagh, 'The monarchy in contemporary political culture', in R. Rose (ed.), *Studies in British Politics* (London, 1976), pp. 19–20; Billig, *Talking*, p. 146.

[26] The Coronation in 1953, the Silver Jubilee in 1977 and the Golden Jubilee in 2002 all prompted such fears: see Ziegler, *Crown and People*, pp. 98, 192–3, 104; P. Brendon and P. Whitehead, *The Windsors* (London, 1994), pp. 190–1; *Observer*, 29 Jul. 2001, 17 Feb. 2002; *Guardian*, 24 Jan. 2001.

[27] See below, p. 620, for opinion poll evidence.

[28] *The Diaries of Evelyn Waugh*, ed. M. Davie (London, 1976), p. 415.

year ending October 1996, seven per cent of the coverage in national and regional daily newspapers was devoted to the Royal Family, surpassed only by the economy, crime, and fashion and beauty.[29] Princess Diana was – and to a surprising extent still is – the greatest royal draw.[30]

When it comes to popularity, there has been a tendency to exaggerate. José Harris stated that 'the British monarchy, which had spent much of the 1930s in a state of squalid crisis, was by 1945 probably more universally popular than at any previous moment in its history of nearly a thousand years'.[31] Nairn wrote in 1994 that over the previous fifty years the monarchy had enjoyed 'permanent and almost unshakeable adoration quite divorced from profit-and-loss accounts'.[32] The right-wing monarchist Ferdinand Mount accepted Nairn's term 'enchantment' to describe the unique nature of the monarchy's appeal.[33] A problem with such hyperbole was that by the early 1990s the permanent, intense adoration had vanished. Nairn was left struggling to justify his view that the end of the 'near-universal romance' simply 'came incredibly quickly', at the time of the Windsor Castle fire in 1992.[34] Moreover, most other European monarchies enjoy comparable or even greater levels of support.[35]

Since the last quarter of the nineteenth century the British monarchy has been a 'most stable and enduring institution', with high overall levels of support by almost any criterion.[36] But there are two important qualifications. Firstly, there have been fluctuations in support, and it is instructive to note when these occurred. Secondly, age, gender, class and region have probably always accounted for marked variations in support, with age responsible for the 'most pronounced differences in view' at the present time.[37] The fluctuations in support for the monarchy in the 1990s were undoubtedly extreme and dangerous, but not unprecedented or terminal.

The absence of regular royal opinion polls until after the Second World War means that imperfect sources have to be used for earlier periods; but even opinion polls present difficulties because of a tendency to ask different questions at different times. Since the early nineteenth century,

---

[29] *Guardian*, 11 Dec. 1996.   [30] *Guardian*, 8 Aug. 1997, 22 Oct. 1997, 14 Feb. 1998.

[31] J. Harris, 'War and social history: Britain and the home front during the Second World War', *Contemporary European History* 1 (1992), 25.

[32] Nairn, *Enchanted Glass*, pp. 19–20.

[33] F. Mount, *The British Constitution Now* (London, 1992) p. 102.

[34] T. Nairn, 'Death of a great British romance', *Observer*, 3 July 1994.

[35] Around 2002, 66 per cent of Swedes, 80 per cent of the Dutch and 90 per cent of Danes supported their monarchies: Fabian Society, *The Future of the Monarchy* (London, 2003), p. 19.

[36] B. Jessop, *Traditionalism, Conservatism and British Political Culture* (London, 1974), pp. 87–8; Fabian Society, *Future of the Monarchy*, pp. 18–19.

[37] Ibid., p. 22.

the 'large crowds in attendance at royal occasions were turned into a confirmation of the strength of support enjoyed by the monarchy'.[38] Yet emphasizing the vastness of crowds can be misleading. Reports of their size and mood are often inaccurate, sometimes deliberately so. In his study of the blitz, Tom Harrisson considered a royal visit to Southampton on 5 December 1940. A local historian recorded in 1951 that the royal party had been received with 'fervent demonstrations of love, loyalty, and enthusiasm', and that 'excited multitudes lined the wintry streets'. Yet Mass-Observation's contemporary account stated that the visit had been poorly handled, much of the route had been unlined, and the royal party had passed almost unnoticed.[39]

Moreover, many journalists and writers assume something like Le Bon's 'law of the mental unity of crowds'. They expect that all members of a crowd will look up to a prestigious figure, and 'being only capable of thinking in images are only to be impressed by images', of the kind produced by grand royal ceremonies.[40] Jack London, for instance, described a coronation crowd in 1902 in these terms:

And now the Horse Guards, a glimpse of beautiful cream ponies, and a golden panoply, a hurricane of cheers, and crashing of bands – 'The King! the King! God Save the King!' Everybody has gone mad. The contagion is sweeping me off my feet – I, too, want to shout, 'The King! God Save the King!'[41]

But in reality there is no 'mental unity' in a crowd; individual personalities and expectations remain intact.

With these qualifications in mind, the existing literature suggests that from the late nineteenth century to the end of the Second World War, the monarchy enjoyed overwhelming popularity in all classes; and that while never more than a tiny minority were publicly critical, private expressions of hostility were perhaps at their greatest during the two world wars. This can be no more than impressionistic, and it is futile even to try to gauge the intensity of people's attachment, reaching from 'unshakeable adoration' to polite, indifferent toleration.

The seclusion of Queen Victoria after 1861 elicited a good deal of sympathy;[42] and the republican criticism it provoked, though unpleasant, was manageable for two main reasons. Firstly, much of the criticism focused on the narrow terrain of royal cost, which could be answered

---

[38] Plunkett, *First Media Monarch*, p. 17.
[39] T. Harrisson, *Living through the Blitz* (London, 1976), pp. 163–4.
[40] G. Le Bon, *The Crowd* (London, 1895; 1977), pp. 55, 68, 130.
[41] J. London, *The People of the Abyss* (New York and London, 1903), p. 148.
[42] J. Wolffe, *Great Deaths* (Oxford, 2000), pp. 194–206; R. Williams, *The Contentious Crown* (Aldershot, 1997), pp. 204, 215.

by disputing figures;[43] and secondly, the idea that Britain had an exemplary constitutional monarchy under which any desirable reforms could be achieved was well established among the public.[44] The day of national thanksgiving in 1872 for the recovery of the Prince of Wales from typhoid was a carefully orchestrated opportunity to demonstrate public support for the monarchy;[45] but no amount of orchestration could have created the sense of public relief and gratitude.[46] By the time of the Diamond Jubilee in June 1897, Victoria was probably justified in writing that 'no one ever, I believe, has met with such an ovation as was given to me . . . every face seemed to be filled with real joy'.[47] The American commentator on British government, A. L. Lowell, wrote of the monarchy in 1908 that there was 'no doubt of its universal popularity . . . there is no republican sentiment left today in parliament or the country'.[48] Edward VII's reign was crucial in reviving, elaborating and meticulously executing royal ceremonies and he realized fully, in a way that Victoria never had, that established institutions had to court popularity.[49]

At the start of George V's reign, a marked increase in political and industrial conflict presented 'by a long distance the most testing constitutional experience for a British monarch since the early days of the reign of George III'; but crucially the public perception of royal neutrality was maintained.[50] The First World War was both an opportunity and a danger for the monarchy. It increased the chances of ordinary people outside London seeing their Royal Family in the flesh as they visited hospitals, shipyards and munitions factories;[51] but it also saw criticism of the 'kingly caste of Germans' on the British throne, and the king receiving regular reports on the extent of republican sympathy among the working class. The royal refusal of asylum for the Russian imperial family, the adoption of the name Windsor and the creation of the Order of the British Empire in 1917 were all royal initiatives to retain popularity.[52] Even so, Lord

---

[43] See e.g. J. Charles Cox, *The Cost of the Royal Household* (Derby, 1871).

[44] Williams, *Contentious Crown*, pp. 48–9, 116–23.

[45] W. M. Kuhn, 'Ceremony and politics: the British monarchy, 1871–1872', *Journal of British Studies* 26 (1987), 137, 150–60.

[46] For a good example, see F. Kilvert, *Kilvert's Diary, 1870–79*, ed. W. Plomer (London, 1944), pp. 156, 158.

[47] E. Longford, *Victoria R. I.* (London, 1964), p. 688.

[48] A. L. Lowell, *The Government of England* (New York, 1908), vol. 1, pp. 51–2.

[49] D. Cannadine, 'The context, performance and meaning of ritual: the British monarchy and the "invention of tradition", c. 1820–1977', in E. Hobsbawm and T. Ranger (eds.), *The Invention of Tradition* (Cambridge, 1983), p. 136; S. Lee, *King Edward VII* (London, 1927), vol. 2, pp. 20–2.

[50] H. C. G. Matthew, 'George V', *Oxford Dictionary of National Biography* (online edition).

[51] K. Rose, *King George V* (London, 1983), p. 179.

[52] F. Prochaska, 'George V and republicanism, 1917–19', *Twentieth Century British History* 10 (1999), 32–9, 42; Rose, *George V*, pp. 170–5, 208–18.

Cromer noted that 'the position of the Monarchy is not so stable now, in 1918, as it was at the beginning of the War'.[53] Victory celebrations reinvigorated popular enthusiasm for the monarchy,[54] and John Buchan felt that monarchism was now 'the willing creed of all':

Its most impressive manifestation was not the crowds around Buckingham Palace . . . but what happened on the late afternoon of Armistice Day. In the wet November dusk the King and Queen drove in a simple open carriage through the city of London, almost unattended and wholly unheralded. The merrymakers left their own occupations to cheer, and crowds accompanied the carriage through the newly-lighted streets, running beside it and shouting friendly greetings. It was an incident which interpreted better than any formula the meaning of a People's King.[55]

The remainder of George V's reign consolidated a style of royal discourse and behaviour to which George VI and Elizabeth II continued to adhere – 'democratic', constitutional, ceremonial, religious, dutiful, familial, reserved, compassionate, philanthropic, national and imperial. The Silver Jubilee in May 1935 displayed this amalgam.[56] The republican Kingsley Martin even wondered whether George V's immense popularity during the jubilee, and the universal sense of loss following his death in January 1936, did not owe something to his having come to be seen as the 'father' of his people.[57]

The course of public opinion during the Abdication crisis is difficult to chart.[58] One of Edward VIII's supporters, Compton Mackenzie, contrasted the London crowds singing 'God Save the King' with provincial disapproval of the king wanting to marry another man's wife.[59] Ziegler judges that the government had more support than the king, and regards the critical moment as the weekend of 5–6 December 1936, when MPs gained the strong impression that the country was shocked that the king was placing 'his affection for a second-rate woman' above his royal duty.[60] George VI's reign started uncertainly with the ill-at-ease new monarch facing the task of restoring public 'faith in the Royal Family's dedication to duty'.[61] It was not until after the coronation in May 1937 that popular support was secure amid an 'ever-evolving fantasy' of an ideal Royal

[53] T. Aronson, *Royal Family* (London, 1983), p. 83; Prochaska, 'George V', 50.
[54] B. Waites, *A Class Society at War* (Leamington Spa, 1987), pp. 234–5.
[55] J. Buchan, *The King's Grace, 1910–35* (London, 1935), p. 240.
[56] *His Majesty's Speeches: The Record of the Silver Jubilee* (London, 1935), pp. 12, 21–2, 37, 50.
[57] K. Martin, 'Public opinion and the coronation', *Political Quarterly* 8 (1937), 434.
[58] F. Donaldson, *Edward VIII* (London, 1976), pp. 276–7; P. Ziegler, *King Edward VIII* (London, 1991), pp. 319–23.
[59] C. Mackenzie, *The Windsor Tapestry* (London, 1938), p. 481.
[60] Ziegler, *Edward VIII*, p. 321.   [61] B. Pimlott, *The Queen* (London, 1996), p. 40.

Table 10.1 *Percentage of Mass-Observation diarists listening to George VI's wartime broadcasts.*

Broadcast, 3 Sep. 1939	20.7
Christmas Day 1939	22.7
Empire Day 1940	14.5
Christmas Day 1940	12
Christmas Day 1941	9.3
Christmas Day 1942	16
Christmas Day 1943	9
Christmas Day 1944	8

Source: Ziegler, *Crown and People*, p. 70.

Family (although Mass-Observation noted some continuing affection for the Duke of Windsor).[62]

The Second World War appears like the First to have provoked some hostility; but this now centred on the social privilege of the Royal Family. Despite the propaganda focus on them as the 'family of families',[63] a Kensington housewife told Mass-Observation:

It's all very well for them traipsing around saying how their hearts bleed for us and they share all our sufferings, and then going home to a roaring fire in one of their six houses.[64]

Harold Nicolson noted in late 1940 that 'everybody is worried about the feeling in the East End . . . It is said that even the King and Queen were booed the other day when they visited the destroyed areas.'[65] Even if this degree of resentment was limited, there is evidence of what Ziegler termed 'swelling indifference': as one middle-aged working-class woman said, 'I think it's all a bit silly – kings and queens in wartime. I don't think they're wanted'.[66] Though Mass-Observation diarists were probably more sceptical about the monarchy than the rest of the population, the number who listened to George VI's broadcasts was strikingly low, especially since nearly all of them listened to Churchill's broadcasts (Table 10.1).

The monarchy was once again the popular focus of victory celebrations at the end of the war, and grief for a man who had 'sacrificed practically everything for his country' was a common reaction to George VI's death

[62] Ibid., 40–55; Ziegler, *Crown and People*, pp. 39, 68; Jennings and Madge, *May the Twelfth*, p. 287.

[63] Pimlott, *The Queen*, pp. 58–61.   [64] Ziegler, *Crown and People*, pp. 72–4.

[65] H. Nicolson, *Diaries and Letters, 1939–45*, ed. N. Nicolson (London, 1967), p. 114.

[66] Ziegler, *Crown and People*, p. 72.

in 1952.[67] Interviewed half a century later, Prince Philip recalled the extraordinary 'level of adulation' in the first years of Elizabeth II's reign,[68] though in the 1950s Richard Hoggart detected a contrast between 'the fervours of London crowds on special occasions', and the provinces where the working man was 'either quite uninterested in Royalty or vaguely hostile'.[69] Even so, the level of support for the monarchy was 'high by almost any criterion' in all classes in the early 1970s, with between 80 and 90 per cent of the population believing that Britain needed the Royal Family.[70] Age differences accounted for the greatest variation in support; but these were 'a source of variation around a very high average' with 59 per cent of the 18–24 year olds in a 1969 poll agreeing that the Queen was 'a symbol of Britain at its best'.[71] Surveys also find that around 30 per cent in the 1950s and 1960s believed that the Queen was specially chosen by God.[72] Above all, the cult of an idealized Royal Family intensified to such an extent that the editor of The Times opposed Princess Margaret's proposed marriage to Peter Townsend in 1955 on the grounds that it would tarnish the model family.[73] Pimlott argues that there was a shift away from such idealization round about 1977 with stories about Princess Margaret and Roddy Llewellyn.[74] If so, it soon shifted back as the family life of the Prince and Princess of Wales was idealized between their marriage in 1981, and newspaper stories about their marital problems in 1985.[75]

Opinion polls indicate that into the 1980s and early 1990s support for a British republic generally remained low (Table 10.2); and more people consistently believed that Britain would be worse off without a Royal Family (Table 10.3). A majority, including of young adults, believed that the monarchy was an important institution (Table 10.4).

Yet the evidence of these polls also points to a significant change occurring in the 1990s. Table 10.3 does not suggest that the fire in Windsor Castle in November 1992, and the £60 million from the taxpayer for its restoration, had on their own an immediate and disastrous impact.[76] Nonetheless, it coincided with the 'War of the Waleses' in the mid-1990s,

[67] Ibid., pp. 85–6.
[68] Brandreth, Brief Encounters, p. 116. See also Pimlott, The Queen, chs. 11–13; Rose and Kavanagh, 'Monarchy in contemporary political culture', p. 25.
[69] R. Hoggart, The Uses of Literacy (London, 1957; Harmondsworth, 1981), p. 111.
[70] Jessop, Traditionalism, pp. 87–8.
[71] J. G. Blumler, J. R. Brown, A. J. Ewbank and T. J. Nossiter, 'Attitudes to the monarchy: their structure and development during a ceremonial occasion', Political Studies 19 (1971), 170.
[72] Harris, Long to Reign, p. 43. [73] Pimlott, The Queen, p. 238. [74] Ibid., pp. 439–40.
[75] See e.g. L. Leete-Hodge, The Country Life Book of Diana, Princess of Wales (London, 1982); R. G. Martin, Charles and Diana (London, 1986), which still regarded the marriage as 'the greatest royal romance of our time'.
[76] Guardian, 10 Jan. 1995.

Table 10.2 *Support for a republic in Britain, 1953–2005.*

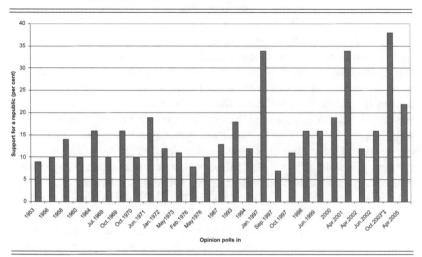

Opinion polls in

* Only adults aged 18–24 were interviewed.
‡ The question was: 'When the Queen dies, do you think that Prince Charles should inherit the throne or should the next head of state be elected instead?'
Sources: Ziegler, *Crown and People*, p. 127; Fabian Society, *Future of the Monarchy*, p. 19; *Sun*, 8 Jan. 1997, 18 Jun. 1999; *Guardian*, 14 Sep. 1997, 25, 28 Apr. 2001, 3 Jun. 2002, 10 Apr. 2005; *Daily Telegraph*, 11 Oct. 1997; royalty poll, Oct. 2003, www.icmresearch.co.uk/reviews.

and the combination proved very damaging for the viability of the monar-chy (Table 10.5). When asked in 1995 whether Britain would still have a monarchy in fifty years, 49 per cent said no against 32 per cent yes, which represented 'the lowest point in the reputation of the Windsors since the abdication of Edward VIII in 1936'.[77]

The death of Princess Diana in August 1997 took that reputation lower still: a month after her funeral, 71 per cent thought the monarchy would not exist in fifty years' time. For the republican *Observer*, the mourn-ers in the Mall denoted a nation united against tradition, and a 'floral revolution' which would leave the nation redefined.[78] This wishful think-ing was very wide of the mark. Firstly, the mourners laying floral trib-utes who strongly disapproved of the Queen and Prince Charles were representative not of the population as a whole but of 'middle Britain' (Table 10.6).[79]

[77] Ibid., 9 Jan. 1995.   [78] *Observer*, 7 Sep. 1997.
[79] Ibid. See also J. Thomas, *Diana's Mourning* (Cardiff, 2002).

Table 10.3 *Would we be better off or worse off without a royal family?,*
1968–2005.

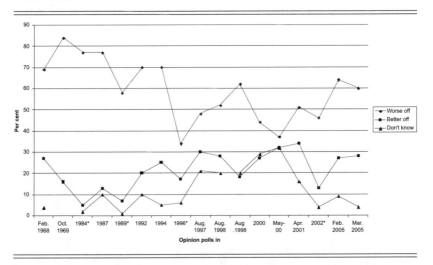

Sources: Rose and Kavanagh, 'Monarchy in contemporary political culture', p. 21;
Guardian, 12 Aug. 1997, 15 Aug. 1998, 12 Jun. 2000, 25, 28 Apr. 2001; Fabian Society, *Future of the Monarchy*, p. 21; www.icmresearch.co.uk/reviews.

Secondly, the harshness of the tabloid headlines reflected a near universal feeling that national mourning could only be adequately expressed
through the Royal Family.[80]

The Windsor fire and the death of Princess Diana did have a decisive
impact on the type of monarchy that people favoured. In 1969, 85 per
cent wanted the monarchy to remain as it was; by the time of Diana's
funeral only 15 per cent did (Table 10.7).

A year later, however, the impact of Princess Diana's death was fading
and a large majority of people believed that the Royal Family had learned
from the public reaction to her death (Table 10.8).

But the idea that the Royal Family was out of touch with ordinary
people was still endorsed by 79 per cent in 1997, and 69 per cent in
1998.[81] This represented a striking change from the earlier years of the
reign, when a poll at the time of the Investiture in 1969 found that
51 per cent believed that the Royal Family mixed adequately with ordinary
people.[82]

---

[80] E.g. 'Your people are suffering. Speak to us ma'am', *Daily Mirror*, 4 Sep. 1997.
[81] *Observer*, 14 Sep. 1997; *Guardian*, 15 Aug. 1998.
[82] Blumler *et al.*, 'Attitudes to the monarchy', 154.

Table 10.4 *How important an institution do you think the monarchy is in Britain today? 1983–2003 (per cent).*

	Important	Not important	Don't know
1983	87	11	
1994	66	23	
1996	67	22	
Jun. 1997	66	27	7

	Very important	Quite important	Not very important	Not at all important	Don't know
1998	28	36		24	
2000	31	34		25	
May 2000*	8	39	33	14	5
2002	37	33	21		
Oct. 2003**		67			

* Only 16–24 year-olds were interviewed.
** Only adults aged 18–24 were interviewed.
Sources: Fabian Society, *Future of the Monarchy*, p. 21; *Sun*, 18 Jun. 1999; Prince William poll, May 2000, www.icmresearch.co.uk/reviews.

Table 10.5 *Looking to the future, do you think Britain will or will not have a monarchy? 1994–2005 (per cent).*

	In ten years			In fifty years			In 100 years		
	Yes	No	Don't know	Yes	No	Don't know	Yes	No	Don't know
1994					65				
1995				32	49				
Jan.1997					48				
Oct. 1997					71				
Aug. 1998					54				
May 2000	72	15	14	39	34	27	22	46	32
Oct. 2003*	66	26	8	50	40	10	39	50	12
Feb. 2005				59	34	7			
				58	37	5			

* Only adults aged 18–24 were interviewed.
Sources: *Guardian*, 9 Jan. 1995; 6 Jan. 1997; *Daily Telegraph*, 11 Oct. 1997; www. icmresearch.co.uk/reviews.

Table 10.6 *Mourners in the Mall, Sep. 1997 (per cent).*

SEX		Women			Men	
		80			20	
CLASS		Middle class			Working class	
		56			44	
ETHNICITY		White			Black and Asian communities	
		90			10	
AGE	Under 18	18–24	25–44		45–64	65+
	8	17	43		26	5
APPROVAL	8–10	6–7	4–5		1–3	Don't know
Queen	21	16	23		25	15
Charles	16	17	28		26	14

Source: *Observer*, 7 Sep. 1997.

Table 10.7 *What kind of monarchy should Britain have? 1969–2003 (per cent).*

	Stay pretty much as are now	Exist but more democratic and approachable	Abolished and non-executive president	Don't know
1969	85‡			
1992	51	31	13	
1994	29	54	12	6
1996	51	34	30	
Sep. 1997	15	71	11	2
Oct. 1997		81		
Apr. 2002	54	30	12	4
Oct. 2003*	46		38‡‡	

* Only adults aged 18–24 were interviewed.
‡ Monarchy should be allowed to continue, perhaps changing with times.
‡‡ When the Queen dies.
Sources: Jessop, *Traditionalism, Conservatism and British Political Culture*, p. 89; Fabian Society, *Future of the Monarchy*, p. 20; *Guardian*, 14 Sep. 1997; *Daily Telegraph*, 11 Oct. 1997; *Independent*, 9 Apr. 2002; royalty poll, Oct. 2003, www.icmresearch.co.uk/reviews.

Most significant was the fact that at the turn of the millennium, for the first time ever, fewer than half of respondents believed that Britain needed a Royal Family, while the 'don't knows' were between a fifth and a third. In the view of the *Guardian*, 'while the disenchantment of the last decade was fuelled by scandal, the current sentiment is something deeper – and surely more alarming for the palace: plain indifference'.[83]

[83] *Guardian*, 13 Jun. 2000.

Table 10.8 *The impact of the death of Diana, August 1998 (per cent).*

Do you still feel sorry over the death of Princess Diana?		
Yes	No	Don't know
67	31	2

Has the death of Diana affected the way you live your life today?

Yes	No	Don't know
8	91	1

Do you think members of the Royal Family feel more relaxed about doing their jobs now that Diana is not around?

Yes	No	Don't know
47	30	23

Do you think royals have learned from the public reaction to Diana's death?

Yes	No	Don't know
75	18	7

Do you think the death of Diana helped or harmed the standing of the Royal Family with ordinary people?

Helped	Harmed	Don't know
40	45	15

Do you think the Queen and the Royal Family are now more in touch with ordinary people?*

Yes	No	Don't know
35.3	62.4	2.3

Source: Royal poll, Aug. 1998, www.icmresearch.co.uk/reviews; * *News of the World*, 27 Sep. 1998.

Support for this view came from the age profile of royal support, for only among those aged 55 or over, did a majority believe that Britain would be worse off without a monarchy (Table 10.9).

The young by a decisive margin, and all adults by a substantial one, rejected the status of being 'royal subjects' rather than 'citizens' (Table 10.10).

There was also evidence of public dissatisfaction over the expense and extravagance of the monarchy and its poor performance (Table 10.11).

These developments coincided with persistent public dissatisfaction with Prince Charles. In the year following Princess Diana's death, support for Prince William succeeding the Queen varied from 51 to 73 per cent.[84] The decade before Prince Charles's marriage to Mrs Camilla Parker Bowles in April 2005 saw a large minority of over 40 per cent who did not want a remarried Prince of Wales to become king,

[84] Ibid., 7 Sep. 1997; *Daily Telegraph*, 11 Oct. 1997; royal poll, Aug. 1998, www.icmresearch.co.uk/reviews

Table 10.9 *Would we be better off or worse off without a Royal Family?: age breakdown, 1997 and 2000 (per cent).*

1997 age breakdown

	Total	18–24	25–34	35–64	65+
Worse off	48	34	46	49	56
Better off	30	36	29	30	27
Don't know	21	30	23	20	6

2000 age breakdown

	Total	18–24	25–34	35–44	45–54	55–64	65+
Worse off	44	24	33	39	49	55	58
Better off	27	40	30	27	22	24	22
Don't know	29	35	37	34	28	21	20

Source: *Guardian*, 12 Aug. 1997; 12 Jun. 2000.

Table 10.10 *Would you prefer to be royal subjects or citizens? 2000 (per cent).*

	Royal subjects	Citizens	Don't know
May 2000*	16	73	11
Dec. 2000	32	60	6

* Only 16–24 year-olds were interviewed.
Sources: Prince William poll, May 2000, www.icmresearch. co.uk/reviews; *Guardian*, 6 Dec. 2000.

and a large majority of between 70 and 76 per cent who did not want the new Duchess of Cornwall to be eventually recognised as queen.[85]

Yet poll evidence also indicates areas of persisting support, and the monarchy's ability to regain lost support. A poll in the aftermath of the Queen Mother's death in 2002 found that support for leaving the monarchy as it was had risen to 54 per cent, and suggested that the monarchy could continue to attract broadly-based support (Table 10.12).

Many or most young adults appeared as convinced by the conventional monarchist arguments in favour of the Royal Family in 2003 as people had been in 1969 (Table 10.13). Blumler's observation in 1971 that approval

[85] *Guardian*, 6 Mar. 1996, 12 Aug. 1997, 22 Aug. 2001; royal poll, Aug. 1998, Charles and Camilla marriage survey, Mar. 2005, www.icmresearch.co.uk/reviews.

Table 10.11 *Royal cost and performance, 1969–2003 (per cent).*

	Yes	No	Don't know
Do you think the Royal Family still get too much money from the public purse?			
1969	32	60	8
1972	48		
Sep. 1998	76.4	20.8	2.8
Oct. 2003*	68		
Do you think the Royal Family provide value for money?			
May 2000**	24	59	17
2001	10		
Oct. 2003*‡	44	54	2
Do you think the Royal Family need to be slimmed down?			
Sep. 1998	63.6	32	4.4
Oct. 2003*	73		
Feb. 2005	62	34	4
Do you think the Queen should cut down the number of royal servants?			
1969‡‡	55	32	13
Aug. 1998	54	29	17
Do you think the Queen should sell off some royal palaces?			
Aug. 1998	42	49	9
Do you think the Royal Family are hard working?			
2001	25		
Oct. 2003*	31		

* Only adults aged 18–24 were interviewed.
** Only 16–24 year-olds were interviewed.
‡ 'The royals are an expensive luxury Britain can no longer afford.'
‡‡ 'Is surrounded by too many hangers-on.'
Source: Blumler *et al.*, 'Attitudes to the monarchy', 154; Jessop, *Traditionalism, Conservatism and British Political Culture*, p. 89; *News of the World*, 27 Sep. 1998; *Guardian*, 29 May 2001; royal poll, Aug. 1998; Prince William poll, May 2000; royalty poll, Oct. 2003; Charles and Camilla marriage survey, Feb. 2005, www.icmresearch.co.uk/reviews.

of monarchy 'derived from almost all the available grounds of pro-royalist sentiment' remained very largely true.[86]

There appeared to have been a marked shift in the numbers who believed that the Royal Family set a moral example as compared to other public figures (Table 10.14).

But even here public attitudes were not clear-cut. When asked about the moral example set by individual royals, the respondents were far more favourable, with 69 per cent in 2003 believing that the Queen set a good

[86] Blumler *et al.*, 'Attitudes to the monarchy', 154.

Table 10.12 *Support for an unreformed monarchy by sex,*
age, class and geography, April 2002 (per cent).

	Left as it is now	Radically reformed	Abolished altogether	Don't know
TOTAL	54	30	12	4
SEX				
Male	55	26	14	4
Female	54	33	10	3
AGE				
15–24	58	20	14	8
25–34	47	36	14	3
35–44	49	36	12	3
45–54	48	36	12	4
55–64	61	25	10	2
65+	64	24	10	2
CLASS				
AB	50	35	13	2
C1	53	30	14	3
DE	60	23	10	6
GEOGRAPHY				
Scotland	48		21	
Wales	62		9	
East Anglia	65			

Source: *Independent*, 9 Apr. 2002.

Table 10.13 *What does the Royal Family achieve for Britain?*
1969 and 2003

Which, if any of the following, do you think the Royal Family achieves
for Britain? (per cent)

	1969			2003*
	Agree	Disagree	Don't know	Agree
Boost tourism	90	5	4	81
Help charity	80	6	13	79
Give Britain prestige abroad				71
Provide a moral example	78	17	4	49
Boost exports for companies				49
None of these				3
Don't know				1

* Only adults aged 18–24 were interviewed.
Source: Blumler *et al.*, 'Attitudes to the monarchy', 154; royalty poll,
Oct. 2003, www.icmresearch.co.uk/reviews.

Table 10.14 *Which do you think demonstrate the moral values which you would wish everyone to try to follow? 1996 (per cent).*

Doctors	78
Teachers	78
Police officers	76
Judges	66
Armed services	60
Church of England leaders	54
Lawyers	51
Other religious leaders	50
Sports personalities	46
Business leaders	41
Trade union leaders	37
Royal Family	31

Source: *Guardian*, 7 Nov. 1996.

Table 10.15 *The monarchy as national symbol, 1969 (per cent).*

1969	Agree	Disagree	Don't know
Helps to hold the country together	80	14	5
Gives us something no other country has	80	15	4
Is a symbol of Britain at its best	70	23	8
Makes no useful contribution to British life	20	76	4

Source: Blumler *et al.*, 'Attitudes to the monarchy', 154.

example of how to live – close to the 71 per cent who believed that she had at least one favourable attribute in 1969.[87]

The claim that the monarchy is a national symbol also needs careful consideration. In 1969 the claim was certainly justified (Table 10.15).

By the 1990s, however, national identities were more diverse and fragmented. The *British Social Attitudes Report* for 1995, for example, investigated national identity by asking respondents how proud they were of the national heritage, and whether they wanted to exclude foreigners. This produced four categories of nationalist, of roughly the same size: the 'supranationalists' (low pride, low exclusion); the 'patriots' (high pride,

---

[87] Royalty poll, Oct. 2003, www.icmresearch.co.uk/reviews; Rose and Kavanagh, 'Monarchy in contemporary political culture', p. 20.

low exclusion); the 'John Bulls' (high pride, high exclusion); and the 'belligerents' (low pride, high exclusion). It seems plausible to believe that those who had low pride in national culture were not strongly attached to the monarchy as a national symbol. If so, this accounted for 39 per cent of respondents.[88] In a 2005 poll which asked which words or phrases were 'very important' in defining Britain only 39 per cent said 'the monarchy' and 29 per cent 'God save the Queen'.[89]

Polls further indicate that the draw of the Royal Family is fading. In 1969, 60 per cent agreed that it was worth putting yourself out to see royal ceremonies. In 2002, only 6 per cent thought receiving an invitation to a Golden Jubilee tea at Buckingham Palace would make Britain a magical place for them that summer.[90] The royal family is important in the lives of only 10 per cent of young adults, and 70 per cent would not take the chance to be Prince William.[91]

To summarize, it seems probable that at no time in the last 130 years have more people believed that Britain would be better rather than worse off without a monarchy, but support has fluctuated, with the public mood possibly being especially uncertain during the two world wars, and with age, gender, class and region sometimes accounting for differences. Many writers have perhaps exaggerated the extent of royal popularity in the four decades following the Second World War, leading them also to exaggerate the significance of the marked rise in disaffection in the 1990s. Recently the monarchy has regained some support, though not to the levels once enjoyed, and opinion polls indicate other unwelcome developments for monarchists.

II

How, then, can we explain the extent and fluctuation of popular support the uniquely privileged Royal Family enjoyed among ordinary people who were aware that, because of the system of social stratification, they themselves were not privileged?

The ubiquity of national and local royal occasions or visits has played a part in sustaining royal popularity, making it impossible for any individual to ignore or be unaware of them, or to be uninfluenced by the reaction of other groups of people. In these circumstances it is less psychologically damaging for people to participate in these royal events than

---

[88] *Guardian*, 21 Nov. 1996.　　[89] *Daily Telegraph*, 27 Jul. 2005.

[90] Magical Britain poll, May 2002, www.icmresearch.co.uk/reviews.

[91] Royalty poll, Oct. 2003, Prince William poll, May 2000, www.icmresearch.co.uk/reviews.

to resist or oppose them. Social psychologists have long investigated the 'pressures towards uniformity' around an exaggerated stereotype of what people think is their group's position.[92] Already in the 1840s newspapers and manufacturers ensured this royal ubiquity.[93] The Golden Jubilee in 1887 saw one of the largest advertising campaigns in nineteenth-century Britain.[94] After Edward VII's funeral in May 1910, Arnold Bennett wrote in his journal that 'it is a tremendous relief to a newspaper reader to have that funeral done with'.[95]

After the first Christmas Day broadcast in 1932, BBC microphones were present at many royal ceremonies.[96] During the preparations for George VI's coronation, 'the point was continually stressed that by means of broadcasting and modern communications the whole British Empire – and thence by a short step the whole world – was sharing in the celebrations'. Four special 'atmosphere' microphones reproduced the sounds of the waiting crowds. The procession was also televised and watched by an estimated 60,000 viewers. Street and shop decorations were everywhere. Westminster City Council decorated nearly four and a half miles of streets, including most of the route of the procession, with masts 28 feet high, topped with a crown of gold and bearing a banner with the initials 'G-E', on every pavement. There were red, white and blue goldfish, mice, pianos, 'undies' and maids' uniforms. Flags were put out by ordinary families and 'there was much veiled competition between streets and even individual houses'.[97]

The effect, Mass-Observation found, was that on the day 'it is interesting that even those persons who shut themselves up most completely could not escape the day entirely', but 'found themselves going back to the radio on one ground or another, or showed a sense of guilt, or found themselves interested after all'.[98] Mass-Observation was especially interested in those cases which 'illustrate an attempt to resist or escape from the Coronation, and the resulting problems and troubles':

---

[92] E.g. E. Van Avermaet, 'Social influence in small groups', in M. Hewstone *et al.*, *Introduction to Social Psychology* (Oxford, 1988), pp. 351–9; M. Wetherell (ed.), *Identities, Groups and Social Issues* (London, 1996), pp. 24–39.

[93] Tyrrell and Ward, 'God bless', 115–6.

[94] T. Richards, 'The image of Victoria in the year of jubilee', *Victorian Studies* 30 (1987), 8–32, at 11; M. Harkness ('John Law'), *Out of Work* (London, 1888), p. 92.

[95] A. Bennett, *The Journals*, ed. F. Swinnerton (Harmondsworth, 1984), p. 323. See also K. Tetens, '"A grand informal durbar": Henry Irving and the coronation of Edward VII', *Journal of Victorian Culture* 8 (2003), 257–91.

[96] P. Scannell and D. Cardiff, *A Social History of Broadcasting* (Oxford, 1991), vol. 1, pp. 279, 283.

[97] Jennings and Madge, *May the Twelfth*, pp. 11, 15–6, 34–5, 169, 284n., 300–1.

[98] Ibid., pp. 91, 267.

Swansea. (CO.28) The charlady also proceeded to tell me that she had attended the Street tea although on Tuesday she had implied that she was not going to it but explained now that she did not want my mother to know as the latter had been very antagonistic towards it all and that she (my mother) would give her no peace over it. But she 'didn't want to be different' and had paid her 1d. a week.

London. (CO.41) Female Typist. Single. 39. I became very bored with the word 'Coronation'. Could not buy cigarettes, sweets, biscuits – not even a suspender belt – without finding crowns and what-not on them . . .

I was surprised how much I responded to the atmosphere of the crowd, the cheering, etc. I felt a definite pride and thrill in belonging to the Empire which in ordinary life, with my political bias, is just the opposite of my true feeling.

Yet I felt a definite sense of relief that I could experience this emotion and be in and of the crowd. One becomes very weary of always being in the minority, thinking things silly which other people care about; one must always be arguing, or repressing oneself, and it is psychologically very bad. One is fighting against the herd instinct all the time. Therefore you will understand that the carnival spirit of the actual Coronation Day *really* was a holiday for me, and I say this without cynicism. I wonder how many others felt the same.

Reviewing it all calmly afterwards, once sees how very dangerous all this is – the beliefs and convictions of a lifetime can be set aside so easily.[99]

This is not in fact a 'herd instinct' or the 'mass hysteria and empty shouting' that Winifred Holtby's militant socialist feared and felt superior to[100] – the typist's self-awareness demonstrates as much. It was the 'weariness' of non-conformity in this particular set of circumstances which pushed people to conform.

This ubiquitousness has continued to characterize all grand royal events. The 1969 Investiture of the Prince of Wales, for example, was the most highly publicized royal event since the 1953 coronation. Full details were reported weeks before it, the unprecedented documentary, *Royal Family*, was screened twice, and a half-hour interview with Prince Charles aired three times in the fortnight before the Investiture. On the day itself there were live transmissions of the ceremony on both BBC1 and ITV lasting over six hours, with 90-minute edited highlights in the evening on all three channels and an unscheduled five-minute address to the nation by Prince Charles.[101] Similarly in June 2002 the Queen's Golden Jubilee dominated television and radio schedules.[102] And the same lack of escape often characterizes local royal visits.[103]

[99] Ibid., pp. 299, 300, 303–5.
[100] W. Holtby, *South Riding* (London, 1936), p. 576. The epilogue to the novel describes George V's Silver Jubilee in 'Kiplington'.
[101] Blumler *et al.*, 'Attitudes to the monarchy', 149.
[102] See the television and radio listings for 2–3 June 2002.
[103] A. Rowbottom, 'Royal symbolism and social integration' (Ph D thesis, University of Manchester, 1994), pp. 173–207. The contemporary image of popularity is also shaped

Newspapers in particular make the Royal Family a presence in everyday life,[104] and the historical preoccupation with infrequent grand ceremonies needs to be balanced by the investigation of this 'banal monarchism', and the 'illusion of intimacy created by the mass media'.[105] The importance of the social psychologist Michael Billig's *Talking of the Royal Family*, based on recordings of sixty-three English families discussing in depth the monarchy in late 1988 and 1989, is that it is the only such investigation.[106] It is a complex book, but at its core are three key ideas. First is the understanding of how 'the popular acceptance of monarchy must say something about the popular acceptance of inequality and national identity'. The second is the expectation of the public that the Royal Family 'earn its privileged position'. Third, the centrality of 'double-declaiming', whereby 'as people make claims about the Royal Family, justifying its position of privilege, so they will be heard making claims about the desirability of their own underprivileged lives'.[107]

Billig found a deep equation of monarchy and nation which guaranteed the future continuity of the nation and constituted a source of superiority over other nations. In this respect royals were 'uniquely different' from celebrities or soap opera characters.[108] Yet time and again respondents spoke of royals as ordinary, and doing a job:

The royal job was to set standards, or to give the image of setting standards. As such, said one father, it was 'part of the job' that 'they have to behave themselves' . . . It was like a contract of employment. A mother spoke as if the contract stipulated privileges in return for the public display of moral responsibility . . . The royals had all 'the material things of life' and 'they' could do the very things 'that we'd love to do'. But there were restrictions; 'their' life was 'governed by rules and regulations' and 'that's probably why they're given the privileges' . . . 'They' must be seen to be earning 'their' golden payment. Taking the money and living a life of immoral luxury was inexcusable.

---

by the presence during local visits of a dedicated and organized self-defining group of royalists, prepared to travel throughout the kingdom and stand for hours in all weathers to cheer and give bouquets and other gifts to the royal visitor: Rowbottom, '"The real royalists": folk performance and civil religion at royal visits', *Folklore* 109 (1998), 77–85.

[104] *Great Royal Front Pages*, introduction by A. Holden (London, 1983), and R. Lacey, *The Queen Mother's Century* (London, 1999) give some sense of the changing character of royal front pages throughout the twentieth century.

[105] Craig, 'Crowned republic?', 174.

[106] On its methodology of 'discursive psychology', see Billig, *Talking*, p. viii, 15–9; Wetherell, *Identities*, pp. 150–70. Billig noted that the 175 people who took part was 'a comparatively large sample for a qualitative study'. Most of the discussions lasted between one and two hours.

[107] Billig, *Talking*, pp. 12, 23, 56–8, 64–7; Billig, 'Rhetorical and historical aspects of attitudes: the case of the British monarchy', *Ideology and Opinion* (1991), p. 159.

[108] Billig, *Talking*, pp. 29–35, 52–4, 220; Rowbottom, 'Real royalists', 85–6.

Billig emphasized the absence of deference as '"we" are imagining "ourselves" to be in the position of command'.[109]

Although 'their' job was well paid, it was unenviably hard; the 'enviable privileges of ordinary life' were absent for them. A middle-aged fitter said, 'they can't say sort of like "We'll nip off to the pictures tonight"'. When a son attacked the wealth and frequent holidays of the Royal Family, his father observed that 'they don't seem to have any freedom at all', and his mother that 'I mean their lives aren't their own, their lives belong to the people.' A woman commented, 'our life is governed nine till five; you're told what your work [is] . . . and after that you do your own thing . . . But their whole life . . . is governed by rules and regulations, which I would absolutely hate'. Billig wrote of this double-declaiming:

The talk about the Royal Family's unenviable life is a variant of the general common-place 'money doesn't bring happiness'. The maxim offers reassurance to those without fortunes, in a society in which money is commonly valued and desired . . . [R]oyals, imprisoned within 'their' unauthentic lives of restricting wealth, can also be imagined to envy 'us' . . . The unfreedoms of ordinary life can be momentarily imagined away in the imagining of the royal envy.[110]

Anne Rowbottom's participant-observer study of the 'real royalists' also revealed this structure of beliefs and emotions. She found as well the reaffirmation of their ideal of the Royal Family when faced by the refusal of a royal to embody it: when the Princess Royal gave no acknowledgment of their presence outside a meeting she was attending, the royalists reasoned that it was because the meeting was private, and that 'if we went to see her again at a more public function on another day, she would probably be in a different mood and respond to us in a friendlier way'; or that 'the Princess was "her own woman" who would not pretend to qualities and interests that she did not possess'.[111] Hoggart too had noticed this pattern among working-class women in the 1950s:

---

[109] Billig, *Talking*, pp. 111–2, 113, 115.
[110] Ibid., pp. 124–5, 137, 140–2. This thought has often appeared in writings on royalty in several disciplines. Freud explored the phenomenon of 'fettering and paralysing a holy ruler through taboo ceremonial' in *Totem and Taboo* (1919; Harmondsworth, 1938), pp. 70–8. Roger Caillois, in *Man, Play and Games* (1958; English trans. 1962), pp. 123–4, observed of a monarch: 'It is evident that the simplest pleasures are forbidden to him, and it is stressed repeatedly that he is not free to love, that he owes himself to the crown, etiquette, and affairs of state. A bizarre mixture of envy and pity thus surrounds the royal personage, and even while people acclaim kings and queens, they seek to persuade themselves that they are no different from them and that the sceptre entails boredom, sadness, fatigue, and servitude, even more than it confers good fortune and power . . . despotic court protocol is a reminder that the lives of monarchs are only happy to the degree that they retain something of the common touch, thus confirming that not too great an advantage accrues from even the most inordinate endowments of fortune'.
[111] Rowbottom, 'Royal symbolism', pp. 292–306, 320–6.

It is this ability, to think of the members of the Royal Family as individuals, caught up in a big machine manipulated by 'Them', having 'a real family life' only with difficulty, which allows a great many women in the working-classes to feel well-disposed towards Royalty today . . . 'It's a rotten job,' people will say, 'they get pushed around as much as we do.' Then they feel a lot of sympathy for all that is expected of the monarch.[112]

As George VI's coronation drew closer, newspaper anxiety grew that he 'is rather highly strung, [and] might conceivably break down under the increasing strain as the ceremony draws nearer'. People of all kinds expressed sympathy for the King. A schoolmaster who described himself as 'inactive Left' wrote: 'as I got up I thought how nervous the King and Queen must be'; and when he later saw the King go by in the heavy gilt coach looking 'very small', he thought him 'frozen nervous'. A Conservative schoolmaster too noted that as the procession went by, the King looked 'extremely uneasy', which caused him to cheer more fervently on the King's return 'in the overwhelming desire to show my appreciation of what I felt the King was doing'. The remark that 'the man I feel most sorry for is the King' was common. A Cambridge diarist watched the procession on television with acquaintances who 'exchanged anecdotes about the Royal Family, all of which had the same point – that the Windsors are really quite human. They were very concerned lest the King and Queen be over-tired by the ceremonies.'[113] Mass-Observation noted that the hesitation in the king's radio address 'seems to have aroused general sympathy, even among anti-monarchists, and to have operated as a factor in his favour'. A Southport diarist wrote that 'being sympathetically conscious of the King's nervousness was the only sensation the business produced in me'. A North Shields family 'made a special point of listening to the King's speech', and 'noticed the long pause before he began and sympathized with him in his difficulty'.[114] This interest and sympathy persisted: one working-class women told Mass-Observation in 1940 that 'he's speaking much better now – much stronger – you can't help but admire him'.[115]

The structure of their own lives predisposed ordinary people to think of and feel for the Royal Family in these terms. But this predisposition was reinforced for most of the twentieth century by the success of monarchist writers in sustaining an appropriate image of royals whose 'whole life . . . is

---

[112] Hoggart, *Uses of Literacy*, p. 111.
[113] Jennings and Madge, *May the Twelfth*, pp. 44 (*Daily Record*, 8 Mar. 1937), 119, 121, 128, 284–5, 300–1.
[114] Ibid., pp. 270, 279, 292. There had been rumours that the King would not speak on the radio.
[115] Quoted in R. Tomlinson, *Divine Right* (London, 1994), p. 106.

governed by rules and regulations', but who remain ordinary.[116] A few instances of an enormous ideological barrage must suffice here. In a short story of 1896, the popular novelist Marie Corelli imagined the reaction of an old woman who failed to see Queen Victoria once before she died: 'the country ain't got no business to keep 'er shut up, first in one prison an' then another . . . it's a plot to keep 'er away from us, you see if it ain't!'[117] The newspaper editor A. G. Gardiner described Edward VII as 'pursued by the intolerable limelight wherever he goes':

No man in his senses would be a King if he could be a cobbler. For a cobbler has the two priceless privileges of freedom and obscurity, and a King has only a prison and publicity.[118]

Gardiner found that when George V was in Lancashire, 'he goes through the mills and the foundries, looking at the machinery with the eye of a mechanic and rubbing shoulders with the operatives in the spirit of a fellow-workman'.[119] *The Times*'s commemoration of his passing presented him as 'an ordinary man called upon to play an extraordinary part'.[120] One aspect of his 'ordinariness' was his willingness to share the pleasures of his peoples, notably football and cricket matches.[121] His middle-brow remarks and tastes were assiduously reported by monarchists.[122] For Sir Hugh Walpole writing in the *Daily Mail* in 1937, George VI was 'the one great self-abnegating figure in this present world'.[123] The author of a commemorative volume for the Coronation described the King as a man who 'loves "thrillers" of the Edgar Wallace kind, as a change from the stiff works about industrial and economic subjects which he studies so that he may know how to rule his subjects the better'.[124] Even his heavy cigarette smoking showed 'the common touch'.[125]

These claims of royal ordinariness were essential in allowing monarchists (and many socialists) to make four related claims: Britain was a

---

[116] J. Williamson, 'Royalty and representation', *Consuming Passions* (London, 1986), pp. 75–88.

[117] M. Corelli, 'An Old Bundle', *Cameos* (London, 1896), p. 178.

[118] A. G. Gardiner, *Prophets, Priests and Kings* (London, 1908), p. 2.

[119] Gardiner, *Pillars of Society* (London, 1916), p. 6.

[120] *Hail and Farewell: The Passing of George V* (London, 1936), p. 99.

[121] H. W. Wilson, *His Majesty The King, 1910–1935* (London, 1935), p. 15; R. Holt, *Sport and the British* (Oxford, 1990), p. 269. George V also attended the first Royal Command Performance in 1912: Stedman Jones, *Languages*, pp. 230, 233.

[122] Matthew, 'George V'. Dennis, *Coronation Commentary*, p. 60, recorded George V's remark that he would rather abdicate than sit through *Hamlet* a second time.

[123] Martin, 'Public opinion and the coronation', 440.

[124] J. T. Gorman, *George VI, King and Emperor* (London, 1937), p. 24.

[125] P. Clarke, *Hope and Glory* (London, 1996), p. 211.

'monarchical republic'; all were equal citizens, with the monarch simply the 'first citizen'; the monarch was 'democratic'; and the monarchy safeguarded the government's democratic character.[126] These claims effectively foreclosed any extensive public discussion of the idea that 'democracy and monarchy are an unthinkable connection'.[127]

The present Royal Family has been well served in the construction of a comparable royal image in the early years by (among many other, less prominent figures) Richard Dimbleby, Dermot Morrah (Arundel Herald Extraordinary), Godfrey Talbot (from 1948 the BBC's first officially accredited court correspondent) and probably even their disgraced and exiled governess, Marion Crawford; and more recently by Lady Elizabeth Longford, Ingrid Seward (editor of *Majesty* magazine), Brian Hoey, and Robert Lacey.[128] People probably have some sense of the rigid rules governing court and civic ceremonial.[129] Occasionally royals themselves – either when they have been sure of their ground, or inadvertently – have reminded the public of their royal burdens. Princess Margaret's statement renouncing marriage with Townsend in 1955 was seen as 'a great act of self-sacrifice, and the country will admire and love her for it'.[130] Indeed, when she died in 2002 some tributes from members of the public still portrayed her as 'a courageous lady who put duty before personal happiness'.[131] When the Queen visited Paris in 1957, she was heard to say that 'I can't even buy a newspaper'.[132]

The most crucial support, however, came from the discretion of the media. The future Edward VIII had little respect for his father's sense of duty and conventional morality. Bruce Lockhart of the *Evening Standard* wrote in his diary in October 1931:

Millie [Duchess of Sutherland] was staying with the Prince at Bayonne when his father telephoned to him about the money crisis and the need for him [the Prince] to give up £10,000 a year. The Prince was in a night haunt at the time and was

---

126 See e.g. M. Amos, *The English Constitution* (London, 1930), p. 9; *Hail and Farewell*, p. 153; Gorman, *George VI*, ch. 5; J. R. Clynes, *Memoirs, 1869–1937* (London, 1937), p. 93.

127 The words are Keir Hardie's in 1897: K. Hardie, *Speeches and Writings*, ed. E. Hughes (Glasgow, 1924), p. 61.

128 All of these authors have several volumes on the Royal Family: see e.g. R. Dimbleby, *Elizabeth Our Queen* (London, 1953); D. Morrah, *To Be A King* (London, 1968); G. Talbot, *The Country Life Book of Queen Elizabeth The Queen Mother* (London, 1973); M. Crawford, *The Little Princesses* (London, 1950); E. Longford, *Royal Throne* (London, 1994); U. Hall and I. Seward, *By Royal Invitation* (London, 1988); B. Hoey, *At Home with the Queen* (London, 2002); R. Lacey, *Royal* (London, 2002).

129 See e.g. F. B. Fawcett, *Court Ceremonial and Book of the Court of King George the Sixth* (London, 1937); P. Millward, *Civic Ceremonial* (London, 1953; 4th. ed. 1998).

130 Nicolson, *Diaries and Letters*, p. 290 (31 Oct. 1955).

131 *BBC News*, 9 Feb. 2002, http://news.bbc.co.uk/1/hi/uk

132 Caillois, *Man, Play and Games*, p. 124.

furious: 'The King and I are being had for a pair of mugs', he said. Millie and Tommy [Lady Rosslyn] both say that the Prince is more irresponsible than he was.[133]

Yet the newspapers presented a prince respectful of his father, conscious of his duty, and leading a campaign for social service on behalf of ex-servicemen.[134] So too did commemorative books marking his accession to the throne, many produced by newspaper publishers.[135] American newspapers were running the story of Edward and Mrs Simpson by October 1936, but the British press abided by 'gentleman's agreements' and ignored it until 3 December.[136] Keynes imagined that W. H. Smith 'spend all their time tearing pages out of American magazines to keep secret the King's affair'.[137] Even after 3 December, newspapers treated the affair as a momentous constitutional and religious matter, rather than a lurid human interest story.

Elizabeth II could continue to count on press discretion in the first four decades of her reign, despite signs of strained relations in the 1950s.[138] The decisive change came with the rise of the Murdoch press,[139] as Prince Philip has recognized. Asked when it all started to go wrong, he pinpointed 1987: 'after Murdoch bought the *Today* newspaper . . . Day after day there was a derogatory story about one member of the family or another.'[140] By 1992 the monarchist James Lees-Milne was dismayed that 'all the intellectual commentators' were now writing 'horrid articles' criticizing the Queen: 'these people do not realise how destructive they are.'[141] By 1996 negative royal stories outnumbered the positive by eight to one, and the monarchy felt forced to go to the Press Complaints Commission to seek injunctions.[142] Critically, although in the months following Princess Diana's death 81 per cent of opinion poll respondents agreed that the Royal Family should be protected by a privacy law, no action was taken.[143] Radio and television have lost much of the reverence

---

[133] *The Diaries of Sir Robert Bruce Lockhart*, ed. K. Young (London, 1973), vol. 1, p. 190.

[134] Donaldson, *Edward VIII*, pp. 122–3, 132–4.

[135] See e.g. B. Maine, *Our Ambassador King: His Majesty King Edward VIII's Life of Devotion and Service as Prince of Wales* (London, n.d.).

[136] K. Martin, 'Public opinion and the king's marriage', *Political Quarterly* 8 (1937), 105–21; S. Koss, *The Rise and Fall of the Political Press in Britain* (London, 1984), vol. 2, ch. 15.

[137] R. Skidelsky, *John Maynard Keynes* (London, 1992), vol. 2, p. 628.

[138] K. Martin, *The Crown and the Establishment* (Harmondsworth, 1963), pp. 126–34.

[139] Koss, *Political Press*, ch. 18.

[140] Brandreth, *Brief Encounters*, p. 117.

[141] J. Lees-Milne, *Ceaseless Turmoil: Diaries, 1988–1992*, ed. M. Bloch (London, 2004), pp. 288, 333.

[142] *Guardian*, 16 Aug., 10 Oct., 11 Dec. 1996, 15 Oct. 1998, 30 Apr. 1999; *Observer*, 7 Apr. 1996.

[143] *Guardian*, 12 Nov. 1997. Instead, the current practice is to use tough tactics to warn off the press: *Guardian*, 15 Aug. 2005; 19 Oct. 2005.

Figure 10.1. The monarchy and the tabloids © Steve Bell 2002.

that they had between the wars for 'the power of monarchy as a transcending value, above the levels of social and political strife, which united all classes'.[144] Channel Four in particular has brought tabloid values to royal programmes.[145]

The tabloids have undoubtedly undermined if not overturned the dutiful and moral royal image: just about anything can now be printed about the Royal Family.[146] However, revelations may elicit sympathy for its victims, by demonstrating the high personal cost the royals pay in the job they do.[147] Many tabloid stories are probably not wholly believed:

[144] P. Scannell, '"A conspiracy of silence": the state, the BBC and public opinion in the formative years of British broadcasting', in G. McLennan, D. Held and S. Hall (eds.), *State and Society in Contemporary Britain* (Cambridge, 1984), p. 152; J. Curran and J. Seaton, *Power Without Responsibility* (London, 1985), p. 141. But the monarchy continues to receive 'extra fair' treatment on television – in that the 'other side' of the argument is not normally presented – and to benefit from favourable scheduling, notably the Queen's Christmas Day message: J. Tunstall, *The Media in Britain* (London, 1983), p. 143.

[145] From many examples, see *The Real Prince Philip* (31 Oct. 2000); *Charles: the Battle with Diana* (5 Apr. 2003); *James Hewitt: Confessions of a Cad* (24 Jul. 2003).

[146] It is difficult to select the most extraordinary allegation of recent years: perhaps 'Rape cover-up at the Palace', *Daily Express*, 14 Mar. 2003.

[147] A noteworthy example was the apology the *Sun* was forced to give to Sophie Rhys-Jones after it published topless pictures of her: *Guardian*, 27 May 1999, 3 Jun. 1999.

a poll in 1999 found that 68 per cent of tabloid readers usually did not trust the tabloids to tell the truth.[148] Again, although the monarchy continues to be extraordinarily secretive about the extent of its wealth,[149] accusations of royal and courtly extravagance are not automatically damaging. They have often been levelled against minor royals, yet with the effect of underlining the probity of the Queen and other senior royals.[150] Royal officials and even government ministers have countered that royal finances show good business sense and offer clear value for money.[151] The number of annual engagements the royals fulfil is normally paraded as evidence of their hard work.[152] Most importantly, the tabloids have not concentrated solely on the Royal Family, but have indiscriminately condemned extravagance in all walks of life, from 'dole cheats' to 'fat cats'.[153] In such a climate the publication of annual accounts of the civil list since 2002 does not appear to have had a significant effect on royal fortunes.[154] Indeed, the only royal whose financial extravagance was decisive in her downfall was the Duchess of York, and then only because the Queen chose not to help her financially as she has the Wessexes,[155] and because public opinion showed little sympathy for her.[156]

The fact that former royal servants have recently been the sources for many of the most extraordinary tabloid stories has been a matter of great concern for the monarchy. Books by royal servants have a long pedigree; but where they were once discreet and decorous,[157] now they are the

148 *Observer*, 30 May 1999. This compared with 83 per cent of broadsheet readers who trusted their newspapers, and 85 per cent of viewers who trusted the television news.

149 The first-ever complaint by the Queen to the Press Complaints Commission was over a report in the *Business Age* naming her as the richest person in Britain and speculating about the extent of her wealth: *Guardian*, 7 Apr. 1996. See also H. Brooke, *Your Right to Know* (London, 2005), pp. 68–71.

150 The Kents and the Wessexes have been favourite targets. See e.g. 'The greedy Rent-a-Kents are a right royal disgrace', *Sun*, 18 Apr. 2001; 'Edward and Sophie go on royal duties "strike"', *Observer*, 19 Aug. 2001.

151 E.g. in June 2004 most newspapers carried a headline along the lines that 'royals cost each of us just 61p a year': *Daily Mail* and *Daily Express*, 23 Jun. 2004; *Daily Telegraph*, 25 Jun. 2004; *Guardian*, 25 Jun. 2005.

152 E.g. 'Members of the Royal Family carried out 2,900 official engagements in the year to April 2004, compared to 2,600 in the previous 12 months. The Queen undertook 486 engagements, entertaining around 37,000 people at six garden parties and holding 27 investitures for 2,900 people and 9,000 guests': *Daily Telegraph*, 25 Jun. 2004.

153 E.g. 'Blair's court costs more than Queen's', *Sunday Times*, 7 Jul. 2002; 'How the fat cats offer slim returns', *Observer*, 29 Feb. 2004.

154 *Guardian*, 10 Jun. 2002; 9 Jul. 2002.

155 *Guardian*, 18, 27 Jan. 15, 30 Apr., 5 Nov., 10 Dec. 1996; *News of the World*, 29 Sep. 1996.

156 In 1998, 52 per cent did not think that the Royal Family had been too hard on the Duchess of York since Diana's death: royal poll, Aug. 1998, www.icmresearch. co.uk/reviews; Billig, *Talking of the Royal Family*, p. 112.

157 E.g. C. Grey, *The Early Years of His Royal Highness The Prince Consort, Compiled Under the Direction of Her Majesty The Queen* (London, 1867); L. Cust, *King Edward VII and His Court: Some Reminiscences* (London, 1930); P. Russell, *Butler Royal* (London, 1982).

opposite.[158] Moreover, the fact that the most sensational royal book of all – Andrew Morton's *Diana: Her True Story* (1992)[159] – was true, has given this genre a legitimacy it has proved difficult to dispute. Royals appear powerless to prevent publication.[160]

Again, such revelations are not inevitably destructive. Such intolerable intrusion could generate sympathy among people thankful for the privacy of their own lives and the trustworthiness of their own family and colleagues. But in fact they have been enormously damaging, because for many they could not but call into question – and for others destroy completely – the wishful thought that the 'royal job was to set standards'. In the 1990s, above all because of the 'war of the Waleses' and the behaviour of other younger members,[161] the Royal Family was felt by many more people not to be doing its 'job' (Tables 10.11 and 10.14).

III

This chapter has argued that royal popularity is related to royal ubiquity and social inequality. The ubiquity of the monarchy and monarchists in everyday life in the shape of 'banal monarchism' as well as on grand ceremonial occasions, creates great psychological pressure to conform. Moreover, an important social function of the Royal Family has been to reassure people that lives shaped by social forces over which individuals have little control – and little confidence in being able to change for the better – are universal and immutable, not the product of a particular class position within a particular kind of society. The Royal Family has been taken as proof that immense wealth and privilege cannot bring happiness and freedom, and often as proof that it causes greater misery and makes intolerable demands. H. G. Wells' jealousy of 'all the freedoms' of his royal contemporaries has simply seemed misplaced to most people. For most of the twentieth century, the Royal Family projected an image which lent credence to this wishful thinking. It took care to appear politically neutral. In public it performed its many, onerous duties without complaint and gave the impression that the private lives of its members were exemplary. It presented itself in what it said and how it acted as at once an ordinary and an extraordinary family. What was written about it in

---

[158] E.g. W. Berry, *The Housekeeper's Diary* (London, 1995); P. D. Jephson, *Shadows of a Princess* (London, 2000); P. Burrell, *A Royal Duty* (London, 2003).

[159] A. Morton, *Diana: In Pursuit of Love* (London, 2004) confirmed the full extent of Princess Diana's collaboration on the earlier book.

[160] *Guardian*, 3 Nov. 2003; *Daily Telegraph*, 25 Jun. 2004.

[161] E.g. the Duchess of York was voted the second most badly behaved female of 1996: *Guardian*, 8 Jan. 1997.

books and newspapers and how it was presented in the cinema and on television was respectful, formal and discreet. This was partly the result of calculated royal cultivation of these media, but to an even greater extent of their overwhelming monarchism.

The two world wars created extreme deprivations for many people which led them to see the Royal Family in a less sympathetic light.[162] The lustre of the 'traditional' royal image began to dull a little in the 1970s as the media became more searching. The 1990s, however, were the nadir. In that disastrous decade, most – though critically not all – of the components of that image were seen to be shams. It became more difficult for all, and impossible for many, to continue wishfully imagining the Royal Family to be 'ordinary' and powerless to do as they please. Crucially the Queen remained as selfless and duty-bound as ever; but the next royal generation did not.

How secure then is the future of the monarchy? That the monarchy will survive into the next reign and beyond – and probably in its present form – seems certain. The idea that 'we could nag the Windsors off the throne'[163] reckons without the Queen's determination that it is her religious and filial duty to 'keep struggling on as best we can'.[164] Even in the 1990s, when there was overwhelming support for change, no political party considered even reforming the monarchy. It was striking that the reform of another largely hereditary institution which lacked popular support – the House of Lords – did not provoke an open debate about the monarchy.[165] If the wish to be citizens and not royal subjects is genuinely held (Table 10.10), there is no political mechanism to bring this about. Nevertheless, it is possible that the monarchy will never be as popular as it was before the 1990s (Table 10.3). The present royal strategy to demonstrate that the Queen is more like ordinary people – the Queen having tea in a Glasgow council house in 1999 was highly publicized – has met with mixed reactions.[166] The obvious discomfort of the monarch on these occasions has probably won her much sympathy, but done little to establish a new royal image. Much of the framework which sustained the royal image established by George V throughout most of the twentieth century has disappeared. But many monarchist arguments in favour of the monarchy still appear credible to a substantial majority of

---

[162] Billig, 'Rhetorical and historical aspects', p. 161.

[163] *Observer*, 10 Mar. 1996.   [164] Quoted in Lees-Milne, *Ceaseless Turmoil*, p. 272.

[165] In November 1997 only 29 per cent thought the House of Lords should remain as it was, down from 57 per cent in 1983; only a third favoured retaining the monarchy as it was, down from two thirds: *Guardian*, 19 Nov. 1997.

[166] E.g. 'We love the common touch ma'am', *News of the World*, 27 Sep. 1998; *Guardian*, 8, 9 Jul. 1999.

Figure 10.2. The Queen has tea with Mrs. Susan McCarron in her housing association home at Castlemilk, July 1999.

people (Table 10.13),[167] though it is unlikely that the monarchy will ever again be near-universally regarded as providing a moral example and the identification of the nation with the monarchy weakened in the 1990s. Nonetheless, the psychological mechanisms in relation to the Royal Family identified in this chapter are bound to survive – in however attenuated a form – since, fundamentally, these, rather than 'a jealous hatred', make living with inequality tolerable.

[167] Billig, 'Rhetorical and historical aspects', p. 156; F. Prochaska, *Royal Bounty* (New Haven, 1995), pp. 274–83. There is evidence that charities are beginning to favour celebrities over royals as patrons: *Guardian*, 4 Dec. 2002.

Index